LESSLIE NEWBIGIN

Missionary Theologian

A READER

LESSLIE NEWBIGIN

Missionary Theologian

A READER

*Compiled and
introduced by*

Paul Weston

WILLIAM B. EERDMANS PUBLISHING COMPANY
GRAND RAPIDS, MICHIGAN / CAMBRIDGE, U.K.

Published 2006

in Great Britain by

SPCK

Society for Promoting Christian Knowledge

36 Causton Street

London SW1P 4ST

and in the United States of America by

Wm. B. Eerdmans Publishing Co.

255 Jefferson Ave. S.E., Grand Rapids, Michigan 49503 /

P.O. Box 163, Cambridge CB3 9PU U.K.

www.eerdmans.com

Printed in the United States of America

11 10 09 08 07 06   7 6 5 4 3 2 1

Library of Congress Cataloging-in-Publication Data

Newbigin, Lesslie.

Lesslie Newbigin: missionary theologian: a reader /

compiled and introduced by Paul Weston.

p.   cm.

Includes bibliographical references (p.   ) and indexes.

ISBN-10: 0-8028-2982-1 / ISBN-13: 978-0-8028-2982-5 (pbk.: alk. paper)

1. Missions — Theory. 2. Newbigin, Lesslie.

3. Ecumenical movement — History. 4. Church of South India.

I. Title: Missionary theologian.   II. Weston, Paul, 1957–   .   III. Title.

BV2063.N4175   2006

266 — dc22

2006006708

Scripture quotations are from the Revised Standard Version of the Bible, copyright © 1946, 1952 and 1971 by the Division of Christian Education of the National Council of the Churches of Christ in the USA, used by permission, all rights reserved; and also from the Revised Version of the Bible, 1881.

Every effort has been made to acknowledge fully the sources of material reproduced in this book. The publisher apologizes for any omissions that may remain and, if notified, will ensure that full acknowledgements are made in a subsequent edition.

Contents

Preface

By any reckoning, Lesslie Newbigin was a giant in the fields of ecumenical and missionary theology in the twentieth century. When he died in 1998, the obituary in *The Times* described him as 'one of the foremost missionary statesmen of his generation', and amongst 'the outstanding figures on the world Christian stage in the second half of the century'.[1] Geoffrey Wainwright, who recently wrote a 'theological life' of Newbigin, has even likened him to one of the 'Fathers of the Church',[2] and points to 'the similarities and continuities' between Newbigin 'and the great bishop-theologians in early ecclesiastical history'.[3]

But Newbigin's reputation lives on – not just as a figure of past importance, but as a writer of continuing significance. There are a number of reasons for this. The first is that his writings are consistently characterized by an ability to identify ahead of time the most significant missionary questions and issues. On themes like contextualization, pluralism, church unity, and mission in the context of the end of Christendom, Newbigin was frequently in advance of contemporary thinking, mapping out the territory to be explored and identifying the questions to be addressed. On a wider canvas too his insights were often visionary. His 'trinitarian' reflections on the nature of mission in the early 1960s, for example, were pioneering, as was his prediction in the early 1950s that the 'Pentecostal' stream within the world Church would play a vital part in its growth and health. Partly as a result of this intuitive instinct, his writings still resonate today with relevance and insight. Rooted in an unapologetic grasp of the missionary character of God and of his ever-present self-disclosure in Christ, they bristle with the contention that Christian 'faith' has as much right to a public hearing *today* as it ever did.

In addition, there is the fact that his writings consistently draw from a wealth of cross-cultural experience. His thirty-six years' missionary experience in India were combined with an extensive and personal knowledge of the worldwide Church to produce missionary theology that is deeply attentive to the interplay of mission and culture. Always sensitive to the needs and questions of the society in which the missionary task is focused, Newbigin's work is also alert to the implications of the cultural 'baggage' that missionaries themselves carry. By taking seriously the subtle interplay involved in this 'pluriform' manifestation of culture, Newbigin helps us to explore vital dimensions of the missionary task that are often overlooked.

---

[1] *The Times*, 31 January, 1998.
[2] Wainwright 2000: v.
[3] Wainwright 2000: 390.

For many readers, of course, it is Newbigin's work on contemporary mission in the West that has sparked interest in his writings. Certainly, his unique contribution to the development of a 'missionary' encounter with our increasingly secularized, 'post-Enlightenment' culture continues to merit serious attention. In this contemporary missionary frontier there have been few more powerful or influential thinkers, a fact made all the more remarkable when one considers that his writings in this area in the 1980s and 90s (some 15 books and over 160 articles) came from a man already in his mid-seventies. As the extracts in this book demonstrate, Newbigin continues to speak into our context with a fresh insight and clarity.

The aim of this book is to introduce the thinking of Lesslie Newbigin to a larger audience by making available extracts from a wide variety of his writings. There is such a wealth of material to choose from, and I have had to make difficult decisions about which pieces to use. Clearly one could concentrate upon his engagement with Western post-Enlightenment culture, as this is perhaps more familiar to those who have already dipped into Newbigin's work. But this would leave the many riches of his earlier writing untouched. I have therefore attempted to provide a flavour of both his earlier and later work, choosing selections which span some 60 years of writing, from his early theological reflections on the nature of knowledge while he was still a theological student at Cambridge in the 1930s to some of his last work on the nature of 'public' truth in the late 1990s.

Following an 'introductory biographical sketch', Part One is designed around six chapters that seek to introduce the main 'Theological foundations for mission' that undergird Newbigin's thinking. Each chapter or part-chapter begins with a short section of introduction and commentary, and is followed by extracts from Newbigin's writings that illustrate and explore this theme. (For this first part, I have chosen texts taken largely from Newbigin's earlier writings.) Each chapter or part-chapter is concluded with suggestions for further reading from Newbigin's other writings. Part Two ('Missionary theology in practice') follows the same basic pattern, and seeks to explore and illustrate the key ideas and practices that characterize Newbigin's later work.

Some words of explanation: I have chosen to reprint Newbigin's texts almost entirely as they were originally published. This means that the extracts reflect quite a range of American and British publishing practices in terms of spelling and punctuation, and some of the language in the earlier extracts may now appear slightly outmoded. In addition I have left the footnotes as they occur in the originals (except in moving 'in-text' notes to the bottom of the page in order to maintain a consistent 'style' throughout the book). Where it seemed appropriate, however, I have added footnotes with additional bibliographical or other information about people or historical events referred to in the text. (These extra footnotes are placed in brackets in order to distinguish them from Newbigin's originals.)

Occasionally, I have edited the extracts in order to remove material relating to events or discussions that are less relevant today, and that might hinder the flow of the argument for contemporary readers. This has occasionally meant that some of the numbering in the originals has been changed in the interests of smooth reading. At other places, I have omitted smaller sections of text. At such points, I have used the following indicators:

- an ellipsis of three dots within square brackets [. . .] indicates that one or more *words* have been omitted
- an ellipsis of four dots within square brackets [. . . .] indicates that one or more *sentences* have been omitted
- an ellipsis of four dots in square brackets on a separate line indicates that one or more *paragraphs* have been omitted.

(Where I have omitted one or more paragraphs from the beginning or end of extracts which were in the original chapters or articles, I have indicated this in the footnote following the extract title by placing an ellipsis of four dots before or after the page numbers.)

I should like to express my sincere thanks to Alison Barr and the editorial and production teams at SPCK for their help in bringing the project to completion; to Tom Faust, Michael Goheen, David Kettle and Wilbert Shenk for their helpful comments on an earlier draft, and to Eleanor Jackson who saved me from a number of errors in the biographical introduction and made many helpful suggestions.

Finally, I would like to thank following for permission to reproduce material in this book:

- Margaret Beetham (Lesslie Newbigin's daughter and literary executor) for permission to use many of the extracts.
- The University of Chicago Press for the extracts on pp. 67–80 from 'The Quest for Unity through Religion', *Journal of Religion* 35 (1955): 17–21, 23–33.
- Western Theological Seminary for the article on pp. 143–8, 'Evangelism in the City', copyright 1987 *Reformed Review*. Used by permission of the publisher, Western Theological Seminary, Holland, Michigan, USA.
- *Scottish Journal of Theology* for the article on pp. 159–72, 'The Basis, Purpose and Manner of Inter-Faith Dialogue', *Scottish Journal of Theology* 30 (1977): 253–70.
- *Studia Missionalia* for the article on pp. 172–84, 'Religious Pluralism: A Missiological Approach', *Studia Missionalia* 42 (1993): 227–44.

Abbreviations

————⋙◆⋘————

BCC   British Council of Churches (1942–90; now CTBI)
CSI   Church of South India (formed 1947)
CTBI   Churches Together in Britain and Ireland
CWME   Commission on World Mission and Evangelism (formed 1961)
IMC   International Missionary Council (formed 1921; became CWME of WCC in 1961)
SCM   Student Christian Movement (founded 1889)
SIUC   South India United Church (formed in 1908)
SPG   Society for the Propagation of the Gospel (founded 1701; now USPG)
URC   United Reformed Church (formed in 1972 by the union of the Congregational Church in England and Wales and the Presbyterian Church of England)
WCC   World Council of Churches (founded in 1948)

Introduction
A biographical sketch

Early life

James Edward Lesslie Newbigin was born in Newcastle upon Tyne on 8 December, 1909. He was the second of three children, a brother among two sisters. His father, a native Northumbrian and an able businessman, had founded his own shipping company in 1895, and became chairman of the North of England Shipowners Federation in 1922. He was widely read, politically energetic, and remained a devout and deeply thoughtful Christian – actively concerned to apply his faith to politics and business. Lesslie's mother was of Scottish stock, and a very different kind of character. Less forthright than her husband, she was a highly accomplished pianist, and was – in Lesslie's own words – 'the most loving and devoted mother that one could wish for'.[1]

After attending a private kindergarten and preparatory school in Newcastle, Lesslie was sent away at the age of 12 to 'board' at Leighton Park, a Quaker boarding school in Reading, Berkshire. His father had chosen it because of its Quaker ethos and because – being a committed pacifist – he approved of the fact that it did not have an Officer Training Corps. It took Lesslie some time to get over his sense of desolation at being left on his own far from home, but he gradually began to adapt to his surroundings and to make the most of the new opportunities they offered. He was to remember little of his formal class education, except for the influence of one particular teacher: his geography master, S. W. ('Bill') Brown, whom Newbigin described as a 'man of genius' and from whom he learned to question received knowledge and to think for himself.

> He created a capacity to think, to break out of stereotypes, to explore new ideas and to question old ones. He taught us to read voraciously and to get to the heart of the argument of a big book so that we could expound and defend it in debate. He made learning a thrilling exercise. And at the end of it he made you laugh at yourself.[2]

---

[1] Newbigin 1993d: 3. (This is the updated edition of Newbigin 1985c.)
[2] Newbigin 1993d: 5. Newbigin remained an avid and inquisitive reader throughout his life. Even towards the end, when his eyesight was failing, he had a 'team' of readers who visited his home and read to him. His ability to digest and recall this material was extraordinary.

Newbigin excelled in a range of subjects at school, but though he was much involved in the school's social work projects and took part in debates on politics and ethics, he had by the end of his schooldays abandoned his parents' Christian faith. He had found his scripture lessons 'utterly boring'; had learned from his chemistry studies that life was a 'disease of matter', and had adopted a 'deterministic' view of history from his wider readings in historical geography. As a result, by the age of 18, Newbigin found that the idea of God was no longer 'a tenable hypothesis'.[3] Despite this, he did read William James's 1896 essay, 'The Will to Believe', and although he was not persuaded by its arguments for Christian faith, it did at least demonstrate to him that faith was not entirely irrational.

Cambridge and conversion

Newbigin went up to Queens' College, Cambridge in the autumn of 1928. He was to read geography, but soon found that the University's academic expectations were much lower than those he had been used to at Leighton Park. So he spent most of his time in more congenial pursuits: he took part in debates at the Union, sang in chamber groups, and indulged his favourite hobby of rock-climbing – fitting in as many trips to the Lake District as he could.

Significantly, during his time at Queens' he also came across the Student Christian Movement (SCM). A small group met in college, and Newbigin began to find the company of its members 'very attractive'. He liked their readiness to ask difficult questions about Christian faith, and began to find himself being drawn unexpectedly towards the possibility of personal belief. As yet he remained unsure whether 'God' existed, but – as he wrote later – 'with William James to support me I knew that I was not being irrational in seeking the help of One of whose existence there was no proof'.[4]

Then in 1929, during his first summer vacation, Newbigin offered to help out at a Quaker centre at Maes-yr-haf in South Wales to bring relief and provide recreation for unemployed miners living in the Rhondda valley. Characteristically, Newbigin had been attracted by the Quakers' efforts to help those at the margins of society, and had agreed to go to help out for several weeks with a student friend he had known since Leighton Park days. It proved to be a life-changing experience. They were based at a recreation centre at Trealaw, and were involved in organizing games and other pastimes for the men. But Newbigin began to feel that what they really needed was something more than the odd game of table-tennis. He described it as 'some kind of faith that would fortify them for today and tomorrow against apathy and despair' and concluded that they too 'needed the Christian faith that was beginning

---

[3] Newbigin 1993d: 5.
[4] Newbigin 1993d: 10.

to draw me'.[5] Towards the end of his time he accompanied around 60 of the men as they set out to spend some nights under canvas near the coast. One evening some of them had managed to smuggle large quantities of alcohol into the camp, and before long not only were they completely drunk, but they had started to fight with each other. Newbigin gradually felt more and more out of his depth, acutely aware of his own inability to resolve the situation; although things eventually quietened down, he went to bed 'with the feeling of total defeat'. But then, while lying awake on his bed, he experienced something of a spiritual awakening. It was a vivid vision of the cross of Christ 'spanning the space between heaven and earth, between ideals and present realities, and with arms that embraced the whole world'.

> I was sure that night in a way that I had never been before, that this was the clue that I must follow if I were to make any kind of sense of the world. From that moment I would always know how to begin again when I had come to the end of all my own resources of understanding or courage.[6]

Newbigin returned to Cambridge in the autumn of 1929 as a committed Christian, and he immediately threw himself into the activities of the SCM with great energy and enthusiasm. He went to many of its meetings, and heard a rich variety of speakers from around the world, including such eminent leaders as John R. Mott, William Temple and John Mackay.[7] It is no surprise, therefore, that from such early experiences Newbigin's faith was to grow in ways that were both sensitive to social questions and profoundly ecumenical in dimension. He was of course to make a major contribution to the ecumenical movement, but he also remained passionate about social issues, and his later work – both in church leadership and in the writing that came out of it – is consistently marked by a desire to apply his Christian faith to the social and political questions of the time.

During the summer of 1930, at the end of his second year at Cambridge, Newbigin was to reach another significant turning point in his life. He had turned down an opportunity to go climbing with friends in the Alps so that he could attend the annual SCM conference at Swanwick in Derbyshire. Up to this time, he had naturally assumed that after graduating he would go into

[5] Newbigin 1993d: 11.
[6] Newbigin 1993d: 11–12. In an unpublished 1962 lecture, Newbigin probably had this experience in mind when he referred to the idea of faith as something which is 'born at the point of ultimate despair', and as a commitment made 'when all other commitments end in a precipice' (Newbigin 1962c).
[7] John Mott (an American Methodist) had presided at the World Missionary Conference at Edinburgh in 1910. He was awarded the Nobel Peace prize in 1946. William Temple became Archbishop of York in 1929, having been previously Bishop of Manchester. He became Archbishop of Canterbury in 1942, but died in 1944. John Mackay was a leader of the growing ecumenical movement. A former missionary in South America, he became President of Princeton Seminary in 1936, where he served for 23 years not only as President, but as Professor of Ecumenics – the first such post in an American seminary.

his father's shipping business. (With this in mind, he had at the time become something of an ardent advocate for the view that Christians ought to pursue callings in secular professions rather than seeing ordination as the only real option.)

The Swanwick conference was to change how Newbigin viewed his future. An annual event since 1909, the conference brought together over 600 students from a wide range of backgrounds and experiences, providing a rich and stimulating environment for devotion, discussion and debate. In Newbigin's words, it 'opened up a new world'. Alongside the more formal lectures and discussions, there were also times set aside for quiet reflection and prayer, as well as opportunities for creativity and recreation. But it was the plenary addresses in the specially erected marquee that contributed most to what Newbigin was later to describe as 'a kind of transfiguration experience' in which he felt 'lifted up into the heights'.[8] Two significant things happened for Newbigin during the week. To begin with, while praying alone in a tent set aside for private reflection, he felt the distinct call to ordination. He found it difficult to describe in words, but later wrote:

> I suddenly knew that I had been told that I must offer for ordination. I had not been thinking about this. But I knew that I had been ordered and that it was settled and that I could not escape.[9]

Shortly after this, he was approached by Willie Tindal (the study-secretary of SCM) about the possibility of working full-time on the SCM staff.

Newbigin's life was taking significant new directions. He returned for his final year at Cambridge (for which he decided to change from geography to economics), and it was during that year that discussions were held as to where he might be employed as an SCM secretary. The suggestion was made that he might become men's inter-collegiate secretary in Glasgow, and it was at an interview for this post that he met Helen Henderson, who was a women's inter-collegiate secretary for Scotland. Newbigin later wrote: 'I fell in love with her there and then and made up my mind that whether or not the whole committee decided to take me on, I would try and ensure that she did.'[10] They became colleagues for three years in the work in Glasgow, and were married in 1936.

It was together that they decided that God was calling them to missionary service in India, where Helen's parents had been missionaries. Accordingly, they offered themselves to the Foreign Mission Committee of the Church of Scotland, and Newbigin applied to train for ordination at Westminster College, Cambridge, where John Oman (an old family friend) was principal. Newbigin took up residence in autumn 1933 for a three-year course, while

---

[8] Newbigin 1993d: 15.
[9] Newbigin 1993d: 15.
[10] Newbigin 1993d: 17.

Helen went to Moray House, Edinburgh for a statutory year of training, followed by teaching at her old school and a period of language study.

In his own words, Newbigin's three years back in Cambridge 'profoundly changed and deepened' his understanding of the Christian faith.[11] He was due to study for the theological tripos, but managed to find an ancient regulation that exempted him from this obligation; and so – apart from the requirement to take the college exams for ordination in the Presbyterian Church – he was able to embark upon a course of wider reading and study of his own choosing, which he felt would be a much better preparation for what lay ahead. He decided to study Paul's Epistle to the Romans, as it seemed to him to be 'probably the most complete and condensed statement of the gospel' he could find. He duly spent the following months 'wrestling with the Greek text' of the letter with the help of a number of commentaries. He described the effect of these studies as follows:

> I began the study as a typical liberal. I ended it with a strong conviction about the 'finished work of Christ', about the centrality and objectivity of the atonement accomplished on Calvary. The decisive agent in this shift was James Denney. His commentary on Romans carried the day as far as I was concerned. Barth I found incomprehensible. C. H. Dodd seemed to have made the Epistle palatable by removing its toughest parts – the parts where I found strong meat. His 'demythologizing' of the wrath of God seemed to me effectively to remove the love of God, for if 'wrath' was only an anthropomorphic way of describing the consequences of sin, then 'love' would have to be explained along the same lines. At the end of the exercise I was much more of an evangelical than a liberal.[12]

Marriage and India

Newbigin's offer of service to the Foreign Mission Committee of the Church of Scotland was accepted in late 1935, and he and Helen were assigned to the Madras Mission. He graduated in the summer of 1936, and in July was commissioned for service as a foreign missionary by the Edinburgh Presbytery. A month later, he and Helen were married in Edinburgh, and on 26 September 1936, the Newbigins departed from Liverpool docks on the *City of Cairo*, bound for Madras.

They arrived in India nearly four weeks later, Lesslie having spent much of the voyage finishing his first book, an SCM study guide entitled *Christian Freedom in the Modern World*.[13] Then, on arrival in India, the Newbigins immediately found themselves transported into a completely new world. Lesslie wrote in his diary:

---

[11] Newbigin 1993d: 28.
[12] Newbigin 1993d: 29.
[13] Newbigin 1937.

I couldn't help being horrified by the sort of relation that seems to exist between the missionaries and the people. It seems so utterly remote from the New Testament. [. . . .] We drive up like lords in a car, soaking everybody else with mud on the way, and then carry on a sort of inspection, finding all the faults we can, putting everyone through their paces. They all sort of stand at attention and say 'Sir'. It's *awful*. [. . . .] But one thing is as sure as death: surely they won't stand this sort of thing from the white man much longer.[14]

During the following nine months, the Newbigins spent a large part of each day trying to master the complexities of the Tamil language,[15] but early progress was hampered by a serious bus accident in which Lesslie badly smashed his left leg. A series of operations in Madras failed to resolve the problem, and so they were reluctantly compelled to sail back to the UK for further surgery in Edinburgh. It was feared at one point that Lesslie's leg would have to be amputated, but miraculously, after much prayer, healing at last began to set in, and within a few months he was back on his feet again – albeit on crutches. In June 1939, the Newbigins' first child (Margaret) was born, and in September they once more set sail for India – this time for Kanchipuram, where they were to be stationed for the next seven years.

Kanchipuram is one of the seven most sacred Hindu cities in India, and Lesslie was soon pitched into a busy schedule as a district missionary. Alongside continuing language study there were villagers' problems to sort out, and many and varied opportunities for street preaching and other evangelistic ministry. During this time, an experience of far-reaching significance for Newbigin's future development arose out of Kanchipuram's reputation as a Hindu centre of learning. Each week, Hindu scholars would gather at the Ashram of the Ramakrishna Mission for study and reflection. Newbigin was invited to share the leadership of this group with the head of the community, and each would take turns to read and lead discussions on the Svetasvatara Upanishad and St John's Gospel. Newbigin's weekly visits were to have a profound impact upon his thinking. On the one hand they made him deeply conscious of the rationality of Hindu belief; but they also made him aware of the lack of any idea of redemption within its world view. Moreover, he found that the religious mindset of Hinduism did not provide any real point of contact with the good news of Jesus Christ. In fact it erected a barrier to it. If there were to be a point of contact, he concluded, it would be in the secular experience of human life rather than in the realm of 'religion'.[16]

Newbigin was also involved in a wider village ministry in the area around Kanchipuram, spending time in the surrounding settlements where 'untouchable' Indians lived in exclusion from mainstream Hindu life. He was responsible for a number of mission agents in each village, whose task it was to teach

---

[14] Newbigin 1993d: 39.

[15] A mark of Newbigin's skill and commitment to cross-cultural work was that he later became indistinguishable from the locals in his grasp of the language.

[16] Newbigin 1993d: 45–55.

and catechize new believers. He developed systematic teaching materials for use in these villages, which resulted in the annual publication of the *Village Workers' Almanack*, a booklet that provided week-by-week material for catechists who had little or no formal theological education.

Bishop in the Church of South India

Gradually, Newbigin began to take on wider responsibilities, not only at home – where the births of Alison in 1941 and Janet in 1944 were followed by that of John in 1947 – but also in the developing and expanding work of the mission. Notably, he began to be drawn into discussions about the vision for church union in South India. The original congregations brought into existence through the work of the mission of the Scottish Churches formed part of what was known as the South India United Church (SIUC), which had been set up in 1908 by a union of Congregationalists and Presbyterians, and had included a number of congregations sponsored by the American Board of Commissioners for Foreign Mission. This association – together with Anglicans and Methodists, and missionaries of the Reformed Church in America – formed part of the Madras Church Council, whose annual three-day meetings Newbigin had attended since his arrival in Kanchipuram. On the agenda of its meetings each year was the matter of the so-called South India Scheme – a vision for a united church that had first been proposed in general terms by William Carey as far back as 1810. Significant in the development of this vision was the meeting at Tranquebar in 1919 at which the movement towards formal negotiations was given impetus by local Indian leadership. However, as a result of various setbacks and tensions among the different elements within the Council, the movement for unity had reached something of an impasse by the 1940s.

In 1942, Newbigin was elected as convener of the Union Committee of the Madras Church Council, and in the following year as convener of the Committee of the SIUC as a whole – the same year that a dynamic new Bishop of Madras, A. D. Hollis, was consecrated. A high Anglican, he was determined to see that negotiations began again in earnest between representatives of the three denominations, although protracted debates continued over questions of episcopal and presbyteral oversight. Newbigin's role in this process was particularly significant in persuading the mission authorities back in Edinburgh to give up their control of mission property, and in encouraging Indian leadership within the South India Churches. In addition, he spent much of his 1946–7 furlough in the UK seeking to defend the proposed scheme against its critics – both in Scotland (where certain pronouncements by the Society for the Propagation of the Gospel had fanned fears of 'popery'[17]) and also in the Church of England (where he encountered much opposition

---

[17] The SPG refused to recognize the new United Church.

from the Anglo-Catholics). However, after much further discussion and debate, the Union of the Church of South India (CSI) was at last agreed and formally inaugurated in Madras Cathedral in September 1947. After the presiding bishop announced that the three Churches had now become the Church of South India, the great congregation 'rose and burst into the Te Deum'.

> It was as though all the agonizing fears and delays of [. . .] 28 years had dammed up a flood that was now bursting through. I have never heard such singing, and I think there were very many like myself who found it hard to keep back tears of joy as one remembered all that had gone before and all that might lie ahead.[18]

The service served to strengthen and confirm the convictions he had long held about unity in the Church, and made him 'so utterly sure that what we are doing is not patching things together, but being led by the Holy Spirit back to the fullness and simplicity of gospel truth'.[19]

It was at the same service that Newbigin was consecrated as bishop in Madurai. He had allowed his name to go forward as one of a long list of candidates for possible election as one of nine newly appointed bishops, but he was confident that he would be passed over. However, he duly received a cable a short time later that simply read: 'You are appointed bishop Church of South India Madura. We pray God's blessing.' As he was later to write, 'The prayer was comforting but the news was shattering.'[20] He was to have episcopal responsibility for the new diocese of Madurai and Ramnad. He was just 37 years old.

Newbigin was to serve as bishop of the new diocese for the following 12 years, setting in place new structures, seeking to provide a focus for unity amid the continuing tensions between the various partners in the Union, and travelling extensively around the small villages, often preaching up to ten times a day.[21] But it was also during this period that he first began to gain an international reputation within the worldwide ecumenical movement. Partly as a result of his position within the CSI, he was invited to be a 'consultant' at the first assembly of the World Council of Churches (WCC) held in Amsterdam in 1948, and went on to chair the committee responsible for preparing the WCC's second assembly at Evanston, Chicago, in 1954 (under the title 'Christ the hope of the world'). Two years later he became vice-chairman of the WCC's Commission on Faith and Order[22] and was instrumental in laying out the ecumenical agenda for the third assembly in New Delhi in 1961.

---

[18] Newbigin 1993d: 90.

[19] Newbigin 1993d: 91.

[20] Newbigin 1993d: 85. The nine new bishops were added to the six bishops already working within the existing structures.

[21] Newbigin's vivid recollections of this period are recorded in Newbigin 1951.

[22] Together with the movement for 'Life and Work', and the 'International Missionary Council', the 'Faith and Order' movement was the precursor of the WCC, providing much of the impetus of the ecumenical agenda between the Edinburgh world missionary conference of 1910 and the inaugural WCC assembly of 1948.

Throughout these and the following years, he continued to be a powerful advocate for a wider recognition of the CSI – especially within the Anglican communion. He attended the Lambeth Conferences of 1948 and 1958 (as a 'special guest' of Archbishop Geoffrey Fisher), but although at the 1958 conference 160 bishops received Holy Communion at a service that used the CSI liturgy, 'full communion' was not granted to the Union. This was a cause of deep disappointment to Newbigin to the end of his life. He felt not only that a key opportunity had been missed in the cause of Christian unity, but that the CSI represented in his own thinking a pioneering pattern for other churches in the WCC.

Ecumenical statesman and Bishop of Madras

Meanwhile, during the 1950s Newbigin became more involved in the work of the International Missionary Council (IMC). Set up in 1921, the IMC had held meetings at Jerusalem in 1928, Tambaram (India) in 1938, and Whitby (Canada) in 1947, prior to the inaugural meeting of the WCC in 1948.[23] Newbigin now took significant responsibility for the 1952 conference at Willingen in Germany (with its theme, 'The Missionary obligation of the Church'), and was subsequently invited to consider the post of general secretary, with a view to integrating the Council into the structures of the WCC. Should this be agreed, it was hoped that the new general secretary would in turn become the director of the proposed WCC Division of World Mission and Evangelism. The idea for integration was very close to Newbigin's heart, not least because it would bring mission and evangelism more fully into the structures of the WCC. But he was torn about taking on the role because of his continued sense of commitment to his diocesan tasks back in India. After much discussion, however, he agreed to be appointed to the IMC on condition that he would be free to return to India after a five-year posting. The CSI agreed to second him for five years from July 1959 'as a bishop of the Church of South India without diocesan charge, released for service with the International Missionary Council'.[24]

Newbigin was very reluctant to leave, for he had built a precious relationship of love and trust with the people of Madurai. He described his departure in his diary:

> There was a great crowd at the station. At the end they just stood in a great mass and gazed and gazed at me till I felt I would weep. We sang (a Tamil lyric) and at last the train moved off and the group became only a blob in the distance [. . .] There was a group at Kodai Road station with fruit and flowers and honey and they asked me to bless them before the train left. At Dindigul there was another big group with many presents.[25]

---

[23] The WCC had been 'in process of formation' since 1938 when W. A. Visser't Hooft became the first general secretary.

[24] Newbigin 1993d: 149.

[25] Newbigin 1993d: 157.

Hard though it was to leave, Newbigin quickly became engrossed in the new challenges facing him. He set to work energetically on plans for the integration of the IMC with the WCC, believing it to be a true realization not only of the ecumenical vision characterized by the World Missionary Conference at Edinburgh in 1910, but of the gospel imperative to take the good news to the whole world – with ecumenism and mission as part and parcel of the same mandate.[26] The integration was achieved by a formal declaration at the opening act of worship at the New Delhi assembly of the WCC in 1961, and Newbigin thus became the first director of the newly formed WCC Division of World Mission and Evangelism, and an assistant general secretary of the World Council of Churches.

This period of Newbigin's life was especially hectic as he juggled the various demands and responsibilities of the integration process, attended further meetings of the Commission on Faith and Order, and sought also to tie up the loose ends of his diocesan responsibilities back in Madurai. On top of all this, he undertook extensive tours in connection with his role with the IMC, visiting 15 countries during a long tour of Africa in 1960, travelling around the Pacific and Latin America in 1961, and visiting the Caribbean in 1962. In addition there were also shorter trips to Thailand, Japan, North America and Africa, as well as to his mother's home at Rothbury (in Northumberland), where he and the family spent as much holiday time as possible until her death in 1962. With his appointment to the new role of director of the Division of World Mission and Evangelism, Newbigin moved to Geneva, leaving the rest of the family in Bromley, South London, where they had lived during his initial spell with the IMC and which became home while the younger children were at school in England. The new Division had offices in Geneva, London and New York, which not only meant 'filing in triplicate', but frequent flights across the Atlantic. On top of all this, he continued to lecture and publish[27] and – as part of the director's role – took on the editorship of the *International Review of Missions*, which involved, among other responsibilities, writing annual editorial surveys of missionary developments around the world.[28]

When his five-year secondment ended in 1965, Newbigin returned to India, this time – after much consideration – to take up the appointment as

---

[26] See e.g. Newbigin 1960a and 1962a.

[27] During this period he published *A Faith for this One World?* (Newbigin 1961), a significant pamphlet entitled *The Relevance of Trinitarian Faith for Today's Mission* (Newbigin 1963), and prepared the bulk of the material later published as *Honest Religion for Secular Man* (Newbigin 1966), as well as several smaller pieces.

[28] As editor, Newbigin insisted (despite much pressure) on keeping the 's' on the end of 'Mission' in the title of the journal in order to preserve the significance of 'missions' – as the task of making the gospel known where it is not known – in the midst of the more general and wider concept of 'mission' (see Newbigin 1993d: 189). The journal had been started by Joe Oldham in 1912 as a follow-up to the Edinburgh Conference of 1910.

elected Bishop in Madras. It was a welcome return to the country he loved, but the challenges of the new job were very great. In the mid-1960s Madras was already a sizeable city of nearly three million, and was reckoned to be growing at the rate of around 100,000 a year. It was much bigger than the diocese of Madurai, which Newbigin had left six years earlier, and it had a stronger sense of tradition and prestige. There had been an Anglican bishop there since 1835 (who until 1942 had been paid out of colonial revenues), and the early bishops under the British Raj occupied a position of importance superseded only by the Governor and Chief Justice. The city itself boasted around 120 congregations (some of them numbering over a thousand members). Looking back on his earlier ministries in Kanchi and Madurai, Newbigin felt that he had been 'too narrowly ecclesiastical' in his concerns. As a result he resolved to 'try to challenge the strong churches of Madras City to think less of their own growth and welfare and more of God's purpose for the whole of the vast and growing city'.[29]

Following his consecration, therefore, Newbigin quickly became involved not only in initiatives to promote evangelism and outreach, but also in developing programmes for social welfare among those who lived in the slums around the city. In addition to these diocesan initiatives, Newbigin continued to be involved in wider responsibilities. He was elected deputy moderator for the whole of the CSI, and continued to travel extensively either to give lectures or to contribute to ecumenical gatherings as time and diocesan responsibilities allowed. He was a prominent delegate at the WCC's general assembly at Uppsala, Sweden in 1968, at the Louvain meeting of the WCC Commission on Faith and Order in 1971, and at the Commission on World Mission and Evangelism conference at Bangkok in 1973 (with its theme of 'Salvation Today').

Retirement

Newbigin eventually reached retirement age in 1974 – at the age of 65. The rules of the CSI allowed that extension be made for a further five years in certain circumstances, but Newbigin felt strongly that he should make way for an Indian leader. His mode of departure was characteristically enterprising: he chose to return to the UK with Helen by land, fulfilling a long-term wish for an 'emotional shock-absorber'[30] between the demands of the work in Madras and whatever might lie ahead. After an emotional farewell at Madras Central Station to a large gathering of well-wishers (which included the Chief Minister), the Newbigins set out on the two-month journey home carrying

[29] Newbigin 1993d: 203.
[30] Newbigin 1993d: 226.

only two suitcases and a rucksack. They made their way north through Delhi and Lahore, into Pakistan and across Afghanistan and Iran, then along the border between Turkey and Russia (via Mount Ararat). Their journey through Turkey then took them west to Erzurum, Kesari and on to Cappadocia. Once a great centre of Christian thought and activity, Cappadocia turned out to be the only place on the entire trip where the Newbigins had to worship on their own on Sunday, because they could find no other Christians with whom to share fellowship. This had a profound effect upon Lesslie and helped to energize his later reflections on European culture, for it brought home just how completely a once-strong Christian heritage could all but disappear. From Cappadocia they travelled on south to Tarsus, along the 'Turkish Riviera' to Antalya, then north through Ephesus, Smyrna and on to Istanbul. From here they continued their journey through Bulgaria, Yugoslavia and Austria until they reached the centre of Munich in mid-May. Here they began to experience 'real culture shock'.[31]

The long trek home had indeed helped to cushion the departure from India, giving a whole new set of challenging experiences and memories to reflect on during the summer months back in their beloved Edinburgh. It was here that Newbigin also fulfilled another ambition: to read all eleven volumes of Karl Barth's *Church Dogmatics*. He wrote later:

> It was an immensely rewarding experience. Barth condensed and Barth quoted I had found totally unimpressive. But the real Barth, and especially the famous small-print notes, was enthralling. It was a needed preparation for the much more difficult missionary experience which (as I did not then realize) lay ahead.[32]

'Retirement' for Newbigin initially involved taking up a teaching post at Selly Oak Colleges in Birmingham in September 1974. He turned down an invitation to become an assistant bishop in the Anglican Diocese of Birmingham, and applied instead to be received as a minister in the United Reformed Church (URC), later becoming its national moderator for the year 1978–9. Then, after five years' teaching at Selly Oak Colleges, he felt it right to give up his salaried position, but found himself chairing a meeting of the Birmingham District URC at which a local vacancy was being discussed. It was to lead a small, struggling, inner-city congregation opposite Winson Green prison in Birmingham. If no one came forward, the church would have to be closed. After much thought and prayer, Newbigin decided to take the position, and in 1981 (at the age of 72) became its pastor – a post he was to hold for the following seven years.

---

[31] Newbigin 1993d: 227.
[32] Newbigin 1993d: 229.

Mission and the West

Meanwhile, the early 1980s saw Newbigin's ministry take a remarkable and profound new turn. He had been invited to join a small working party convened by the British Council of Churches to prepare for a major conference on 'Church and Society', which was being planned for 1984. Newbigin was unhappy about the initial proposals for the conference, feeling that it did not address the fundamentally important questions, and asked whether it might be postponed in order to allow for more thorough preparation. This was agreed, and Newbigin was asked to write a discussion document, setting out the questions that needed to be considered. As a result of this process, Newbigin wrote a small booklet, published in 1983 under the title *The Other Side of 1984*. It soon became a bestseller, and was to be the first in a series of publications by Newbigin concentrating on the missionary challenges posed by the dominance of a post-Enlightenment culture in the West. Up until the publication of *The Other Side of 1984*, the Churches' wider process of reflection had been loosely entitled the 'British Council of Churches 1984 Project', but thereafter it assumed Newbigin's suggested alternative of the 'Gospel and Our Culture' programme. It quickly gathered pace, developing into two regional conferences (at High Leigh, Hertfordshire in 1990, and Swanwick, Derbyshire in 1991) and culminating in an international conference of 400 delegates held at Swanwick in July 1992.

It was to be a characteristically busy and energetic final phase to an already full life. In addition to the hectic schedule of travel that often characterized his various ministerial and ecumenical responsibilities, Newbigin had already published some 17 books (and over 50 articles) before his retirement in 1974. Often written *en route* to meetings and engagements around the world, these had concentrated upon the broad themes of ecclesiology, ecumenism and mission that had been the focus of his life's energy and convictions. But during his post-retirement years in the UK he published a further 15 books and over 160 smaller pieces, most of them exploring the missionary challenge facing the Church in the West. Particularly significant were *The Other Side of 1984* (1983), *Foolishness to the Greeks* (1986), *The Gospel in a Pluralist Society* (1989), and *Proper Confidence* (1995).

His final years were spent in Herne Hill, South London, where the Newbigins had moved in 1992 from Birmingham in order to be nearer three of their children, and it was here that he died unexpectedly on 30 January, 1998, succumbing suddenly to heart disease following a brief illness. He was 88 years old.

Part 1

THEOLOGICAL FOUNDATIONS FOR MISSION

1

The knowledge of God

The question 'What does it mean to know God?' is central to many of Newbigin's writings. The following two extracts (which are separated by some 30 years) address some of the issues and underlying assumptions raised by it. Both set the question in its widest context, and focus on aspects of 'knowing' that were to remain at the heart of Newbigin's discussions of epistemology throughout his life. They revolve around two fundamental convictions: first, that the meaning of the universe is ultimately to be understood in 'personal' terms, and second, that the deepest clues to the meaning of that universe are to be found in the fact of God's self-disclosure in the person of Jesus Christ.

The first extract is taken from an essay written as early as 1936, while Newbigin was still a theological student at Westminster College, Cambridge. It is a fascinating piece, not least because it outlines the essential lines along which Newbigin's later thinking was to develop. Here he discusses the challenges to the Christian doctrine of revelation, and develops the argument that in contrast to the assumption that real knowledge must be 'factual' (and therefore somehow 'impersonal'), divine revelation is the ultimate demonstration that true knowledge is fundamentally 'personal': 'we know a person only as he chooses to reveal himself, and only as our own spirit is sensitive and trustful to respond to his revelation'. In this context, the knowledge of God is pictured as a gift of grace imparted to those who would receive it. It is not a piece of metaphysical 'information', but a personal revelation of the loving will of the Creator who longs for his creatures to be reconciled to him. The Church – as the recipient of this searching love – is pictured as the community through whom God reaches out to his creation.

This remarkable early essay provides the foundations for Newbigin's later treatments of revelation, and helps to explain why he found the writings of Michael Polanyi so conducive to his thinking when he first came across them some 30 years later.[1] The second extract illustrates this development, and is taken from his 1966 book Honest Religion for Secular Man, *in which Newbigin devotes a chapter to the theme of 'knowing God'. Here (partly in answer to the book* Honest to God

---

[1] Michael Polanyi (1891–1976) was Hungarian by birth and came to England as Professor of Physical Chemistry at Manchester University in 1933. He devoted much of his time to the investigation of scientific enquiry and to the nature of its 'truth' claims. The university created a special 'Professorship of Social Studies' for him in 1948 to enable him to continue work in this field. The book that most influenced Newbigin was published in 1958 and called *Personal Knowledge: Towards a Post-Critical Philosophy* (= Polanyi 1958).

published by Bishop John Robinson in 1963, which had tended to depersonalize the doctrine of God), Newbigin develops Polanyi's insights and argues that the context and precondition of all knowing is to be found in the mutual knowledge of persons. The ultimate expression of this knowledge is the personal self-revelation of God in Christ, remembered and shared with others through the life of the Church. The book was based on the Firth Lectures Newbigin gave at the University of Nottingham in 1964.

* * *

Extract 1
'Revelation' (1936)[2]

It is the mark of religion, among the activities of the human spirit, to claim to be the bearer of revelation; to claim, that is to say, that the message which it delivers and the facts with which it deals are not the fruit of unaided human processes of observation and inference, but have their root in transactions in which man plays the part of recipient and not of originator. In Christianity this is central. There have been divergences, sometimes wide, but the main current of Christian thought has echoed the words of Christ: 'I thank thee, Father, Lord of heaven and earth, that Thou didst hide these things from the wise and understanding and didst reveal them unto babes.'[3] It has been the glory of Christianity to find its saints among those whom the world counts babes, and to exclude from the sphere where it is most intolerable the snobbery which makes blessedness dependent upon abilities which must always be the possession of a few.

In a preliminary consideration of the subject we may fairly say that the central importance ascribed to revelation in Christianity depends upon two beliefs about the nature of the world and of man. Firstly the belief that the meaning of the world is personal. For if the final meaning of the world is less than personal, then it [is] best understood by those methods of scepticism and experiment which are the requisites of scientific enquiry, but which would be the complete destruction of any personal understanding. For we know a person only as he chooses to reveal himself, and only as our own spirit is sensitive and trustful to respond to his revelation, and if the meaning of the world is personal then revelation is the only path by which it can be made known to us.

Secondly the belief that the meaning of man's life is in fellowship: if it were otherwise, we should not only expect that every man would be able to achieve for himself, apart from co-operation with his fellows, the necessities of physical existence and culture, and that pain and pleasure would always be

---

[2] Newbigin 1936: 1–3, 23, 33–6.
[3] Matt. 11.25.

distributed in mathematical accordance with sin and merit; but also that every man would be able to receive by direct revelation from God – apart from human telling – the knowledge necessary for blessedness. But if it be true that man was made for fellowship then we can understand not only the meaning of the co-operation which economic facts make necessary, and the strange incidence of pain and pleasure, so monstrously unjust by the standards of the law courts; but we can also understand the immensely significant fact that the revelation which is the key to our highest blessedness does not descend to us straight from heaven, but has to reach us passed from hand to hand of our fellow men along the chain of a historic community.

It is to be noted that both of these beliefs are essential elements in the Christian view of revelation: the first without the second would make way for an individualistic mysticism very remote from the genius of Christianity; while the second without the first – a belief in human solidarity apart from a personal interpretation of the world – is perfectly compatible with that tyranny of second-hand information which is the characteristic of the age called 'scientific'.

The problem which revelation raises for human thought may be said to be a part of the problem of Grace – the problem of stating the relations of God and man in a way that shall not either annihilate man, or reduce God's revelation to a mere phrase covering nothing more than human discovery. It may also be said to be a part of the problem of knowledge – of how we can know any truth seeing that knowledge must on the one hand be wholly our own inward understanding and valuing, and on the other hand must be wholly concerned with reality external to our mind.

[. . . .]

We may sum up [the] two-sided examination of the teaching of the New Testament about revelation by saying that, on the one hand, God's purpose for man is made known not by the up-reach of human moral and intellectual striving, but by the down-reach of God's saving grace. But that – on the other hand – that saving grace achieves its end only as it is recognised and accepted by men's deepest insights, and that it will take no other road. Our own un-aided insight will not bring us to God; yet only as it accepts Him will He come to us; we only receive His light as we recognise it for the light; yet it may be very different from what we had expected. God's saving word is not spoken *through* our highest faculties; but it is spoken *to* them.

[. . . .]

The modern situation

To the present tendency to distrust and misunderstand the idea of revelation two factors seem to have mainly contributed. In the first place, there has been the movement which – on a wider scale than that described in the last section – has seen the dissolution of the externally guaranteed infallibilities and the growing conviction that nothing is to be accepted as truth except as it is seen to be true. This tendency is not so universal as is sometimes supposed; science – for all but a very few experts in each field – is a matter of infallibly guaranteed dogmas accepted with a credulity which might have been the envy of past theologians; nevertheless it has been a movement of decisive importance for theology.

But secondly, and possibly even more important, there has been the immense – because largely unconscious – influence of scientific thought in depersonalising our view of the world. The atmosphere of scientific thinking is one in which the active and originative part appears to be entirely played by the self, while the external world with which we are dealing lies inert and passive for our manipulation and exploitation. Such a world offers us no final resistances, and the mind moves in a solitary omnipotence, governed only by its own desires. And in this matter the triumphs of applied science powerfully reinforce the psychological effects of the dominance of scientific thinking. Even man is caught up into this world view, and by the various sociological sciences reduced to a mere counter to be moved about at will. How different from all this is the real world of persons! [T]here the self is confronted not with dead counters for his manipulation, but with the irreducible fact of a living will which may oppose his own. Not only does he question; he may himself be questioned. In judging he finds that he himself is judged. Not only is the world his discovery; it is also a revelation.

From the point of view of the Christian understanding of the world it seems that the first tendency is something to be whole-heartedly accepted, and the second to be whole-heartedly attacked. Yet the issue is complicated by the fact that in practice there has often been pollution of the first stream by the second, in that the statement that man's insight is a condition of receiving God's revelation has passed by a subtle transition to the view that man's insight is the only reality in the transaction at all. Here the protest of Barth is surely on the right lines; the voice that speaks to our religious insight is the voice of another person and another will which confronts us with a question and a judgement which is emphatically not that simply of our own highest selves.

The fundamental and unifying fact is the personal nature of God and of man. Only in the light of this fact can we see how God's self-disclosure and man's valuation are inseparable parts of one whole relationship. Only so do we see God's revelation not as a piece of information, but as the love which discloses its nature in the act of seeking its object, and man's response not merely as the mastering of an advanced lesson in metaphysics, but as the answer of heart and mind and will to the love that is seeking him. As long as revelation is seen as primarily concerned with the abstract reason, then the wise and prudent who continue to give such learned indications of the obscurity, not to say opacity, of its contents, can only serve to prove that the babes must have mistaken it for something else. But if it be the revelation of a loving will in the act of beseeching us to be reconciled to itself, then even he who does not fully understand the doctrine may yet make his true response by his doing of the will. And, finally, in the light of this fact, we can understand how Christ could ascribe the Mosaic Law to divine revelation, and yet set it aside as out of date; for revelation – being the divine education of children – must take account of the stages of our development and speak so as to be understood by such insight as we already have.

The understanding of and response to the love which is seeking us through all life begins when we see that life which was both the perfect response to and the perfect expression of that love. And the light of that life reaches us through the Church, through the community of those who – bound together in the love which it brought down to men – are forever shedding that love abroad, and manifesting in the grace of Christlike character the reconciling purpose of God; and through the records of that life and those transactions in which the Church was born. And as we allow that love to pierce our clouded vision and are gathered into the Christian fellowship, we exchange the eyes of resentment for those of reconciliation and learn to see in the world of daily life that same love which first broke into our hearts because it was revealed in Christ.

Extract 2
Honest Religion for Secular Man *(1966)*[4]

What does it mean to speak of knowing God?

[. . . .]

I think we cannot tackle this question without trying to say something, however inadequate, about what we mean by knowing anything. Here, more perhaps than in most other matters, we tend to take over uncriticized the assumptions of our culture, and it is therefore the more important to be aware of these assumptions and of the fact that other assumptions are possible. Our present culture accustoms us to regard as the ideal of knowledge the kind of knowledge which can ultimately be stored in an electronic computer. We are accustomed to regard other kinds of knowledge as being reliable in the measure that they approach that standard. But quite other views can be and are held. One who has absorbed the thought-forms of Hinduism, at least in its central tradition, sees as the ideal and standard of knowledge that which can be attained by abstraction from all the impressions of sense. The data provided by the five senses, so far from being regarded as the foundation of all else, are regarded as basically unreliable and even illusory. The true knowledge by which all else is to be measured is found by withdrawal from them into an

---

[4] Newbigin 1966: 77, 79–89, 92–5 [. . . .].

inner citadel of pure subjectivity. The language of the Bible introduces us to yet a third view of knowledge. The central use of the verb 'to know' in the Old Testament is its use in respect of the mutual knowledge of persons. It expresses a relationship in which much more is involved than knowledge of facts, of concepts, or of mathematical or logical operations. One of the most significant uses of the verb in the Old Testament is its use to describe the act of love between a man and a woman. There is expressed, if you will, the ideal of knowledge from the biblical point of view – the total mutual self-revelation and surrender of persons to one another in love. And the Bible repeatedly uses the analogy of the sexual relation to describe the mutual knowledge of God and his people.

It is from within this biblical tradition that I speak if I try to say something of what is meant by the knowledge of God. But I believe that this under-standing of knowledge helps us to understand the nature of all knowing, and to understand that the knowledge of God is not unrelated to all our other kinds of knowledge, including that which can ultimately be stored in a computer.[5]

1   In the first place let us note the obvious point that all knowing is a skill. One must learn to know. This is true from the very first beginnings of per-ception when an infant learns to focus its eyes and to distinguish objects from their background and from the total blur of lights and shades around it. This skill which is acquired by the process of learning and practice contains ele-ments which cannot be specified in any formula which would thenceforth obviate the necessity of learning. The skills involved in riding a bicycle depend for their effectiveness upon laws of motion and gravity which can be stated in terms of formulae which can be fed into a computer. But the availability of these formulae does not eliminate the process of learning necessary to acquire the skill. The same is true at all stages of learning, whether it be in acquiring skill in riding a bicycle or in using a mathematical or logical process. Knowledge does not impose itself upon us – at any stage. It is acquired by being learned, and it is learned by acquiring the skills necessary to carry through the mental operations involved in learning. Knowing is a personal achievement which, in appropriate cases, is rewarded by the gift of a prize. Knowing is an activity of persons.

2   Knowing is an activity of persons in community. This is also true from the first beginnings of knowing in infancy. The earliest knowledge of a new-born baby is knowledge of its mother. As it grows, its knowledge of things around it is knowledge of a world shared with its parents and other members of the family. The names by which it learns to distinguish one thing from another are names learned from them. This communal aspect of learning remains essential from start to finish. All progress in knowledge depends upon the existence of a community of persons who share their experience and

---

[5] Readers of Polanyi 1958 will recognize in what follows my debt to this book.

who mutually trust one another to accept certain standards. Throughout the whole process there are personal decisions to be made, about which personal conflict may ensue between different scholars. In these conflicts much more is involved than purely intellectual activities. There are involved the total personalities of those concerned. This combination of mutual trust with the readiness for mutual resistance and conflict are part of the stuff without which there can be no advance in knowledge. From beginning to end our knowledge of the world is a shared knowledge; indeed without this communal element we could have no assurance even of the reality of what we think we see and feel. No human being is strong enough to go on asserting the existence of something in face of the unanimous denial of the rest of mankind. If he tries, he is put in a mental hospital. Not only our appreciation of music, of poetry, of architecture and of philosophy, but also our knowledge of the physical world depends upon our participation in a community of persons within which there is at least some real measure of mutual knowledge and trust.

3   Knowing involves a risk and a commitment. It involves the acceptance, at least provisionally, of beliefs which might be mistaken. One cannot even speak a sentence without accepting provisionally the framework of thought which this language expresses and which is itself the result of the particular history of the people who speak it. One comes to realize this when one is trying to master a language which belongs to a totally different family of languages from one's own as, for instance, when an Englishman learns to speak Tamil. The very structure of the language and the use of the words arises from an immensely long experience different at important points from that which has formed the English tongue. And yet one cannot begin to speak without provisionally accepting that framework of thought. As we use words reflectively, we become aware of assumptions underlying them which we had taken over uncritically with the word when we first heard it used. We then use other words in order to try to correct the false assumption, but in order to carry out this critical activity we have to accept for the moment and use uncritically another set of words. There is no way of speaking except by taking these risks. The true seers, the poets and the original thinkers, create new patterns of words and run the risk of writing nonsense. But this is the necessary risk involved in the efforts to know more deeply. The same risk is run by the artists and the composers and the architects who create new patterns of colour or shape or sound, often at the risk of uttering nonsense. But the risk has to be run in order that the possibility may be created for the human community to discern beauty which it had not before discerned. And the same is also true of the great advances in mathematics and the natural sciences. The great scientific advances have been creative and imaginative leaps in which the scientist was taking the risk of being declared wrong. One does not need to be reminded of the fierce controversies which have surrounded the first announcement of some of the great new theories. Science has not advanced by the method of sticking to facts which cannot be contradicted. Quite the opposite. It has advanced by the daring of those who created completely new patterns of

thought even when there were still plenty of facts that could be used to refute them.

[. . . .]

It is therefore wholly erroneous to say, as is often said in discussions about re-ligious knowledge, that real knowledge is only achieved by a scrupulous care in avoiding any possibility either of believing anything which is beyond the evidence or of saying anything which is not entirely clear and immediately verifiable. In fact the extension of knowledge in all realms of human experi-ence is achieved in defiance of these two rules. Anyone is, of course, free to invent games as he wishes and to lay down the rules. But reality, if one may be excused for using the word, is almost by definition that which does not submit to our rules but requires us to submit to its. All the evidence of human experience, the evidence of the greatest of men, the poets, the artists, the sci-entists and the saints, goes to suggest that knowledge is accessible to those who are ready to keep the doors open, to venture beyond what is clear and unques-tionable, even if it involves the risk of being mistaken or talking nonsense. It is difficult to read the whole story of the human quest for knowledge with-out coming to the conclusion that it is more dangerous to be afraid of mak-ing a mistake than to be afraid of missing something real. To put it in another way, it is possible to be led astray both by too much faith and by too much doubt, but there can be no question that the active principle in knowing is faith. The ancient word of Anselm is true of much more than theology: one must believe in order to understand.

To say this is not for a moment to deny that doubt and scepticism have an indispensable role to play in the art of knowing. Some facts alleged by reli-gious believers are untrue, some words written under the name of poetry have been nonsense, and some scientific theories have been mistaken. Not to stray outside my own proper field, there is a great deal in the world of religious language and practice which calls for a much more rigorous scepticism than it often gets in religious circles. To be prepared to face sceptical scrutiny is the necessary mark of any belief which is belief in what is real. But scepticism is not the active principle in the advance of knowledge. The active principle is the willingness to go out beyond what is certain, to listen to what is not yet clear, to search for what is hardly visible, to venture the affirmation which may prove to be wrong, but which may also prove to be the starting-point for new conquests of the mind. In the traditional language of Christianity the name for that active principle is faith.

4   However, it is obvious that neither in ordinary speech nor in the speech of the Bible are 'faith' and 'knowledge' synonymous. In many contexts faith is used for a state of mind which may be a preparation for knowledge but cer-tainly falls short of knowledge. A man may be sustained in a long course of difficult research by the faith that he is on a fruitful line and that it will even-tually bring results. But the result he expects is something different from the faith which sustains him: it is assured knowledge, let us say, in principle,

knowledge of the kind which could be fed into a computer. No one is going to confuse these two things. And it might seem natural to go on the very common view that the highest role which can be assigned to faith is that it is an element in the achievement of knowledge, but can never be more than that. Where we have to be content with faith, it is simply because knowledge is not available, or because of invincible ignorance.

However, the matter is not quite so simple as that. The result of our scientist's research may be such that in due course it becomes part of what is regarded as assured knowledge. It goes into the textbooks and becomes the basis for further research. Yet, in spite of the fact that it is in this sense regarded as 'knowledge', our scientist knows that it is perfectly possible that in a few years' time it will be superseded as the result of further research. When that happens he will not fight for its retention. It is, in truth, provisional. But if a school of thought were to arise which attacked not his particular findings, but the whole scientific method; if, let us say, due to some unforeseen swing of the political pendulum there should be a demand by government that the medical faculty should begin to teach the Ayur Vedic system of medicine, or that astrology should be introduced as an optional paper for the BSc degree, then our scientist, if he is worth his salt, will fight back. The conviction for which he will fight is not 'knowledge' of the kind that could be fed into a computer. It is faith in the validity of the scientific method over against its predecessors. It is faith in the integrity of the community of scientists to which he belongs and to which he owes loyalty. It is not knowledge. It is not assured in the sense of the 'assured findings' which have passed into the textbooks. But he will fight for it, as he would not fight for the other. If reality is that which has to be reckoned with, which requires us to alter course, which cannot be simply walked through as one walks through a phantom, then it would seem that the objects of faith may have a higher degree of reality than the objects of our knowledge. It is difficult to deny, unless we are to condemn as irrational the kind of behaviour which we normally applaud as noble, that faith may bring us into contact with reality no less surely than knowledge. Or, to put it in another way, it is difficult to deny there are realities which we *know* by faith.

5   There is one realm where this is obviously true, namely the knowledge which we have of other people. [I have referred to] the distinction between two ways of knowing, knowing an object and knowing another person. This distinction has been made familiar in the writings of Martin Buber, with their sharp reminder of the difference between the relation I–Thou and the relation I–It.[6] The knowledge of an object is achieved by processes of inspection and experiment in which the knowing subject is the only active agent. Knowledge of another person involves the recognition of another centre of decision which it is not in my power to control. True knowledge of that other person [. . . .] can only come as the result of a mutual trust leading to a mutual

---

[6] (See e.g. Buber 1958.)

self-revelation. This is a self-revelation which the other can, if he will, finally withhold. I may even use torture and the threat of death to extract from another some secret about himself, but he can still withhold from me that trust and love which are the substance of personal knowledge. What is true of all knowing is supremely true of the knowledge of another person, that one must believe in order to know. It is possible to learn by observation and even by experiment a great deal about a person. It is possible to use a person, and to discover how he can be used. But to treat the person in this way is to exclude oneself from the possibility of knowing the person as he or she truly is. That knowledge is a matter of self-revelation which depends wholly upon mutual trust, mutual respect, mutual caring.

[. . . .] The argument of the present chapter seeks to show that knowledge is all of a piece, and that even our knowledge of the kind of facts which can be stored in an electronic computer cannot be understood except as personal knowledge, knowledge which is the achievement of persons, living in a community of persons, and, in a very real sense, living by faith. The mutual knowledge of persons is not something apart from our other knowledge. It is not an exception to the general rule which might be allowed for but which could not govern our basic thinking. It is, on the contrary, the context and the precondition of all knowing. Without it there can be no other kinds of knowledge. The biblical usage in which the primary meaning of the verb 'to know' refers to this mutual knowledge of persons is not an archaeological oddity. It is a profoundly significant witness to the truth about all knowing.

6   In the light of this discussion about knowing in general we must now approach our central question: what does it mean to speak of the knowledge of God? Manifestly, in the first place, our language about knowing God is to be interpreted in terms of what we have described as personal knowledge. To know God is not to know of the existence of an object over and above the sum of objects whose existence is known to unbelievers. Nor is it a kind of knowledge separate from our whole knowledge of the world of things and persons. Such knowledge is not accessible to us. Even our most intimate personal knowledge of one another is possible only through our sharing together in a common world of things and persons. There is no other personal knowledge available to us. It has been suggested that some kinds of insects communicate with one another by direct psychic means and that this explains the extraordinary order and cohesion of insect communities. We have known of human relationships in which one person had such a psychic power over the other that he could enforce his will almost without the use of explicit speech. But this is not true personal knowledge. Such knowledge is only achieved through sharing together in a common world of things, of experiences, of ideas. *A fortiori* it is only through the shared world of nature and history that we have knowledge of God. It is in, with, and under this shared world of things and persons that we can know God.

[. . . .]

26

We cannot argue ourselves into knowledge of another person. That person must meet us, and we must learn by speech, action, event, to know that person in the concreteness and particularity of his person. The Christian testimony is that God has so acted, so spoken, so given himself to us in Jesus, that we know that he loves us, and that that knowledge is constantly confirmed and enriched through the events of daily life.

[. . . .]

It is obvious that the existence of God can be doubted, is in fact doubted, even by believers. This seems to some [. . .] a reason for trying to find some way of stating religious faith which is not open to doubt. I think this rests on a wrong concept of knowledge. It rests, that is to say, upon the conception which dominates our contemporary culture, that the ideal form of knowledge is knowledge which is proof against doubt. I am arguing that this is a false ideal of knowledge, and that we are on the wrong track if we try to describe the knowledge of God in terms which eliminate the possibility of doubt. For myself I have to confess that the heart of the whole matter is at the point [. . .] where I know that I am dealing with the living God who is, if you like, the eternal Thou, but who is emphatically not a category but a living personal being. If this be illusion, then it seems to me that the rest of the language about ultimate concern, about self-transcendence, about the ground of our being, is robbed of real meaning. They are phrases which echo an experience whose substance has disappeared. I am concerned about knowing God, knowing him as one who is other than myself, as the Father whom I worship, whose forgiveness I seek, whose will I desire to know, and from whom I ask those things that he knows I need. When I so worship and pray it is not enough for me to remember that arguments can be found for believing in the ultimacy of the personal. I want to know whether he is there, and whether he hears me. And I want to know why it is that, if he is there, it is possible for me to doubt it. I want to know why he seems to hide himself. [. . . .]

7 [. . . .] Personal knowledge depends upon mutual trust. And this trust includes as one essential ingredient respect for the independence and integrity of the other. If I feel, in respect of another person, that 'I've got him where I want him', and can be sure that he has no further surprises in store for me, then my relation with him falls short of true mutual personal knowledge. The greater and richer the personality of the other, the more certain is it that, even in a lifetime of contact, my knowledge of him will not be exhaustive. He will still have surprises to spring which make me realize that there was more to him than I understood. In true personal relations, the other always remains free. Even in the most intimate of such relations, in marriage at its very best, there is, and there ought to be, more on each side than can be fully known to the other. Each person remains free, with depths of consciousness, of memory, of desire, and of imagination which the other can never completely grasp and must always respect. True personal knowledge is threatened by the

possessiveness which is not willing to accept this, but which lusts for the kind of relationship in which one can take the other for granted, in which everything is under control, in which there are no more unfathomed depths and no more surprises.

If this is true in the mutual knowledge of men and women, it must certainly be true of man's knowledge of God. Man can know God only in so far as God manifests himself in events which are accessible to man's observation and which are interpreted as God's doing. These events will enable man to know God in so far as man grasps them as occasions for trusting God and obeying him. Without this response there is no personal knowing. But this knowing can never be complete. 'We know in part.' The full richness of God's being must far transcend all that we have grasped by grasping these events as the disclosure of his character. We must be ready for surprises, be constantly aware that the God who is so revealed is also hidden; that a lifetime is not enough to fathom the depths of his being. We must, to use the biblical imagery, be pilgrims, always ready to move on, to leave even the most hallowed place, to take down even the sanctuary where God has shown himself to us, and move on. But we do not want to do this. We want the religion that we have, rather than the risky faith that God has somewhere more in store for us. The story of the children of Israel in the wilderness is the mirror which the Bible holds up to us to show us the whole story of human religion.

We know God as he reveals himself to us. There is no other way to the knowledge of persons. He reveals himself in what he does. We cannot forecast or control it. Suddenly we know that he was there, in that bush burning in the desert, in that storm sweeping aside the waters and making a path for the escaping slaves, in that man hanging upon a gallows. That was the moment when we saw, and we go back to it; we must go back to it again and again to renew the vision. The whole believing community goes back again and again to the place where the disclosure was made. The words and acts of Jesus are read and expounded, his baptism is re-enacted for each believer, his death and resurrection are shown forth again in the breaking of bread and the sharing of the cup. These acts, repeated, formalized so that they may become the common possession of all races and all generations, constitute the visible substance of religion. By them the believing community relives the moment of revelation, renews its participation in it, reaffirms its faith in its truth.

Further reading

Newbigin 1968: 12–16.
Newbigin 1989b: 52–65.
Newbigin 1996.

2

The death of Christ

Newbigin described his discovery of the 'finished work of Christ' on the cross while still a theological student at Cambridge as a 'turning point' in his theological journey.[1] He had decided to study Paul's letter to the Romans in order to find out 'what I could believe' and spent several months 'wrestling with the Greek text of Romans' surrounded by half a dozen of the major commentaries. However, it was James Denney's commentary[2] that 'carried the day' as far as Newbigin was concerned, and as a result he came to understand the cross as both the demonstration of God's patient love and the manifestation of his righteous judgement.

The first extract is taken from the 1956 book Sin and Salvation, *which Newbigin originally wrote in Tamil to help train village preachers in the district of Madurai, where he was Bishop from 1947 to 1959. Here we find Newbigin's emphasis on the cross as the supreme revelation of the love of God. It is 'at the cross we understand the infinite depths of God's love [. . . .] He has come down to bear upon Himself the burden of sin, to receive the wages of sin, to suffer the dread penalties of sin.'[3] He was later to write that this one of the 'mighty certainties upon which we rest all that we have and are, and which we proclaim to every man who will hear'.[4]*

This conviction about the cross not only characterized the content of Newbigin's missionary preaching, but also laid the groundwork for his approach to Christian unity (see chapter 5). It was also to undergird his later discussions about Christian involvement in public affairs. The second extract is taken from his 1989 book The Gospel in a Pluralist Society, *which was based on the Alexander Robertson Lectures he gave at Glasgow University in 1988. Here Newbigin develops the idea that the cross reveals God's 'unmasking' of the spiritual 'principalities and powers' that are at work in the social and political structures, and that assume a power not rightfully theirs. In the light of the cross, nothing is left absolute 'except God as he is known in Jesus Christ'.[5] The basis of Christian action in the world is therefore founded on the fact that all other powers are shown up for what they are, and must be brought into the light of God's redemptive action in Christ.*

* * *

[1] Newbigin 1993d: 29.
[2] Denney 1904.
[3] Newbigin 1956: 91.
[4] Newbigin 1960b: 157. See Newbigin 1951: 32, 39 for his experience of preaching the cross in South India.
[5] Newbigin 1989b: 208.

Extract 1
Sin and Salvation *(1956)*[6]

'God so loved the world, that he gave his only begotten son that whosoever believeth in him should not perish but have everlasting life.' In that sentence which every Christian knows and loves, the good news of salvation is briefly expressed. [. . . .]

1   The first thing we notice is that the author of our salvation is God. We have seen [. . .] that man is unable to extricate himself from the net of sin. Like an animal trapped in a clever snare, mankind trapped in the snare of sin struggles to free himself, but the more he struggles, the more the snare fastens its grip on him. His efforts to be free of sin are themselves infected by sin and drive him deeper into sin. Because sin is a corruption of the very centre of man's will, even when he wills to be free from sin he is driven deeper into sin.

[. . . .] The more God's people strove to draw near to Him, the more deep was the gulf which separated them from Him. That is the tragedy of the Old Testament. And it reaches its climax in the Pharisees of the New Testament. These were the most zealous and energetic of the Jewish churchmen. They laboured unceasingly to bring the whole Jewish people under obedience to the Law of God. It was their aim to root out every trace of uncleanness in their lives and the life of their people. And yet it was these men who took the lead in the murder of Jesus. In that fact we see the nature of sin revealed. More than any other men, the Pharisees willed to escape from sin, but that very will drove them to the most terrible sin in the history of the world. Man can never by his own power or will extricate himself from the grip of sin; only God can extricate him. And God has done it. That is the good news which we preach.

2   Secondly we notice that this act of God sprang from His love for the world. We have seen that the whole world is in the power of sin, and is therefore in a state of enmity against God. And yet God loved the world and still loves it. That is the reason why He has put forth His power to save it. This is a fact which we must never forget. Sometimes Christians in trying to explain the cross of Christ have suggested that it was the love and self-sacrifice of Christ which turned away the wrath of God and so secured our salvation. This is a perversion of the truth. It is true that – as we have seen – the wrath of God is revealed against the sin of the world. The wrath of God is a reality. In order to understand the cross we must understand that. But the love which secured our salvation also comes from God. In Him there is both wrath and love. The wrath is the reverse side of His love. But God's wrath is not turned away by anything from outside of God. It was because God loved the world that He gave His Son to be its Saviour.

---

[6] Newbigin 1956: 56–68 [. . . .].

3   It is by giving His only begotten Son that God has saved the world. In order to understand this we have to speak briefly about the doctrine of the Holy Trinity. This is a mystery which is beyond the power of our human minds to understand fully. We must expect that the nature of God will be greater than our minds can grasp. But we have to try to understand what God has revealed to us. He has revealed His nature to us as perfect love. In His being there is the complete fulness of love. This being so, we must say that God is personal but that He is not a person. For a single person cannot possess the fulness of love. Love in its fulness only exists where there is a giving and receiving of love, where love is mutual. If God were a single person, He could not know the perfection of love because there is no one who can give Him perfect love in return for His love. But what is revealed to us through Christ is a God in whom there is both giving and receiving of love, love in mutuality and in perfection. The Father loves the Son, and the Son loves the Father, and they are bound together in the same Holy Spirit. Of course this is more than our minds can grasp. There is one God, but He is not one Person; he is Father, Son and Holy Spirit. He is an ocean of love and joy beyond anything that we can conceive and beyond anything that could exist in one person. Out of that fulness the Son has come forth into the world to win our salvation. In so doing He has come under the power of sin and therefore under the sentence of suffering and death which is the wages of sin. But yet He remained and remains one with the Father in the unity of the Godhead. When He poured out His soul to death, He did not pour it out like water into sand; He poured it out into the hands of His Father. 'Father, into thy hands I commend my Spirit.' And the Father accepted the offering. Thus when God came forth to undertake the salvation of the world from sin, He did not abandon His Godhead. He remained and remains God, an ocean of love ever full, ever given and ever received, and therefore ever full of joy. How then did the Son come forth from the Father for the salvation of the world? He came 'in the likeness of sinful flesh';[7] He was 'made flesh';[8] He emptied Himself, taking the form of a servant, being found in fashion as a man.[9] All these different phrases mean that He, being God, took upon Himself our manhood – that manhood which has come under the power of sin and death. The manhood which He took was a complete manhood – body, mind and soul. He was not a divine soul in a human body; He was completely and perfectly a man. Nor was His manhood a temporary appearance. He took upon Him our manhood for eternity. As man he rose from the dead and ascended into heaven. This union of godhead and manhood in one person is certainly a mystery beyond our comprehension. But the record of the apostles shows that it is a fact. In the Gospel story we find that He is in every respect a man like us. He is tempted by sin;

---

[7] Rom. 8.3.
[8] John 1.14.
[9] Phil. 2.7.

He is wearied, hungry, thirsty; He is disappointed and surprised by unbelief; He longs for the companionship of His friends; He is fully man. And yet at the same time He says things and does things which only God can say and do. He takes the Law of God from the Old Testament and says: 'Ye have heard that it was said to them of old time thus . . . But I say unto you . . .' Who but God can speak thus – unless He be a blasphemer? Or consider such words as these: 'He that loseth his life for my sake shall find it[10] or these: 'Whosoever shall be ashamed of me and of my words in this adulterous and sinful generation, of him shall the Son of man be ashamed when he cometh in the glory of his Father with the holy angels.'[11] It is not necessary to give many examples; Jesus was a man who lived among men in Palestine 19 centuries ago; but He also spoke and acted as God's own representative with full powers to claim the obedience which man owes to God. When the lord of the vineyard in Jesus' parable had sent all His servants to claim His dues from the wicked cultivators and when there was nothing more that He could do, He sent His own beloved son.[12] That is what God did for the world. He being 'God of God, Light of Light, Very God of Very God', came down from heaven and took upon Him our sinful manhood, was born of a virgin, lived a perfect human life, died, rose again, and ascended into heaven. Taking upon Himself our sinful nature, so that He became subject to the fierce temptations of sin as we are subject, He lived a life of sinless perfection in the midst of sin. Never for one moment did any evil come between Him and His Father. He remained at every instant 'in the bosom of the Father' in perfect intimacy with Him. Thus He met and overcame sin in our nature, from within the enemy's territory.

But when we have said this we have not yet reached the heart of the matter. The heart of the matter is His death. About that there can be no doubt. The New Testament makes this very clear. In the Gospels – where an account is given of His birth, life, teachings and miracles – the main attention is concentrated upon His sufferings and death and resurrection. In the Epistles this is even more clear. When St Paul gives a summary of the Christian message to the Corinthians,[13] it is entirely concerned with the death and resurrection. The rest of his teaching bears this out. His preaching is 'the word of the cross'.[14] And in the Epistles of Peter and John we find the same emphasis. In fact, as is well known, the cross has become the universal symbol of Christianity. The cross is the place where the decisive battle between Christ and sin took place, where the powers of Satan brought all their strength to the attack, and where they were defeated. It is the place where the wages of sin[15] were accepted on behalf of the whole human race.

---

[10] Matt. 10.39.
[11] Mark 8.38.
[12] Mark 12.6.
[13] 1 Cor. 15.1–11.
[14] 1 Cor. 1.18–25.
[15] Rom. 6.23.

Of course the cross must not be isolated from the whole work of Christ. Without His incarnation there could be no cross and no salvation. Without His words and works we should not know who it was that died for us there. Without His resurrection the cross would not be known to us as victory but as defeat. Without His ascension to the Father and the gift of the Spirit, we who live at other times and places could have no share in Christ. All these things are parts of the one complete work of Christ for the salvation of the whole world. But the centre and focus of that work is the cross, and it is about the cross that we shall especially be speaking in the following chapters.

4   The verse which we are studying (John 3.16) goes on to say that the purpose of God's sending His Son was that 'those who believe on him should not perish but have everlasting life'. Everlasting life – that is the purpose. There is a way which goes to death. The whole world is on that way. It is going the way to death, destruction, emptiness, darkness. But God in His love does not will thus. He wills life for His creatures, He wills them to have it now. It is true that we cannot have the perfect fulness of life until God brings in the new heavens and the new earth which He has promised. The fulness is for all, and we cannot have it alone. We still have to take our place and bear our witness in the midst of this world which is under the power of death. Even our bodies must also die. But it is His will that, even now, we should be sharers in that eternal life. He gives this share through the Holy Spirit. By the gift of the Spirit we are able even now, while living in this world, to know that we are heirs of eternal life. It is given to us to have in us 'a well of water springing up unto life eternal'.[16]

5   Finally, our text tells us that it is by faith that we are to take hold of this great blessing. What Christ has done once for all, in Palestine, 19 centuries ago, can be made mine here today if I believe. Faith is the hand that grasps what Christ has done and makes it my own.

We have seen that the centre and heart of God's saving acts is the death of Jesus Christ on the cross. It is about that that we must now chiefly speak. It is important never to forget the whole saving work of which the cross forms only the centre. We must not isolate the cross and treat it in forgetfulness of what went before and what came after. Nevertheless the New Testament teaches us that when we seek the source of our salvation, it is primarily about the death of Christ that we have to speak.

As we try to do so, we must remember that, here too, we have a mystery which the mind of man can never fully grasp. Thousands of books have been written on the death of Christ. Many theories have been developed to explain how Christ's death saves us. And yet none of these theories really 'explains' it. All of them can only suggest, hint at, point to, the truth. The truth is that there is nothing else in all human experience which is equal to the cross, and

---

[16] John 4.14.

therefore no general theory can explain it. But there are many helpful pictures and symbols given to us in the New Testament itself which – taken all together – help us to understand it. In what follows we shall first listen to what Jesus Himself taught about His death, and then look in turn at the main symbols which have been used to point to the meaning of the cross.

The teaching of Jesus about His death

1 His death is necessary. Even in the earliest part of His ministry it appears that Jesus expected His death. He likens Himself and His disciples to a marriage-party,[17] and says that the days are coming when the Bridegroom will be taken away. In many places the Messiah is likened to a bridegroom, and His coming to the joy of a marriage; but here He definitely warns them that the bridegroom will be taken away. Similarly in Mark 3.1–6 He makes it quite clear that he knows the Jews are planning His death. But it is after Peter's confession that He is the Christ, that Jesus begins very clearly to tell His disciples that He must die. 'The Son of man must suffer' is His repeated and emphatic word to them.[18] And in accordance with this we read that 'He steadfastly set his face to go to Jerusalem',[19] knowing that He was going to His death.

2 His death is the will of the Father. It is clear that Jesus did not merely accept His death as unavoidable on account of the forces which were ranged against Him; He accepted it as the will of His Heavenly Father. There is much evidence to show that He found the will of His Father expressed for Him in the prophecy of the Suffering Servant of the Lord[20] [. . .]. There are very frequent echoes of the language of this chapter in the Gospels. When He says to the 12 disciples, 'How it is written of the Son of man that he should suffer many things and be set at naught'[21] He must have been referring to this chapter. And in Luke 22.37 He directly quotes it: 'I say unto you that this which is written must be fulfilled in me, And He was reckoned with transgressors.'

The matter becomes very clear in the prayer which Jesus made in the Garden of Gethsemane, 'Abba, Father, all things are possible unto thee, remove this cup from me; howbeit, not what I will, but what thou wilt'.[22] These words, and the whole of what happened in Gethsemane, make it very clear that Jesus accepted His death not as something merely unavoidable, but as the

---

[17] Mark 2.19–20.
[18] Mark 8.31; 9.31; 10.33–34.
[19] Luke 9.51.
[20] Isa. 53.
[21] Mark 9.12.
[22] Mark 14.36.

means of doing His Father's will. To suffer and die was not an accident but the fulfilment of the vocation which God had given Him.

3 His death arises from His identification of Himself with sinners. At the outset of His ministry Jesus went to be baptized by John in Jordan. This baptism was spoken of as 'A baptism of repentance for the remission of sins'.[23] Those who came to be baptized were men and women who felt the burden of their sin and longed to be free of it. It is very clear from Jesus' own words that He had no personal burden of sin. He spoke always as one who had unclouded fellowship with His Father without any of the sense of sin which the greatest saints feel when they approach God. And yet Jesus felt Himself so much one with men, He loved them so much and identified Himself with them so much that He gladly went with them to share in the same baptism. It was then that He received the definite assurance about His unique nature and calling[24] and about the empowering of God's Spirit for the task.[25] That was the beginning of His ministry as Saviour of the world. And when He spoke about His death, He spoke of it as the fulfilment, or accomplishment of His baptism. 'I have a baptism to be baptized with, and how am I straitened till it be accomplished.'[26] This identification of Himself with sinners reaches its climax in the terrible cry from the cross: 'My God, my God, why hast thou forsaken me?'[27] Here we see the sinless Son of God crucified like a common criminal between two murderers, so completely one with sinful men in their misery and shame, that He cries out – as it were – from the very pit of hell. He is 'made in all things like unto his brethren that he might be a merciful and faithful high priest in things pertaining to God, to make propitiation for the sins of the people'.[28]

4 His death is God's judgment of the world. One of the most memorable of Jesus' parables is the parable of the wicked husbandmen.[29] The basis of this parable is the famous parable of Isaiah about the vineyard.[30] It was a very familiar thought to all Jews that Israel was the vineyard of the Lord, and that He had planted it in order to bring forth fruit. Jesus retells that story with new features. The Lord of the vineyard sends His servants one after another to receive the fruit, which is His due. One after another they are refused and humiliated. Obviously the reference is to the long line of great prophets. At

---

[23] Mark 1.4.
[24] Mark 1.11.
[25] Mark 1.10.
[26] Luke 12.50.
[27] Mark 15.34.
[28] Heb. 2.17.
[29] Mark 12.1–9.
[30] Isa. 5.1–7.

last the Lord of the vineyard sends His 'Beloved Son' saying 'They will reverence my Son'. And at once the wicked husbandmen take Him and kill Him and cast Him forth out of the vineyard. And the question follows: 'What will the Lord of the vineyard do?' It is obvious to all the hearers what this means. Jesus is the final Word of God to men; if they reject Him (as they are going to do) they will bring down upon themselves God's final judgment. And, to drive the point home, He adds another famous passage from the Old Testament: 'The stone which the builders rejected, the same was made the head of the corner; this was from the Lord and it is marvellous in our eyes'. Again the meaning is plain. He is Himself the headstone. And in Luke's Gospel He adds: 'Every one that falleth on that stone shall be broken to pieces; but on whomsoever it shall fall it will scatter him as dust.'[31] The crucifixion of Jesus is the decisive judgment of God upon the world.

5 His death is a ransom. In one of the most famous passages of the Gospels Jesus says: 'The Son of man came not to be ministered unto but to minister, and to give his life a ransom for many.'[32] In Psalm 49 (vv. 7–8) it is said 'No one can by any means redeem his brother, nor give to God a ransom for him.' Jesus says that this is precisely what He has come to do. Men's souls are forfeit, ruined, lost. No man can redeem them. But Jesus has come to give His life as a ransom for them. In the original Greek it is very clear that He is giving His life not only for them but instead of them, that is, in their place. And the word translated 'ransom' is the same word which is translated in the Old Testament as propitiation. This word of Jesus does not tell us how His life is a ransom for many. But it tells us very clearly that He has come to give His life in place of, on behalf of, the lives of men which are forfeit.

6 His death is a sacrifice. We have seen that the word used in the previous saying for 'ransom' is a word which is used in the Old Testament in connection with sacrificial ideas. There is another saying in which the idea of sacrifice is made very clear. At the Last Supper, after Jesus had given bread to His disciples and said 'Take ye; this is my body', we read that He gave them the cup and said: 'This is my blood of the covenant, which is shed for many.'[33] What is meant by 'blood of the covenant'? There is little doubt that it refers to the giving of the covenant on Mount Sinai in the time of Moses. There we read that oxen were offered in sacrifice, part of the blood was sprinkled on the altar, and part of it was sprinkled on the people, and thereafter Moses and the elders of Israel were admitted to a vision of God and to eating and drinking in His presence.[34] Thus was the old covenant inaugurated: the blood of an animal was offered in sacrifice and by means of this God and the people were

---

[31] Luke 20.18.
[32] Mark 10.45.
[33] Mark 14.24; St Matthew's Gospel adds 'unto remission of sins' (Matt. 26.28).
[34] Exod. 24.4–11.

brought together. The meaning of Jesus' words seems to be that in the same way by the offering up of His life in sacrifice a new covenant between God and men is being inaugurated. Again, these words do not explain how a sacrifice such as this could remove sin and establish a new covenant between man and God. To understand that we have to understand the whole story of salvation. But they do show that Jesus regarded His death as a sacrifice which – like the ancient sacrifices – was intended to make atonement between God and man.

7 His death is the means of life to the world. In St John's Gospel there are a great many sayings in which Jesus reveals His belief that His death will be the means of new life for the world. This is the main subject of the long discourse in chapter 6 in which He speaks of Himself as the living bread come down from heaven. He says: 'The bread which I will give is my flesh for the life of the world.' In chapter 10 He speaks of Himself as the good shepherd who lays down His life for the sheep. He says He has come that they may have life and have it abundantly.[35] In chapter 12 he speaks of the corn of wheat which cannot bring forth new life except by falling into the ground and dying,[36] and of His being lifted up to draw all men to Himself.[37] These sayings are similar to His saying in Mark's Gospel: 'Whosoever would save his life shall lose it; and whosoever shall lose his life for my sake and the gospel's shall save it.'[38] We should here refer also to his saying about the temple which is given fully in John's Gospel and also referred to in the others.[39] 'Destroy this temple and in three days I will raise it up.' The disciples did not understand this saying at the time, but afterwards they understood. His death would bring into being a new temple, a new dwelling place for God on earth, namely the Church which is His body and wherein men of every race can come together to find fellowship with God.

8 His death is not to be an isolated event, but others are to follow it and share it. According to St Mark, as soon as Jesus began explicitly to speak of His death, He also told His disciples that they must take up their crosses and follow him.[40] As His death is the means of new life to the world, so those who believe Him are to die with Him and find new life through Him.[41] At the Last Supper He calls upon His disciples to take and eat the bread which is His broken body, and to drink the wine which is His poured-out blood. In other words they are to be sharers in His dying and new life. And in

---

[35] John 10.10–11.
[36] John 12.24–25.
[37] John 12.32.
[38] Mark 8.35.
[39] John 2.19–22; cf. Mark 14.58 and 15.29.
[40] Mark 8.34.
[41] Mark 8.35.

the Garden of Gethsemane He pleads with them to watch with Him, to be sharers with Him in the agony of suffering for the world. When they fall asleep in the midst of His agony, He is deeply wounded and asks them: 'What, could ye not watch with me one hour?'[42] His death is on behalf of all men, instead of all men. He does something which man cannot do for himself. But He wills that men should not stand back and leave Him alone, but should share with Him in His redemptive agony.

Extract 2
The Gospel in a Pluralist Society *(1989)*[43]

The idea that the gospel is addressed only to the individual and that it is only indirectly addressed to societies, nations, and cultures is simply an illusion of our individualistic post-Enlightenment Western culture. Very plainly when we turn to the Old Testament we find no such separation of the individual from the society which nurtures and forms him and of which he is a part. The Torah, God's gracious instruction of his people, is addressed as much to the life of the nation as to that of the individual. It is as much about law and order, hygiene, economics, social welfare, and politics as it is about personal morals. It is Israel as a whole which is addressed in the Torah. That is obvious; but many would say that this is one of the matters on which the teaching of the New Testament is radically different from that of the Old. In the New Testament, they would say, God's word is addressed to the individual, not to a nation, and the new Israel is not a nation but a community of individuals living in many cities and states but bound together by their individual commitment to Jesus Christ. The New Testament, it is said, does not envisage a social or political reformation of Greek and Roman society; it simply accepts that society as the milieu within which individuals have to work out their own salvation. Is this true? I do not believe that it is, and in order to correct what I believe to be a flawed reading of the New Testament, I want to direct attention to an element in its teaching which has been neglected in the modern period of the historical–critical approach to the Scriptures but is – once you open your eyes to it – extremely prominent.

I refer to the whole mass of teaching in St Paul's letters about what are variously called principalities, powers, dominions, thrones, authorities, rulers, angels, and other names. With these we must also look at what the Gospels have to say about hostile spiritual powers, about Satan, and about what the Fourth Gospel calls 'the ruler of this world.' If I am not mistaken, most scholarly readers of the New Testament in the past 150 years have regarded all this language as something which we can for practical purposes ignore because it belongs to a thought-world which we have grown out of. We imagine a host

---

[42] Matt. 26.40.
[43] Newbigin 1989b: [. . . .] 199–210.

of angelic or demonic beings flying around in the air somewhere above our heads, suppose that Paul and his contemporaries believed in these, just as people once believed in fairies and elves, and conclude that we can ignore this part of his writing. The domination of a reductionist materialism, which supposed that when we had discovered the atomic and molecular and biological facts about any phenomenon we had explained it, has prevented us from discerning the realities that Paul and other New Testament writers are talking about, and they *are* realities.

When we read right through the whole New Testament looking for words which speak of power, authority, rule, dominion, or lordship, we find such words on almost every page. The central phrase of the gospel, the kingdom of God, is obviously about power, authority, rule. In a vast number of cases, of course, the words refer to what we would recognize as human rulers and authorities – magistrates, priests, elders, a governor like Pilate, or a petty rajah like Herod. When Paul writes about 'the powers that be' in Romans 13, it is clear that they are human beings, for they wear swords and collect taxes. But what are we to make of the principalities and powers in the heavenly places against which we are to wrestle (Eph. 6.12)? And how on earth is the Church to set about making known the manifold wisdom of God to the principalities and powers in the heavenly places (Eph. 3.10)? Are these powers the same as or quite different from the powers that collect taxes on earth? When Paul says that none of the rulers of this world understood the wisdom of God, for if they had they would not have crucified the Lord of glory (1 Cor. 2.8), is he just talking about Herod and Pilate, or about something else? A couple of verses earlier Paul has said that these rulers are doomed to pass away. But Herod and Pilate had disappeared from the scene before Paul wrote these words. Does he mean that these two men are doomed to pass away? If so, it seems hardly worth saying: they are already dead. So does he mean that their roles, their offices, their authority is doomed to pass away? Are we talking about an individual called Herod or Pilate or Smith or Jones, or are we talking about something which is temporarily embodied in these officeholders, about the role rather than the individual who plays it? And when (according to the Fourth Gospel) Jesus speaks of his coming death and says, 'Now is the judgment of this world; now shall the ruler of this world be cast out' (John 12.31), he cannot be speaking just of Herod or Pilate; neither of them could be called 'ruler of this world.' Clearly this language does not simply refer to certain human beings who hold these offices of power and authority for a few years and are then dead and gone. They refer to something behind these individuals, to the offices, the powers, the authority which is represented from time to time by this or that individual. It is these powers, authorities, rulers, dominions which have been confronted in Christ's death with the supreme power and authority of God. That is why it is the business of the Church to make manifest to them the wisdom of God. That is why we are told in the brief, hymnlike words of 1 Timothy 3.16 that God was 'manifested in the flesh, vindicated in the Spirit, seen by angels, preached among the nations,

believed on in the world.' What was done in the incarnation, death, and resurrection of Jesus confronts the powers before it is preached among the
nations. That is why we are told that the risen Christ has been seated at God's
right hand with all the principalities and powers under his feet (Eph. 1.21).
That is why we are also told that Christ in his cross disarmed the principalities and powers and made a public example of them, triumphing over them
in his cross (Col. 2.14). But what exactly are these principalities and powers?

It seems clear from the examples already quoted that these powers do not
exist apart from the human agencies in which they are embodied – Pilate,
Herod, Caiaphas. Yet they are not identical with these particular individuals.
They refer, I suggested, to that which is behind them, to the power which they
represent and exercise but which is not identical with them. We are talking
about power and authority which is real, which is embodied in and exercised
by individual human beings, but is not identical with them. The king dies, but
the kingship goes on. Another king steps into the place. But what is this thing
that we call 'kingship'? I used a spatial metaphor when I spoke of the authority which is 'behind' the particular person who holds office and exercises
authority for the moment. A spatial metaphor is obviously very inadequate.
You do not find a thing called kingship by looking behind the king's back. We
say that kingship is a reality which is more than, which transcends the particular exercise of kingship by this man or this woman. But we do not escape the
spatial metaphor, for 'transcendence' means being above something else. When
in contemporary English we speak of the relation of a spiritual reality to
its visible embodiment, we tend to think of inwardness – another spatial
metaphor. We cannot avoid spatial metaphors but we can be saved from being
misled by acknowledging that a variety of metaphors is possible. Shall we
speak of the spiritual power within, behind, or above its visible embodiment?
We all know very well that long-enduring institutions have something, an
inwardness which can be recognized in those who form the institution at any
one time, but outlasts and transcends them. This 'something' may be benevolent or malevolent. A good school has a spirit, an ethos, which molds the characters of the pupils. It was there before they came, and it will be there after all
the present pupils have left. A nation similarly has something which is not just
the sum of the attitudes of its individual citizens. And a mob can become an
embodiment of evil, an evil which its individual members would never have
wished for on their own. Clearly this 'something' has reality. But we cannot
locate it spatially within, behind, or above its visible embodiment. It is not
something which hovers in the air above the heads of living human beings.
We have tended to read the New Testament as though this was how its writers conceived of this spiritual reality. We have assumed that 'the heavenly
places,' where the principalities and powers dwell, are above our heads. But
Paul is not a victim of his own inevitably spatial language. According to Paul
those who are in Christ are already seated in the heavenly places where
Christ is (Eph. 1.20). This 'something' which is invisible, and which cannot be
located spatially either within or behind or above its earthly manifestations, is

nevertheless real – terribly real. When Christians have to fight their battles, they are not just fighting with this or that person, this magistrate or that temple priest, or that angry mob in the theater; they are not fighting against flesh and blood. Their conflict is not against human beings. It is against the spiritual power that is – how shall we say it? – behind, within, and above human beings. It is this that we have to address. So when John the Seer addresses the churches in Asia, he does not address their members as individuals whom he could name; he addresses the angels of the churches, the spiritual reality, the power – good, bad, or mixed – which is embodied in the congregation, which is more than the personal conduct of each individual. And so throughout the Book of Revelation, there is always a correspondence between the war in heaven and the wars and disasters on earth. The happenings on earth are only understood in terms of the spiritual battle between the victorious Christ who is seated on the throne in the heavenly places, and the spiritual powers that challenge his rule.

Paul's use of words in relation to these unseen realities is extremely flexible. Such words as principalities, powers, dominions, thrones, angels, authorities, and others are used without any apparent attempt to distinguish between their meanings if indeed there is any difference. Just as no one spatial metaphor can describe the relation between these invisible entities and their visible embodiments, so no one word is adequate to denote them. There is, however, one other word which Paul uses in this connection and which helps us to get to the heart of his meaning. It occurs in the passage of Colossians where we are told that Christ in his cross has disarmed the powers (Col. 2.15). This is the word *stoicheion*, used always in the plural, *stoicheia*. It is variously translated in our versions: 'rudiments,' 'elements,' 'elementary spirits,' 'ruling spirits of the universe.' Its basic meaning is simply expressed in the word 'elements.' It is very frequently used in contemporary Greek writing for the four elements – air, earth, fire, and water. It is used for the letters of the alphabet. It is used in the Letter to the Hebrews (5.12) for the first principles, the elementary matters of the gospel. It may seem strange that Paul brings this word into close relation with his language about principalities and powers, as he does in two places. In Galatians Paul seems to identify it with the law. He tells his readers that before Christ came they were like children under the law which was their custodian, but that now in Christ we have been set free from this control so as to live in the freedom of the Spirit. And to those who want to creep back again under the protection of the law, by receiving circumcision, he says, 'Formerly you were in bondage to beings that by nature are no gods; but now that you have come to know God, or rather to be known by God, how can you turn back again to the weak and beggarly *stoicheia*, whose slaves you want to be once more?' (Gal. 4.8–9). In the Letter to the Colossians his readers are warned against becoming a prey to 'philosophy and empty deceit, according to human traditions, according to the *stoicheia* of the universe and not according to Christ,' and later on they are told that having died to the *stoicheia*, they should not live as if they belonged to this world, submitting to all sorts of rules and regulations (Col. 2.8, 20). In both passages it is the work of Christ which has delivered Christians from the' power of the *stoicheia* and in the Colossians passage it is stated that this is because Christ has disarmed the principalities and powers.

What is clear in these as in other passages is that the powers have been disarmed but not destroyed. They are put under the supreme dominion of Christ by what he has done on the cross, but they still exist. We have to wrestle with them. And the Church has to make manifest to them the wisdom of God as revealed in Jesus (Eph. 3.10). Moreover, in the letter to the Colossians it is explicitly stated that the powers were created through Christ and for Christ and in him alone they have their coherence (Col. 1.15–17). So these things, whatever they are, have a good purpose. They are intended to serve the purpose of God as manifest in Christ. And yet it is these things, these principalities and powers, which crucified the Lord of glory. There has been a rebellion of these powers against their proper sovereign Lord. The rebellion has been put down. The rebellious powers are not destroyed; they are disarmed. They still have a function to perform in God's ordering of the universe, but they must now subserve their Lord. They are under his feet, and in the end they will disappear when (according to 1 Cor. 15.24) Christ destroys them and hands over the kingdom to his Father.

How do we interpret this language? Simply to ignore it as some sort of outdated mythology would be a disastrous mistake. It is obviously an extremely important element in Paul's teaching. Nor are we without clues to its meaning.

Let us begin with the matter which is at issue in Galatians, namely the law. Paul has repeatedly affirmed that the law is a good gift of God. Yet it has become a power that enslaves, from which Christ had to deliver us by his death. It was the representatives of the law who put Jesus on the cross. But Caiaphas and his colleagues were not just a few wicked men. They were acting as the temporary agents and embodiments of something more fundamental and more enduring than their own individual opinions. The Colossians passage speaks of 'human traditions' about eating and drinking and the observance of seasons and festivals. The passage in Romans 13 refers to the state authorities. The passages in 1 Corinthians 2 refer simply to 'the rulers of this age,' which no doubt includes all those elements which had a hand in the decision to destroy Jesus – legal, political, ecclesiastical, and other. If one can summarize all these as referring to the structural elements in human life, one brings them into relation with the language about the *stoicheia*. All human life is lived and has to be lived within limits which are set by certain structural features, both of the natural world and of the world of human society. In the former category belong the fundamental elements of the physical universe (the original meaning of *stoicheia*), the invariances which are the subject of natural science and which make it possible for us to behave rationally in the world. If we could not rely on these invariances, on the fundamental stability of the natural world, we could not live a human life. So also our life in society is structured by law, custom, and tradition. Without these we could not develop into responsible beings. No one lives and no one could live a rational life if there were no given norms (which may be different in different places and times) which govern behavior. Most of the time even the most eccentric human being does from moment to moment what the normal customs and traditions of his or her society indicate. Nor can we function without the help of accepted roles. A person appointed to a public office, or ordained to the Christian ministry, may in course of time develop very fresh and original ways of interpreting his role. But she has to begin by accepting the guidance of the tradition. One cannot begin by a sort of *creatio ex nihilo*, developing a totally original model of behavior unrelated to the expectations of the society which has appointed her to this role. A person who tried to do this simply could not function in her role. So also with our life in larger political units. There has to be some kind of ordered structure of power. Without it, human life would dissolve into anarchy. These structural elements are necessary to guide and protect human life. They serve God's purpose. But, as we well know, they can also become demonic. The God-given authority of the state can be used for tyranny. Roles can become dehumanizing so that even our best efforts at goodness can become – as Jesus said – play-acting, hypocrisy.

I have been speaking of entities which are not just individual human beings, flesh and blood in Pauline language, but which yet exist and have power. I have been speaking of norms, roles, and structures. We have to acknowledge the reality and the power of these things, and we have to ask what the gospel has to do with them. And we have seen that a great deal of New Testament writing is addressed exactly to that question. These things, says Paul, are good creations of God. They have a part to play in his purpose. But they can come to usurp the place to which they have no right, the place which belongs to Christ and to him alone. They can be, as we say, absolutized, and then they become demonic. The power ordained by God of Romans 13 becomes the Beast of Revelation. The Torah, that loving instruction which God gives his people and the beauty of which is celebrated in Psalm 119, becomes a tyrant from which Christ has to deliver us. Tradition, the handing on of good practice from parent to child as it is so beautifully described in Deuteronomy, becomes an evil power which comes between human beings and the living God.

These are examples from the New Testament itself of the ways in which the powers, created in Christ and for Christ, become agents of tyranny. One could give many more examples from outside the New Testament. Number is one of the *stoicheia* which has fascinated thinkers of various schools. Numbering enables us to measure and quantify. It is an element of order in the universe. But it can become a tyrant when, as in modern reductionist thinking, it is absolutized and nothing is valued except what can be measured and quantified.

Chance seems to be a fundamental element in this contingent universe which God has created. In past times it was made into a goddess and named Fortuna. And, though not given a personal name, the same power rules wide swathes of contemporary thought. Chance mutations in the transmission of genes becomes the sovereign power governing the emergence of life. The chance workings of the free market become the 'Invisible Hand' of Adam Smith which mysteriously converts private selfishness into public good. This particular example of an invisible power ruling over human affairs is particularly relevant at present, since it is one of the key arguments of the religious Right against the religious Left that one cannot speak of justice or injustice when describing the huge differences between rich and poor in our society. These, on this view, cannot be called unjust because they are not the work of conscious human agency but the result of chance. Thus in our economic life we are no longer responsible to Christ; we are not responsible at all, for economic life has been handed over to the goddess Fortuna. It is not difficult to recognize that as one of the principalities and powers of which Paul speaks.

Race is another element in the structuring of human life. Family, kinship, tribal community – these are all parts of the structure of human life which play a vital part in the nurturing, the developing of authentic humanity. It was therefore with good intention that missionaries in South Africa insisted that African Christians should be able to organize their churches and conduct their worship in their own traditional ways and using their own languages. But when this good provision was given an absolute status as part of the order of creation, not subject to Christ, it became the demonic power of apartheid. No one who lives in South Africa can doubt its reality and power, and the task of Christians in that country is not to wrestle against flesh and blood, not to attack the God-fearing Afrikaners, but to wrestle against the demonic power which is as real as it is invisible.

Money is perhaps another example of the principalities and powers of our time. As is well known, Marx used the word 'fetishism' to speak of the attitude to money which he found in capitalist society. Money, which is a useful means for facilitating exchange, has become a power in itself, so that we do not measure human wealth in terms of real goodness and happiness but in terms of cash. Money has truly become a fetish, a power which demands and receives absolute devotion. In the vision of Marx the proletariat was to be a sort of corporate Messiah which would overthrow the power of this false god and create a society of free and responsible human relationships. Alas, the proletariat is not Christ. The Marxist ideology has itself become a power in the Pauline sense, which controls human behavior and forces those under its power to crush the free expression of the human spirit. The wrestling of men and women like Solzhenitsyn is not against flesh and blood, not against particular human beings, but against the invisible but terribly powerful spiritual force that controls their actions.

The principalities and powers are real. They are invisible and we cannot locate them in space. They do not exist as disembodied entities floating above this world, or lurking within it. They meet us as embodied in visible and tangible realities – people, nations, and institutions. And they are powerful. What is Christ's relation to them? To recapitulate briefly: they are created in Christ and for Christ; their true end is to serve him; some do – for the New Testament speaks of good angels who perform his service; but they become powers for evil when they attempt to usurp the place which belongs to Christ alone. In his death Christ has disarmed them; he has put them under his feet; they must now serve him; and the Church is the agency through which his victory over them is made manifest and is effected as the Church puts on the whole armor of God to meet and master them. The language is pictorial, mythological if you like, because we have no other language. But the things described are real and are contemporary. They are at the heart of our business as Christians. Let me try to spell this out in terms of contemporary Christian duty.

In the cross Christ has disarmed the powers. He has unmasked them. He has not destroyed them, but – in Johannine language – has cast the ruler of this world out of his usurped throne. What I have called the structural elements in the world as we know it, from the basic structure of the physical world to the social and political structures of the nations, to the customs and traditions by which human beings are normally guided, to what the sociologists call the 'plausibility structures'[44] by which all human thinking is guided: all of these are part of God's good ordering of his creation. Yet it was these things which at the decisive *denouement*, the moment when they were confronted by the living God in person, by him in whom the fullness of Godhead was present bodily, were found ranged in unanimous and murderous hostility against him. The death of Christ was the unmasking of the powers – Caiaphas and Herod and Pilate were not uniquely wicked men; they were acting out their roles as guardians of the political and moral and religious order. They acted as representatives of what the New Testament calls the world, this present age. When God raised the crucified Jesus, this present age and its structures was exposed, illuminated, unmasked – but not destroyed. Cross and resurrection seen together mean both judgment and grace, both wrath and endless patience. God still upholds the structures; without them the world would collapse and human life would be unthinkable. But the structures lose their pretended absoluteness. Nothing now is absolute except God as he is known in Jesus Christ; everything else is relativized. That is the bottom line for Christian thinking and the starting point for Christian action in the affairs of the world. What does it imply in practice?

Let me begin with some negatives. It does *not* mean anarchy. It does not mean an attack on structures as such. Many people are tempted this way. There are those for whom Christian freedom means a rejection of institutions, traditions, laws, and structures. And they can always show good reasons, for all human traditions, institutions, and structures are prone to evil – including religion and including Christianity and the Church. They are all part of this

---

[44] (A term coined by Peter Berger to refer to the structures of thinking and practice that make particular beliefs sustainable.)

present age. They are all prone to make absolutist claims. They are all ambiguous. There are always good reasons for attacking them. But human life is impossible without them, and God in his mercy preserves them in order to give time for the Church to fulfill its calling to make manifest to them the wisdom of God. Our relation to the structures has to contain both the judgment that is inevitable in the searing light of the cross, and also the patience which is required of us as witnesses to the resurrection. We are not conservatives who regard the structures as part of the unalterable order of creation, as part of the world of what we call 'hard facts' beyond the range of the gospel and who therefore suppose that the gospel is only relevant to the issues of personal and private life. Nor are we anarchists who seek to destroy the structures. We are rather patient revolutionaries who know that the whole creation, with all its given structures, is groaning in the travail of a new birth, and that we share this groaning and travail, this struggling and wrestling, but do so in hope because we have already received, in the Spirit, the firstfruit of the new world (Rom. 8.19–25).

But, second, as Paul tells us, our wrestling is not against flesh and blood but against the principalities and powers in the invisible world (Eph. 6.12). What are we talking about when we speak of confronting the institutions of state and market economy and culture with the gospel? We are not fighting against the individuals who perform their roles within these institutions. We know well that when we get a chance to talk intimately with them, they feel themselves powerless. To the outsider they appear to wield great power, but they know that they are under the control of forces greater than their own and that their freedom to change things is very narrowly limited. Those who call for a Christian assault on the worlds of politics and economics often make it clear that the attack belongs to the same order of being as the enemy to be attacked. The aim of the attack is to seize the levers of power and take control. We have seen many such successful revolutions, and we know that in most cases what has happened is simply that the oppressor and the oppressed have exchanged roles. The structure is unchanged. The throne is unshaken, only there is a different person occupying it. How is the throne itself to be shaken? How is the power to be disarmed and placed at the service of Christ? Only by the power of the gospel itself, announced in word and embodied in deed. As Walter Wink reminds us,[45] the victory of the Church over the demonic power which was embodied in the Roman imperial system was not won by seizing the levers of power: it was won when the victims knelt down in the Colosseum and prayed in the name of Jesus for the Emperor. The soldiers in Christ's victorious army were not armed with the weapons of this age; they were the martyrs whose robes were washed in blood. It was not that a particular Emperor was discredited and displaced; it was that the entire mystique of the Empire, its spiritual power, was unmasked, disarmed, and rendered powerless. A con-

---

[45] (A reference to Wink's books on 'The Powers': Wink 1984 and 1986.)

version of individuals which failed to identify, unmask, and reject that spiritual, ideological power would have been as futile as an attempt by Christians to wrest that power from its holders. Evangelism which is politically and ideologically naive, and social action which does not recognize the need for conversion from false gods to the living God, both fall short of what is required.

The principalities and powers are realities. We may not be able to visualize them, to locate them, or to say exactly what they are. But we are foolish if we pretend that they do not exist. Certainly one cannot read the Gospels without recognizing that the ministry of Jesus from beginning to end was a mighty spiritual battle with powers which are not simply human frailties, errors, diseases, or sins. And one cannot read St Paul, or the other books of the New Testament, without recognizing that this drama of Christ's disarming of the powers is central to their meaning. If we dismiss this as merely outworn mythology, we shall be incapable of grasping the central message of the New Testament. If we try to systematize the diffuse and flexible language of the writers and develop a sort of systematic demonology, we shall also go astray. But if we live in the real world and take the Bible as our clue for understanding and coping with it, we shall certainly know what it means that our wrestling is not against flesh and blood but against the invisible principalities and powers, and we shall learn what it means to put on the whole armor of God for the conflict.

Further reading

Newbigin 1956: 69–91.
Newbigin 1982: 157–62.
Newbigin 1993d: 8–18, 28–36.

3

Election and the people of God

— ⬥ —

The doctrine of 'election' is an important theme in Newbigin's thought. The extract I have chosen to illustrate this is from his 1961 book A Faith for this One World? *which was based on the William Belden Noble Lectures delivered at Harvard University in 1958. Here Newbigin explains his understanding of the doctrine in a chapter entitled 'The Presuppositions of Christ's Revelation'. The material is based upon some earlier reflections he had published as part of the preparatory documents for the first WCC assembly at Amsterdam in 1948, under the title 'The Duty and Authority of the Church to Preach the Gospel'.[1] It was a theme to which he returned often, encapsulating what lay at the heart of the calling of God's people.*

Newbigin's approach is not to expound the doctrine primarily in terms of the individual believer's assurance before God, but rather in terms of God's choosing of a people at particular times and in specific places in order to mediate his universal reign – a purpose that finds its fulfilment in the election of Jesus Christ himself. In expounding this theme, Newbigin addresses some key questions for Christian mission. Why should God's universal reign be mediated so 'locally'? And why does God not reveal himself to other peoples in the context of their own cultural history, rather than through the history of the Jewish people? Newbigin's discussions of the doctrine of election not only force him to address the 'scandal of particularity' suggested by the seemingly arbitrary nature of God's choosing. They also enable him to underline the missionary imperative implied by this calling. The Church is brought into being not for its own sake, but for the sake of the world, as the bearer of God's universal message of salvation. In can be argued therefore that the Church carries in its own being the key to the world's existence. It is 'the clue to the meaning and end of world history'.[2]

* * *

---

[1] Newbigin 1948.
[2] Newbigin 1961: 81. For a useful discussion of this theme see Hunsberger 1998: 82–112.

Extract
A Faith for this One World? *(1961)*[3]

The fact of Jesus Christ must be interpreted in relation to the biblical doctrine of election.

Here we meet with an idea which is as offensive to our human reason as it is central to the Bible. The Bible is primarily the story of election, of the people whom God chose, and of the individuals whom he chose to play special parts in the story. According to the Bible, God chose one tribe out of all the tribes of men to be his people, his witnesses, his priests, the agents of his kingship. Again let it be noted that we are not setting up the authority of Genesis and Exodus alongside that of Christ. We understand election, like creation, in the light of Christ's words and deeds. Christ accepted it as his vocation to recall Israel to its true vocation. He reconstituted the chosen people, choosing whom he would and appointing twelve to be the nucleus of a new Israel. These twelve he sent out to be his authorized representatives. Men were to be related to the Kingdom of God by being related to them. To receive them was to receive Christ and to receive Christ was to receive God. Christ is God's chosen and they are chosen in him. To them, and to all who believe, his word is: 'You did not choose me but I chose you'.

This whole conception of election is, as I said, unquestionably offensive to our human reason. How, we are inclined to ask, how can it be that among all the tribes of the ancient world, one should be God's people? How can it be that the Christian Church, one particular strand of human history, should be the exclusive bearer of God's saving grace for mankind? The difficulties which this doctrine creates are, I think, of two kinds, metaphysical and ethical. In the first place, it is felt by many people to be self-evident that particular events cannot demonstrate universal truths, that God is present always and everywhere, and that the idea that one particular series of events could be regarded as in any exclusive sense the acts of God, is impossible. In the second place, on ethical grounds it is felt to be unworthy of a benevolent deity that he should show discrimination and pick out one race among others for his special favour. Let us look at these two difficulties.

The first type of objection rests upon assumptions which, if they are taken seriously, ultimately exclude the possibility of belief in a personal God at all. I am not going to attempt even in the most superficial way to consider the whole question of the possibility of this belief. I must simply affirm that there is here a great divide in human thinking, and you have to stand on one side or the other. If it is incredible that a real personal will, however far beyond anything we know of human wills, is at the heart of reality, then we have to accept the consequences of that position. But if we believe in a personal God, we must believe that it is possible for him to act and therefore to choose the times and places of his actions.

---

[3] Newbigin 1961: [. . . .] 77–83.

The second objection rests upon a misunderstanding of the purpose of election in the Bible. It is election not simply to privilege but to responsibility. God's people have constantly forgotten that fact both under the old covenant and under the new and have therefore brought the whole idea of divine election into disrepute. But one must answer the objector by putting the counter-question: 'What is it that you are really asking for?' Are you asking for a relationship with God which is in principle accessible to everyone individually apart from any relationship with his neighbour? That is in fact what the unredeemed ego in each of us really wants. At the most secret and central place of our being, do we not constantly want to be in the position where we do not have to be debtor to any other man? We ask: 'Why should I have to go there? Why should I have to do that? Why should I have to depend upon them for the salvation of my soul? Cannot God deal with me directly without bringing another person, another religion, another culture into the business?' The answer is that he can but will not. His purpose is precisely to break open that shell of egotism in which you are imprisoned since Adam first fell and to give you back the new nature which is content to owe the debt of love to all men. And so God deals with us through one another. One is chosen to be the bearer of the message to another, one people to be God's witnesses to all people. Each of us has to hear the gospel from the lips of another or we cannot hear it at all. God's plan for the salvation of the world is a consistent whole, the means congruent with the end. The end is the healing of all things in Christ, and the means therefore involve each of us from the very beginning inescapably in a relationship with our neighbour. Salvation comes to each of us not, so to say, straight down from heaven through the skylight, but through a door that is opened by our neighbour. We cannot be saved except through and with one another, for salvation means making whole. And if it be objected that there is a flaw in that argument because, on this showing, the Jews at least received the gospel through the skylight, the answer is that according to the argument of St Paul in Romans, the Jews also can only be saved in the end through the Gentiles. The salvation of God is a consistent whole. From beginning to end it relates us to God only through a relationship with our neighbour. One is related to God's saving acts not by any kind of direct, unmediated spiritual experience, however it may be formulated. One is related by becoming related to God's people and to the history of God's people, and the central and decisive acts in the history of God's people, which are the substance of the apostolic message.

That statement must at once be safeguarded against misunderstanding. When we speak of the history of God's people, we are speaking of one particular strand in world history, but we are not implying that that is something which exists or can be understood in any kind of disjunction from world history. It is part of world history, that part from which we understand the whole. It is the clue to world history. The Bible, you will remember, does not make any sharp break between the special history with which it is concerned and world history as a whole. The Bible is, so to speak, open at both ends. It begins with the creation of the whole cosmos and with all the tribes of men. Only after this does the story narrow down on the principle of election until it reaches the crisis at which Israel is one Man, and the whole purpose of God for the world is concentrated in the single thread of events enacted on a hill outside Jerusalem. Then at once the story broadens out again. The tribes of men, proleptically present on the day of Pentecost, are gathered in, until at the end we have a vision which includes all the nations and the entire cosmos. The Bible is thus concerned with the whole of human history understood from one centre. And moreover as the story proceeds we are reminded again and again that the special story with which it is concerned is in no kind of isolation from the rest of the world's history but is bound up with it. The God who shapes the destiny of Israel shapes also those of Assyria and Babylon and Tyre and Egypt and Rome; the God who calls Abraham and Jeremiah also raises up Pharaoh and Cyrus. Yet the clue to the meaning of the whole is found in the story of the chosen people. Not that the world exists for the sake of the chosen people; precisely the opposite: the chosen people are chosen for the sake of the world. The mission of the Church is the clue to the meaning and end of world history. But the Church does not exist for itself, it exists for the sake of fulfilling God's purpose for the world. It is the people of God in the world and precisely in its concreteness and particularity, it is the bearer of the universal salvation for the world. Therefore we must state, and this is the point that I am trying to make here, that the duty and authority of the Church to preach the gospel to all nations rests upon the fact that God has chosen it for this purpose, to be the witness, the first fruit and the instrument of his saving deeds. He might have chosen others. In the nature of the case, he must choose someone. In the mystery of his will, he has chosen us, the weak and foolish and insignificant. That ought to leave in us no room for pride, but equally it ought to leave no room for disobedience.

One implication of this is so vital that I cannot close without stating it. Everything that the New Testament says about the people of God takes it for granted that it is one people. There is one body as there is one Spirit. Christ has one body, not many, one bride, not a plurality of them. And this one people of God, chosen in Christ before the foundation of the world, the body whose Head is exalted over all things, the ruler of all rule and authority, is not an abstract idea nor a merely eschatological expectation, but a concrete and particular and even sinful body of men and women in Jerusalem and Antioch and Corinth and Ephesus. This is the new man, the new-created human race in Christ, wherein the enmity between Jew and Greek is overcome, wherein men of all kinds and sorts are reconciled in one body through the cross. One has only to call to mind such phrases as these from the New Testament to make it clear that the disunity of the Church is a contradiction of its proper nature and a public abdication of its right to preach the gospel to all nations. We have seen that it is at the heart of the biblical understanding of God's purpose for the salvation of the world, that this purpose is to be effected through a people. This people has its being from God and is the first-fruit and witness and instrument of his saving purpose for all men. The purpose is to reconcile all men to himself in Jesus Christ. But how can those who are not reconciled to one another be the instruments of God's reconciling action? How can he use us to draw all men to himself if we do not let him draw us to one another? How can the world believe our witness to Christ's love if we ourselves have found that love too weak to overcome our natural differences? Our divisions are a public denial of the sufficiency of Christ.

Properly speaking, the Church is just the people of God, just humanity remade in Christ. It should therefore have as much variety as the human race itself. Nothing human should be alien to it save sin. The very vastness of its diversity held together by the single fact of Christ's atonement for the whole human race should be the witness to the sufficiency of that atonement. It should confront man with no sectional or local society, no segregation of people having similar tastes and temperaments and traditions, but simply as the congregation of humanity redeemed, as the family to which every man right-ly belongs and from which only sin can sever him. There is, as I have tried to show, an inescapable particularity about the people of God. It is one people chosen out of all the peoples of the earth; that is the scandal of the divine elec-tion. But its particularity is in order to be universal. We have by our divisions introduced a wholly wrong kind of particularity, so that men see in it not just the people of God but a variety of particular societies held together, and held apart from other Christians, by some peculiarity of practice or tradition or devotional or doctrinal formulation. Thereby we hide from men's eyes the sufficiency of Christ. Only when we are willing to stake our whole existence as churches on the belief that we have in Christ a unity which can hold us in one fellowship in the truth in spite of the variety among us, only then shall we learn for ourselves and show to the world the sufficiency and finality of Christ.

It is sometimes objected, perhaps with the tongue in the cheek, that if we had a single Church (a thing of which we do not appear at present to be in much danger) it would have no safeguard against the temptation to absolutize itself; that in fact the divisions of the Church are needed to keep us humble. I cannot agree with this, for two reasons which I will briefly state. First, I do not think it is necessary to believe that history has taught us nothing. The true antidote to the temptation of the Church to absolutize itself is not schism; it is to take seriously the secular order. There you have the true, God-given reminder to the Church that it is still *in via* and cannot treat itself as the abso-lute vice-regent of God on earth. I do not believe that we shall go back on that insight. And secondly, it is true, though it has not always been true, that our very divisions can help us, help to save us from absolutizing ourselves. Even sin can become a means of grace if it helps to make us humble. Shall we then continue in sin that grace may abound? Doubtless there is no situation in which the Church does not need the grace of God to save it from pride, but I cannot believe that God will ever fail to give his grace to churches which are willing to surrender their separate existence in order that Christ's name may be hallowed and his will for the unity of his people fulfilled.

Further reading

Newbigin 1948: 19–35.
Newbigin 1978b: 75–87. (Reprinted as Newbigin 1995b: 68–78.)
Newbigin 1989b: 80–8.

4

Christic as the clue to history

What is the meaning of 'history', and is there a constructive basis for participation within it? These questions surface again and again in Newbigin's writings, and reflect the fact that he was always seeking to interpret the times in which he lived from a Christian perspective. Perhaps two factors in particular fuelled his engagement with these questions. On the one hand, the tumultuous decades between the 1930s and the 1960s witnessed the rise of the conflicting ideologies of Nazism, Marxism, and the steady growth of materialism in the West. Each offered its own interpretation of history, and each in its own way set forward a vision for an earthly 'utopia'. Newbigin's early response to these developments can be found in his 1937 book Christian Freedom in the Modern World (written during his first sea voyage to India in 1936), or his 1941 lectures entitled 'The Kingdom of God and the Idea of Progress', which were given in Bangalore. Here he argued for a radical re-orientation of the idea of 'progress' in the light of the in-breaking of the Kingdom, thus sharply disagreeing with the idea that humans could sustain progress unaided within history. The other factor that influenced Newbigin's discussions was his immersion in the culture of Hinduism in India. Here of course the meaning of history was conceived in radically different terms from those in the West. History is cyclical not linear, and the meaning of historical existence is interpreted in terms of its training of individual souls for a better life in the next cycle. History as such has no meaning outside of this context.

Newbigin's reflections come together in his description of Christ as the 'clue to history'. Here – in the self-disclosure of God's purposes within history – are to be found the events that are determinative for the meaning of the whole. To grasp this is to enable Christians to commit themselves to constructive action within history (even though the outcome of that history is not yet clear), and to avoid the kind of 'withdrawal' that has often characterized the Christian mindset. These themes are drawn together in a chapter entitled 'The clue to history', which follows. It is taken from Newbigin's 1969 book The Finality of Christ, which was a revision of lectures originally delivered at Yale Divinity School in 1966, and subsequently at Cambridge University.

* * *

54

Extract
The Finality of Christ *(1969)*[1]

[. . . .] To speak of the finality of Christ is to speak of the Gospel as the clue to history. What does it mean thus to speak?

1   In the first place it means that one takes one's stand on one side of what Nicol Macnicol calls 'the great divide among the religions'; one confesses the faith that history means something. If religion is concerned about that which finally controls and unifies all experience, then it is clear that in principle there are two ways which it can go. There are in principle two ways in which one can seek unity and coherence behind or beyond all the multiplicity and incoherence which human experience presents to us. One way is to seek unity as an existent reality behind the multiplicity of phenomena; the other is to seek unity as an end yet to be obtained. The typical picture of the first is the wheel; of the second, the road.

Although the wheel is a human construct, it is a powerfully evocative symbol of the natural world as man experiences it. The cycle of birth, growth, decay and death through which plants, animals, human beings and institutions all pass suggests the rotating wheel – ever in movement yet ever returning upon itself. The wheel offers a way of escape from this endless and meaningless movement. One can find a way to the centre where all is still, and one can observe the ceaseless movement without being involved in it. There are many spokes connecting the circumference with the centre. The wise man will not quarrel about which spoke should be chosen. Any one will do, provided it leads to the centre. Dispute among the different 'ways' of salvation is pointless; all that matters is that those who follow them should find their way to that timeless, motionless centre where all is peace, and where one can understand all the endless movement and change which makes up human history – understand that it goes nowhere and means nothing.

The other symbol is the road. History is a journey, a pilgrimage. We do not yet see the goal, but we believe in it and seek it. The movement in which we are involved is not meaningless movement; it is movement towards a goal. The goal, the ultimate resting-place, the experience of coherence and harmony, is not to be had save at the end of the road. The perfect goal is not a timeless reality hidden now behind the multiplicity and change which we experience; it is yet to be achieved; it lies at the end of the road.

This, very roughly sketched, is what Macnicol calls 'the great divide'. Many writers on religion do not acknowledge it as such. Too often, it seems, writers on the comparative study of religion assume that the essence of religion lies in the mystical experience and therefore take their stand, without argument, on one side of the divide. Starting from this conviction, they find evidences in all religions of this experience in varying forms and with varying

---

[1] Newbigin 1969: 65–87 [. . . .].

depths – but all recognizable as belonging to the same kind. Obviously different religions have different attitudes to history, but these differences are taken to be variations within one fundamentally homogeneous reality, different dialects of one language. There is no 'great divide'.

Paul Tillich, in his report on his discussion with Buddhists,[2] treats what we have called the great divide as a polarity within a single system. Both Christianity and Buddhism, he says, grow out of 'the experience of the Holy here and now'. In one the mystical predominates, and in the other the ethical. In one holiness is what ought to be (the Kingdom of God), and in the other holiness is what is (Nirvana). This leads to divergent attitudes towards history. But, says Tillich, there is a non-historical mystical element in Christianity, and – on the other hand – 'history itself has driven Buddhism to take history seriously'. On this the following comments would seem to be in order.

(a)   Manifestly Christianity and Buddhism, as religious systems which have existed through many centuries and have been involved with other cultural and religious forces throughout these centuries, have been influenced by factors other than those which originally gave them birth. Christianity has, from the moment that the Gospel broke into the Hellenistic world, been in contact with, and influenced by pantheistic religion and by the kind of mysticism which flourishes in a pantheistic environment. Nevertheless the basic structure of the Christian Scriptures, creeds and liturgies is such as to make it impossible for this kind of mysticism ever to have the central place. Nothing can displace the concrete historic figure of Jesus Christ from the centre of the Christian religion. And on the other hand the modern development of a unified secular world-society has compelled Buddhism to take history seriously. Nevertheless this development is not just an accidental fact of history; it is intimately related to the worldwide spread of the secularized form of the biblical conception of the Kingdom of God which has its roots in Christendom. From a Christian point of view this development is part of the consequences of the incarnation – the drawing of all men out of a non-historical form of existence into a single global history dominated by issues which have been raised for man by the biblical revelation.

(b)   We may accept the statement that both religions grow out of 'the experience of the Holy here and now'.[3] But the question is: 'What is the character of the Holy?' or, 'Who is the Holy One?' It is an obscuring of the issues to speak of 'Holiness as what is' and 'Holiness as what ought to be' as though they were the end-readings on a scale across which the needle could swing back and forth without a break. The revelation of God which is concentrated in the Cross of Jesus Christ is the revelation of a holiness which *is* and which is in agony until what ought to be is. That agony is in history, and if history is

---
[2] Tillich 1963: 58.
[3] Tillich 1963: 74.

not taken seriously the revelation is not received. For Christianity the deepest meaning of history lies in the fact that in it God, who is, is wrestling with the estranged and rebellious wills of men, until his own perfect love is embodied and reflected in a redeemed and restored creation. That is necessarily involved in taking the total fact of Christ, with its burning centre in the Cross, as the object of faith. *Per contra* I have found in discussion with Hindu friends that, while they will generally seek to interpret Christian experience and doctrine from within the perspective of the Vedanta, they generally acknowledge that at the point of the attitude to history there is a radical difference between what Christians believe and what the Hindu view of life permits. There is, it seems to me, good reason for agreeing with Macnicol that this is 'the great divide' among the religions.

2   To speak of Christ as the clue to history means that history is under-stood as in some sense a coherent whole. This is not obvious. History appears to be full of incoherence and meaninglessness. Moreover history as normally understood is the history of some part of the human race or of some aspect of human culture. One can understand what is meant by the history of India, or the history of European architecture, or of Arctic exploration. Until very recent times the conditions did not exist for writing a universal history which could include in one work substantial material covering all the continents and all the races of mankind through all the millennia of human existence on the planet. There was not enough mutual contact between the great races and cultures, and there was not enough knowledge of the past. What was called 'universal history' was – until relatively recent times – history based upon the Bible, written by men who were ignorant of vast tracts of human history, but who took their stand upon the biblical faith concerning the origin and destiny of man. In recent times it has been common to regard this kind of 'universal history' as invalid; it is easy to point to its limitations and to con-clude that it is really a very local or provincial essay in history, not different basically from, say, a history of Europe into which the rest of the world comes only as it impinges upon the consciousness of European man.

Since Voltaire there have been many efforts to construct a universal history which would be genuinely universal – free from the limitations and prejudices of the Western Christian tradition, history written in an objective, impartial spirit which sees all mankind and all human history as equally worthy of record. But the matter has only to be stated in that way to reveal its intrinsic impossibility. All historical writing involves the selection of the most significant from among the almost infinite mass of records. The selection is necessarily based upon the provisional judgment of the historian, which again depends upon his own understanding of and commitment to the course of events in his own time. Histories which claim to be free from any sectional or provincial prejudice cannot conceal from the critical reader the convictions which led the historian to proceed in the way he did. His convictions may be so much the unexamined convictions of his age and place that his first read-ers do not notice them, and are convinced by the claim to objectivity and impartiality. But readers of another age and place will immediately recognize that his axiomatic convictions are indeed highly questionable.

If all history is to be grasped as a unity, it must be from some standpoint, and, as I have already said, there is no standpoint which is above all particular standpoints. A man can only see things from where he is. How then can there be such a thing as a universal history?

Normally a story can only be well told by a man who sees the point of the story before he begins to tell it. If he does not see the point, his tale will get lost in a mass of irrelevant detail. If the detail includes (as it does in the story we are considering) all the available records of the whole life of man in every age and country, the possibility of getting lost is very great. But how does one grasp the point? Normally the point is only clear at the end; we are still in the middle of the story. How, then, can there be a universal history? Only if, by some means, the teller has become convinced about the end of the story while he is still in the midst of it. Such a conviction will necessarily be at the same time a commitment to act in a certain way in the history which is being written today and tomorrow.

To speak of the finality of Christ is to express such a conviction and such a commitment concerning the point of the human story as a whole. A secular historian writing a universal history is – explicitly or implicitly – expressing such a conviction and commitment. It is a conviction which can be criticized. It is not a point of vantage above all sectional standpoints. It is vulnerable. But without accepting the risks which it involves, there can be no universal history.

In this respect there is no difference in principle between the Christian theologian's way of handling the historical records of his faith and those of a secular historian. Both of them are taking the risks which are involved in making a judgment about the data; they differ about the 'end' which determines the meaning of everything that goes before it. 'The faith which is needed to interpret the Bible is not in principle different from the faith with which any secular historian handles his material.'[4]

Once again, therefore, to speak of the finality of Christ is to speak of him as the clue to our interpretation of history as a whole. It implies that our conviction about Christ, and our commitment to serve him in the present hour, gives us the standpoint from which we can truly understand human history as a whole. It therefore involves us in a discussion not merely with the adherents of other religions but with all men who are seeking to understand the human situation and to discern the kind of commitment which is required for playing a responsible part in the ongoing history of which we are a part.

3   What, exactly, is it for which we claim finality? It is not 'Christianity'. On that probably all Protestant Christians would agree. We have seen how

---

[4] Alan Richardson. (Source unquoted, though see Richardson 1947: 89–109 for this line of argument.)

both at Edinburgh in 1910 and at Tambaram in 1938[5] – though with differing terminology – the point was clearly made that we claim no sort of finality for the body of beliefs and practices which is included under the heading 'Christianity'. Christianity is a changing and developing corpus of belief, practice, association, cultus, which is all the time assimilating new elements from other religions and other world views, and which needs, therefore, criteria by which it can determine what is true development and what is distorted or cancerous growth. We cannot claim finality for Christianity.

[. . . .]

[We] claim finality for Christ. But what does that claim mean, when differentiated from a claim on behalf of Christianity? What are the implications of making a radical disjunction between Christ and Christianity or between the Gospel and Christianity? It is one of the small ironies of history that the same Tambaram Conference which witnessed the most resounding statement of the distinction between the Gospel and Christianity was also the meeting which insisted upon the centrality of the Church to the missionary task, which insisted that the Church is in fact part of the Gospel. It is well known that the missionary thinking of the years preceding the Tambaram Conference had given little place to the Church and had been inclined to speak more of the Kingdom of God. Tambaram emphatically and deliberately turned the thinking of the Churches in a different direction, and made the Church the centre of its thinking about the missionary task. The Tambaram discussion is therefore a good starting-point for posing the question: what exactly is involved in making a disjunction between Christianity and the Gospel?

(a) I have already referred to the argument of Hogg that a distinction analogous to that made by Kraemer between the Gospel and Christianity must also be made between Hinduism as a total system of belief and practice, and the faith of a devout Hindu.[6] In reply to this Kraemer had little difficulty in showing that it was not a true analogy, for the thing for which he claimed finality was not the faith of the devout Christian but the Gospel – the message of God's unique and decisive self-revelation in Jesus Christ, Incarnate, Crucified, Risen.

---

[5] (The World Missionary Conference was held at Edinburgh in 1910, and the second meeting of the International Missionary Council at Tambaram, Madras, in 1938.)

[6] (Hendrik Kraemer (1888–1965) was a Dutch Reformed missionary in the East Indies and author of the influential work *The Christian Message in a Non-Christian World* (Kraemer 1938). He argued that because Christian faith is founded upon God's unique self-disclosure in Jesus Christ, a sharp distinction must be made between this revelation and religious experience generally – whether Christian or non-Christian. Alfred Hogg (1875–1954) was for many years the Principal of the Christian College in Madras, India, and argued that though the revelation of Christ is decisive, there is evidence in the heart of true Hindu faith of a partial but real response to the divine calling.)

(b)   This reply of Kraemer's is [itself] open to criticism. [. . .]. It is impossible to make a total disjunction of revelation and faith, for if there is no faith by which the revelation is grasped, there is no revelation. Revelation happens when God actually communicates himself to men, and that communication happens only if there is human response. The decisive revelation cannot be described altogether apart from the human response of faith. Moreover at this point we have again to listen to the historian. I have already drawn attention to the fact that historians cannot make a total disjunction between so-called 'facts' and their interpretation. A 'fact of history' is an interpretation of evidence. The 'fact of Christ' (to use the phrase beloved of my old teacher Dr Carnegie Simpson) is the life, death and resurrection of Jesus interpreted by the apostles. Apart from their faith, the very name of Jesus would be unknown to us; there would be no 'fact of Christ' for us to believe in. Like other facts of history, the fact of Christ is available to us now because of the judgment of contemporaries about its significance. The 'fact' cannot be had in isolation from the judgment, even though the judgment is always subject to our critical examination. E. H. Carr's definition of the nature of history could also be applied to the work of Christian theological thinking: it is a continuous conversation between the believer of today and the first believers – the apostles.

(c)   To claim finality for Christ is to endorse the judgment of the apostles that in this life, death and resurrection God himself was uniquely present and that therefore the meaning and origin and end of all things was disclosed; it is to join with the apostles in making this judgment.

This does not mean that, whereas God is always revealing himself in all times and places, it happened that at this time and place there were those who recognized and responded; that would be to claim uniqueness for the apostles, not for Christ. If this were all we meant by the fact of Christ, then we could not claim finality for this; for we could expect others at other times and places to respond even more adequately. The Christian faith, based upon the apostolic testimony, is that in the whole course of history, which is in some sense a unity, this is the decisive point, the turning-point; and that at this turning-point both the event and the true interpretation of the event were – by God's overruling activity – made possible. It is of the substance of what we mean by 'the fact of Christ' that in God's long and patient wrestling with the human race, this time and place were made ready, this people was prepared, these men were chosen and trained in order that they might be the witnesses and interpreters of this unique and decisive event.

(d)   I have said that to speak of the finality of Christ is to endorse the apostolic testimony concerning him. But a further point has now to be made. We do not know about this apostolic testimony in the way that an archaeologist learns about a remote and long-buried civilization. We know about it because we have been made part of a continuous tradition, carried by a community in which the writings of these apostles have been continuously treasured, reproduced, studied, expounded, interpreted and applied to changing situations. It is as part of this living, doubtless changing, but also continuing tradition that we speak about the finality of Christ. Without this, the apostolic testimony would not be a significant fact of our own present experience. To claim, for instance, that some event which took place during the history of the Mohenjo Daro civilization or among the Incas of Peru was the decisive turning-point of human history would be meaningless. We are not connected with it in any way which involves our present experience. The claim that the fact of Christ is decisive for all human life is a meaningless claim except as it is interpreted in the life of a community which lives by the tradition of the apostolic testimony. There cannot, therefore, be a total disjunction between the Gospel and 'Christianity'. To claim finality for Christ means *in some sense* to claim a decisive role in history for the Church.

The answer to the obvious question: 'In what sense?' will have to be developed when we come to speak of conversion to Christ and his Church. Here, however, the following point must be made. The original apostolic witness remains permanently at the centre of the life of the Church in order to provide the norm by which all subsequent development is judged and by which aberrations are corrected. There must be development. It is impossible simply to go on repeating the original words. They have – in the first place – to be translated, and all translation changes meaning. They have, then, to be reinterpreted to meet new situations. It is precisely by the vigour and courage with which the work of reinterpretation is done that the claim to finality is made good in the actual course of human history. Only when the Church has the boldness to reinterpret the original testimony in the face of new human situations is it able to make plain and effective the claim to finality. Reinterpretation always carries risks, but to evade risks always means to court disaster. Syncretism is not the only danger against which the Church has to be alert. The New Testament is equally clear in its warnings against the opposite danger – the danger of timidity, of trying to avoid risks by tying up the talent in a napkin to be preserved in useless safety until the Lord's return. In this necessary and dangerous work of reinterpretation the Church has to take its bearings by means of the original witness of the apostles. This acts as a norm of development, a source of reform when life and message have been distorted by being conformed to the whims of a passing age, and a fount of renewal when life has been stifled by too much caution and by a false isolation from the world.

(e) The apostolic testimony to Jesus as Lord is a claim for his finality in respect of matters of which the apostles themselves were necessarily ignorant. They knew nothing of Buddhism or Hinduism, yet claimed that Jesus was the only name given under heaven whereby we must be saved. They knew nothing of the sort of future for the human race which we are glimpsing in the second half of the twentieth century, yet they confessed him as the *alpha* and the *omega*, the beginning and end of all things.

In this respect Christian faith is analogous not only to the judgment of a historian, but also to the generalization of a natural scientist or mathematician. Like the great theorems of science and mathematics, it is a statement which, if true, implies much more than the person who first made it could possibly be aware of. Its truth will be confirmed by discoveries which lie far beyond the horizon of its originator. This has implications which may be stated both negatively and positively.

(i) Negatively it means that faith in Christ does not give the believer a total picture of human history which excuses him from the necessity of making new discoveries. He is not in a position to read off a chart of world history from creation to consummation out of the material given in the Bible. This is a point at which Christians have frequently been mistaken. There is a real sense in which the Bible is a universal history, telling the story of the world from its origin to its end. But its accounts of the beginning and the end are imaginative and parabolic proclamations of its faith that the clue to the whole is to be found at the centre; of its faith that the origin and end not only of human history but of cosmic history (and the Bible requires us to work with this conception) are to be understood in terms of that series of events in which God has decisively acted and thereby revealed his character and his intention.

(ii) Positively one can state the claim in the following way. The community which lives in the fellowship of commitment to Christ as Lord, while not thereby given any detailed map of the course of history, is enabled by faith to participate in the struggles of human history in such a way as not to be in vain. To put the matter in another way: the kind of commitment to action in history which arises from faith in Christ will be found – in all the vast and unforeseeable changes of the human situation, changes which the first apostles could never have imagined – to be fruitful, creative, constructive.

Thus the claim is certainly not that Christianity is final. It is that through participation in the corporate life of the community which – founded upon the apostolic testimony – is committed to Christ as Lord, one is enabled rightly to interpret God's work in human history, and thereby rightly to commit oneself to constructive action in history. It is the claim that, at the end of the story, this will be seen to have been the true, the proper, the relevant commitment.

4 But can we, even on the basis of faith in Christ, really interpret history? There is a mass of depressing evidence which could be cited against any claim to be able to do so. One thinks of all the cranks and fanatics down the ages, and in our own day, who claim to understand exactly what God is doing in contemporary history. One thinks of all the expert students of the Books of Daniel and Revelation who claim to foretell the events of the 1970s. One thinks of the German Christians in the 1930s confidently interpreting the rise of the Nazi movement as God's cleansing action on behalf of the German people. It is understandable that those who went through the terrible experiences of Nazi rule, and others also, should express some alarm when they hear Christians claim to know what God is doing in the political and cultural and technological revolutions of our time.

One may grant that there is ground for this alarm, and yet one must press the question: how can we possibly refuse to try to interpret what God is doing in the secular events of our time? If we were to do so, we should be parting company with the prophets and with Jesus himself. The very heart of the prophetic message was their inspired interpretation of the events of their time – wars, enslavements, liberations, droughts, plagues and famines – in terms of the purpose of the living God. And Jesus himself, it seems, repeatedly told his hearers that they ought to be able to discern the signs of the times just as they knew how to interpret the changes in the sky and the winds. Whatever be the dangers of this enterprise, are we permitted to abandon it?

Moreover, what is the alternative? If I am to commit myself in any way to taking part in the public life of my time, it must be on the basis of some interpretation of what is going on, of what are the issues, of what are the forces at work. If I decline to attempt any interpretation, I must also avoid any commitment and confine myself to keeping my own personal record clean – if that is possible in a world so full of evil. And if I refuse that dereliction of duty and commit myself to action in the public realm, where am I to find the guidelines if not in my faith in Jesus Christ?

[. . . .] If history is not a meaningless jumble of events, if God is working out a purpose in it, it is necessary to try to interpret – even if only in very modest, tentative and provisional terms – what he is doing. If we are to know where to act, where to throw our weight, where to commit ourselves, we must have some provisional answer to the question: 'Where is God at work and where is the Devil?'

Perhaps our greatest temptation lies at the following point: it is easy, in effect, to translate the faith that God is at work in history into the proposition that where a movement appears to be successful there God must be at work. It is easy to think of examples of what – at least with the benefit of hindsight – looks like this fatal error. The assurance, for instance, with which many Western Protestant Christians regarded the spread of Western power all over the world, and the consequent expansion of the opportunities for missionary work as a sign of the activity of God, is an example that comes readily to mind. Other similar convictions may be more disputable because they are nearer to our own day. Obviously there is here a very plausible temptation. Moreover no one can deny that the conviction that God is on our side can give an unequalled vigour and vitality to any movement.

Recognizing these dangers, what practical content can we give to the faith that God is working out his purpose in history and that the clue to this purpose is to be found in Jesus Christ? How are we to interpret God's action in history and so learn to commit ourselves to obedient partnership?

In this difficult matter I would suggest the following three-fold statement of the Christian claim:

(a)   That which is disclosed in Jesus Christ is the very character and will from which all that is proceeds. For the believer who, by the work of God's

Spirit, has been brought to stand before the Cross of Christ and to give his Amen to the apostolic testimony about it, this is thenceforth the commitment by which all else is judged. It arises from a total personal experience, which the New Testament calls the new birth, in which a man is brought to abandon all other commitments and to commit himself wholly and without reserve to Jesus Christ in the fellowship of those who share the same commitment.

To one who has made that commitment, the disclosure of God in Jesus Christ is determinative of his interpretation of all the events of history. Wherever he sees men being set free for responsible sonship of God; wherever he sees the growth of mutual responsibility of man for man and of people for people; wherever he sees evidences of the character of Jesus Christ being reflected in the lives of men; there he will conclude that God is at work, and that he is summoned to be God's fellow worker, even where the Name of Christ is not acknowledged. By contrast, wherever he sees the reverse process at work, men being enslaved, mutual responsibility being denied, and the opposite of the character of Christ being produced in men; there he will recognize the work of the Devil and will know himself summoned to resist.

Jesus Christ is the sole criterion. Here we have to take our stand with the Barmen Declaration.[7] There is no other source of revelation, once we have known Christ.

(b) This disclosure of the character and will of God in the midst of human history is met not by success but by rejection. Jesus is crucified; his Church is persecuted; those who follow him are promised suffering, rejection and death. There is emphatically no equation between faithfulness to God's will and success in history. To follow Christ means to deny self and accept the Cross. Therefore the Christian who commits himself to the kind of action in history just described will not be deflected or defeated when he and the causes which he supports meet rejection. He will accept this as part of his participation in God's struggle with man which is the stuff of history.

(c) But this is not the last word. If it were, Christian discipleship could only be a flight from history. Jesus rises from the dead. The tomb is empty. Jesus is declared to be the Son of God with power. This is a fact of history in the only sense in which we can speak of a fact of history, namely a judgment of the evidence. The Christian believes that this judgment is determinative for the understanding of all history, that it is the point at which the meaning of the whole story is disclosed, and that the whole story must therefore be understood from this point.

While recognizing the very great problems which these assertions raise, I would submit that if, at this point, we fall back into a dichotomy of inward and outward, making the resurrection only an event in the internal spiritual history of the disciples and not an event in the history of Jesus and therefore

---

[7] (The Barmen Declaration of 1934 comprised six 'evangelical truths' issued by German Protestant representatives in opposition to the Nazi-supported 'German Christian' movement. It emphasized strongly the unique and final revelation of God in Jesus Christ.)

of the world, then we abandon the possibility of claiming that Jesus is the clue to history.

Because of his resurrection faith, the Christian will expect and will find that defeat is turned into victory; that even in the midst of the appalling triumph of human blindness and wickedness, evidences will be continually forthcoming – manifest to eyes of faith – of the victory of God. 'Manifest to eyes of faith.' Like the resurrection itself, these evidences of God's victory in the life of the world will be – not 'facts' which could be demonstrated irresistibly to any person irrespective of his personal judgment – but confirmations of that judgment of faith which recognizes in the resurrection of Jesus the decisive act of God. The claim that Jesus is final is the claim that at the end of the story this judgment will be seen to be the true judgment, the true interpretation of history, and the action arising out of commitment to that judgment to be the ultimately significant action.

I think that we can go a step further. As the Christian looks back over the course of human history, as it is unfolded by the work of scholars, and over the still vaster course of cosmic history as it is deciphered by biologists, palaeontologists and astronomers, and as he seeks to interpret it from the standpoint of the revelation of God in Jesus Christ, he sees signs which confirm the understanding which is given to him in the Bible: a growing mastery of man over nature, a growing interdependence of all men with one another, larger areas of freedom and therefore of responsibility. As he looks to the future, the Christian sees the pattern of Cross and Resurrection as the key to its interpretation: the rejection by man of God's love; the use of the greater and greater freedom and power which God gives to man for more and more disastrous rebellion against God; and yet the infinite power and resourcefulness of God to use men's rebellion as the means to his victory; the pattern of Cross and Resurrection thrown on to the screen of world history in the shape of the New Testament figures of the Antichrist and the Millennium; the ultimate assurance of God's victory in this world and over this world – even though the relation between this 'in' and this 'over' remains hidden from us.

To claim finality for Christ is to claim that this is the true clue to history, the standpoint from which one truly interprets history and therefore has the possibility of being relevantly committed to the service of God in history now.

Further reading
Newbigin 1941: 1–55.
Newbigin 1989b: 103–15.

5

The ecumenical vision

————•◆•————

In his autobiography, Newbigin wrote that from the start of his Christian experience as an undergraduate at Cambridge, the SCM had taught him 'to see unity and mission as two sides of a single commitment'.[1] This conviction – strengthened through the visits to Cambridge of ecumenical statesmen such as Joe Oldham and John Mott – was to play its part in forming a passion for the cause of Christian unity that Newbigin was never to lose. For him this conviction was always a matter of theological principle rather than pragmatic expediency. Writing in 1976, for example, he argued that 'to give up the quest of [. . .] unity is to settle for something less than the Gospel'.[2] Or again, in 1992, he stated that 'We cannot, with any hope of being believed, preach to men the word of our Lord that he, when he is lifted up from the earth, will draw all men to himself, if we continue stubbornly to say that even his love is not enough to draw us close to one another and enable us to live together as brethren in one family.'[3]

The pinnacle of his own ecumenical achievements was undoubtedly the formal inauguration of the United Church of South India in 1947, which was to remain a source of great joy and excitement to him, and in which he served as a founding bishop. So committed was he to its vision that he saw its establishment as somehow pioneering a way for the whole Church worldwide. This was never to be, and Newbigin was to experience desperate disappointment in his struggles to defend the CSI against its detractors in the years that followed its foundation. Newbigin's passion for unity remained undaunted, however, and during the 1950s in particular he was deeply and energetically involved in the discussions over the nature of the unity espoused by the WCC, which was to become a key theme of its third assembly at New Delhi, India, in 1961. The debates around this question had been gathering momentum for some years, and in 1954 (shortly before the second assembly in Evanston, Chicago) Newbigin delivered the Thomas Memorial Lecture at the University of Chicago on the theme 'The quest for unity through religion'. The following extract is taken from it. Here Newbigin contrasts the Christian vision for unity with that of Hinduism, before setting out in clear and robust terms the grounds for unity implied by the gospel of Jesus Christ, and the local forms in which this might be expressed. His lecture, published in the Journal of

---

[1] Newbigin 1993d: 239.
[2] Newbigin 1976: 306.
[3] Newbigin 1992c: 4.

Religion *in 1955, made a significant contribution to the ecumenical discussions that followed.*

* * *

Extract
'The Quest for Religion through Religion' (1955)[4]

[In] India [. . .] the belief that all religions are in essence one has become not merely an article of faith but almost an axiom of thought. Anyone who doubts its truth is regarded as semi–illiterate. [. . . .] Against that background, the Christian missionary has to face the charge of sectarianism and separatism. The slogan, 'Christ, the Hope of the World,'[5] is met by indignant repudiation: 'If by the word "Christ," you mean the same universal religious principle which is also in Buddha, in Krishna, in Mohammed, in Gandhi, we agree that this is the Hope of the World. But, if you mean that all the world is to follow one way, to be enrolled under one banner, to accept one dogma, namely, the one you bring us, then we say, "No." That is not the way to unity, but the way to sectarian strife. Your religious imperialism is out of date; it is the survival of an earlier day, when every frog in its own little pond thought that that pond was the ocean. We are happy to hear what you have to tell us about your religion; we recognize in Jesus an incarnation of the one universal religious principle. We shall gladly worship him as we worship others. But if you insist that we must all join your flock, we must tell you that you are still in the kinder-garten stage of religion; that if you want to make your contribution to our national life, you must abandon these ridiculous claims to exclusive truth, recognize the truth in all religion, and join with us as brothers in the one religious task.'

[. . . .]

The most eminent and persuasive exponent of this Hindu claim today is the great philosopher and statesman, who is at present vice-president of the Indian republic, Dr S. Radhakrishnan. He says:

> The Hindu attitude to other religions is based upon a definite philosophy of life, which assumes that religion is a matter of personal realization. Spirit is free being, and its life consists in breaking free from conventions and penetrating into true being. The formless blaze of spiritual life cannot be expressed in human words. We tread on air so thin and rare that we do not leave any

---

[4] Newbigin 1955: [. . . .] 17–21 (extracts), 23–33.
[5] (The theme of the second assembly of the WCC that met in Evanston, Chicago in 1954.)

visible footprints. He who has seen the real is lifted above all narrowness, relativities, and contingencies.[6]

This inability to express the real in human words does not, however, as
Radhakrishnan makes very clear, mean that there is anything vague about it.
The basis of the Hindu position, as he says, is a very definite philosophy,
which, like other philosophies, is capable of statement and of criticism and
which, in turn, is based upon an experience which is described as 'personal
realization,' 'penetration into true being,' 'seeing the real.' That philosophy is
what India calls the 'Vedanta,' the end and summation of all revelation. It
teaches that the reality behind all the manifold appearance and all the ceaseless change which our five senses report to us is one undifferentiated and
unchanging spirit and that that spirit is identical with our own spirit.

[. . . .]

The ultimate basis of the whole Hindu position is thus the experience of mystical union with the ultimate. On this Radhakrishnan is very explicit: 'The
religions of the world can be distinguished into those which emphasize the
object and those which insist on experience. For the first class, religion is an
attitude of faith and conduct, directed to a power without. For the second, it
is an experience to which the individual attaches supreme value. The Hindu
and the Buddhist religions are of this class.'[7] That experience has been
described many times by mystics, East and West, and the essential features of
their description are the same. The essence of it is, first, a gradual withdrawal
of the mind from the world of sense perception by exercise in ascetic discipline; second, the concentration of all the mental powers upon a single object,
upon an image, a text, upon a single sound, such as the sacred syllable '*om*,' or
upon some part of the body, until the soul becomes empty of everything
except the object of its meditation; and, finally, the point is reached where
even the object of meditation ceases to be an object distinct from the subject.
Subject and object are dissolved in a single unitary awareness, which is not an
apprehension of any object but only, if one may put it so, awareness in an
intransitive sense. 'The soul, holding itself in emptiness, finds itself possessing
all.' And those who have visited these sublime heights tell us that they have
experienced a rapture beyond any earthly joy, a knowledge beyond logic, a
peace beyond understanding.

It is that experience which provides the basis of certitude upon which the
Hindu attitude to other religions rests. From that standpoint, every expression
of the religious sense, whether it be the most primitive idolatry or the most

---

[6] Radhakrishnan 1939: 316–17.
[7] Radhakrishnan 1939: 21.

refined and spiritual theism, is seen to be but a refraction of the one ultimate truth seen through human natures which are at various stages of development — that is to say, at various stages of liberation from the toils of *maya*. Within such a view of reality, there is room for almost infinite tolerance. Human nature varies, and each man is free to join the stream of living religion at the place to which his nature and environment lead him. There is no place for mutual criticism or hostility. Each man must be encouraged to be faithful to the religious path of his choice but, at the same time, to penetrate behind the forms of religion, its alleged revelations, its creeds and dogmas and rituals, to find through them (and it does not matter what they are) the one truth, which is not a dogmatic statement or a personal meeting but an experience of identity with the Supreme Being.

The one thing which on this view cannot be tolerated is the one assertion which Christianity is bound to make, namely, that the Supreme Being has, once and for all, revealed himself in a historic person; that truth is to be found only by relating one's self to him; and that he is the center around which the unity of mankind here in history is to be built. To such a claim, when it is clearly understood, Hinduism, in obedience to its own fundamental tenets, can only present an unrelenting opposition. From the point of view of the Vedanta, the preaching of the Christian gospel is an assertion of ultimate validity for something which belongs to the world of illusion.

[. . . .]

Thus the Hindu offer of reconciliation between religions is a consistent whole from start to finish. It begins with the assumption with which it ends, namely, that the phenomenal world of multiplicity and change is illusory. It therefore begins by a process of withdrawal from that world, and it ends with a conception of salvation which can have no organic relation to any particular historic events or to any visible historic community. Its claim to be the truth transcending all religions is necessarily at the same time a negation of the truth of those religions as their adherents understand them. So far from providing the basis for a permanent truce between the religions, it is — when properly understood — a declaration of war upon all religion which claims to be based upon a historic revelation.

There is no escaping the fact that the unity of mankind can be achieved only around some center, and therefore the question 'What is the true center?' is the vital question. There is no way to unity by mere amalgamation, wholesale syncretism, or universal toleration. Men are not made one except by something which draws them together. When the Hindu says, 'All rivers flow into the ocean; all ways lead to God,' he is, in fact, bearing witness to a very definite faith as to the ultimate nature of man, of the world, and of God, and we cannot avoid asking the question 'Is it true?' Once that question is raised, we are again in the realm of conflict between religions. The unity of mankind cannot be achieved except as a unity in the truth; and truth cannot make concordats with falsehood. The quest for unity must itself involve the steady repudiation of every claim to achieve unity around a false center.

[. . . .]

What, then, shall we say of the claim implicit in the existence of the World Council of Churches and explicit in the title of the assembly which is about to meet: 'Christ, the Hope of the World.' The World Council of Churches [. . .] draws together bodies which hold profoundly different interpretations of the truth. Within its membership are to be found teachings which mutually contradict one another on important issues. Its member churches are not able in all cases to recognize one another as churches. Yet, by their covenanting together to form this Council and by many public statements, they have confessed that there is a truth which holds them together in spite of the differences which hold them apart. We have to ask: 'What is the basis upon which this unity is affirmed in spite of disagreement on large and important matters of truth?' We have seen that, in the case of the Hindu claim to reconcile all religions, the basis is the mystical experience and the claim that this is the path to identification with the Supreme Being. What, in the case of the ecumenical movement, is the basis upon which unity is affirmed in the face of diversity?

The first assembly of the World Council of Churches at Amsterdam[8] answered that question in these words: 'We are divided. . . . But Christ has made us one, and He is not divided.' What exactly does the phrase 'Christ has made us one' mean? The subject of the sentence is the name of a person who lived at a particular and somewhat remote place and time in human history. The predicate is a statement of personal experience. How exactly are they related?

I have only once attended a meeting of the Central Committee of the World Council of Churches, and at that meeting two new churches were admitted – the Holy Orthodox church of Greece and the Presbyterian church of Formosa. If one were to ask representatives of each of those churches to sit down with us and together answer the question: 'In what sense has Christ made you one?' how would they answer? Leaving aside the fact – so helpful to the ecumenical movement – that distance lends enchantment to the view, we should find that our two friends were obliged to make the most radical criticisms of each other, that, in fact, each would have very grave reservations about applying the term 'Christian church' to the other. Why, then, have they both accepted membership in a council of churches? In what sense has Christ made them one? The answer which we might expect would be something like this: 'We both recognize that in Jesus Christ, incarnate, crucified, dead, buried, and risen again, in Palestine under Pontius Pilate, God was reconciling the

---

[8] (Held in 1948.)

world to himself; that he died to take away our sin and the sin of the world, and that in him we have been born again to a new life in the Spirit; as we listen to one another confessing this faith in Christ and this debt to Christ, we acknowledge these as a reality in one another; and we acknowledge that this reality is of such transcendent importance that it ought to govern our relations to one another; therefore, while not surrendering the truth which we hold or admitting the error which we see in one another, we agree to live, work, talk, and pray together in the faith that Christ will complete in us his work and make us one as he wills us to be.' Let us try to analyze this more carefully.

1   The starting point is an event alleged to have happened in Palestine, under Pontius Pilate. The Vedantin finds the clue to all experience in a particular kind of individual spiritual experience which is, in principle, equally available to all men and women at all times and places; starting from that, he develops his whole world-view in logical order and consistency. The Christian finds the clue in a particular historic event, unique, unrepeated, and unrepeatable. Everything hangs on that. If that event did not, in fact, happen, the whole Christian religion falls to the ground. That is why accurate, critical historical study is essential to Christianity. To the Vedantin this is incredible folly; it is, for him, self-evident that no universal truth can be established on the basis of a particular event in the flux of history. To the Christian, on the other hand, everything hangs upon this. His creed is a statement of historic happenings, and at its center stands the phrase 'under Pontius Pilate.'

2   Consistent with his starting point, the Christian insists that he is related to that once-and-for-all event through a continuous, living, historic process. The report of the event comes to him in a tradition which is both oral and written and which is continuous from the original event until today. Christians may differ as to the relation between these two strands of tradition, but all in fact acknowledge and depend upon the double strand. The Roman Catholic, with all his emphasis on tradition, treats the written Scripture as inerrant; the most redoubtable Protestant receives the Scriptures in and through a living tradition of spiritual experience.

3   The character of the once-and-for-all event governs the character of the unity which it creates. The experience which lies at the base of the Vedanta does not issue in a visible community. The typical *sannyasi* is an isolated figure; if he has company, it consists of those who have come to him to receive for themselves the secret of enlightenment. The experience of enlightenment does not create community; on the contrary, it frees him who attains it from the bonds of all human community, including those of family. He is henceforth at one with all that is, and there is no place for any particular attachments. The death of Jesus, on the other hand, has, from the beginning of the Christian tradition, been interpreted as an atonement. It is an event by which atonement is wrought between God and men and therefore between man and his fellow man. The unity thus created between men is not simply an intellectual one; it does not consist in the sharing of a common set of beliefs,

though that is involved in it. It is the reconciliation of persons in their totality to one another. It is the mutual forgiveness of sins, based upon that fact that in Christ the sins of all have been forgiven by God. It is the replacement of mutual hostility by mutual love.

Here we introduce a set of terms completely alien to the whole vocabulary of the Vedanta. For the Vedantin, the disunity of humanity is the product of man's involvement in *maya*; it is the result of *aviddya*, of man's failure to know and to realize his identity with the one spirit. For the Christian, the disunity of mankind is due to his sin, to his having abused the divine gift of responsibility, turned the divine gift of love into self-love, and so fallen into fear, envy, and hatred towards his neighbor. In Christ, God has, by a new creative act in the very midst of a humanity corrupted by sin, provided a place of atonement, a *hilasterion*, a mercy-seat, to which sinful men may come for reconciliation. This reconciliation involves a complete inward revolution, a breaking-up of the deeps of human nature, a death and rebirth, a redirecting of the whole vital power of human nature by which what had formerly been harnessed to the task of self-seeking is turned outward in active love towards the neighbor. It places a man in a completely new situation in a new field of forces, as the result of which his whole powers are set free from the task of self-preservation and self-justification and are directed upward and outward in gratitude for the free gift of forgiveness.

The relationship thus created between men is of a quite different character from that which arises out of unanimity of opinion or even out of common participation in one type of experience. It has its base in the faith that the Holy One died for the unholy, that the source of all loveliness loved the unlovely. Therefore, it rejoices to bear tensions and even incongruities. On any matter which would call in question the reality and sufficiency of the atoning act upon which it rests, it must be intransigent; on every other matter it can afford to be, and rejoice to be, infinitely forbearing. But its forbearing will not be of the kind which easily lets every man go his own way because in a world of illusion clear-cut distinctions are folly. It will be earnest in wrestling for the truth. But yet the unity does not depend upon intellectual unanimity. It is the relationship of mutual love and responsibility which is created by the recognition of a common obligation to infinite love.

It is of the very essence of such a relationship that it must issue in a visible community. Love is nothing if it does not issue in words and deeds by which the lover binds the beloved to himself. Love is infinitely more than tolerance. Tolerance requires no visible community to express it, but love does. The deeper and stronger the love, the more binding will be the mutual obligations to which it will lead. Therefore, it belongs to the very essence of the atonement wrought by Christ, that it leads to the creation of a visible community binding men together in all nations and all generations.

4   How, then, are we to understand the bond which binds together churches in the World Council which are deeply divided from one another on matters of truth? As in the case of the Hindu conception of religious unity,

so here we must go to the starting point and understand the whole from there. The starting point is the faith that, in the once-and-for-all events which we confess in the Creed, the clue to all existence has been given.

In Jesus Christ, God the Holy One has died for sinners. The holiness is wholly his; the sin is mine. Even my understanding of what he has done is clouded by my sin. My formulation of what he has done and my obedience to him have no finality. It is only in him and his finished work that there is finality. When, therefore, I meet another body of Christians which acknowledges the lordship of Christ and the finality and sufficiency of what he has done, but differs from me in its interpretation of the saving events and of the life which flows from them, I am placed in an existential relation with its members which I cannot deny, even though I may find myself in acute disagreement with them about its nature and implications. All who have shared in the life of the ecumenical movement will recognize the situation which I am trying to describe. As one talks and prays with the fellow Christian of another confession, one is driven to recognize that here is the same acknowledgment of an infinite obligation to the One Redeemer. The common acknowledgment of this infinite obligation makes it impossible for the one to disown the other. The same Holy Spirit by whose working in the heart I am driven to acknowledge Christ's sole lordship drives me to acknowledge also his presence in the other's confession. The bond that unites us is not a mere feeling, not a mere agreement in thought, not a merely natural sympathy, it is an actual knitting-together of two persons, which can be described either by saying that the Holy Spirit unites us or by saying that the death of Christ for us both places us in a relation to each other wherein we can but acknowledge each other as brothers. Within this acknowledgment there is room for the possibility of wide difference of belief. Just because the very basis of our relationship is the fact of the all-sufficient death of the Holy One for sinners, our recognition of one another is compatible with the recognition that each of us may, in his formulation of the nature of Christ's work, be led far astray by sinful blindness. We must claim absoluteness and finality for Christ and his finished work; but that very claim forbids us to claim absoluteness and finality for our understanding of it. The resulting relationship between us is characterized, therefore, by a complete intransigence in regard to the central ground of our faith, along with a willingness to recognize and learn from one another in the realms where we differ. For this mutual recognition the word 'toleration' is not appropriate, because the relationship is much more than tolerance. 'Tolerance' suggests leaving one another alone, and this is precisely what Christians cannot do. If contradictions of belief and practice are not allowed to destroy fellowship, it is because they are recognized as the results of that sin and its resultant blindness from which Christ has redeemed us. Therefore, the relationship of mutual responsibility into which Christ puts us by his atoning work lays upon us the obligation to wrestle with these differences in frankness and humility, until they yield deeper insight into God's nature and will.

Everything depends upon the starting point. For the Christian, it is the person and work of Christ as the clue to all reality. About that the Christian has to be as intransigent as the Hindu is about his. The characteristic fruit of the Hindu starting point is toleration, in the form of which I have tried to speak earlier. The characteristic fruit of the Christian starting point is the creation of a new relationship, a relationship of binding mutual responsibility between persons. Within that relationship a right understanding of the starting point issues in an attitude which can hold profound differences of belief and practice within a tension of love. But it is a tension. It is not static but dynamic, full of movement and of conflicting force. The resolution of the tension comes as and when difference leads to penitent acknowledgment of our sinful blindness, and from that to a fresh apprehension of the divine will and nature revealed in Christ. Above all, the Christian starting point requires and creates a visible community. Binding mutual responsibility can be expressed only in a visible community. So, from the beginning, the gospel has the church at its heart, and so also the ecumenical movement could not remain a mere movement, but must necessarily give birth to something like the World Council. The unity which Christ creates must, of its own nature, take to itself some such visible and tangible embodiment.

To the question: 'What is the proper form of that embodiment?' I shall return in a moment. But first the line of argument must be pursued in another direction. I have asserted that the starting point of the whole Christian understanding of the world is the series of historic events centering in the death of Jesus Christ under Pontius Pilate, interpreted as the all-sufficient atonement between God and man and between man and his neighbor. This event, so understood, places those who understand it in a relation with one another which can be expressed only in the form of a visible community. The church is organic to the gospel. But, in saying this, we have only said the first half of what has to be said. The atoning work of Christ places me in a new existential relationship not only with my fellow believer but also with every human being, whether he is a believer or not; for that atoning act is directed to the whole human race, and not to anything less. Christ died for all men. Speaking of his own death, he is reported to have said: 'I, if I be lifted up, will draw all men unto myself.' No limit can be drawn to the potential reconciling power of his sacrifice, short of the limits of humanity itself. Those who have been, by the power of the Holy Spirit, brought within the circle of that reconciling power and reborn into the new system of relationships which it creates are by that very fact committed to participation in that reconciling ministry. They are bound to go out to all men with the words that the apostles used to the Corinthians: 'We are ambassadors therefore on behalf of Christ, as though God were entreating by us: we beseech you on behalf of Christ, be ye reconciled to God.' In other words, by their membership in the church they are committed to a mission to the world. They cannot abandon the latter without forfeiting the former.

It is precisely here that the Christian, looking at the world today, is liable to find himself in a dilemma. If he goes out into the non-Christian world to prosecute vigorously the Christian mission, he must appear in many places to be the agent not of unity but of separatism. That is especially true in India today. The evangelistic missionary is looked upon as, at best, an anachronism leftover from the age of colonialism and, at worst, a positive menace to national unity and progress. That attitude is, of course, far from universal among non-Christians, but it is dominant. In the face of it the missionary is assailed by three temptations: the first is to bury himself in the affairs of the church and to evade real meeting with the non-Christian culture. The second is to engage in a flurry of welfare activities of the kind most likely to be popular at the moment with the powers that be. The third is to align himself with the most sympathetic leaders of the other religions in a profession of loyalty to 'Truth,' the implication being that 'Truth' is something which transcends and includes both his message and theirs. Examples of all three are to be found in India today. The first, which is perhaps the most popular, requires no comment. It is a simple evasion of the church's fundamental task. The second may earn quick popularity, but it is mocking men with false hopes. It is only by deliberately blinding ourselves that we can persuade ourselves to believe that the world will be saved by the universal dissemination of the economic and cultural achievements of Europe and America. The third is a frank abandonment of the central message of Christianity, which is the offer of reconciliation with God and men through the death of Christ. It is not possible to undertake such an abandonment in the face of the non-Christian world and at the same time to retain any living reality of faith within Christendom. This is no longer a remote issue. The world is now a neighborhood, and the implications of the missionary character of Christianity are forced right upon our attention, whether we like it or not. If Christianity is true, then it is the center – not merely in theory but in a concrete visible community – for the reconciliation of mankind. If it is not that center, then it is untrue in its central affirmations and ought to be abandoned.

It ought by now to be clear to all that the ecumenical movement can have no enduring substance if it is not missionary through and through. The claim to transcend religious differences must, as has been said already, rest upon some claim of truth, unless it be a merely cynical indifference to truth or a merely loveless indifference to the eternal destiny of our fellow men. The Hindu claim rests upon a definite conception of religious truth which we have examined. The ecumenical movement within Christendom rests upon something different, upon the once-and-for-all atonement wrought by Jesus Christ. But that very fact involves it in a mission to the world. If, in seeking to be faithful to him who said, 'I will draw all men unto myself,' we appear to others to be separatists and sectarians, we can comfort ourselves by the reflection that every claim to draw men together must rest upon some truth, must derive from some center, and that whatever the truth be, and whatever the center, it must be one liable to human criticism and opposition. There is no standpoint available to man which is not some particular standpoint, and every claim to reconcile men must share the precariousness which arises from that fact.

But we must immediately add a second reflection which is a source not of comfort but of deep shame. And this brings us back to the question which we were discussing a moment ago. The Christian claim that Christ is the center round which all mankind must be made one has to encounter much more than the necessary amount of resistance in the minds of good men just because that claim is so flagrantly contradicted by the disunity of Christendom itself. The real scandal of this situation is only fully manifest when the church is in a missionary situation in the face of a dominant non-Christian religion. The claim of a small minority, in the midst of a vast and ancient religious civilization, to have the ultimate secret of man's reconciliation would in any circumstances be likely to arouse disbelief. But when that small minority is itself divided into a multitude of yet smaller sects, the claim becomes not merely incredible but laughable. It is not possible for the same group of men in one context − when facing the non-Christian world − to assert that the death of Christ is the one sufficient event by which all men may be made one family under God, and, at the same time, in another context − when dealing with one another − to assert that the event is not sufficient to enable those who believe in it to live as one family. The disunity of the church is a public denial of the sufficiency of the atonement. It is quite unthinkable that the church should be able effectively to preach that atonement and to become, in fact, the nucleus of the reconciled humanity, while that denial stands. So long as it stands, the world will see in the church not the one place where all men may at last come home, but a series of separatist bodies, each marked by a whole series of cultural peculiarities and idiosyncrasies of belief and practice. Even those who love the church best would surely stand appalled before the thought that the whole human race should find its unity in any of the sects as we now know them. Yet it is not possible to proclaim Christ as the center for the world's reconciliation as an experienced fact.

Thus the question of the visible embodiment of the unity of mankind in Christ becomes one of pressing urgency. If the heart of the Christian message is the good news of atonement for the human race wrought out in the death of Christ and issuing in a newly created community of reconciled men and women, and if the preaching of the gospel to the whole world is inseparable from the existence of that community, then the question: 'What is the proper form of this new community?' is plainly central to our whole task. I have repeatedly stressed the fact that it is a visible community, an actual human fellowship offering to all men the center for a reconciled humanity. But where on earth today can we find that fellowship? The Roman Catholic church is confident that the answer is to be found without remainder in its own communion. The Orthodox churches make a similar claim, though in a less exclusive form. The ecumenical movement is the recognition of Orthodox, Anglican, and Protestant churches that an answer must be given. If the world is to be made one in Christ, the world must be able to see the nucleus of that unity embodied in some sort of visible community. There is no more urgent task than to seek to meet that need. But we have to face the fact that there is no general agreement among Christians even as to the direction in which we ought to go in order to do so.

On that issue the World Council of Churches is (necessarily) officially neutral. It is itself a form of Christian unity, and one of the dangers of the present situation is that the very success and value of the Council's work should lead to an obscuring of the other elements which are necessary to a full embodiment of unity in Christ. Nevertheless, there is to be found within the Council itself a very wide range of views on the proper form of the church's visible unity. The Orthodox churches believe that they themselves contain the fulness of the church's being maintained in unbroken continuity from apostolic time and that it is only by reconciliation with them that other Christian bodies can participate completely in the fulness of churchliness. The Anglican churches have generally made it clear that they regard as essential to the church's being the acceptance of the historic episcopate and that the proper form of the church's unity would be a federation of regional churches, all episcopally ordered and having complete fellowship with one another on that basis. Among others there is wide diversity; some regard doctrinal agreement as the one essential and do not see any need for a uniform ministry; some look for the linking-together of existing denominations in a federal union, each retaining its own separate existence and traditions, but all being regarded as parts of one church and therefore enjoying complete intercommunion; some again – though probably the majority of these are outside the membership of the World Council – see no need for any all-embracing organization and would be content to have the maximum liberty for every group of Christians to organize itself as and how it wishes, without reference to others, but with the hope that all would be willing to treat one another with brotherly charity and respect.

It is not my business here to comment in any detail upon this babel of opinion. I shall make only a few general comments on the issues which are involved.

1   The question of visible organization cannot be evaded and is, in fact, central to our present task. The very essence of the Christian claim to be the way to unity for mankind is that it springs from an atonement wrought out in history and issues in an actual community. Therefore the question: 'What is the proper form of that community?' cannot be evaded.

2   Those who fear and resist the formation of vast organizational structures deserve to be heard with respect. There is at least a very good case to be made out for the view that large-scale centralized organization is harmful to the development of man's personality and incompatible with the nature of the atonement wrought in Christ.

3   It is not possible to believe that any of the existing ecclesiastical structures, or even all of them together in one organization, could provide the

home for the whole human race. The proper nature of the church is that it should be simply the new man, humanity recreated in the last Adam, Jesus Christ. It should be the place wherein mankind would see its own true image, its own self according to the original divine intention. One of the effects of division is that the divided parts have been led to emphasize and develop those elements of belief and practice which distinguish them from one another; the result is a series of societies, each marked by some peculiarity of tradition, and that very peculiarity makes it impossible that it should be the home for all mankind. It is possible to hope and pray that all mankind should be made one in Christ; it is not, I think, possible for the most devout Christian to pray that the whole of mankind should become Baptist, Presbyterian, Anglican, or Methodist. These separated bodies which we have come to call (in defiance of the usage of the New Testament) 'churches' have necessarily developed a kind of life, a kind of structure, a kind of organization, which makes it impossible to believe that any one of them or all of them tied together in a superorganization of the same kind could ever be the home for all mankind.

4   Nevertheless, these broken fragments, distorted by their divisions, are yet, in fact, the place where the atonement in Christ is being continuously and ever afresh made available for the life of mankind. They have at the heart of their being the one secret of healing for the world. What is required of them is a return in fellowship to that source, to the place where self-sufficient humanity is brought to death and rebirth, to the place where forgiveness and reconciliation are alone to be had. Their coming together must necessarily be a kind of corporate dying, in order to live anew in Christ. It is impossible to say in advance exactly what that dying will involve. What is certain is that while the separated churches cling to their own individuality and seek to evade that dying, they cannot be reborn into the one fellowship which mankind will recognize as the nucleus of its remaking into one.

5   If we ask: 'What is to be the character of the fellowship which issues from such a dying and rebirth; what – in other words – is the proper form of the church's unity?' I believe that at least these things can be said in answer: first, that it must be such that all who are in Christ in any place are, in that place, visibly one fellowship. Second, that it must be such that each local community is so ordered and so related to the whole that its fellowship with all Christ's people everywhere, and with those who have gone before and will come after, is made clear. That will mean at least this: a ministry universally recognized and visibly linked with the ministry of the church through the centuries. But within these wide limits there are vast areas where we must simply say that we have yet to learn what is required of a fellowship which is truly to embody Christ's atonement in and for the world. What degree of uniformity in belief and practice is necessary in order to safeguard the fundamental truth upon which the very existence of the fellowship depends? What are the nature and method of organization proper to such a fellowship? How are authority and freedom to be related within it? What is the nature of the discipline which it must exercise in order to safeguard its true character as a

fellowship founded upon Christ's atoning work for sinners? On each of these matters a vast amount might be said. It is quite certain that the church has repeatedly demanded more uniformity than was necessary for the safeguarding of its essential nature, and has thereby obscured its essential nature; quite certain that it has often adopted methods of organization and kinds of authority which were not proper to it, and thereby obscured the gospel; quite certain that it has often abandoned the task of discipline or exercised it in a way that destroyed instead of creating. Our experience in South India has been that it was only the fact of union which compelled us to recognize and face these questions. It was when we were brought into one fellowship with others of widely differing traditions and when we were led to abandon our own separate existence as churches and throw ourselves together into a common life that we were compelled to listen to one another's criticisms, to face these questions, and to go back together to the center of our faith in order to seek for the answers.

6   This leads me to my final comment. All our thinking and acting has to be controlled by our starting point, which is the atonement wrought by Christ for men. That atonement is the clue to unity for mankind, because it is the place at which men's sins are forgiven and they are enabled to forgive one another. It is the only place at which the fundamental problem of humanity is dealt with. It is only at that point that the churches can be made one. The essential nature of the unity which the church can offer to mankind is the unity that issues from mutual forgiveness in the presence of the Crucified. The church can offer that unity to mankind only when it is the substance of its own life. And it can be the substance of its own life only when its members are daily and weekly rediscovering for themselves that experience of mutual forgiveness. In a divided church that does not happen. The fundamental problems of human community are evaded when men are offered a variety of churches from which they can take their choice. In that situation men are not compelled to face the issue of mutual forgiveness. They can simply avoid one another, and the churches become a series of clubs for the like-minded. When, on the other hand, the churches begin to tackle the issue of unity at the local level, then they are brought back to the starting point, to the Cross; for it is only there that sinful men and women can find the secret of community – there where sin is forgiven. The search for unity drives us back to the Cross, which is the place alone where unity can be born.

But from that place we are bound to go out also beyond the bounds of Christendom to proclaim to the whole world that this is the place where it may be made one. Unity and mission, mission and unity, these must ever be the two foci of the ecumenical movement. The unity which the ecumenical movement seeks, transcending the differences between Christian denominations, is not – as some perhaps have thought it was – the first step towards a unity that would ultimately transcend all religious differences in some larger truth still to be discovered. The situation is precisely the opposite. The unity which the ecumenical movement acknowledges is a unity created by Christ in his atoning death, and that finished work of his means unity not only for the churches but for the world in him. The same impulse that drives us to dig below our differences to find one another as forgiven sinners in the face of our crucified and ascended Lord drives us also to the ends of the earth to proclaim to all men that he alone is the secret of their unity. And the great task before the ecumenical movement is just this: to help to make that claim credible to the world by the demonstration of a Christian fellowship which the world could recognize as the nucleus of its own recreation into one; it is, in fact, to be the instrument in the hands of Christ for the fulfilment of his own prayer that his people may be one, that the world may know.

The unity of mankind is no longer the dream of a few philosophers; it is the clamant necessity of today. But it will not be achieved by any amalgam of religions. It will not be set forward by any device which pretends to bypass the fundamental differences between the religions of mankind. There is no way of evading the necessity to take a stand. The greatest task before the church today is simply to take her stand humbly but decisively upon the accomplished work of Christ upon the Cross and to go forth into all the world with the proclamation that here, and here alone, at the place where all men are made nothing, is the place where all men may be made one.

Further reading

Newbigin 1958.
Newbigin 1981b: 240–6. (Reprint of Newbigin 1962b.)
Newbigin 1981a: 247–55.

6

Trinitarian mission

———◆————

Newbigin's approach to the theology of mission underwent a significant change of emphasis in the 1960s, particularly as a result of the WCC's New Delhi assembly in 1961. Before this, he had been influenced by the emphasis – advocated within WCC circles since the Tambaram Conference of 1938 – that the primary 'agent' in the work of world mission was the Church. During the New Delhi assembly, however, he came to realize that this approach was inadequate, and that only a 'fully trinitarian doctrine' of mission would do justice to what the Bible had to say, setting 'the work of Christ in the Church in the context of the overruling providence of the Father in all the life of the world and the sovereign freedom of the Spirit who is Lord and not the auxiliary of the Church'.[1]

The first fruits of this revision were to be seen in his 1963 booklet entitled The Relevance of Trinitarian Doctrine for Today's Mission,[2] *from which the first extract is taken. It was a pioneering work, written for his colleagues in the WCC as a kind of 'manifesto' for the newly formed WCC Division of World Mission and Evangelism.[3] But Visser't Hooft (the general secretary of the WCC) 'disapproved of its theology', and so it did not get the recognition within the WCC that it deserved. Wider recognition of Newbigin's approach was heralded by the publication in 1978 of* The Open Secret, *based on lectures he gave at Selly Oak Colleges in Birmingham following his return to the UK. Here, Newbigin had the chance to develop his earlier thinking, arguing that a trinitarian approach to mission holds together three facets of the work of God in a dynamic and creative tension: the 'proclamation' of the Kingdom (in the authority of the Father), the 'presence' of the Kingdom (in and through the Son), and the 'prevenience' of the Kingdom (through the ministry of the Spirit who 'goes before' the Church in its missionary work). 'This threefold way of understanding mission', he concluded, 'is rooted in the triune being of God himself. If any of these is taken in isolation as the clue to the understanding of mission, distortion follows.'[4]*

At a time today when trinitarian thinking is so much in vogue, it is noteworthy that Newbigin's work in this area was well ahead of its time. It was to underpin much of

---

[1] Newbigin 1993d: 187.
[2] Newbigin 1963.
[3] Newbigin 1993d: 187–8. The new Division was the result of the integration of the International Missionary Council within the structures of the WCC at the New Delhi assembly.
[4] Newbigin 1978b: 72.

his later writing, providing both a framework for thought and a testing ground for conclusions.

* * *

Extract 1
The Relevance of Trinitarian Doctrine for Today's Mission *(1963)*[5]

[. . . .] We have stated that the present situation of the missionary movement has brought us to the point where the question of the uniqueness and finality of Christ is presented with a new sharpness. We have now to say that this question will not be rightly answered, nor will the question of the relation between what God is doing in the mission of the Church and what he is doing in the secular events of history be rightly answered, except within the framework of a fully and explicitly trinitarian doctrine of God.

This statement may not, at first sight, appear to contain anything which is not familiar to all Christians. But the familiar may sometimes be rendered inoperative just by its familiarity. The point has several times been made that a true doctrine of missions must make a large place for the work of the Holy Spirit; but it is equally true that a true doctrine of missions will have much to say of God the Father. The opinion may be ventured that recent ecumenical thinking about the mission and unity of the Church has been defective at both these points. The church-centric view of missions has perhaps been too exclusively founded upon the person and work of Christ and has perhaps done less than justice to the whole trinitarian doctrine of God. Such phrases as 'the Lordship of Christ over the Church and the World', and such images as that of the building up of the body of Christ, have had almost exclusive occupancy of the central places in ecumenical thinking about the nature of the mission of the Church. We have already borne testimony to the immense importance and fruitfulness of this period of missionary thinking. But it may be that the time has come to ask whether it does not require some correction.

If one looks to the New Testament one certainly does not find a formally developed doctrine of the Trinity – any more than one finds other doctrines formally developed. But an attentive reader will note how constantly a trinitarian pattern underlies the language of St Paul, and how large a place is taken by the work of the Holy Spirit, and by the reference of all things finally to God the Father. And when the Church began to take the message of salvation through Jesus Christ out into the pagan world, it very soon found itself compelled to articulate a fully trinitarian doctrine of the God whom it proclaimed. It is indeed a significant fact that the great doctrinal struggles about

---

[5] Newbigin 1963: 31–4.

the nature of the Trinity, especially about the mutual relations of the Son and the Father, developed right in the midst of the struggle between the Church and the pagan world. These trinitarian struggles were indeed an essential part of the battle to master the pagan world view at the height of its power and self-confidence. The Church had to articulate the Christian message of God's Kingdom in a world which interpreted human life mainly in terms of the interaction of 'virtue' and 'fortune'. Put in terms more relevant to our day, human life was interpreted as the interaction of man's intelligence, skill and courage with the forces of his environment. It is significant that the Church found itself driven to articulate the Christian message in this situation in terms of trinitarian doctrine, and that, during the period in which the intellectual struggle took place to state the Gospel in terms of Graeco-Roman culture without thereby compromising its central affirmation, it was the doctrine of the Trinity which was the key to the whole theological debate. In other words, it was in terms of this doctrine that Christians were able to state both the unity and the distinctness of God's work in the forces of man's environment and God's work of regeneration within the soul of man. The vehemence of the doctrinal struggles which centred on the formulation of the trinitarian doctrine, and especially on the question of the relation of the Son to the Father is evidence of the centrality of this issue for the whole Christian witness to the pagan world of that time.

By contrast, during the era of 'Christendom' the doctrine of the Trinity has not occupied a comparable place in the thought of Christians. Not that there has been any widespread tendency among devout Christians to deny the doctrine, but simply that it has usually been regarded as a venerable formulation handed down from the past, or perhaps – if we are in an apologetic situation – a troublesome piece of theological baggage which is best kept out of sight when trying to commend the faith to unbelievers. It is significant that during the great theological struggle to the Reformation, the doctrine of the Trinity was never in dispute.

But it is also significant that, when one goes outside the 'Christendom' situation to bring the Gospel to non-Christians, one soon discovers that the doctrine of the Trinity is not something that can be kept out of sight; on the contrary, it is the necessary starting point of preaching. Even in the simplest form of missionary preaching, one finds that one cannot escape dealing with this doctrine. When an evangelist goes into an Indian village where the name of Jesus is unknown and preaches the Gospel for the first time, how is he to introduce the Name? How does one say who Jesus is, in a pagan situation? Presumably the hearers have already the word 'god' in their vocabulary. How is the name of Jesus to be related henceforth in their minds to that word? I have sometimes heard the Gospel preached in such a way that the hearers – accustomed to many gods – were led to think that the name of Jesus represented yet another god, this time more powerful and beneficent than those they already knew. Clearly that would not be the Christian faith as the New Testament understands it. I have always found, in talking to such village groups, that they had already in their minds the consciousness, however vague, of one God behind all the gods, One who was their creator and judge. If this consciousness is present, how does one relate the name of Jesus to it? Does one say that 'Jesus' is the name of that one God? Clearly, again, this would not be the New Testament faith. The truth is that one cannot preach Jesus even in the simplest terms without preaching him as the Son. His revelation of God is the revelation of 'an only begotten from the Father', and you cannot preach him without speaking of the Father and the Son.

Moreover, if the evangelist is wise, he will take time to listen before he talks. And if he does so, he will probably find that things have happened in the experience of his hearers which – without any human planning – have prepared the way for them to receive the Gospel. A time will come when they will look back upon these things as Christians and will recognize them as the prevenient work of the Spirit, the same Spirit who spoke to them in the preaching of the evangelist, the same Spirit who enabled them to receive the human words of the Evangelist as the Word of God. The true evangelist knows that the faith of these new Christians is not the effect of which his words were the cause; he knows that his words were but instruments of the work of the Spirit, a work which began before he arrived and continues after he left, of which their faith is the fruit.

Thus even in its most elementary form the preaching of the Gospel must presuppose an understanding of the triune nature of God. It is not, as we have sometimes seemed to say, a kind of intellectual capstone which can be put on to the top of the arch at the very end; it is, on the contrary, what Athanasius called it, the *arche*, the presupposition without which the preaching of the Gospel in a pagan world cannot begin.

This is not to suggest that an explicit trinitarian theology will be the substance either of the preacher's talk or of the new converts' understanding. We have already said that even in the New Testament itself such an explicit trinitarian theology is not found. But it is to say that a true understanding of the questions which God raises for us in our time, and a true restatement of the meaning of the missionary task will rest, as the New Testament rests, upon the revelation of God as Father, Son and Spirit. [. . . .] At this stage it may perhaps be accepted as at least a reasonable suggestion that a fresh articulation of the meaning of the missionary task in terms of the pluralistic, polytheistic, pagan society of our time may require us likewise to acknowledge the necessity of a trinitarian starting point.

Extract 2
The Open Secret (1978)[6]

To the question of authority [for mission] the first answer is, as we have seen, 'In the name of Jesus.' It is by this name that Paul introduces himself in his

---

[6] Newbigin 1978b: 20–31 [. . . .]. (Reprinted as Newbigin 1995b: 19–29.)

letters: he is a messenger sent by Jesus, called and sent by one greater than himself. There is no authority beyond that to which he can appeal.

But that answer necessarily prompts the next question: 'Who is Jesus?' How is that question to be answered? The first and most natural answer finds its model in the first answer to Jesus' question: 'Who do men say that I am?' He is 'one of the prophets.' This, as Jesus suggests, is the natural answer of 'flesh and blood' (Matt. 16.17). For the Hindu he is one of *jeevanmuktas* who have attained in this life the full realization of the divine. For the Muslim he is one of the messengers of Allah. For the man of modern Western society he is one of the world religious leaders to whom one will find reference (along with Buddha, Muhammad, Moses, and Guru Nanak) in the 'Religion' section of *Time* magazine but not in the section on 'World Affairs.' He is one of an acknowledged class. His introduction does not disturb the structure of ideas of which this classification is a facet.

This, as I have said, is the 'natural' answer. As a first step it is unavoidable. As a missionary in India I often shared in evangelistic preaching in villages where the name of 'Jesus' had no more meaning than any other strange name. I have heard speakers use many different Tamil words to explain who he is. He is *Swamy* ('Lord'). Or he is *Satguru* ('the true teacher'). He is *Avatar* ('incarnation of God'). Or he is *Kadavul* ('the transcendent God') who has become man. What all these words have in common is that they necessarily place Jesus within a world of ideas which is formed by the Hindu tradition and which is embodied in the language of the people. *Swamy* is usually translated 'Lord,' but it does not have the meaning that the word *Kurios* had for a Greek-speaking Jew. It denotes not Yahweh, the Lord of the Old Testament, but one of the myriad gods who fill the pages of the Hindu epics. *Avatar* is usually translated 'incarnation,' but there have been many *avatars* and there will be many more. To announce a new *avatar* is not to announce any radical change in the nature of things. Even to use the word *kadavul* will only provoke the question: 'If Jesus is *kadavul*, who is the one to whom he prays?'

The example which I have taken from personal experience is simply a reminder of the fact that one cannot begin to answer the question 'Who is Jesus?' without using a language – and therefore a structure of thought – which is shaped by the pre-Christian experience of the one who asks the question. There is no way of avoiding this necessity. And yet the introduction of the name of Jesus placed the structure under a strain which it cannot bear without breaking. Jesus is now not just Lord, but unique Lord, not just *avatar*, but unique *avatar*. The word *kadavul* can no longer refer to a monad: it must refer to a reality, within which there is a relationship of hearing and answering. The event by which the old structure is broken is not a natural happening. Jesus tells Peter that the confession 'You are the Christ, the Son of the Living God' is not the work of 'flesh and blood' but a gift of the Father (Matt. 16.17). It is not a human achievement but a gift from above. It is the primary work of the Spirit of God himself (1 Cor. 12.1–3; 1 John 4.1–3). It is the action of God by which he chooses and anoints the messengers of his reign.

It is the work of the sovereign Spirit to enable men and women in new situations and in new cultural forms to find the ways in which the confession of Jesus as Lord may be made in the language of their own culture. The mission of the church is in fact the church's obedient participation in that action of the Spirit by which the confession of Jesus as Lord becomes the authentic confession of ever new peoples, each in its own tongue.

But how do we begin to say who Jesus is? As the first generation of Christians moved out of the culture of Judaism into the cosmopolitan culture of the Graeco-Roman world it had to develop a way of doing this. The way it developed is embodied in the new style of literature of which Mark's Gospel is our earliest exemplar. Here a story is told in such a way as to provide, not a biography in the modern style, but an answer to the question: 'Who is Jesus?'

> The beginning of the gospel of Jesus Christ, the Son of God. As it is written in Isaiah the Prophet,
>
>> 'Behold, I send my messenger before thy face, who shall prepare thy way; the voice of one crying in the wilderness: Prepare the way of the Lord, make his paths straight –'
>
> John the baptizer appeared in the wilderness, preaching a baptism of repentance for the forgiveness of sins. And there went out to him all the country of Judea, and all the people of Jerusalem; and they were baptized by him in the river Jordan, confessing their sins. Now John was clothed with camel's hair, and had a leather girdle around his waist, and ate locusts and wild honey. And he preached, saying, 'After me comes he who is mightier than I, the thong of whose sandals I am not worthy to stoop down and untie. I have baptized you with water; but he will baptize you with the Holy Spirit.' In those days Jesus came from Nazareth of Galilee and was baptized by John in the Jordan. And when he came up out of the water, immediately he saw the heavens opened and the Spirit descending upon him like a dove; and a voice came from heaven, 'Thou art my beloved Son; with thee I am well pleased.' The Spirit immediately drove him out into the wilderness. And he was in the wilderness forty days, tempted by Satan; and he was with the wild beasts; and the angels ministered to him. Now after John was arrested, Jesus came into Galilee, preaching the gospel of God, and saying, 'The time is fulfilled, and the kingdom of God is at hand; repent, and believe in the gospel.' (Mark 1.1–15)

In this brief introductory paragraph Jesus is introduced as the one who announces the coming of the reign of God, the one who is acknowledged as the Son of God and is anointed by the Spirit of God.

1   He announces the reign of God. God was known already in Israel as one who reigns. He had made known his sovereignty in delivering Israel out of the slavery of Egypt. He was indeed sovereign over all the earth, though the nations did not know it. In age after age Israel had been summoned to 'say among the nations' that 'the Lord reigns' (Ps. 96.10). Through centuries of crushing defeat and humiliation a remnant in Israel had kept alive the faith that the sovereign Lord would in the end reveal his hidden kingship, tear aside

the illusions behind which evil carries on its work, dethrone the idols, and come to reign in justice over the nations.

Jesus announces that that day has dawned. But the announcement is also a call to a radical reversal of normal attitudes. Israel has been eagerly awaiting the coming of the Lord's rule but looking for it in the wrong direction. The announcement is therefore at the same time a call to turn around and look the other way – to repent. Only as part of such a radical turnabout can Israel receive the gift of faith – faith to believe that the reign of God is indeed present, faith to know the secret of the kingdom of God (Acts 4.11). This secret is the 'good news' which the church publishes, the 'gospel.' Jesus is thus not the initiator or founder of the kingdom. It is God's kingdom. Jesus is the one who is sent as herald and bearer of the kingdom.

2   Jesus is acknowledged as the Son of God. The most characteristic word on the lips of Jesus seems to have been the Aramaic word *Abba*, a word used as the most informal and intimate mode of speech from a son to his father. It was not, apparently, a word that was ever used in prayer to God. But it seems to have been so much the characteristic way in which Jesus prayed that it was carried over into the language of the Greek-speaking church. Paul can speak of it as the sign of our sonship given to us by the Spirit (Rom. 8.12–17). Jesus' characteristic use of this word points to the deepest secret of his being. He was 'the Son.' In the fourth Gospel this is very specially emphasized and we are told that the glory which his disciples saw in him was 'glory as of the only Son from the Father' (John 1.14). Though Jesus is the bearer of the kingdom, he is yet at the same time the obedient Son. The sovereignty which he brings and which puts to flight the demonic powers (Mark 1.27) is not exercised in his own name but in the name of the Father. It is exercised by one who looks up in loving obedience as a son to a father.

3   Jesus is anointed by the Spirit. In the Old Testament the Spirit is the living active power of God, giving life to all and empowering men to perform special service or to receive special revelation. It is the 'breath of the Lord,' and the life and power of the Lord are in it. In many passages of the Old Testament the promise is made that the Spirit of the Lord will rest upon the one whom he sends to be the agent of his justice. The voice which Jesus heard at his baptism echoes the words of Isaiah 42.1: 'Behold my servant, whom I uphold, my chosen, in whom my soul delights; I have put my spirit upon him, he will bring forth justice to the nations.' And according to Luke's Gospel Jesus interprets the words of Isaiah 61.1–2 as foreshadowing his ministry. 'The Spirit of the Lord God is upon me, because the Lord has anointed me to bring good tidings to the afflicted, he has sent me to bind up the brokenhearted, to proclaim liberty to the captives, and the opening of the prison to those who are bound; to proclaim the year of the Lord's favor' (Luke 4.18–19).

The acknowledgment of Jesus as Son and his anointing by the Spirit took place, according to the record, at his baptism by John in the Jordan, the event which is described as 'the beginning of the gospel.' John's baptism seems to have been a symbolic action in the tradition of the prophets of Israel. Jeremiah had smashed an earthenware pot as a vivid and unforgettable sign of God's impending judgment on Jerusalem, and Isaiah had gone naked and barefoot as a sign of the coming calamities in Egypt and Ethiopia. Other examples can be cited. The message of John was one of impending judgment; God was coming to purge his people with fire, to cut down the barren trees (Matt. 3.10; cf. Isa. 5), and to sift the wheat from the chaff (Matt. 3.12). John called people to repentance in order that they might escape the coming judgment. The baptism in the Jordan was a symbolic action which affirmed the call to a radical new beginning for Israel, and the acceptance of baptism was a symbol that the call had been heard and accepted. But it was only a symbol. The real thing, when it came, would not be water but a devouring fire, the very breath of the Lord (Mark 1.8; cf. Luke 3.16–17).

Jesus was one of those who heard and accepted the call. His first appearance in the story was as one of a crowd of unnamed men and women who had been convicted of sin and had heard and accepted the call to repentance. As one of them Jesus was baptized. He took his place as part of sinful humanity. And in that action he received the anointing of the Spirit. At the same moment the word of God spoken through Isaiah sounded in his ears. He is the beloved Son, anointed by the Spirit to bring forth justice to the nations.

The baptism in the Jordan was only a beginning. It had to be completed by a crowded ministry in which Jesus acted out his identification with sin-burdened humanity (Matt. 8.17). It had to be consummated on Calvary, where his baptism was complete (Luke 12.50; Mark 10.38). And that consummation of his baptism opened the way for the whole company of his chosen apostles to receive the same anointing of the Spirit, to be acknowledged as children of God, and to be sent out to bring God's justice to the nations.

Here, then, is the first answer to the question: 'Who is Jesus?' He is the Son, sent by the Father and anointed by the Spirit to be the bearer of God's kingdom to the nations. This is the Jesus who was proclaimed by the first Christians to the world of their time.

Any missionary, in fact anyone engaged in the business of communication, knows very well that what is spoken and what is heard are by no means always the same. What is heard is necessarily shaped by the thought-world of the hearer. What was it that was heard when the story about Jesus was spoken into the thought-world of the Roman Empire of the first two centuries?

To attempt to describe that thought-world in a few paragraphs would be absurd. But what can be said, simply and truthfully, is that it was a world controlled by presuppositions radically different from those which governed the thought-world of the Judaism of which Jesus was a part. Fundamental among these presuppositions was that the really real, the ultimate source of all being, must be beyond and above the ordinary world which we see and hear, taste and handle. It must be beyond time, for time implies change and change implies imperfection. It must be beyond space, for space is the arena of our sense experience, which can never give us absolute truth. No particular event in history, therefore, can be more than an illustration or symbol of the time-less, changeless, passionless, purely spiritual entity which is ultimate being.

This meant that all thinking was controlled by certain inescapable dichotomies. In science there was the dichotomy between the intelligible world and the sensible world, between that which can be known of pure being by the rational and spiritual powers of the mind and that which can be experienced through the five senses, which can never give access to being itself. In history there was the dichotomy between virtue and fortune. The world of external happenings is not under the undisputed control of pure rea-son. It is the sphere either of the purely irrational, or of fate. Man's history is the story of the conflict between this and whatever equipment of intelligence, skill, and courage he can bring to the conflict.

Within such a world view there is room for, and in fact necessity for, a whole range of intermediate entities to bridge the gap between the pure being which is essentially unknowable and unapproachable and the ordinary world of things and events. As in the similar thought world of India, it was natural to place Jesus somewhere in this intermediate range. Jesus, an actual man with a place in history, could not be identified with the One who is beyond all change and all multiplicity. That would be simple nonsense. But the very name 'Son' implies subordination, and therefore Jesus could be under-stood either as some kind of emanation from the One, or even as among the first of creatures. Or else he could be understood as a man who had been brought into an exceptionally or even uniquely close relationship with the One – in Indian terms, a *jeevanmukta*. The story of the first three centuries of the Christian era furnishes a rich variety of variations on these themes. What they have in common is that they leave intact the classical thought world. They leave unhealed its dichotomies. Above all they leave it with a God finally uninvolved in human history.

Against this the mind of the church fought a long, stubborn, often confused but finally successful battle. It did so because at the very heart of its life, its thought, and its worship was the figure of the one who had died on the cross and had been raised from the dead – 'the Son of God,' as Paul says, 'who loved me and gave himself up for me.' There is a famous graffito in Rome which depicts a man lifting up his hands in worship before a figure with an ass's head stretched out on a cross. Underneath is written 'Anexamenos worships his god.' Presumably some pagan slave was mocking his Christian fellow slave. The picture vividly suggests both the stubborn strength of the Christians' insistence on the deity of Christ, and the horror and contempt which this aroused in that classical world. The absolutely crucial point was this: in the man Jesus God had actually suffered for the sin of the world. For that assurance Christians were ready to go to the lions. If it was true, the whole classical world view was false and had to be replaced by something radically different.

In his book *Christianity and Classical Culture*[7] C. N. Cochrane tells the story of the development of classical thought from its brilliant restoration under Augustus to its disintegration in the fifth century. By that time a new way of understanding the whole human situation had been developed, and it was the work of Augustine to build on this foundation the beginnings of the new world view that would shape the thought of Western Christendom for a thousand years. This new way of understanding was embodied in the doctrine of the Trinity. As we have seen, this doctrine is already implicit in our earliest written answer to the question: 'Who is Jesus?' – implicit but not yet fully thought out. It was the work of the great theologians of the first three centuries, especially of Athanasius, to develop this implicit understanding into a model which would replace the classical axioms with a new set of axioms. The ultimate reality, according to this new view, is not to be understood as a timeless, passionless monad beyond all human knowing, but as a trinity of Father, Son, and Spirit. This understanding is not the result of speculative thought. It has been given by revelation in the actual historical life and work of the Son.

Accepted thus by faith it becomes the starting point for a new way of understanding the world. It cannot be understood and much less can it be verified by reference to the assumed axioms of classical thought. It is verified only by the action of the Holy Spirit present in the witness of the martyrs. But accepted by faith it becomes the basis of a new way of making sense of the world, not just by speculative science, but by practical wisdom.

Thus, on this new basis the dichotomy between the sensible and the intelligible worlds is healed, for God himself has actually been made flesh. The Son who offered the perfect sacrifice of loving obedience to the Father on the cross is not the Father, but he is truly God as the Father is God. The being of God himself is involved in the suffering of history. And through the Spirit the Christian can share this suffering, knowing that in doing so he is in touch with the very being of God himself (Rom. 8.18–27).

Likewise the dichotomy between virtue and fortune is healed, for the Christian who thus shares in the travail of history also knows that God works everything for good to those who love him (Rom. 8.28). His life here in the midst of history is thus not a hopeless battle against fate, but the faithful following of Jesus along the way of the cross in loving obedience to the Father whose rule is over all. A wholly new way is opened up to accomplish what classical science and philosophy could not accomplish – a way of grasping and dealing with the reality of human life as part of a meaningful history within a world created and sustained by the God who had revealed himself in Jesus and who continued by his Spirit to guide the followers of Jesus into the fullness of the truth.

The language in which this trinitarian faith was wrought out was necessarily the language of that time and place. The crucial word upon which the

---

[7] (Cochrane 1940.)

central conflict turned was the word *homoousios*, a word which expressed in the language of contemporary philosophy the conviction that the being of the Son and the being of the Spirit are the very being of the Godhead and are not something intermediate between a remote and ultimately unapproachable Supreme Being and the known world of nature and history. On the firm maintenance of that conviction everything depended. In that sense the church can never go back on what was then decided. But it is also true that it is not enough for the church to go on repeating in different cultural situations the same words and phrases. New ways have to be found of stating the essential trinitarian faith, and for this the church in each new cultural situation has to go back to the original biblical sources of this faith in order to lay hold on it afresh and to state it afresh in contemporary terms.

It has been said that the question of the Trinity is the one theological question that has been really settled. It would, I think, be nearer to the truth to say that the Nicene formula has been so devoutly hallowed that it is effectively put out of circulation. It has been treated like the talent which was buried for safekeeping rather than risked in the commerce of discussion. The church continues to repeat the trinitarian formula but – unless I am greatly mistaken – the ordinary Christian in the Western world who hears or reads the word 'God' does not immediately and inevitably think of the Triune Being – Father, Son, and Spirit. He thinks of a supreme monad. Not many preachers, I suspect, look forward eagerly to Trinity Sunday. The working concept of God for most ordinary Christians is – if one may venture a bold guess – shaped more by the combination of Greek philosophy and Islamic theology which was powerfully injected into the thought of Christendom at the beginning of the High Middle Ages than by the thought of the fathers of the first four centuries.

If, as I have argued, we are forced to answer the question of authority by the words 'In the name of Jesus'; and if we then have to answer the question: 'Who is Jesus?', we shall only be able to answer that question in terms which embody the trinitarian faith. Like the earliest Christians we shall have to expand our first answer so that it runs, 'In the name of the Father, the Son, and the Holy Spirit.' And this means that, like them, we shall be offering a model for understanding human life – a model which cannot be verified by reference to the axioms of our culture but which is offered on the authority of revelation and with the claim that it does provide the possibility of a practical wisdom to grasp and deal with human life as it really is.

I have been encouraged to think that this is a fruitful approach to the subject of this book by reading the parallel which Michael Polanyi has drawn between our time and the time for which Augustine wrote. At the crucial turning point of his great book, *Personal Knowledge*, Polanyi writes:

> The critical movement, which seems to be nearing the end of its course today, was perhaps the most fruitful effort ever sustained by the human mind. The past four or five centuries, which have gradually destroyed or overshadowed the

whole medieval cosmos, have enriched us mentally and morally to an extent unrivalled by any period of similar duration. But its incandescence had fed on the combustion of the Christian heritage in the oxygen of Greek rationalism, and when this fuel was exhausted the critical framework itself burnt away. Modern man is unprecedented; yet we must now go back to St Augustine to restore the balance of our cognitive powers. In the fourth century AD, St Augustine brought the history of Greek philosophy to a close by inaugurating for the first time a post-critical philosophy. He taught that all knowledge was a gift of grace, for which we must strive under the guidance of antecedent belief: *nisi credideritis, non intelligitis.*[8]

Polanyi's plea is for a 'post-critical philosophy' without which he believes science must destroy itself. In developing his reference to Augustine, Polanyi insists that 'the process of examining any topic is both an exploration of the topic, and an exegesis of our fundamental beliefs in the light of which we approach it; a dialectical combination of exploration and exegesis. Our fundamental beliefs are continuously reconsidered in the course of such a process, but only within the scope of their own basic premisses.'[9]

The Christian mission, as I understand it, has an analogous logical structure. It is an acting out of a fundamental belief and, at the same time, a process in which this belief is being constantly reconsidered in the light of the experience of acting it out in every sector of human affairs and in dialogue with every other pattern of thought by which men and women seek to make sense of their lives.

Further reading

Newbigin 1978b: 32–72. (Reprinted as Newbigin 1995b: 30–65.)
Newbigin 1977b: 209–18.
Newbigin 1994c: 2–5.

---

[8] Polanyi 1958: 265.
[9] Polanyi 1958: 267.

Part 2

MISSIONARY THEOLOGY
IN PRACTICE

7

Christic and the cultures

—◆◆◆—

*Many of Newbigin's writings are in effect an exercise in cross-cultural analysis, explor-
ing the relationship between the 'Christ' of missionary proclamation and the 'culture'
to which the message of Christianity is being brought. But Newbigin's approach brings
something new to the more traditional discussions of this theme. He builds on the classic works of writers like Richard Niebuhr[1] and Paul Tillich,[2] but takes the 'pluriform'
nature of culture seriously — that of the missionaries as well as that of the culture to
which they go.*

*As a result, one writer comments that Newbigin's work displays a truly 'integrative
force, bringing into intimate relationship discussions which have tended to remain too
much in isolation from each other'.[3] The background to this 'inter-cultural' perspective
arose inevitably out of Newbigin's long missionary experience in India. As he initially
attempted to share the gospel with Hindus, his own inherited European assumptions
were gradually thrown into sharp relief. As he was later to put it: 'I often confused the
gospel with my assumptions as a "modern" European.'[4] A similar process took place
when Newbigin returned to the UK in the 1970s. 'Having spent most of my working
life in India and then come back,' he said in an interview in 1988, 'I have discovered
— in a way, to my own astonishment — that one faces the same problem here, and that
one is again in a culture where, when you attempt to communicate the gospel, you are
going completely against the stream.'[5]*

*The two extracts that follow illustrate Newbigin's exploration of these themes.
The first comes from* The Open Secret *(1978) and represents his mature reflections
on cross-cultural communication following his return from missionary service. The
book is a revision of lectures he gave at the Selly Oak Colleges in Birmingham in
the mid-1970s. The second extract is taken from his later book,* Foolishness to the
Greeks *(1986), in which he turns his attention specifically to the task the Church faces
in the West as it seeks to engage its own culture with the gospel. Newbigin's approach
here was striking in its freshness, not least because it took the ambivalent nature of
the Church seriously — on the one hand called to be a witness to the in-breaking of the
Kingdom, while on the other in danger of accommodating itself to the assumptions*

---

[1] Niebuhr 1952.
[2] Tillich 1959.
[3] Hunsberger 1998: 277.
[4] Newbigin 1985b: 8.
[5] Newbigin 1988b: 30.

of the culture of which it is a part. In the interplay between these various 'parties', Newbigin's analysis remains fresh and vital, as relevant to the Churches today as when it was first written.

* * *

Extract 1
The Open Secret (1978)[6]

[O]ne can speak of the path which the church must take as lying between two opposite dangers. The first danger is that the church may so conform its life and teaching to the culture that it no longer functions as the bearer of God's judgement and promise. It becomes simply the guardian and guarantor of the culture and fails to challenge it. The other danger is that the language and the life-style of the church should be such that they make no contact with the culture and become the language and life-style of a ghetto. Between these two extremes there is a wide spectrum of possibilities, parts of which have been explored in Richard Niebuhr's *Christ and Culture*. This classic work deals with the relation of church and culture within a single culture and does not raise the difficult and complicated questions which arise in the communication of the gospel from one culture to another. How, in seeking to preach the gospel to people of another culture, does the church find the proper path between a kind of accommodation which robs the gospel of its power to challenge traditional ways of life, and a kind of intransigence which either fails to communicate altogether or else alienates the converts from their culture? To this difficult question we must now turn.

1 (a) Any attempt to preach the gospel involves using the language spoken by the hearers. That language has been shaped by and has shaped their experience of life. It is the form in which they seek to grasp and make sense of the whole range of human experience. It embodies their beliefs about life and death, about sin and virtue, about guilt and forgiveness, about salvation and damnation, about soul and body, about time and eternity, about God and man. None of the language is 'neutral'; it embodies beliefs to which its users are committed. These beliefs are not the same as those of the evangelist. Nevertheless the evangelist has no alternative except to use this language, doing the best he can to find words which will come as near as possible to creating in his hearers the belief he wants to share with them. When he has done his best to find idioms of speech, of life-style, of rite and liturgy which will most effectively embody the truth of the gospel, he will still have to re-cognize that these idioms, shaped as they are by a different set of beliefs, will distort the truth which they are employed to embody. There is no way of avoiding this fact.

---

[6] Newbigin 1978b: [. . . .] 163–80. (Reprinted with minor changes as Newbigin 1995b: 145–59.)

(b)   But in putting the matter in this way I have oversimplified it. I have left out of account the fact that the idioms of speech and conduct by which the evangelist grasps and expresses the gospel are themselves shaped by his culture. If he has had no experience of the sharp clash of cultures he may be unaware that this is so. He may suppose that the way he understands the gospel is the way it 'really is.' No doubt – especially if he is well instructed in the Reformed faith! – he will agree that his understanding of the gospel is always subject to correction by reference to the Bible. He will be confident that the Bible provides the sure standard of teaching and that it will confirm the truth of the gospel as he has tried to communicate it. And so the evangelist takes early steps to ensure that the Bible is translated and placed in the hands of the receptor community and that they are taught to read it.

(c)   But the introduction of the Bible changes the situation. It is not long before the Bible begins to make its own impact on its readers in the receptor community. In its stories, its prayers, its ethical teachings, and above all in the figure of Jesus as he presents himself to fresh eyes through the medium of print, the readers are confronted with something which raises questions both about their traditional culture and about what has been offered to them by the evangelist as 'Christianity.' A three-cornered relationship is set up between the traditional culture, the 'Christianity' of the missionary, and the Bible. The stage is set for a complex and unpredictable evolution both in the culture of the receptor community and in that of the missionary. As an illustration of the former one could point to the massive development of the so-called African Independent churches. These have developed by a process of ferment, renewal, and schism within the churches established by Western missions, and the studies of David Barrett[7] have demonstrated an extremely close correlation between the formation of the Independent churches and the availability of the Scriptures in the languages of the communities concerned. That is to say that the Bible has operated as an independent source of criticism directed both against the Christianity of the missionaries and against the traditional culture of the tribe. The Independent churches are marked not only by the rejection of certain aspects of Western Christianity but also by an equally sharp rejection of elements in the traditional African culture. Werner Hoerschelmann has documented comparable movements in South India.[8]

It must be admitted that the Western churches which have sent missions to Asia and Africa have remained very largely unaffected by the development which I have described because their missionaries have operated at a distance from the sending churches and on the extreme periphery of their consciousness. But like others who have spent long periods in foreign missionary service, I have to bear witness that the experience of living for most of four decades as part of an Indian church has made me acutely aware of the cultural

---

[7] Barrett 1968.
[8] Hoerschelmann 1977.

conditioning of the Christianity in which I was nurtured, and of the culture-bound character of many of the assumptions which are unquestioned by English Christians. I shall have to revert to this point later.

(d)   I said that this triangle of forces made up by the culture, the invading culture, and the Bible sets the stage for a complicated and unpredictable evolution. This is no uniform pattern. Sometimes the impact of the experience of salvation in Jesus Christ is such that questions concerning the traditional culture drop into insignificance. They are regarded as *adiaphora*. Only after some time do the converts begin to draw from their new experience critical questions about their traditional culture. More often the first response is a strong reaction against the traditional culture. It is 'the world' which is still in the power of evil. The new life in Christ is so absolutely new that the old must be put away. At this stage it is the Christianity of the invading culture that is accepted and welcomed. The message is so closely linked with the messenger who brought it that there is no desire to separate them. There is a sharp rejection of elements in the old culture which, even if not evil in themselves (such as music, drama, and visual art), are felt to be evil because of their association with the rejected world view.

After the passage of some years, often in the second or third generation of the church, a new situation arises. The church has now become so much at home in a new thought-world that the old no longer poses a threat. The old culture has been for these Christians desacralized. Its music, art, dance, and social customs are no longer feared because of their pagan associations; in fact they begin to be prized as part of the world which God loves and which he has given to men. The church begins for the first time to think about the relation of Christ to culture. It begins to experiment with the variety of possible models for this relation. In some cases, as for example in many of the South Pacific Islands, a new *Corpus Christianum* comes into existence. There is a practical identification of church and society, and Christ is seen as the one who harmonizes and reconciles the old culture. In other situations, especially where the church is a small minority, there is a strong effort to reverse the alienation from local culture which marked the first conversions and to approach the older culture in a spirit of acceptance and openness. The tendency then will be to search for christological models which can be accommodated within the thought-world of the older culture. And again there will be movements of renewal which often take the form of a sharp attack upon elements both in the church and in the old culture. There is an almost infinite variety of different situations, and none of them is static.

(e)   It is already clear that we have moved a long way from the simple picture of a culturally uncontaminated gospel being planted in a series of culturally isolated, stable, and homogeneous communities. In fact the Christianity which the missionary brings is already conditioned by his own culture, and the community to which he brings it is a changing entity exposed to contact without and tension within. I have suggested that within the receptor community there is a complex evolution determined by three factors: the traditional culture, the Christianity of the missionary, and the witness of the Bible. But it is clear that this also is far from being the full picture. In the modern world all human communities, with very few exceptions, are exposed to cultural influences of many kinds from one another. We do inhabit one single planet, and we are more and more closely crowded together. The three-cornered relation of which I have spoken is not isolated from this contact. Each of these patterns of development is part of the vast and infinitely complex pattern of intercultural influence on a global scale. And the Christian communities within each culture, being bound together in the growing fellowship of the ecumenical movement, have to be open both to the cultures in which they participate as members of nations, citizens of cities, workers, thinkers, etc., and also open to the Christian testimony of those who inhabit other cultural worlds but share a common allegiance to Jesus Christ. This openness to Christians of other cultures and the experience of ecumenical fellowship which it makes possible, will provide a continuing critique of the ways in which the church within any culture is related to that culture. All will acknowledge in principle that the gospel cannot be completely domesticated within any culture. The Christ who is presented in Scripture for our believing is Lord over all cultures, and his purpose is to unite all of every culture to himself in a unity which transcends without negating the diversities of culture. But, as we well know, the Scriptures alone do not suffice to prevent us from the attempt to domesticate him within our cultures. The bewildering variety of ways in which Jesus has been portrayed by Christian artists who have the same Bible in their hands but belong to different cultures is sufficient evidence of the cultural conditioning of our reading of Scripture. We need the witness of Christians of other cultures to correct our culturally conditioned understanding of Scripture.

Starting from the simple case of a missionary preaching the gospel for the first time in a community which has not previously heard it, I have moved on to a picture of the church as a global fellowship in which the same three-cornered pattern of relationships is continuously developing. At the level of the local church one can picture an ideal situation in which there is at the same time full openness to the local culture, to the Scriptures, and to the witness of other Christians in the ecumenical family. The day-to-day worship and work and witness of the local church has to be developed in relationship to all of these in such a way that it becomes credible to the inhabitants of the local culture as sign, instrument, and foretaste of that one universal reign of God which is the true origin and goal of this and every human culture. It must communicate in the idiom of that culture both the divine good which sustains it and the divine purpose which judges it and summons it to become what it is not yet. At the world level the corresponding picture would be of a fellowship of Christian churches open to and rooted in all the cultures of mankind within which they are severally placed, and so renewing its life through ever-fresh obedience to Christ as presented in the Scriptures that it becomes an increasingly credible sign, instrument, and foretaste of God's reign over all nations and all things.

The contemporary ecumenical movement is a frail, limited, and stumbling move towards such a vision of the universal fellowship of churches. I shall say something of its limitations in a moment. But first it is proper to acknowledge with thankfulness that within these limitations it is a real movement towards this goal. Like multitudes of others who have shared in ecumenical meetings I have experienced the strain and even contradiction between different under-standings of the gospel which have arisen out of different cultural situations. I have been tempted to ask whether the contradiction was not total, whether we were really speaking of the same reality when we used our different lan-guages about Jesus and the gospel. But I have also known again and again, as others have, the experience of finding – as we prayed together, studied the Scriptures together, and listened to one another's experiences of Christ – that there was and is one Lord Jesus Christ to whom we are in our different ways bearing witness, and that he has indeed bound us together in himself in bonds which are stronger than those which bind us to our several cultures. It is out of such experiences that we return to our local churches with fresh awareness of the sharpness of the Word of God as it is addressed to our own cultures.

But with these thankful and positive statements I must also speak of the limitation of the contemporary ecumenical movement. And here I am not speaking of the limitations which beset any movement because of the weak-ness and sinfulness of those who participate. I am referring to a very specific defect which has far-reaching implications for the present discussion of church and culture. The contemporary ecumenical movement was born among the churches which share in common the culture that has developed in Western Europe and North America in the past centuries and which has undergone enormously rapid transformation since the Age of Reason in the eighteenth century. All its work is conducted in the languages of Western Europe. Only those who have had long training in the methods of thinking, of study and research, and of argument which have been developed in Western Europe can share in its work. These ways of thinking have become so dom-inant throughout the world during the past two centuries that it is very difficult for those who have never known anything else to realize that they are only one of the possible ways in which men and women have found it possi-ble to make sense of their experience. I may perhaps be able to make the point clear by the following illustration. Anyone who has lived within the Tamil churches knows that there are rich resources of living Christian faith and experience embodied in the continuing stream of Tamil Christian lyrical poetry, a stream which has flowed for a century and a half and is still flowing strongly. The people who write and read and sing these lyrics do not take any part in the work of the ecumenical movement. Their lyrics cannot be trans-lated into a European language without losing their power and beauty. The world of thought, the concepts through which they capture and express the deepest Christian experiences are not those which appear in the documents of ecumenical meetings. Only those Tamil Christians who have undergone a long and rigorous training in Western methods of study, argument, and experiment can participate in these meetings. It is almost impossible for them to communicate in these meetings what is most vital and powerful in the life of the churches from which they come. I am sure that similar testimony could be given about the Christian culture of many parts of Asia, Africa, and the Pacific.

For those who have never lived in any other cultural world than that of the contemporary West it is very hard to see that theirs is only one of the tribal cultures of mankind. They are inclined to see it simply as the 'modern scientific world view.' It is the only way in which systematic and rigorous thinking can be done. Anything else has to be translated into these forms before it can be seriously studied. Even so sensitive a thinker as Hans Küng advises the theologians of the great world religions that they will have to 'develop scientific theologies in the modern sense' before we can have a really fruitful dialogue among the world faiths.[9] Because of this cultural dominance of one set of cultural patterns the whole ecumenical movement is severely limited, and Christians who inhabit this cultural world do not receive from Christians of other cultures the correction which they need. It is true that there is at present some enthusiasm for 'third world theologies,' but these are normally theologies written in the language of Europe and (it must be frankly said) are too often echoes of earlier phases of European thought – Marxist, Hegelian, or other. The real power of Asian and African Christianity does not lie in these productions. It lies in the very heart of the Christian life and practice of peoples who naturally live out their Christian faith in the idiom of their own culture and who continue to win their own people to Christ's service through this witness. Theologians of the 'older' churches have often expressed their anxiety lest the 'younger' churches of Asia and Africa should yield to the temptation of syncretism and should develop theologies too closely shaped by their traditional cultures. Just because of the total dominance of European culture in the ecumenical movement there has seldom been any awareness among Western theologians of the extent to which their own theologies have been the result of a failure to challenge the assumptions of their own culture, and because theologians of the younger churches have been compelled to adopt this culture as the precondition of participation in the ecumenical movement they have not been in a position to present the really sharp challenge which should be addressed to the theologies of the Western churches. The point which I have to make in the final section of this chapter will perhaps illustrate this contention.

2 I have described the interaction between gospel and culture as a continually developing relationship within a triangular field of which the three

---

[9] Küng 1976: 105.

points are the local culture, the ecumenical fellowship representing the witness of Christians from other cultures, and the Scriptures as embodying the given revelation with its center and focus in the person of Jesus Christ. In discussion of these matters with colleagues who belong to the cultural world which understands itself to be committed to the modern scientific world view I have found that while there is no question about the first two points of this triangle, there is considerable questioning of the third. In other words, the modern Western theologian will fully recognize the necessity for openness to and dialogue with the local culture, and for the ecumenical dialogue with the whole Christian fellowship. The question will be whether, and in what sense, the Scriptures can be said to function as a third and independent party in this development. When such a place is claimed for Scripture in a discussion within the modern scientific world, three objections are likely to be raised.

(a)   The Bible itself represents the experiences of one particular culture or complex of cultures. The New Testament speaks the languages and uses the models of a particular time and place in human history. It is no Switzerland among the cultures of the world, no 'neutral zone,' no 'non-aligned state.' It arises out of the experience of a people, or a group of peoples, among all the peoples of mankind. It is indelibly marked by their cultural peculiarities and it is embodied in their languages. How, then, can it be absolutized, given an authority over the products of other cultures?

(b)   Within the New Testament itself there is a variety of interpretations of the gospel. Some appear to be shaped by models drawn from the Old Testament, some from Iranian mythology, some from the world of Greek philosophy. How can this collection of varied models, all related to particular temporary and local forms of culture, provide criteria by which all future models, based on the whole range of human culture, may be tested?

(c)   Critical study of the New Testament, using the tools of modern historical research, has led many scholars to believe that it is impossible to have any knowledge of the life, character, and teaching of Jesus sufficiently reliable to provide a criterion for judging the future developments. We cannot, it is said, be sure how far the material in the New Testament represents the character and message of Jesus himself and how far it represents the beliefs of the primitive church.

These questions obviously raise issues which could only be adequately discussed in a series of volumes, but the present discussion requires some attention to them because they obviously affect the integrity and authority of the Christian mission.

(a)   It is, of course, unquestionable that the Bible has its locus in one particular part of the whole fabric of human culture. This fact is indeed the constant horizon of the biblical narrative from the time it is said God chose the clan of Eber from among all the seventy nations that made up the human family. Here is a primitive expression of the dogma, which is central to the Christian tradition, that God has chosen one people among all the people to be the unique bearer of his saving purpose for all nations. In contemporary

Western culture this is confronted by the statement that it is impossible to believe that one among all the cultures should have this unique position. The alleged impossibility rests upon another dogma regarding the meaning of human experience. Here two different dogmatic systems confront one another, and I know of no set of axioms more fundamental than either of them, on the basis of which it would be possible to demonstrate the truth of one of these dogmas and the falsity of the other. According to one dogma, world history is in some sense a coherent whole, and it is therefore possible to affirm that certain events have a unique significance for the entire story. According to the other dogma, there are no events which have such unique significance and therefore no universally valid affirmation can be made about the meaning of history as a whole. The Christian affirmation about the unique significance of these events is a dogmatic statement made as part of the total faith-commitment to Jesus as Lord. The contrary affirmation rests upon a different dogma which belongs to the dominant 'myth' of contemporary Western culture. Here the question at issue is not one of 'translation' from one cultural world to another, but the clash of ultimate faith-commitment.

However, the acknowledgment that this particular part of the whole fabric of human culture has a unique place still leaves open the question about the manner in which this uniqueness is to be interpreted. Does it mean that the cultural forms of the Semitic world have authority over all other cultural forms? Are those who accept the uniqueness and finality of God's revelation of himself in a Jewish male of the first century obliged to accept the cultural forms in which that revelation was given? Plainly no, for the New Testament itself records the debate which arose within the primitive community at the point when the testimony about Jesus moved from a Jewish into a Greek culture. The answers given to the question were not clear-cut, for the 'decrees' recorded in Acts 15.29 include purely Semitic elements which could not be and have not been accepted as permanently valid. But the answers given do make plain that incorporation into the community of Jesus Christ did not mean acceptance of the cultural world in which Jesus himself had lived and which he had accepted. Jesus himself apparently never questioned the law of circumcision. The decisive mark of membership in the new community was nothing definable in terms of culture; it was a reality – apparently quite unmistakable – recognized as the presence of the Holy Spirit.

With this I have already moved into the second of my three questions, that of the variety of voices with which the New Testament speaks of Jesus.

(b) The fact that the New Testament contains not one but several interpretations of Christ prompts the following reflections:

(i) The first is a negative one. There is a variety, but not an unlimited variety, of Christologies in the New Testament. In determining which of the traditions regarding Jesus should be included in the canon and which should be excluded, the church was guided by the belief that the name of Jesus referred to a real man who had lived at a known time and in a known place, and that therefore traditions must be verified against the testimony of original witnesses or of those who were related to the original witnesses by a continuous tradition of public teaching. By this test certain interpretations of the person and teaching of Jesus had to be rejected. Those which were accepted, varied as they are, were united by the fact that they were judged to be reliable reports about the same person. The inclusion of a variety of differing accounts, and the absence of any attempt to iron out these differences so as to create a single picture, is evidence of the fact that the controlling factor was the actual person who had lived – not the doctrines about him.

(ii) The second reflection is positive. It is important for a faithful doing of Christian theology that we should affirm and insist that the New Testament contains not one Christology but several. This is not an unfortunate defect to be regretted or concealed. It is, on the contrary, of the essence of the matter because it makes clear the fact that Christology is always to be done *in via*, at the interface between the gospel and the cultures which it meets on its missionary journey. It is of the essence of the matter that Jesus was not concerned to leave as the fruit of his work a precise verbatim record of everything he said and did, but that he was concerned to create a community which would be bound to him in love and obedience, learn discipleship even in the midst of sin and error, and be his witnesses among all peoples. The varied Christologies to be discovered in the New Testament reflect the attempts of that community to say who Jesus is in the terms of the different cultures within which they bore witness to him. If there were to be discovered in the New Testament one definitive Christology framed in the *ipsissima verba* of Jesus himself, the consequence would be that the gospel would be forever bound absolutely to the culture of first-century Palestine. The New Testament would have to be regarded as untranslatable, as is the Qur'an among Muslims. We would be dealing with a different kind of religion altogether. The *variety* of Christologies actually to be found in the New Testament is part of the fundamental witness to the nature of the gospel: it points to the *destination* of the gospel in all the cultures of mankind. The *unity* of the New Testament, the fact that it contains, not every Christology, but only those which were judged to be faithful to the original testimony, reflects the *origin* of the gospel in the one unique person of Jesus.

(iii) These two reflections, negative and positive, lead to the affirmation that the New Testament, read as it must always be in the context of the Old, provides us, in the variety and unity of its interpretation of Jesus, with the *canon* – the guide and regulator of our doing of Christology. It shows us that Christology must always be something which is *in via*, incomplete, but it shows us that the road has a real starting point in the historic fact of Jesus Christ who lived, taught, died, and rose again under Pontius Pilate; that it has a real destination in the universal confession of this Jesus as Lord; and that the two conditions for the journey are faithful confession within the varied cultures, and faithful mutual openness within the ecumenical fellowship.

(c)   This brings us, however, to the third of the questions which modern critical study of the New Testament poses: do we, in fact, have such reliable knowledge of 'the historic fact of Christ' as would enable us to speak thus of a known starting point for the journey of Christology? Obviously it is impossible to discuss such a large and much debated question here; it is, however, necessary to draw attention to one point in the debate which is relevant to the discussion.

[. . .] [T]he application of modern methods of critical historical research to the contents of the New Testament involves two distinct issues from the point of view of the present discussion. On the one hand it involves the use of greatly improved tools for examining the origins of each tradition and the factors which have shaped its formation and influenced its transmission. But it involves also the presuppositions which control the use of these tools. Every attempt to write history involves, as I have already argued, assumptions about what is significant, and therefore assumptions about the ultimate meaning of the story which alone can give significance to any part of it. But the question of the ultimate meaning of history is the question of one's ultimate faith-commitment. The question has to be pressed whether the skepticism of many Western theologians about the possibility of a reliable knowledge of the 'Jesus of history' does not arise from an uncritical acceptance of the implicit faith-commitment which has dominated the culture of the (admittedly large and influential) tribe to which they have belonged since the Enlightenment of the eighteenth century.

The body of the New Testament writing was formed within a community which believed that the ultimate meaning of the whole human story had been declared in the total fact of Jesus Christ as the first witnesses had known him. Within the limitations of the historical methods available to them within their culture, they sought to create and hand on a record which was faithful to the original testimony of those who had known Jesus in the flesh and who were the witnesses of his resurrection. The controlling belief which shaped the selection and handling of the material was that in Jesus the meaning of the whole of history is revealed. Within this perspective the Jesus of history is the Christ of faith.

It is of course possible to hold a completely different view of the meaning of the story or to hold (as the Indian tradition has generally done) that the story has no meaning. It is clear that a momentous shift took place about two hundred years ago in the thinking of the people of Western Europe about the way in which the story was to be understood. The idea of progress, that is to say the idea that the meaning of the story is to be found in the progressive mastery of man's reason over the powers of nature and over tradition and social structures inherited from the past, seems to have become operative in the European mind during the eighteenth century. When history is understood in this way, it is obvious that the story about Jesus cannot have the decisive place. In fact, from the period of the Enlightenment to the present day, world history is normally taught in schools and universities from a point of view which puts into the decisive place such things as the development of modern science, the industrial revolution, and the evolution of modern forms of political order. The story about Jesus may still have a central place in 'religious instruction,' but it will have only a marginal place in 'world history.' It retains a place in the sphere of personal religion, but it does not determine the way history as a whole is understood.

It is natural that a scholar operating within the assumption of modern European culture, when he comes to study the biblical records as history, will bring to them these assumptions. His work as a historian will be governed by assumptions other than those which are expressed in the hymns and prayers used in church. He will have to try to understand Jesus from the standpoint of a 'modern critical historian,' and it will inevitably follow that the historical Jesus whom he discovers will be a different figure from the Christ of the Christian faith. It is not that there are two different realities. There is only one Jesus and only one set of records. The difference lies in the prior assumptions which are brought to the study of the records.

Of course, it has to be added immediately that the Christ of faith is seen very differently from different cultural perspectives. I have already fully acknowledged this. I have affirmed my belief (part of the fundamental commitment upon which the whole mission of the church rests) that these different perceptions are perceptions of one real person who is decisive for all that it means to be human. I have insisted that these different perceptions are never to be absolutized but have always to be subject to correction within the believing, worshiping, serving, and witnessing fellowship of churches. But – and here is the essential point for the moment – I have argued that this ecumenical fellowship is distorted by its dependence almost entirely upon one set of cultural models, namely, those of the Western world. Consequently the necessary ecumenical correction is not applied to the theology that arises within this culture. Its practitioners find it hard to recognize that the 'modern scientific view of history' is only one among a number of possible ways of looking at history. They find it difficult to recognize the culturally conditioned nature of their fundamental presuppositions. They are therefore tempted to absolutize these presuppositions and to relativize the traditional testimony about Jesus. It is the urgent need of the hour that the ecumenical fellowship of churches should become so released from its present dependence upon one set of cultural forms that it can provide the place wherein we are able to do theology in the only way that it can be done properly – by learning with increasing clarity to confess the one Lord Jesus Christ as alone having absolute authority and therefore to recognize the relativity of all the cultural forms within which we try to say who he is.

Extract 2
Foolishness to the Greeks *(1986)*[10]

My purpose [. . .] is to consider what would be involved in a genuinely missionary encounter between the gospel and the culture that is shared by the peoples of Europe and North America, their colonial and cultural off-shoots, and the growing company of educated leaders in the cities of the world – the culture which those of us who share it usually describe as 'modern.' The phenomenon usually called 'modernization,' which is being promoted throughout much of the Third World through the university and technical training network, the multinational corporations, and the media, is in fact the co-option of the leadership of those nations into the particular culture that had its origin among the peoples of Western Europe. For the moment, and pending closer examination of it, I shall simply refer to it as 'modern Western culture.'

The angle from which I am approaching the study is that of a foreign missionary. After having spent most of my life as a missionary in India, I was called to teach missiology and then to become a missionary in a typical inner-city area in England. This succession of roles has forced me to ask the question I have posed as the theme of this book: What would be involved in a missionary encounter between the gospel and this whole way of perceiving, thinking, and living that we call 'modern Western culture'? There is, of course, nothing new in proposing to discuss the relationship between gospel and culture. We have Richard Niebuhr's classic study of five models of relationship in his book *Christ and Culture*.[11] We have had the massive work of Paul Tillich,[12] who was so much concerned with what he called, in the title of his first public lecture, the 'theology of culture.' But this work has mainly been done, as far as I know, by theologians who had not had the experience of the cultural frontier, of seeking to transmit the gospel from one culture to a radically different one.

On the other hand, we have had a plethora of studies by missionaries on the theological issues raised by cross-cultural missions. As Western missionaries have shared in the general weakening of confidence in our modern Western culture, they have become more aware of the fact that in their presentation of the gospel they have often confused culturally conditioned perceptions with the substance of the gospel, and thus wrongfully claimed divine authority for the relativities of one culture.

For some on the liberal wing of Protestantism, such as W. E. Hocking, Christian missions were to be almost absorbed into the worldwide spread of Western culture, and this was quite explicit. But those at the opposite end of the spectrum, the conservative evangelicals, were often unaware of the cultural conditioning of their religion and therefore guilty, as many of them now

---

[10] Newbigin 1986b: 1–10, 20.
[11] (Niebuhr 1952.)
[12] (Tillich 1959.)

recognize, of confusing the gospel with the values of the American way of life without realizing what they were doing. In the last couple of decades there has been a spate of missionary writings on the problem of *contextualization*. This has been preferred to the terms *indigenization* and *adaptation*, earlier much used by Protestants and Catholics respectively. The weakness of the former was that it tended to relate the Christian message to the traditional cultural forms – forms that belonged to the past and from which young people were turning away under the pervasive influence of 'modernization.' The effect was to identify the gospel with the conservative elements in society. The weakness of the latter term, adaptation, was that it implied that what the missionary brought with him was the pure gospel, which had to be adapted to the recep-tor culture. It tended to obscure the fact that the gospel as embodied in the missionary's preaching and practice was already an adapted gospel, shaped by his or her own culture. The value of the word *contextualization* is that it sug-gests the placing of the gospel in the total context of a culture at a particular moment, a moment that is shaped by the past and looks to the future.

The weakness, however, of this whole mass of missiological writing is that while it has sought to explore the problems of contextualization in all the cul-tures of humankind from China to Peru, it has largely ignored the culture that is the most widespread, powerful, and persuasive among all contemporary cultures – namely, what I have called modern Western culture. Moreover, this neglect is even more serious because it is this culture that, more than almost any other, is proving resistant to the gospel. In great areas of Asia, Africa, and Oceania, the church grows steadily and even spectacularly. But in the areas dominated by modern Western culture (whether in its capitalist or socialist political expression) the church is shrinking and the gospel appears to fall on deaf ears. It would seem, therefore, that there is no higher priority for the research work of missiologists than to ask the question of what would be involved in a genuinely missionary encounter between the gospel and this modern Western culture. Or, to put the matter in a slightly different way, can the experience of missionaries in the cross-cultural transmission of the gospel and the work of theologians who have worked on the question of gospel and culture within the limits of our modern Western culture be usefully brought together to throw light on the central issue I have posed?

Let us begin with some preliminary definitions. By the word *culture* we have to understand the sum total of ways of living developed by a group of human beings and handed on from generation to generation. Central to cul-ture is language. The language of a people provides the means by which they express their way of perceiving things and of coping with them. Around that center one would have to group their visual and musical arts, their techno-logies, their law, and their social and political organization. And one must also include in culture, and as fundamental to any culture, a set of beliefs, ex-periences, and practices that seek to grasp and express the ultimate nature of things, that which gives shape and meaning to life, that which claims final loyalty. I am speaking, obviously, about religion. Religion – including the Christian religion – is thus part of culture.

In speaking of 'the gospel,' I am, of course, referring to the announcement that in the series of events that have their center in the life, ministry, death, and resurrection of Jesus Christ something has happened that alters the total human situation and must therefore call into question every human culture. Now clearly this announcement is itself culturally conditioned. It does not come down from heaven or by the mouth of an angel. The words *Jesus Christ* are the Greek rendering of a Hebrew name and title, *Joshua the Messiah*. They belong to and are part of the culture of one part of the world – the eastern Mediterranean – at one point in history when Greek was the most widespread international language in the lands around the Mediterranean Sea. Neither at the beginning, nor at any subsequent time, is there or can there be a gospel that is not embodied in a culturally conditioned form of words. The idea that one can or could at any time separate out by some process of distillation a pure gospel unadulterated by any cultural accretions is an illusion. It is, in fact, an abandonment of the gospel, for the gospel is about the word made flesh. Every statement of the gospel in words is conditioned by the culture of which those words are a part, and every style of life that claims to embody the truth of the gospel is a culturally conditioned style of life. There can never be a culture-free gospel. Yet the gospel, which is from the beginning to the end embodied in culturally conditioned forms, calls into question all cultures, including the one in which it was originally embodied.

[. . . .]

I begin by looking at what is involved in the cross-cultural communication of the gospel. The New Testament itself, which chronicles the movement of the gospel from its origin in the cultural world of Judaism to its articulation in the language and practice of Greek-speaking Gentile communities, provides us with the models from which to begin. As a starting point, I find it illumin-ating to consider Paul's speech in the presence of King Agrippa and his court (Acts 26). The cultural setting is that of the cosmopolitan Greek-speaking world of the eastern Roman Empire. Paul is speaking in Greek. But at the decisive point of his story he tells the court that when God spoke to him it was not in Greek but in Hebrew: 'I heard a voice speaking to me in the Hebrew language,' the language of the home and the heart, the mother tongue. Paul is a citizen of that cosmopolitan Greek-speaking world. But the word that changed the course of his life was spoken in Hebrew, the language of his own native culture.

But – and this is equally important – the word spoken to his heart, while it accepts that language as its vehicle, uses it not to affirm and approve the life that Saul is living but to call it radically into question: 'Why do you persecute me?' It is to show him that his most passionate and all-conquering conviction is wrong, that what he thinks is the service of God is fighting against God, that he is required to stop in his tracks, turn around, and renounce the whole direction of his life, to love what he had hated and to cherish what he had sought to destroy.

And – this is my third point – a voice that makes such a demand can only be the voice of the sovereign Lord himself. No one but God has the right and the power to contradict my devotion to God. 'Who are you?' is Paul's trembling question. It is the same as Moses' question at the burning bush: 'What is your name?' The answer, 'I am Jesus,' means that from henceforth Saul knows Jesus as simply and absolutely Lord.

We have here, I suggest, a model of what is involved in the communication of the gospel across a cultural frontier. (1) The communication has to be in the language of the receptor culture. It has to be such that it accepts, at least provisionally, the way of understanding things that is embodied in that language; if it does not do so, it will simply be an unmeaning sound that cannot change anything. (2) However, if it is truly the communication of the gospel, it will call radically into question that way of understanding embodied in the language it uses. If it is truly revelation, it will involve contradiction, and call for conversion, for a radical *metanoia*, a U-turn of the mind. (3) Finally, this radical conversion can never be the achievement of any human persuasion, however eloquent. It can only be the work of God. True conversion, therefore, which is the proper end towards which the communication of the gospel looks, can only be a work of God, a kind of miracle – not natural but supernatural.

This pattern is brilliantly exemplified in the Johannine writings. 'John' freely uses the language and the thought-forms of the religious world for which he writes. Much of it is suggestive of the sort of world view that is often very imprecisely called 'Gnosticism' and has obvious affinities with Indian thought. For this reason the Fourth Gospel was early suspected of Gnostic tendencies and has later been eagerly welcomed by Hindus as placing Jesus firmly within a typically Indian world view. Yet 'John' uses this language and these thought-forms in such a way as to confront them with a fundamental question and indeed a contradiction. The *logos* is no longer an idea in the mind of the philosopher or the mystic. The *logos* is the man Jesus who went the way from Bethlehem to Calvary. In my own experience I have found that Hindus who begin by welcoming the Fourth Gospel as the one that uses their language and speaks to their hearts, end by being horrified when they understand what it is really saying. And so, logically, we move to the third point to which 'John' gave equal emphasis: that – as Jesus puts it in the sixth chapter – 'No one can come to me unless the Father draws him' (John 6.44). The radical conversion of the heart, the U-turn of the mind which the New Testament calls *metanoia*, can never be the calculable result of correct methods of communication. It is something mysterious for which we can only say that our methods of communication were, at most, among the occasions for the miracle.

The same threefold pattern is exemplified in the experience of a mission-ary who, nurtured in one culture, seeks to communicate the gospel among people of another culture whose world has been shaped by a vision of the totality of things quite different from that of the Bible. He must first of all struggle to master the language. To begin with, he will think of the words he hears simply as the equivalent of the words he uses in his own tongue and are listed in his dictionary as equivalents. But if he really immerses himself in the talk, the songs and folk tales, and the literature of the people, he will discover that there are no exact equivalents. All the words in any language derive their meaning, their resonance in the minds of those who use them, from a whole world of experience and a whole way of grasping that experience. So there are no exact translations. He has to render the message as best he can, draw-ing as fully as he can upon the tradition of the people to whom he speaks.

Clearly, he has to find the path between two dangers. On the one hand, he may simply fail to communicate: he uses the words of the language, but in such a way that he sounds like a foreigner; his message is heard as the bab-blings of a man who really has nothing to say. Or, on the other hand, he may so far succeed in talking the language of his hearers that he is accepted all too easily as a familiar character – a moralist calling for greater purity of conduct or a guru offering a path to the salvation that all human beings want. His mes-sage is simply absorbed into the existing world view and heard as a call to be more pious or better behaved. In the attempt to be 'relevant' one may fall into syncretism, and in the effort to avoid syncretism one may become irrelevant.

In spite of these dangers, which so often reduce the effort of the mission-ary to futility, it can happen that, in the mysterious providence of God, a word spoken comes with the kind of power of the word that was spoken to Saul on the road to Damascus. Perhaps it is as sudden and cataclysmic as that. Or per-haps it is the last piece that suddenly causes the pattern to make sense, the last experience of a long series that tips the scale decisively. However that may be, it causes the hearer to stop, turn around, and go in a new direction, to accept Jesus as his Lord, Guide, and Savior.

The Jesus whom he thus accepts will be the Jesus presented to him by the missionary. It will be Jesus as the missionary perceives him. It is only necessary to look at the visual representation of Jesus in the art of different people through the past 18 centuries, or to read the lives of Jesus written in the past 150 years, to understand that Jesus is always perceived and can only be per-ceived through the eyes of a particular culture. Think of the Christ of the Byzantine mosaics, a kind of super Emperor, the Pantocrat; the Christ of the medieval crucifix, a drooping, defeated victim; the Christ of liberal Protestantism, an enlightened, emancipated, successful member of the bour-geoisie; or the Christ of the liberation theologians portrayed in the likeness of Che Guevara. It will inevitably be the Christ of the missionary to whom, in the first instance, the new convert turns and gives his allegiance. This may express itself in the adopting of styles of worship, dress, and behavior copied from the missionary – sometimes to the embarrassment of the latter.

111

But this will be only the first expression of it. The matter will not stop there, for the new convert will begin to read the Bible for himself. As he does so, he will gain a standpoint from which he can look in a new way both at his own culture and at the message he has received from the missionary. This will not happen suddenly. It is only as the fruit of sustained exposure to the Bible that one begins to see familiar things in a new light. In this light the new convert will both see his own traditional culture in a new way and also observe that there are discrepancies between the picture of Jesus that he (from within his culture) finds in the New Testament and the picture that was communicated by the missionary. From this point on, there are various possible developments. The convert, having realized that much of what he had first accepted from the missionary was shaped by the latter's culture and not solely by the gospel, may in reaction turn back to his own culture and seek, in a sort of hostile reaction to the culture that had invaded his own under the cloak of the gospel, to restate the gospel in terms of his traditional culture. Some of what is called Third World theology has primarily this negative orientation, rather than being primarily directed towards the communication of the gospel to those still inhabiting the traditional culture. What can also happen is that the missionary, and through him the church he represents, can become aware of the element of syncretism in his own Christianity, of the extent to which his culture has been allowed to determine the nature of the gospel he preaches, instead of being brought under judgment by that gospel. If this happens, great possibilities for mutual correction open up. Each side, perceiving Christ through the spectacle of one culture, can help the other to see how much the vision has been blurred or distorted. This kind of mutual correction is at the very heart of the ecumenical movement when it is true to itself.

But even where this mutual correction does begin to take place, it is still – in the modern world – under the shadow of the overwhelming predominance of modern Western culture. All the dialogue is conducted in the languages of Western Europe, and this in itself determines its terms. Only those who have had what is called a modern education are equipped to take part in it. That is to say, it is confined to those who have been more or less co-opted into the predominant modern Western culture. Most of the missionary outreach across cultural boundaries still comes from churches that are part of this culture. How, then, can there be a genuine encounter of the gospel with this culture, a culture that has itself sprung from roots in Western Christendom and with which the Western churches have lived in a symbiotic relationship ever since its first dawning? From whence comes the voice that can challenge this culture on its own terms, a voice that speaks its own language and yet confronts it with the authentic figure of the crucified and living Christ so that it is stopped in its tracks and turned back from the way of death? One might think that the vision of the mushroom cloud that has haunted the mind of modern Western people ever since it first appeared over Hiroshima would be enough. But we know that fear does not bring deliverance. From whence can the voice, not of doom but of deliverance, be spoken so that the modern Western world can hear it as the voice of its Savior and Lord?

[. . . .]

Here, surely, is the most challenging missionary frontier of our time.

Further reading

Newbigin 1978a: 1–22.
Newbigin 1988a: 50–3.
Newbigin 1993a: 98–100.

8

The nature and calling of the Church

8.1 The nature of the Church

Newbigin's seminal study on the Church, The Household of God, *from which the first extract is taken, was published in 1953. It was based on the Kerr Lectures, delivered at Trinity College, Glasgow, during November 1952, and has remained a classic ever since. In it Newbigin deliberately avoided detailed discussions about the structure of the Church's ministry, or questions about its sacraments or ordinances. Instead, he chose to concentrate upon the question: 'By what is the Church consti-tuted?' The originality of the book arose out of his decision to deal with this question in the light of the answers given by three 'streams' of Christian life and thought with-in the worldwide ecumenical movement. In Chapters 2 and 3 he discusses the contri-bution of two more traditional streams, which he 'loosely' describes as 'Protestant' and 'Catholic': the one with its emphasis upon salvation by faith alone, the other with its commitment to the continuing 'body of Christ' and its emphasis upon sacramental incor-poration. But Newbigin adds to these a third stream with its emphasis on the Church as 'The community of the Holy Spirit', which he calls the 'Pentecostal'. Writing in the early 1950s, he was convinced that the contribution of the Pentecostal movement was largely yet to be made. But he also believed it would be both timely and much needed if what he called 'the ecumenical conversation' was to 'bear its proper fruit'.[1] Newbigin's analysis proved to be prophetic in its insight into the subsequent development of the worldwide Christian movement.*

The second extract is a contribution Newbigin made to a 1988 book of essays exploring the relationship between the traditional notion of 'parish' churches and their role within a society that was fast becoming detached from the very idea of 'church'. Originally delivered as a paper at a colloquium set up by the Grubb Institute to explore this issue, Newbigin's contribution − entitled 'On Being the Church for the World' − provides a sustained theological reflection on the nature of the Church. It reflects his long missionary experience in India, and his (then) setting as a minister of a local church in inner-city Birmingham, predominantly populated by Hindus, Sikhs and Muslims. It concludes with some typically trenchant remarks about 'denominationalism'.

* * *

---

[1] Newbigin 1953: 108.

Extract 1
The Household of God *(1953)*[2]

I

The doctrine of the Church has come in recent years to occupy a central place in theological discussion. The reason for this is to be found in the interaction of several closely related factors, and it will be well at the outset to look briefly at these, since they provide the context for our discussion. I am going to refer to three such factors: the breakdown of Christendom, the missionary experience of the Churches in the lands outside of the old Christendom, and the rise of the modern ecumenical movement.

1 The breakdown of Christendom

By this phrase I mean the dissolution – at first slow, but later more and more rapid – of the synthesis between the Gospel and the culture of the western part of the European peninsula of Asia, by which Christianity had become almost the folk-religion of Western Europe. That synthesis was the work of the thousand-year period during which the peoples of Western Europe, hemmed in by the power of Islam to east and south, had the Gospel wrought into the very stuff of their social and personal life, so that the whole population could be conceived of as the *corpus Christianum*. That conception is the background of all the Reformation theologies. They take it for granted. They are set not in a missionary situation but in this situation in which Christendom is taken for granted. This means that in their doctrines of the Church they are defining their position over against one another *within* the context of the *corpus Christianum*. They are not defining the Church as over against a pagan world. It is not necessary to point out how profoundly this affects the structure of their thinking.

The dissolution of the medieval synthesis and the transition to the world which we know today have brought the Church once again into direct touch with the non-Christian world in two ways, through the experience of foreign missions, and through the rise of anti-Christian movements within Christendom.

A study of the beginnings of the modern missionary movement shows how strongly this movement was still controlled by the old Christendom idea. Missions were conceived of as the extension of the frontiers of Christendom and the conveyance of the blessings of Christian civilisation to those who had hitherto been without them. The first converts shared these presuppositions, and were in most cases glad to adopt the culture of the missionaries along with their Gospel. But the rise of substantial Churches in Asia, Africa and the Pacific islands compelled rethinking of these presuppositions. A distinction

------

[2] Newbigin 1953: 11–31.

had to be drawn between the Gospel and Western culture, and this in turn meant that the Church, as the body which – in whatever cultural environment – lives by the Gospel alone, had to be distinguished from the society in which it was set. In the first phase of missions, the colony of the *corpus Christianum* had been very clearly marked off as a totally distinct cultural community from the society round about it. The line of demarcation was very prominently represented by the high wall of a mission compound. But now the Church had outgrown the mission compound. Its members were scattered over city and countryside, sharing in a wider and wider variety of occupations with their non-Christian neighbours. Obviously a new kind of line had now to be drawn, a line dividing the Church from the world but not separating the Christian community from the local culture. The drawing of that line was the work of thousands of practically minded men and women immersed in the daily care of the churches rather than of professional theologians. But its theological implications, which we shall consider in a moment, have been profound.

In the meantime, within the old Christendom the same issue was being forced upon the churches by the rise of non-Christian forces, at first more or less accepting the *mores* of Christendom while challenging its theology, but eventually launching a full-scale attack upon the whole ethical tradition of Western Europe and seeking to replace it by something totally different. In this situation Christian worship, teaching, and service could no longer be regarded as the religious activities of the whole community. The Church was compelled more and more to define itself both in theory and in practice as a body distinct from the community as a whole, and therefore to reflect upon its own nature. The present widespread discussion both in England and in Scotland of what has been called 'indiscriminate baptism' is one element in the present phase of that task.

But there is a further reason for the fact that the breakdown of Christendom has placed the doctrine of the Church in the centre of our thinking. One phase of that breakdown has been the dissolution of the ties which bound men and women to the natural communities of family, village, or working group, to which they had belonged. I do not need to labour this point, which is the constant refrain of the social diagnostician. Western European civilisation has witnessed a sort of atomising process, in which the individual is more and more set free from his natural setting in family and neighbourhood, and becomes a sort of replaceable unit in the social machine. His nearest neighbours may not even know his name. He is free to move from place to place, from job to job, from acquaintance to acquaintance, and – if he has attained a high degree of emancipation – from wife to wife. He is in every context a more and more anonymous and replaceable part, the perfect incarnation of the rationalist conception of man. Wherever Western civilisation has spread in the past one hundred years it has carried this atomising process with it. Its characteristic product in Calcutta, Shanghai, or Johannesburg is the modern city into which myriads of human beings, loosened from their old ties in village or tribe or caste, like grains of sand fretted by water from an ancient block of sandstone, are ceaselessly churned around in the whirlpool of the city – anonymous, identical, replaceable units. In such a situation it is natural that men should long for some sort of real community, for men cannot be human without it. It is especially natural that Christians should reach out after that part of Christian doctrine which speaks of the true, God-given community, the Church of Jesus Christ. We have witnessed the appalling results of trying to go back to some sort of primitive collectivity based on the total control of the individual, down to the depths of his spirit, by an all-powerful group. Yet we know that we cannot condemn this solution to the problem of man's loneliness if we have no other to offer. It is natural that men should ask with a greater eagerness than ever before such questions as these: 'Is there in truth a family of God on earth to which I can belong, a place where all men can truly be at home? If so, where is it to be found, what are its marks, and how is it related to, and distinguished from, the known communities of family, nation and culture? What are its boundaries, its structure, its terms of membership? And how comes it that those who claim to be the spokesmen of that one holy fellowship are themselves at war with one another as to the fundamentals of its nature, and unable to agree to live together in unity and concord?' The breakdown of Christendom has forced such questions as these to the front. I think there is no more urgent theological task than to try to give them plain and credible answers.

2   The experience of the Christian mission

I have already referred to the fact that the contact of the Church with dominant non-Christian religious cultures outside of Europe raised practical questions about the relations of the Church to the world, and therefore about the nature of the Church itself. As a result of the effort to handle these practical issues, the question of the Church has come to dominate missionary thinking for the past two decades. It is necessary now to explain these statements more fully.

It is, I think, difficult for those who have lived only in Western Europe to feel the enormous importance of the fact that the Church is surrounded by a culture which is the product of Christianity. One needs to have had experience both of this, and of the situation of a Church in a non-Christian culture, to feel the difference. The Churches in most of the countries of Western Europe take it for granted that by far the greater part of the secular affairs of their members are conducted without any direct relationship to the Church. Education, medicine, art, music, agriculture, politics, economics, all are treated as separate spheres of life, and the Christian who plays his part in them does so as an individual, looking for guidance in them not to the Church but to acknowledged masters in each sphere who may or may not be Christians. It is no longer expected, nor would it be generally tolerated, that the Church should control these activities directly. Yet the fact that this whole body of secular culture has grown up within Christendom still profoundly affects its character. Christian ideas still have an enormous influence in the thinking and practice of those who take part in it. Individual Christians can make great contributions to it precisely because it is still so much shaped by its origin in a single Christian conception and practice of life. The Churches can, without immediate and obvious disaster, confine themselves to specifically 'religious' concerns, to the provision of opportunities for worship, religious teaching, and fellowship, knowing that their members will, in their secular occupations, still have some real possibility of maintaining Christian standards of thought and practice. Thus the Churches tend to become loosely compacted fellowships within a wider semi-Christian culture, providing for only a small part of the total concerns of their members. Membership in a church may often involve only slight and relatively superficial contacts with other members, because the church is – for each member – only one among the many different associations to which he belongs.

I am well aware that this picture is only partially true, that all Churches in the West are not in the same position in this matter, and that many Christians deplore this development, are awake to its enormous dangers, and are seeking to reverse it and to find a deeper involvement of the Church in the 'secular' order. Yet the general picture is fair enough to provide a true contrast with the situation of the Church in the midst of an ancient non-Christian culture such as Hinduism. Let me now seek to sketch that situation in a few very rough strokes.

(i)   In the first place, becoming a Christian in such a situation involves a radical break with the whole of the non-Christian culture. That culture may contain a vast amount of good, but it is determined by the dominant religious idea, and the convert therefore generally feels compelled to make a complete break with it. Later on, when he is securely established within the new community, he can assess the culture which he has left with a discriminating eye, seeking to preserve what is good. But that is only possible because he is now a member of a new community which is controlled by quite different principles. The majority of his contacts will now be with his fellow members in the church. He will look to them at every decisive point. His whole being is now enveloped in a new atmosphere, controlled by a new environment. He is, if one may put it so, not so much a man who has joined a new club as a child adopted into a new family. The church is the total environment of his life, rather than one among the circles in which he moves.

(ii)   Looking now at the situation from the side of the Church rather than from that of the individual, we see that the Church going out into new territories has in most cases felt itself bound almost at once to involve itself in all kinds of service to the community – educational, medical, agricultural, industrial. It has felt compelled to try to demonstrate in these ways not merely a new pattern of personal behaviour within the pagan culture, but a new pattern of corporate activity extending beyond the strictly religious sphere. It may possibly be argued that this is a feature of post-Constantinian missionary work, and does not properly belong to the real business of the Christian mission. It is not necessary to argue the point here, for my concern is only to show that this, which has been a universal feature of missionary work in the modern era, has been one of the factors leading to a rethinking of the doctrine of the Church.

(iii)   Thirdly, the Church in a non-Christian cultural environment has to take seriously the business of discipline. That is a commonplace in the experience of every one of the younger Churches. It is necessary because, in the first place, the removal of the convert from the sphere of the traditional discipline of caste, community, or tribe, puts upon the Church the responsibility for seeing to it that this is replaced by a new kind of social discipline; and secondly, because without this the Church's witness to the non-Christian world becomes hopelessly compromised. It is often in this sphere that the sharpest necessity arises for the rethinking of traditional attitudes derived from the Christendom background. Within Christendom one is familiar with two contrasted attitudes: on the one hand there is the attitude, typical of a national Church, which accepts a certain responsibility for the whole life of the community, but fails to make it clear that the Church is a separate community marked off from the world in order to save the world; on the other hand, and in opposition to this, there is the attitude of the gathered community – the body which is very conscious of being called out from the world, and from a merely nominal Christianity, but which yet can wash its hands completely of any responsibility for those of its members who fail to fulfil its conditions for membership. A missionary Church in a pagan land can take neither of these attitudes. On the one hand it must be a distinct body, separate from the pagan world around it. But, on the other hand, it cannot divest itself of responsibility for those whom it has uprooted from their ancient soil and transplanted into a totally new soil, or for their children. Perhaps this issue is less acute in some areas than in India. Certainly there the Church would be guilty of shocking irresponsibility if it did not accept some responsibility for all who, by baptism, have been removed from their ancient setting in the solidarity of caste and community, and brought into the community of Christ. In their baptism they have decisively broken the old ties of social discipline by which the common life was ordered, and if the Church does not make itself responsible for giving them a new and better kind of social discipline, it will stand condemned as an enemy of human well-being. But – as will at once be obvious – the effort to meet this need, to provide a type of discipline which is truly evangelical, which leads to Christian freedom and not to ecclesiastical tyranny, is one that raises the most difficult questions about the nature of the Church itself.

(iv)   Fourthly, it is in this situation, as a new community set in, and yet separated from, the ancient religious cultures of the non-Christian lands, that the question of unity has become inescapable. Everything about such a missionary situation conspires to make Christian disunity an intolerable anomaly. Within the assumed unity of Christendom, the Churches could fall apart, increasingly leaving the main direction of the life of the world to secular forces, and concentrating on rival interpretations of the life in Christ, expressed in the form of religious fellowships which made a less and less total demand upon their members. But when they were thrust – for the first time for more than a thousand years – into a really missionary situation; when they were called to bear witness to one Lord and Saviour in the face of vast and ancient religious cultures which did not know Him; and when they began to see that to speak of Christ as Redeemer of the world was mere empty talk if the hard geographical implications of that phrase were not accepted: then it began to be clear that the division of the Church into rival and hostile bodies is something finally incompatible with the central verities of the Gospel. Much has been written in the last few years to bring to light again the profound connection at the very heart of the Gospel between mission and unity, and it is not necessary to repeat what has already been said. At the centre of the whole missionary enterprise stands Christ's abiding promise, 'I, if I be lifted up, will draw all men unto myself', and its goal is 'to sum up all things in Christ'. When the Church faces out towards the world it knows that it only exists as the first fruits and the instrument of that reconciling work of Christ, and that division within its own life is a violent contradiction of its own fundamental nature. His reconciling work is one, and we cannot be His ambassadors reconciling the world to God, if we have not ourselves been willing to be reconciled to one another. It is the result of this deep connection at the heart of the Gospel itself that Churches which – within Christendom – had accepted their disunity as a matter of course, found that when they were placed in a missionary situation their disunity was an intolerable scandal. Out of this new missionary experience arose those forces by which the Churches were drawn from isolation into comity, from comity into co-operation, and – in some areas at least – from co-operation into organic union.

And that leads us to the third factor in the context of our discussion – the rise of the ecumenical movement.

3 The ecumenical movement

The ecumenical movement has been a by-product of the missionary movement, arising out of the missionary experience of the Churches outside of the old Christendom, and enormously reinforced by the experience of Churches within Christendom which have found themselves here also in a missionary situation face to face with new paganisms. It is important to bear this fact in mind, for the ecumenical movement will become fatally corrupted if it does not remain true to its missionary origins. The very name ought to be a safeguard, were it remembered that in the New Testament *oikumene* never means the worldwide Church but always the whole inhabited earth to which the Church is sent. There is a real danger at the present time of a false sort of ecumenism, an attempt to find consolation amid the wreckage of the old Christendom in the vision of a new and wider Christendom, yet without the acceptance of the hard demands of missionary obedience. The attractions of this broad and comfortable blind alley must be resisted. There can be no true ecumenical movement except that which is missionary through and through, for there can be no true doctrine of the Church which is not held, so to say, in the tension of urgent obedience between the Saviour and the world He came to save. The fact that the World Council of Churches and the International Missionary Council, linked as they are in the closest association, are still two separate bodies, is a reminder of the fact that a thoroughly missionary conception of the nature of the Church has not yet been wrought into the ordinary thinking of the Churches.

The decisive feature of the present stage of the ecumenical movement is the formation of the World Council of Churches. The implications of this event are only slowly being realised in the Council itself and in its member Churches. At Amsterdam the member Churches made this statement about what they had done: 'We have covenanted with one another in constituting this World Council of Churches. We intend to stay together. We call upon Christian congregations everywhere to endorse and fulfil this covenant in their relations one with another. In thankfulness to God we commit the future to Him.' These words indicate a very far-reaching change in the relationship of the Churches with one another. The ecumenical movement is no longer to be a matter for individuals or groups, nor is it to be concerned only with limited objectives. The Churches have bound themselves to one another in the sight of God and of the whole congregation of the faithful. Not all the implications of that act could be clearly discerned at the time. The same assembly confessed, in thanking God for unity which the ecumenical movement had helped them to recognise: 'We acknowledge that (God) is powerfully at work amongst us, to lead us to goals which we but dimly discern. We do not fully understand some of the things He has already done amongst us, or their implications on our familiar ways.'[3] Reflection among the Churches as to what those implications were raised searching questions. In this covenant the member Churches had in some sense recognised one another as Churches. In what sense? Had they recognised one another as 'the Church' in the New Testament sense, and – if so – had they agreed to lay aside their own distinctive doctrines about what constitutes the essence of the Church, or to treat them as of merely secondary importance? If not, how could they treat as Churches bodies lacking elements which, upon their own view, are essential to the Church? These questions soon clamoured for an official answer.

Two years after the Amsterdam assembly, the Council's Central Committee issued in 1950 at Toronto an extremely precise and carefully balanced statement of what the implications of membership were. This made it clear that membership did *not* imply that a member Church was obliged to treat the other member Churches as in the full sense Churches, or to regard its own doctrine of the Church as merely relative, or to accept any particular view as to the visible form of the Church's unity. Positively the statement listed

---

[3] Amsterdam Section I Report, para. VI.

the following assumptions as underlying the formation of the Council, and implied in membership. All recognise that Christ is the one Head of His Body, the Church, and that the Church is therefore one; each member Church recognises that the Church Universal exists *in some sense* beyond its own boundaries, that the question 'In what sense?' is a subject for common study and conversation, and that this recognition of elements of the true Church in other Churches makes such mutual conversation obligatory; all recognise that they ought to seek together to learn from Christ what witness they should bear together in the world, to live together in mutual helpfulness, and to enter into spiritual relationships with each other to the building up of the Body of Christ. One may summarise the situation as this document states it by saying that the World Council of Churches gives institutional embodiment to the conviction that the Church ought to be one, while remaining neutral as to the proper form of that unity. It thus provides a place in which very diverse views as to the unity which the Church ought to have can confront one another in fruitful conversation. There are those who hold that the divinely willed form of the Church's unity already exists in their own communion (whether in assent to doctrines as formulated in a particular confession, or in acceptance of a particular historic order) and who therefore cannot regard bodies outside their own communion as, in the full sense, Churches. There are others who, holding a different view of the divine will for the Church, can accept as true Churches bodies of a very wide variety of types of doctrine and order. All of these are invited to become members of the Council and are assured that they are not thereby required to modify their views. The Council is a place where they can all meet and engage in fruitful converse.

And yet, of course, it is more than a meeting-place, a mere forum for discussion. When the Churches at Amsterdam spoke of 'covenanting together' they did not use empty words. Something came into existence there which had not existed before, a mutual commitment, leading to a new sort of unity in witness and action. The World Council exists, and acts more and more effectively in many spheres – in witness, service, the edification of the Body of Christ. This is a new fact, a new reality. And it exists because the member Churches have been unable to refuse to recognise one another as Christ's people. 'We are divided from one another,' said the Amsterdam assembly, 'but Christ has made us His own, and He is not divided.' Whatever their doctrines of the Church, the member Churches could not refuse to make that momentous statement, and they cannot refuse to accept its implication, which is that their togetherness in the Council is – in some sense – a togetherness in Christ. No one who has taken any part in the ecumenical movement can doubt this: its unity is a unity in Christ. The World Council is not a mere neutral meeting-place for differing views of the Church: it has itself a churchly character.

It follows from this that, while we must accept the statement of the Toronto document that the World Council is *in intention* neutral on the question of the form of the Church's unity, we cannot agree that it is neutral *in fact*, for it is itself a form of that unity. And, if the Council be regarded as anything other than a transitory phase of the journey from disunity to unity, it is the *wrong* form. In saying this I am, of course, abandoning any pretence at speaking from a position of neutrality among the conflicting ecclesiologies with which we have to deal. I cannot so speak, for I believe that the divinely willed form of the Church's unity is at least this, a visible company in every place of all who confess Jesus as Lord, abiding together in the Apostles' teaching and fellowship, the breaking of bread and the prayers. Its foci are the word, the sacraments, and the apostolic ministry. Its form is the visible fellowship, not of those whom we choose out to be our friends, but of those whom God has actually given to us as our neighbours. It is therefore simply humanity in every place re-created in Christ. It is the place where *all* men can be made one because all are made nothing, where one new humanity in Christ is being daily renewed because the old man in *every* man is being brought to crucifixion through word, baptism and supper. Its unity is universal because it is local and congregational. Believing this, I am bound to believe that all conceptions of reunion in terms of federation are vain. They leave the heart of the problem – which is the daily life of men and women in their neighbourhood – untouched. They demand no death and resurrection as the price of unity. They leave each sect free to enjoy its own particular sort of spirituality, merely tying them all together at the centre in a bond which does not vitally and costingly involve every member in every part of his daily life. They envisage a sort of unity whose foci are not the word and sacraments of the Gospel in the setting of the local congregation, but the conference table and the committee room. They do not grapple with the fact, which any serious reading of the New Testament must surely make inescapable, that to speak of a plurality of Churches, is strictly absurd; that we can only do so in so far as we have ceased to understand by the word 'Church' what the New Testament means by it; that our ecclesiologies are, in the Pauline sense, carnal (1 Cor. 3.3–4). The disastrous error of the idea of federation is that it offers us reunion without repentance.

I am not wishing to assert that the World Council is a federal union of Churches. That is made clear by the Toronto Statement, and by the fact that the member Churches are not committed to intercommunion. Yet, in so far as it is an embodiment of Christian unity, it is a federal form of embodiment. And precisely because it is much more than a merely neutral meeting-place, because in it a real common life in the Holy Spirit takes place, because it is the locus of much that is most fruitful and precious in the life of Christendom today, because it is the increasingly effective organ of co-operation among Churches for all sorts of service and witness to the world, there is a real danger of our forgetting that the World Council only has a right to exist as a means to something further, as a stage on the way from disunity to unity; and that if it comes to be regarded as itself the proper form of the Church's unity in Christ, it will have become committed to a disastrous error. I believe that membership in the World Council is indeed the way that God has opened up in our time by which the Churches may move from disunity to unity, and that to refuse this way would be to refuse God's call. But it is the way, not the end, and if it comes to be regarded as the end it must be condemned as the wrong end. We have to recognise that the present situation is critical; that the Faith and Order discussions do not at the present moment seem to be leading to any adequate move forward in the direction of organic reunion; and that a very large number of Christians seem to be content to regard our present level of co-operation as sufficient. In other words, there is a real danger that the World Council, while proclaiming itself neutral as regards the form of the Church's unity, should in fact come to be accepted as the organ of a sort of federal union. There can be no doubt that very many Protestants[4] who ardently support the work of the Council do so with this underlying idea; they take seriously the fact that the Churches have, in some sense, accepted one another as Churches, and have covenanted together in the Council; and they are hurt and irritated by the refusal of Catholics to take what seems the next step – complete intercommunion among the member Churches. There are doubtless many who would regard such intercommunion as a step towards organic unity, but the evidence seems to me clear that a vast number would regard it not as a step towards organic unity, but as a substitute for it. The present position of the English Free Churches is an example of the evidence I refer to. In other words, federation is apparently accepted as an adequate goal. In this situation I think that the Catholics may be provisionally justified in their intransigence, that in refusing intercommunion on these terms they are perhaps, in the only way possible to them at the moment, maintaining their witness to the Scriptural truth about the nature of the Church which might otherwise be hopelessly compromised.

But the Catholics also are in a dilemma. For in sharing in the ecumenical movement they have become involved in a situation for which their traditional theology has no place. The Catholic rightly believes that it is of the nature of the Church to be one visible fellowship, and if he is serious he must believe that his own Church is that fellowship. He cannot, then, treat other separated bodies of Christians as Churches. Yet in the World Council he has found himself compelled to recognise them as, in some sense, Churches, and therefore to join with them in a binding covenant. But his own traditional theological language can provide him with no categories to justify what he has done, and he will constantly appear to others as insincere or inconsistent. He maintains, for instance, that episcopacy is essential to the Church. That can only mean that where a body has no bishops it is no Church; that if it regards itself as a Church it is suffering from delusion; and that the only proper exercise of Christian charity towards its members is to deliver them from this delusion, and to bring them out of a pseudo-Church into the true Church.

---

[4] It will be obvious that here [. . .] I am using the two words 'Protestant' and 'Catholic' in a very loose sense to describe the two major points of view represented in the present ecumenical conversation, and that the word 'Catholic' is not here being used as it is in the Creeds.

He repudiates that deduction because in the ecumenical movement he has come to know as a sheer fact that Christ is present in the other Churches. He cannot deny it without feeling that he is guilty of sinning against the Holy Ghost. The logical conclusion would then seem to be that he should correct the statement 'Episcopacy is essential to the Church' to 'Episcopacy is very valuable to the Church'. But that he cannot do without destroying his whole theological position. The Catholic is stuck in a logically impossible position. Yet by sticking to it he is defending a vital Christian truth which would otherwise apparently go by default.

The result is the stalemate with which we are painfully familiar. As an organ of co-operation and conversation, the World Council of Churches goes from strength to strength. But the visible reunion of the Churches makes little progress, and indeed denominational positions tend to harden. Thus the Council, instead of being something essentially transitional, tends to appear more and more as the permanent form of the Churches' unity. Its ecclesiological neutrality is in danger of becoming a screen for ecclesiological federalism. I have already said that I believe that this would be disastrous. Yet there is no way of avoiding that disaster except by finding some way of breaking through the theological impasse in regard to the doctrine of the Church. It is this actual situation in the relations of the Churches that gives its urgency to the subject I have chosen for these lectures.

II

Having said so much about the context of our discussion, let me say a word about the standpoint from which it will be conducted. I have already made it clear that I can make no pretence to neutrality. I can only speak from the place where I serve, which is in the ministry of the Church of South India. Standing in that place, I have very definite views as to the divinely intended form of the Church's visible unity. I have already indicated what they are. But perhaps the most important thing about the Constitution of that Church is the explicit confession that the Church is not what it ought to be. I should like to quote here some sentences from the statement prepared by the Church of South India for the Lund Conference:

> Probably no Church is as static as its fundamental documents suggest, but the Church of South India has the idea of development written into its very constitution. That constitution is explicitly a starting point; it does not pretend to be a final resting place. It was written by three Churches still divided from one another, as a sufficient starting point for the adventure of unity, and in the faith that truth would be more clearly seen in unity than in separation. It confesses its own partial and tentative character by acknowledging that the final aim is 'the union in the Universal Church of all who acknowledge the Name of Christ' and it claims to be tested by the principle that every such local scheme of union 'should express locally the principle of the great catholic unity of the Body of Christ' (Const. II.2). Very obviously in these words the Church of

125

South India confesses that it is not yet the Church in the full sense which the word 'Church' ought to have. It confesses itself to be on the road, and it makes a claim to be on the right road, but it does not pretend to have arrived.

If there is any single constructive feature in these lectures it will simply be the attempt to draw out what is involved in that statement. The Church is the pilgrim people of God. It is on the move – hastening to the ends of the earth to beseech all men to be reconciled to God, and hastening to the end of time to meet its Lord who will gather all into one. Therefore the nature of the Church is never to be finally defined in static terms, but only in terms of that to which it is going. It cannot be understood rightly except in a perspective which is at once missionary and eschatological, and only in that perspective can the deadlock of our present ecumenical debate be resolved. But – and this is of vital importance – it will be a solution in which theory and practice are inseparably related, not one which can be satisfactorily stated in terms of theory alone. There is a way of bringing the eschatological perspective to bear upon our present perplexities which relieves them at no cost to ourselves, which allows us to rest content with them because in the age to come they will disappear. That is a radically false eschatology. The whole meaning of this present age between Christ's coming and His coming again is that in it the powers of the age to come are at work now to draw all men into one in Christ. When the Church ceases to be one, or ceases to be missionary, it contradicts its own nature. Yet the Church is not to be defined by what it is, but by that End to which it moves, the power of which now works in the Church, the power of the Holy Spirit who is the earnest of the inheritance still to be revealed. To say that the deadlock in the ecumenical debate will be resolved in a perspective which is missionary and eschatological is not true unless it is understood that that perspective means a new obedience to, and a new possession by, the Holy Spirit. It is a perspective inseparable from action, and that action must be both in the direction of mission and in that of unity, for these are but two aspects of the one work of the Spirit.

III

Having spoken about context and standpoint, I must proceed to say something by way of definition. We are to be speaking about the Church, and it is necessary at the outset to say that this means a society of human beings, which – so far as those still living in the flesh are concerned – is a visible community among the other human communities. The question, 'What are its boundaries?', is part of the question we have to discuss, but just for that reason it is important to make clear that we are speaking of a society which *has* discernible boundaries. We are not speaking of an abstract noun, or of an invisible platonic idea. It is true that the Church includes those who, having died in faith, are now beyond our sight, but await with us the final day of judgment, resurrection and victory. We are not called upon to determine among them who are and who are not of the Church. They are in God's hands. But in respect of those now living in the flesh that responsibility is given to us. We are called upon to recognise and join ourselves to God's visible congregation here on earth. This congregation is truly known only to faith, because it is constituted in and by the Holy Spirit. But it is a visible congregation. As Schmidt says (in the article in Kittel's Dictionary to which I shall refer several times[5]), it is 'precisely as visible and temporal as the Christian man'. The point is so important that we must devote some attention to it before closing this introductory lecture.

The whole core of biblical history is the story of the calling of a visible community to be God's own people, His royal priesthood on earth, the bearer of His light to the nations. Israel is, in one sense, simply one of the petty tribes of the Semitic world. But Israel – the same Israel – is also the people of God's own possession. In spite of all Israel's apostasy, Israel is His, for His gifts and calling are without repentance. This little tribe, and no other, is God's royal priesthood, His holy nation. And the same is true in the New Testament. There is an actual, visible, earthly company which is addressed as 'the people of God', the 'Body of Christ'. It is surely a fact of inexhaustible significance that what our Lord left behind Him was not a book, nor a creed, nor a system of thought, nor a rule of life, but a visible community. I think that we Protestants cannot too often reflect on that fact. He committed the entire work of salvation to that community. It was not that a community gathered round an idea, so that the idea was primary and the community secondary. It was that a community called together by the deliberate choice of the Lord Himself, and recreated in Him, gradually sought – and is seeking – to make explicit who He is and what He has done. The actual community is primary: the understanding of what it is comes second. The Church does not depend for its existence upon *our* understanding of it or faith in it. It first of all exists as a visible fact called into being by the Lord Himself, and our understanding of that fact is subsequent and secondary. This actual visible community, a company of men and women with ascertainable names and addresses, is the Church of God. It was present on the day of Pentecost, and the Lord added to it day by day those that were being saved.

The phrase Church or congregation or assembly of God (*ecclesia theou*), and the thing itself, are both carried over from the old dispensation. Schmidt shows in the article referred to that the essential meaning of the word depends upon the fact that *theou* always follows – expressed or understood. The word *ecclesia* by itself tells us nothing more than the English words 'meeting' or 'gathering'. We require to know who called the meeting, or who attended it. Here we are dealing with the Church or congregation of God. It derives its character not from its membership but from its Head, not from those who join it but from Him who calls it into being. It is God's gathering. And this

---

[5] Schmidt 1965.

explains the fact that, as Schmidt says, the singular and the plural can be used promiscuously and interchangeably, as they are in Acts and the Epistles, and both with the genitive *theou*. You can speak of God's gathering in Ephesus, of God's gathering in Smyrna, or of God's gatherings in Asia. This does not mean that the Church of Asia is made up of a number of local churches, or that the local churches are, so to say, subordinate 'branches' of the Church regarded as a whole. It means that God is gathering His own, alike in Ephesus and in Smyrna and in all Asia. 'Congregation of God' is equally the proper title for a small group meeting in a house, and for the whole worldwide family. This is because the real character of it is determined by the fact that God is gathering it. This may remind us of Christ's word, 'Where two or three are gathered together in my Name, there am I in the midst of them' (Matt. 18.20).

There is an analogy here with the use of the word 'Kingdom'. In the New Testament the phrase *basileia tou theou* means primarily the presence and action of the kingly power of God. The operative word – so to say – is *theou*. But in loose speech the word Kingdom has been used alone, as though it denoted some sphere or order of things which could be thought of in itself. The situation is similar, says Schmidt, with regard to the word *ecclesia*. The operative word is *theou* or *Christou*. It is the church or congregation which God is gathering in every place. It is God's Church and its whole character derives from that fact. The moment you begin to think of it as a thing in itself, you go astray. The God whose gathering it is may never, even for temporary purposes of thought or argument, be excluded from the picture. But at the same time it is a real gathering. God is really working. Therefore there is a real congregation. It is these people here whom He has gathered, and this is the Church of God.

In contradiction to this, the idea of the invisible Church, in its popular use, derives its main attraction – unless I am much mistaken – from the fact that each of us can determine its membership as he will. It is *our* ideal Church, containing the people whom we – in our present stage of spiritual development – would regard as fit members. And obviously the Church – so regarded – is a mere appendage to our own spirituality. It is not the Church of the Bible, but a mere idea which may take as many different and incongruous visible embodiments as there are varieties of human spirituality. The congregation of God is something quite different. It is the company of people whom it has pleased God to call into the fellowship of His Son. Its members are chosen by Him, not by us, and we have to accept them whether we like them or not. It is not a segregation but a congregation, and the power by which it is constituted is the divine love which loves even the unlovely and reaches out to save all men. There is, of course, a very important truth in the idea of the invisible Church: that which constitutes the Church is invisible, for it is nothing less than the work of God's Holy Spirit. But the Church itself is the visible company of those who have been called by Him into the fellowship of His Son. The great Pauline words about the Church as the Body of Christ, the Bride of Christ, the Temple of God, are addressed to the actual visible and sinful congregations in Corinth and in Asia Minor, and indeed are spoken precisely in connection with the urgent need to correct the manifold sins and disorders which the Apostle found in them.

The idea of the invisible Church must be examined more fully later. It derives its main force from the obvious fact that the visible Church is full of things which are utterly opposed to the will of God as it is revealed in Jesus. But Luther, who employed this concept in his polemic against Rome, also pointed the way to the truth in the light of which the problem of sin in the Church is to be interpreted when he insisted that justification by faith is the article by which the Church stands or falls. The problem of how an unholy concourse of sinful men and women can be in truth the Body of Christ is the same as the problem of how a sinful man can at the same time be accepted as a child of God. *Simul justus et peccator* applies to the Church as to the Christian. It seems to me that our present situation arises precisely from the fact that this fundamental insight which the Reformers applied to the position of the Christian man was not followed through in its application to the nature of the Christian Church, and this is one of the clues which we shall seek to follow in the present course of lectures. As Schmidt says in the phrase already quoted: the Christian community is precisely as visible as the Christian man.

But the acceptance of this truth leaves vast issues unsettled. If we agree that the Church on earth is the visible body of those whom God has called into the fellowship of His Son, we have to ask: 'Where is that body to be found?' We know where it was on the day of Pentecost. It was there in Jerusalem. But where is it today? By what signs or works can a body rightly claim today to be the Church of God? We are all agreed that the Church is constituted by God's atoning acts in Christ Jesus – His incarnation, life, death, resurrection, ascension, His session at God's right hand and the gift of the Spirit. But how are we of the subsequent generations made participants in that atonement? *What is the manner of our ingrafting into Christ?* That is the real question with which we have to deal.

I think that there are three main answers to these questions, and these answers are embodied in great Christian communions which claim to be the Church.

The first answer is, briefly, that we are incorporated in Christ by hearing and believing the Gospel. The second is that we are incorporated by sacramental participation in the life of the historically continuous Church. The third is that we are incorporated by receiving and abiding in the Holy Spirit.

The moment one has stated these three positions in this bald way, it is at once apparent that they are far from being mutually exclusive, that very few Christians would deny the truth of any of them, and that there is an infinite variety of combinations of and approximations to these three positions. Nevertheless I think that we can best approach our problem by isolating these three positions. Classical Protestantism, especially in its Lutheran form, of course ascribes an immense value to the sacraments. But the major emphasis is upon faith, and faith comes by hearing, and therefore the pulpit dominates the rest of the ecclesiastical furniture. It also knows and speaks of the work of the Holy Spirit but does so with reserve. It is shy of enthusiasm, and is reluctant to give a large place to the claims of 'spiritual experience'. Catholicism honours preaching and acknowledges the necessity of faith, but it finds the centre of religious life rather in the sacrament than in the sermon. It acknowledges a real operation of the Holy Spirit sanctifying the believer, but gives the decisive place rather to the continuous sacramental order of the Church. The third type – for which it is difficult to find a single inclusive name – acknowledges and values preaching and the sacraments, but judges them by their experienced effects, and is not interested in the question of historical continuity. All these three answers to the question can obviously make effective appeal to Scripture in support of the truth for which they contend. It will be our aim in the succeeding lectures to look in turn at each of them, its basis in Scripture and in the nature of the Gospel, and – in a very cursory way – at some of the light which the history of the Church has shed upon it. We shall also try to show the distortions which have resulted from taking any one of these answers as alone the clue to the Church's nature. In the two concluding lectures we shall try to consider the nature of the Church in the light of the fact that it is a community *in via*, on its way to the ends of the earth and to the end of time.

Extract 2
'On Being the Church for the World' (1988)[6]

I was ordained in the Church of Scotland for foreign missionary service. I went out with about 11 years of the old British Raj still to go, as an old-fashioned district missionary, monarch of all I surveyed and telling everybody else what to do, but not yet having really learned to do it myself. Then I became a bishop of a diocese, with 12 years of very exciting experience in seeking to knit together two very different traditions, Anglican and Congregationalist – they put a Presbyterian in to keep the peace between the two! After that I became what I suppose one would call an ecumenical bureaucrat, after which I went back to India to the very different kind of role of being Bishop in Madras, an enormously expanding city.

Now, at the very end, I am beginning to learn what I ought to have learned at the beginning. I am the minister of a little United Reformed Church congregation in Birmingham. If you want to visit me you ask for Winson Green Prison and then look for the building just opposite, which Hitler unfortunately missed. That is where I try to minister. This is one of these typical inner-city areas where a demolition order was put on the church 35 years ago, which has neither been withdrawn nor carried out, and most of the houses round about and all the shops, have been knocked down. My congregation point to a field of thistles and say, 'That's where I was born and brought up',

---

[6] Newbigin 1988d: 25–42.

and the folk who have gradually been brought in are, as the local beat police-man said to me, all OHMS. I thought he was saying something about the prison, and said 'What exactly do you mean?' He said, 'Only Hindus, Muslims and Sikhs'. So we have this situation of a loyal congregation of white ageing people who, not of their own will, have been banished to the suburbs and do not have cars to travel in, trying to minister to a local area where it is not just thistles and tin cans but is mostly Hindus, Muslims and Sikhs. That is the sort of background out of which I shall try to speak.

I have a special interest in our topic, because in the days when I worked in Scotland as an SCM secretary I was in close contact with George MacLeod, who recalled the Church of Scotland to the parish principle. The Church of Scotland has a much more dominant position in Scotland than the Church of England does in England and the concept of the parish has been able to exer-cise a much more dominant influence in Scotland than it has in England. Later when I was Bishop in Madras, where we had about 120 congregations in this exploding city of three million people, I was constantly facing the fact that, although these congregations were growing very rapidly (I often used to have to point out that while Our Lord promised to be present where two or three are gathered, He never made that promise for two or three thousand), they were associational congregations. They were not congregations who felt that, intrinsically, they were responsible for that bit of the city. Therefore, I spent a lot of my ten years as Bishop in Madras trying to hammer the parish prin-ciple into congregations which were very largely shaped by the associational perspective.

My second point is the need for clarity about criteria. Obviously, changing sociological and cultural conditions, the enormous and rapid changes that are taking place in our society, are relevant to the way that we understand our task. But I do most deeply believe (and I have tried to carry that belief out in many different situations), that when we are looking for guidance and re-newal, we have fundamentally to go to the scriptures. We do so not in a sort of unintelligent and stupid way, just picking up odd texts, but with the faith by which the Church lives – that the character and the purpose of God is rendered apparent for us in the scriptures, and understood as we read them in the power of the Holy Spirit and in the fellowship of the whole Christian Church in all ages. I think it is important to say this, because all of our society, all of our thinking in the last two hundred years, has been dominated by the inductive principle: namely, that in trying to find our way what we do is to assemble all the facts and then, on the basis of all the facts, make some kind of theory about how we ought to go on.

The inductive principle, which has been so enormously creative in pro-ducing what we call a modern scientific world view, is a method which is of strictly limited application. It is not applicable to the question of our ultimate destiny because, in relation to our ultimate destiny, we shall not have all the data until the universe comes to a conclusion. We have to depend upon another kind of reasoning. The Church exists because God has revealed himself in the story of Israel, in the ministry and death and resurrection of Jesus Christ, and we are in the world as the bearers of a revelation of God's purpose for creation, and that is the only criterion, ultimately, by which we have to be guided. Obviously we have an enormous amount of discussion among ourselves about how we interpret the scriptures, about how we relate what is given to us in the scriptures to the new experiences that come to us as the world goes on its way. But we have to be quite unembarrassed and unambiguous about the fact that we find our ultimate criteria in that which has been given to us in revelation, which is not available by a process of observation and induction from the human situation as we see it.

In the New Testament, the Church is always and only designated by reference to two realities: one, God, God in Christ; and the other, the place where the Church is. And when, as we know from the Corinthian letters, the believers were forming themselves into groups involving another name ('I belong to Cephas, I belong to Paul, I belong to Apollos'), Paul is exceedingly tough in his dealing with them. He says 'You are carnal' – that is a very strong word but it is the appropriate word. Paul responds to that information by simply presenting to them again the Cross of Christ, in relation to which every other name is relativized. No other name can take the place that belongs alone to the name of Jesus Christ and, therefore, when believers propose to identify themselves with another name than that of the Lord Jesus Christ they are, as Paul said, 'carnal'. That is to say, they are falling back upon the flesh, upon *human* wisdom, power or spirituality, and they are therefore falling away from the Spirit, which is simply the life lived through what God has done finally and decisively in Jesus Christ. This is not incidental; it is fundamental.

Look at the interesting word which the New Testament writers use for the Church – *ekklesia theou*. There was a considerable number of words available in the contemporary vocabulary of that Hellenistic world to describe religious groups of people who were drawn together by a common quest for salvation under some kind of name, with some kind of discipline and with some kind of tradition of learning. There were a lot of Greek words for this, like *heranos*, *thiasos*, and so on, and the opponents of Christianity like Celsus constantly used those words to describe the Church. But in the first five centuries of the Christian Church you never find those words used. The Church never defines itself in the language that was used by these various religious groups that were composed of people in quest of salvation. They used only this word – *ekklesia*.

As you know, there are two words used in the Greek Old Testament to translate the congregation of God – there is the word *sunagogos* and the word *ekklesia*. The New Testament writers could have chosen either of those words; the word *sunagogos* was already the word used by the Jews in the Diaspora. But they chose this word *ekklesia*, which is the secular word for the assembly of all the citizens, to which every citizen is summoned and expected to attend, in which the business of the city is dealt with. Paul always used the word, all the New Testament writers use the word *ekklesia tou Theou*, the assembly of God;

the assembly, in other words, to which all are summoned without exception. And they are summoned not by the town clerk, but by God – not by Peter, not by Apollos, not by Paul, but by God. And that is why you have this interesting fact that you can use the word 'Church' or 'Churches' indiscriminately. You can say the Churches in Asia, or the Church in Asia because, in a sense, it is one reality, it is the one God who is summoning all people and, therefore, whether it is simply that group that meets in Thessalonika or whether it is the whole reality in the whole world, it is the same reality. It is the Catholic Church. The local church is not a branch of something else: the local church *is* the Catholic Church. It is the *ekklesia tou Theou*, and Paul uses the most realistic language about it. Even when he has to tell them that they are sinners in all kinds of respects, they are nevertheless the *ekklesia tou Theou*, defined simply by the 'place' where they meet, and any other definition is ruled out. And in the subsequent history of the Church this principle has been carried on. The basic units of the Church – the parish, the diocese – were all determined by secular realities. And that is fundamental.

I remember a fascinating discussion among a group of bishops about the proper size for a diocese. There were those who said that the size of the diocese must be determined by the number of people with whom a bishop can have a real pastoral relation. And in passionate opposition to that, I remember hearing Ted Wickham saying, 'No, the size of the diocese must be determined by the size of the human community. The diocese must be that which represents the purpose of God for this human community, and for the pastoral care of its members. You have got to make the proper arrangements. But you cannot determine the size of the diocese by the internal needs of the Church. It must be determined by the secular reality for which the Church is there'. That has been fundamentally right through the history of the Church, that the structural forms of the Church are determined by the secular reality, and not by the internal needs of the Church; and that I think is true to scripture.

The relation between the Church in a 'place' and the secular reality of that 'place' is intrinsic not extrinsic. It is not just that it happens to be located in that spot on the map. It is the Church of God *for that place*, and that is because the Church does not exist for itself but for God, and for the world which Jesus came to save. I once got into trouble after taking a confirmation service in one of those Madras churches which I think was more 'associational' than 'parish'. In the meeting of the Elders after the service I asked the naughty question, 'What is this church for?'. There was, of course, a long and embarrassed silence and then I received the answer, 'It caters to the needs of its members'. 'Then', I said, 'it should be dissolved.' The Church does not exist for its members.

One possible definition of the Church which I think is worth thinking about, is that the Church is the provisional incorporation of humankind into Jesus Christ. Jesus Christ is the last Adam. All humankind is incorporated in Adam. We are all part of this natural human world. Jesus is the last Adam and the Church is the provisional incorporation of humankind into Christ. It is provisional in two senses: provisional in the sense that not all humankind is so incorporated; and provisional in the sense that those who are so incorporated are not yet fully conformed to the image of Christ. So the Church is a provisional body; it looks forward. It looks forward to the full formation of Christ in all its members, to the growth of its members in holiness to the stature of Jesus Christ. It also looks forward in the other sense, that it is only the provisional incorporation of what is in God's intention the whole of humanity.

That is however nonsense unless we deal with the actual realities of humanity. In talking about the world you have to talk about that segment of the world in which you are placed, and it is in relation to that segment of the world in which you are placed that the Church has to be recognizable as *for* that place. Certainly, the geographical definition of that segment may not be the only one that is relevant, although I think it is the fundamental one. There can be other possible definitions of the 'place', but it is of the very essence of the Church that it is *for* that place, for that section of the world for which it has been made responsible. And the 'for' has to be defined Christologically. In other words, the Church is *for* that place in a sense which is determined by the sense in which Christ is *for* the world. Now, one would need to go into a whole theology of the atonement to develop this, but obviously Christ on his cross is in one sense totally identified with the world, in another sense totally separated from the world. The cross is the total identification of Jesus with the world in all its sin but in that identification the cross is the judgement of the world, that which shows the gulf between God and his world, and we must always, in every situation, be wrestling with both sides of this reality: that the Church is *for* the world *against* the world; the Church is *against* the world *for* the world. The Church is for the human community in *that* place, *that* village, *that* city, *that* nation, in the sense which is determined by the sense in which Christ is for the world. And that must be the determining criterion at every point.

I take, as a basic text, the Johannine version of the Great Commission. Missionary thinking has often been distorted by the fact that when people say 'The Great Commission', they always mean Matthew 28.18–end. There are in fact three basic forms of the Great Commission given to us. There is the Matthaean form. There is the Lukan form in Acts 1.6–8, 'You shall receive power when the Holy Spirit is come upon you and you shall be my witnesses'. Here, the mission of the Church is seen as a kind of overflow of Pentecost, not as a command laid upon us, but as a gift given to us. And then there is the Johannine version (20.19–23), and I would like to take that as a kind of basic paradigm for our understanding. I have said that we must understand the sense in which the Church is for the place Christologically; here it is, spelt out with the greatest clarity. The disciples are huddled together in a room, withdrawing themselves from the world in fear of the world and then, as he had promised, Jesus is present in their midst. 'Where two or three have gathered together, there am I.' And immediately his command, is 'Open the doors, go out into the world. As the Father sent me, so I send you.' And that is the launching of the Church. The Church is a movement launched into the world in the same sense in which Jesus is sent into the world by the Father.

I have always been grateful for the fact that in my first diocese, which was a largely rural diocese, about half of our congregation had no buildings whatsoever. And so for my first 12 years as a bishop I was normally conducting worship in the open street – all the services of the Church without exception. My picture of the Church formed in those years is deeply etched in my mind, the picture of a group of people sitting on the ground and a larger crowd of Hindus and Muslims and others standing around listening, watching, discussing; and, thank God, when one came back a few months later some of those would be in the group in the front. So you get the sense of the Church not as something drawn out of the world into a building, but the Church sent out into the world. And the operative word in our text is the word 'as': in the sentence, 'As the Father sent me, so I send you'.

Now that 'as' in a sense contains the whole crux of the question under discussion. The question is not, 'Does *society* need the parish church?', but 'Does God need the parish church?'. That is really the question we are wrestling with. And this 'as' contains the whole crux of the matter. How did the Father send the Son? Well, one could go back to that basic text in Mark 1.14, where Jesus comes into Galilee preaching the Gospel of God, the good news of God, and saying: 'The time is fulfilled, the Kingdom of God is at hand, repent and believe the good news – believe the good news that I'm telling you'. Now, that is the announcement of a fact. It is news in the strictest sense of the word.

I used to get awfully tired of being asked the same question when I was a bishop in India. My house in Madras was half-way between the airport and the city, so it was a wonderful place for ecumenical travellers to stop off and have lunch. And after lunch one always got the question, 'Are you optimistic or pessimistic about the future of the Church in India?', to which I had to develop the standard reply, which was, 'I believe that Jesus rose from the dead, and therefore the question doesn't arise'. In regard to a fact, one is not optimistic or pessimistic. One is believing or unbelieving. But in regard to a programme, you can be optimistic or pessimistic. We are deceived by the media who constantly suggest to us that the Church is a kind of good cause which we have to support, and if we don't support it, it's going to collapse. Yes, if it's a programme, then one can be optimistic or pessimistic. But about a 'fact', these are not the appropriate words. The question is, 'Do you believe or do you not?' Here is a fact, and of course it is not a religious fact. It does not belong to that little slot in *Time* magazine, between drama and sport, where religion is kept. It belongs to the opening section on world affairs. The Kingdom of God is at hand. The reign of God is at hand. In what sense is that news? It is not news to the Jews that God reigns. That is a fact that they have known for generations. What is new is that the reign of God is now a present reality, with which they have to come to terms. It is no longer a theological idea. It is no longer a vision in Heaven. It is no longer something in the distant future. It is now a reality with which they have to come to terms. But you cannot see it because you are facing the wrong way, you are looking in the wrong direction.

On one occasion I had to visit a village in Madras diocese which, like many of the villages, was miles from any road. In order to get to this village you had to cross a river and you could cross either at the north end or at the south end, and in their wisdom the congregation had decided that I was coming in at the south end. So they had a magnificent reception prepared, such as only a village congregation in India can prepare, with trumpets and drums and fireworks and garlands and fruit and everything you can think of. I came in at the other end and found a totally deserted village, which created a great crisis. I had to withdraw into the jungle and the whole village had to reorganize itself and face the other way, and then I appeared. Well now, that is what the word 'repent' means. It is a total U-turn of the mind. You are expecting something quite different from the reality that is coming upon you, and so you cannot see it.

When you have made the U-turn, it becomes possible to believe. And so there comes the call; 'Follow me', and Jesus calls Peter and Andrew and James and John. But the Kingdom is not obvious. There is the complaint: 'We don't see it. Where is it?' and so there are the parables and the 'mighty works' – the miracles. But finally, there is the final parable and the final miracle, which is the cross. Ultimately, the reign of God is present in the cross. And only to those who have been called as witnesses is the secret given that the cross is in fact not defeat but victory, that it is the victory of God over all the powers of this world. And therefore when Jesus said to them, 'As the Father sent me, so I send you', he showed them his hands and his side. In other words, the Church will be recognizable as the bearer of this mission on which the Father sent the Son and on which the Son sent the Church, in so far as the scars of the Passion are recognizable in its body. So you have that classic definition of mission, which has been so much ignored, in St Paul's letters, where he defines his apostolic mission as 'bearing in the body the dying of Jesus, that the life of Jesus might be manifest in our mortal flesh'.

I think we have often missed something by concentrating entirely on that Matthaean version which can produce the kind of triumphalist picture of the mission of the Church. Here, however, the Church is recognizable as the bearer of the Kingdom, the presence of the Kingdom, in so far as it is marked by the scars of the Passion. And the Passion of Jesus is not passive submission to evil, but the price paid for an active challenge to evil. The Passion is what the theologians call the Messianic tribulation, that which occurs at the frontier, where the reign of God challenges the rulers of this world. And that frontier runs right through the whole of human life and it is when the Church is at that frontier that it bears in its body both the marks of the Passion and the power of the risen life, of the Lord. And so then He immediately says 'Receive the Holy Spirit'. He gives to them the power of his risen life so that they may be the bearers of his reconciling work. 'Whosoever's sins you remit they are remitted, whosoever's sins you retain, they are retained.' The Church bears in its body the reconciling power of the atonement in so far as it is marked by the scars of the Passion, and it is therefore the bearer of the risen life. And, if you see the mission of the Church in that sense, then all this futile discussion between evangelism and social action disappears. It is a discussion which is irrelevant. It is meaningless when you see the mission of the Church in the terms that this Johannine passage offers. I suggest that its version of the Great Commission rules out three wrong ways of looking at the local church.

The first way is that which takes Church growth by itself as the criterion. Now I don't want to be unfair to the Church Growth school, because I know that they have been self-critical. My old friend Donald McGavran, who is the guru of the school, is perhaps a little less self-critical than he might be, but I know that the Church Growth school does try to get away from a kind of crude statistical measuring rod as the one criterion by which the Church is to be judged. Nevertheless, the main thrust of the Church Growth school is that the Church is there simply to make converts.

There you get the associational model neat. When you ask what is the purpose of making converts the answer is that they may make more converts, and when you ask what is the purpose of those further converts it is that they may make more converts. There is, in other words, an infinite regress. And, as we know from the medical analogy, the multiplication of cells unrelated to the purpose of the body is what we call cancer. That is a very hard thing to say, and I don't want to suggest that the folk who are in the Church Growth school are blind to these points. But I do think that there is a very sharp note of criticism that needs to be made against the idea that the Church exists simply to make more members, irrespective of that purpose for which the Father sent the Son into the world, which is that the presence of the reign of God might be a reality now.

The second way is the concept of the local church as simply the religious aspect of the local community, providing a focus for folk religion, but failing to confront people with the sharp call for radical conversion. This is perhaps a particular temptation for the established church. Remember, my background is Scotland, and I think the established church in Scotland is inclined to yield to that temptation even more than the established church in England. But it is the temptation for the established church. And one understands the power of it, the tremendously deep attachment that people have to their parish church, even though they would never under any circumstances go into it until the day of their funeral. I think this concept of folk religion is one The Grubb Institute has been interested in. It is one that certainly needs a good deal of analysis. Having lived most of my life in India, I am bound to say that much of what passes for religion here is just what in an Indian village we would call heathenism. But it is also mixed up with a lot of vestigial Christianity. It's a very complex mixture, this folk religion. One should certainly never be contemptuous of it, or despise it. One should always be on the look-out for the signals that it gives us of a recognition of realities beyond the visible world. But the New Testament is very clear that there is a radical repentance needed, a radical conversion, if one is to see the Kingdom of God.

Having said that, I want to say very strongly that conversion is the work of the Holy Spirit. Conversion is not something which can be programmed or accomplished or manipulated, even by the most expert evangelist. If there is one thing I have learned as a missionary it is that though I was in a situation where, thank God, a great many people were being brought to Christ through conversion, baptism and Church membership, the more I investigated the ways in which it had happened, the less I seemed to have to do with it. God works in a mysterious way. I have talked with scores of people who have come to the Christian faith from a Hindu or Muslim or Marxist or secular humanist background, and I am always impressed by the fact that the conversion of any person to Christ is a mysterious thing, in which there are many, many different elements, but the strategy is always in the hands of the Holy Spirit. The Holy Spirit Himself, and He alone, is the agent of conversion.

Thirdly, there is the concept of the Church in purely functional terms. I constantly hear people talking about 'Kingdom issues' versus 'Church issues'. 'Forget about the Church, all this ecclesiastical stuff which has nothing to do with God's will. On the last day, when the sheep and the goats are finally separated, they are all irrelevant questions. The important things are Kingdom issues: justice, peace, liberation.' This has a certain element of truth in it. But if it's taken by itself, then the Church just becomes a crusader for liberation which is a very different thing. The Church cannot fulfil the Kingdom purpose that is entrusted to it – and certainly the Kingdom is the horizon for all our thinking: that God reigns and that the Church is sent into the world as a sign of the Kingdom – if it sees its role in merely functional terms. The Church is sign, instrument and foretaste of God's reign for that 'place', that segment of the total fabric of humanity, for which it is responsible – a sign, instrument and foretaste for *that* place with its particular character.

I start with 'foretaste': the great New Testament word *arrabon*, which is such a wonderful word if you think about it. I was once making an elaborate explanation of this word *arrabon* in a class in the Selly Oak Colleges and explaining how scholars used to be puzzled by it because it is not a classical Greek word. And then they dug up a lot of parchments in the sands of Egypt and found that they were shopkeepers' accounts and that *arrabon* was just the word that the shopkeepers all used for cash on deposit, a pledge for a bill that you would pay at the end. And an Egyptian student in the class got up and said, 'Well, we still use the same word in Cairo'. Apparently the Arabic word *arbon* is still an operative word. If you want to buy a suit in Cairo you dicker about the cloth and about the style and all that, but before the tailor will start making it he will ask you to put down some cash which is spendable cash, it's not just an IOU. He can go and have a drink with it. The point of that cash, *arbon*, is that it is a pledge that the full bill is going to be paid. And that's the word that St Paul uses over and over again for the Holy Spirit.

If one might use an analogy nearer to home, think of one of those very posh dinner parties where you are kept standing for ages and ages and wonder whether there's ever going to be anything to eat. Then a trolley is brought on and there is a tinkle of glasses, and you are not only extremely glad to get a drink because you're getting very thirsty, but, what is much more important, that trolley is a sign that something is cooking in the kitchen. Now, the Holy Spirit is the *aperitif* for the messianic banquet. It is something which you enjoy now and that is the great thing in the charismatic movement. You enjoy it. There is something really to enjoy and celebrate now. It is not just an IOU, a promissory note. But the whole point of it is that it is a foretaste, that it assures you of a greater reality still to come. And in that sense the Church is a fore-taste of the Kingdom.

Here I think the Orthodox have something to teach us. The Orthodox often criticize us in the Western Church for a too functional view of the Church, and I think they are right. The Orthodox have always stressed the point that the Church is first of all a communion in the Holy Spirit in the life of the triune God, so that you must define the Church in ontological terms and not just in functional terms. The Church is defined by what it is. It is already a sharing in the life of God. I felt that tremendously on the occasions when I participated in Orthodox worship in Moscow, where the Church, in functional terms, is almost powerless. It is not allowed to do anything. It's not allowed to preach; it's not allowed to do social work, or to publish anything. But the Church continues to draw converts, and it's just because when you step out of a Moscow street into an Orthodox Church and find yourself in the middle of the Orthodox liturgy, you know that you have stepped out from under one jurisdiction into another jurisdiction. There is another reality there, which just by being what it is challenges the world outside and draws us, because we are made for God and our hearts are restless until they rest in Him. The first thing, therefore, is that the Church is a foretaste, and that means it will be different from the world. If it isn't, it's no good. Don't let us be afraid of the fact that the Church is different from the world, that the reality which we celebrate, which we share, which we rejoice in in our worship is a reality which the world treats as an illusion. We must not evade that, or try to slide over it or make it seem less sharp.

But in so far as it is a foretaste, it can also be an instrument. It can be an instrument through which God's will for justice and peace and freedom is done in the world. That takes the Church out into the secular world with whatever is relevant to the real needs of that secular world. If that is not hap-pening, how is the world going to know that the reality we talk about is true? I have recently been very much struck by the fact that if you look at what is often called the mission charge in Matthew Chapter 10, it begins by saying nothing about preaching at all; it simply says that Jesus chose these disciples, and gave them authority over unclean spirits to cast them out and to heal every disease and every infirmity. Then the names of the twelve disciples. And then he goes on to say, 'As you go, preach. And say the Kingdom of God is at hand'. If you look at it that way you can see that the preaching is the expla-nation of what is happening. If there is nothing happening, there is nothing to explain. But the preaching is a necessary explanation. Other people were healers. Other people cast out devils in the time of Jesus. But if you asked why are devils being cast out, why are people being healed, the answer is that the reign of God is upon you. The preaching explains the happenings.

I used to think about this often in my first charge. I was in a very sacred Hindu city. It is a place which has almost less Western influence than any other city in India, the ancient capital of the Pallava Empire, with a thousand temples and hundreds of thousands of pilgrims who come there every year. And I used to do a lot of street preaching. And I often used to think to myself, 'Now does this do any good? Is this just words?' And I used to reflect that it was because the people there know that we who are standing up and preaching like that are also healing their sick in the hospital, and are also teaching their boys and girls in the schools, and are also helping their village people to do something about their desperate poverty, and are also involved in attempts to make a more just society; it is because they know that, that the words will have some meaning. In other words, that the words without the deeds lack authority! The deeds without the words are dumb, they lack meaning. The two go together. And the Church, in so far as it is a foretaste of the reign of God, can also be an instrument of the reign of God, an instrument by which its justice is done. Not the only instrument of course. God has other instruments – the State is an instrument for God doing justice in the world. I think we have too much neglected this, that God has other instruments for the doing of His will in the world. But it is only the Church which can be the foretaste, the *arrabon* of the Kingdom.

Thirdly, a sign. The point of a sign is that it points to something that is not yet visible. If you want to go to Winson Green you don't put a sign up in Winson Green; you have a sign in Handsworth or Edgbaston or something, which says 'Winson Green'. The point of a sign is that it points to something which is real but not yet visible – which is not visible, not because it does not exist, but because it is over the horizon. Now the Church is a sign of the Kingdom, in so far as it is a foretaste. The Church is a sign of the Kingdom, pointing people to a reality which is beyond what we can see. And the necessary 'other-worldliness' of the Church seems to me to be something that has to be absolutely held on to. We do not compete with all the other agencies in the world that are offering solutions to human problems here and now. We are not offering utopian illusions. We are pointing people to a reality which lies beyond history, beyond death. But we are erecting in this world, here and now, signs – credible signs – that make it possible for people to believe that that is the great reality and, therefore, to join us in going that way.

In all this I've been presupposing the parish model, and I believe that the parish model is the right one. But I recognize the power of the associational model, particularly in its contemporary form. I have recently come to realize how much the 'denomination' has become the model by which we think of the Church, and yet how recent a thing the denomination is. We all tend to think of the Churches as various denominations. And yet the sociologists of religion point out that a denomination is something quite new in church history. It is not a schism, it is not a sect, it doesn't regard itself as the true Church in contrast to the false churches. It is one optional form for the Church, which is in a sense invisible. We cannot apply to the denomination the language that Paul applies to the Church in Corinth, which is the Church of God, full stop. These people in Corinth, sinners as they are, *are* the Church of God, not an expression of it or a version of it. My impression is that through the enormous power of the American model, which tends to dominate the rest of the world, all our Churches are being drawn into this denominational pattern. And my fear is that one of the results of Vatican II might be that the Roman Catholic Church allows itself to be drawn into that model too.

What the sociologists of religion have pointed out to us is that the denomination is precisely that visible form which the Church takes when a secularized society privatizes religion. The most striking fact about our culture is that we have a dichotomy between the private and the public worlds, a dichotomy which does not exist in pre-modern society. We have a private world of what we call values, where everyone is free to choose his or her own values. We do not say about these that they are true or false. We glory in our pluralism. We say that in the realm of values (and religious beliefs are included in that realm), everyone must be free to have his or her own faith. Pluralism reigns. We also have a public world of what we call facts, where pluralism does not reign, where things are either true or false; and religion does not belong to that field. It does not belong to the public world. Now the denomination is the visible form that the Church takes in a society which has accepted the secularization of public life and the privatization of religion, so that the variety of denominations corresponds, if you like, to the variety of brands available on the shelves of the supermarket. Everyone is free to take his choice.

The denomination, either singly or together, cannot be the bearer of the challenge of the Gospel to our society, because it is itself the outward and visible form of an inward and spiritual surrender to the ideology of that society. And, therefore, if we are to recover the sense that the local church *is* the Holy Catholic Church for that bit of the world in which God has set it (and that is the parish principle), then we have to challenge this whole acceptance of the denominational principle as being the normal form in which Church life is expressed. I find this both a necessary and a frightening thought. I cannot avoid it if I try to be faithful to the scriptures, but I find it terribly challenging.

I have referred earlier to my own personal situation. I am the minister of a very small URC congregation in Winson Green. How do I try to carry out these ideas there? We have the parish church; we have a Pentecostal church; we have another URC church; we have a black church called the Church of the Firstborn; and we, without formally being a Local Ecumenical Project (because I don't think our higher authorities would allow it), simply act together as clergy. We meet together constantly. We pray together constantly. We plan together constantly. We try to ask what, in spite of our divisions, our unity in Christ has to mean for the life of this community in Winson Green.

It seems to me that the development of that kind of local accepting of one another, in spite of our divisions and our misunderstandings, is the Catholic Church in that place seeking to erect the sign of the Kingdom for that place. These two things are mutually involved. I do not think we shall recover the true form of the parish until we recover a truly missionary approach to our culture. I do not think we shall achieve a truly missionary encounter with our culture without recovering the true form of the parish. These two tasks are reciprocally related to each other, and we have to work together on them both.

Further reading

Newbigin 1953: 32–110.
Newbigin 1977c: 115–28.

8.2 *The calling of the Church*

The following two extracts illustrate Newbigin's later writing on the 'calling' of local churches in the communities in which they are placed. The first is an article, 'Evangelism in the City', written in 1987 for the Reformed Review, *in which he explores the question of how the 'strange story of God made flesh, of a crucified Savior, or resurrection and new creation' can be made credible for secularized and post-Christian people 'whose entire training has conditioned them to believe that the real world is the world which can be satisfactorily explained and managed without the hypothesis of God'. In response, he introduces for the first time the idea of the local congregation as the 'hermeneutic of the gospel', which became a characteristic phrase in his later writings. It encapsulates his belief that in the context of a secularized and post-Christian West, the good news of the crucified and risen Jesus can really only be made comprehensible to the citizens of our contemporary culture as it is 'interpreted' through the life, words, and deeds of local church communities.*

The second extract is the chapter entitled 'The Congregation as Hermeneutic of the Gospel' from his 1989 book The Gospel in a Pluralist Society. *Here Newbigin explores what it could mean for the Church to make again the claim it made in its earliest centuries: 'the claim to provide the public truth by which society can be given coherence and direction'. This leads into a biblical and theological reflection on the calling of the local church to signal the reality of the Kingdom of God in the life of society, and to a further exploration of the idea of the local congregation as the 'hermeneutic' of the gospel. In the second half of the chapter Newbigin offers some practical illustrations of what this might mean, describing six characteristics that will mark the life of a congregation authentically seeking to live out its divine calling in the world.*

* * *

Extract 1
'Evangelism in the City' (1987)[7]

A couple of years ago I wrote a book entitled *Foolishness to the Greeks* in which I tried to explore the issues arising in a missionary encounter between the gospel and our contemporary Western culture. I tried in this to bring to bear the experience of a foreign missionary in India upon my present task as pastor of an inner-city congregation in Birmingham, England. In a friendly review of the book, the editor of the *Expository Times* challenged me to say how I would apply the rather abstract reasoning of the book to the concrete business of an ordinary inner-city parish. It was a very reasonable question, but not an easy one to answer. I felt bound to respond, not because I was confident about having the right answers, but because I could not evade the question.

The small congregation with which I now minister worships in a Victorian building situated immediately opposite the Winson Green Prison. In an early document the area served was defined by the following boundaries: 'HM Prison, the Lunatic Asylum, the railway and James Watt's famous factory.' It is now an area of very high unemployment, an exceptionally high proportion of single-parent families, and a rich ethnic mix in which native Anglo-Saxons form a minority. In relation to the nation as a whole, it would be described as an area of severe deprivation. In terms of absolute poverty, or, for example, in comparison with the Indian villages where most of my ministry has been exercised, its people have considerable material resources. Every home has a television and this provides, for most of the time, the visible center of life in the home. The commodity in shortest supply is hope.

The older inhabitants speak much of earlier times when there was a closely packed community in which neighbors knew and helped each other. Much of this was destroyed in the name of 'improvement.' The terrace houses were pulled down and their inhabitants forced to move to the suburbs. One 18-story tower-block was built; those who inhabit it have one main ambition, namely, to escape. Older people comfort themselves with nostalgic memories of the past, and are fearful of the present. For young people, especially for those of the Afro-Caribbean community, there is little reason for hope about the future. There is a famine of hope.

We have good news to tell. Before we think about how it is communicated, it is well to begin with a negative point. It is *not* communicated if the question uppermost in our minds is about the survival of the church in the inner city. Because our society is a pagan society, and because Christians have in general failed to realize how radical is the contradiction between the Christian vision and the assumptions that we breathe in from every part of our shared existence, we allow ourselves to be deceived into thinking of the church as one of the many 'good causes' which need our support and which will collapse if they are not adequately supported. If our 'evangelism' is at bottom an effort to shore up the tottering fabric of the church (and it sometimes looks like that) then it will not be heard as good news. The church is in God's keeping. We do not have the right to be anxious about it. We have our Lord's word that the gates of hell shall not prevail against it. The nub of the matter is that we have been chosen to be the bearers of good news for the whole world, and the question is simply whether we are faithful in communicating it.

But how to communicate? In my experience the hardest part is trying to communicate to the native Anglo-Saxon. The others are, in general, people who know that God is the great reality, even if we may judge that their knowledge of him is imperfect. To the Muslim the gospel is shocking but at least it is significant. To Hindus and Sikhs it is something really worth listening to, even if one finally decides that it is just another version of the 'religion' which is common to us all. Many of the Afro-Caribbean people in our inner cities are devout Christians whose faith, hope, and love put most of us to shame. But for the majority of the natives, the Christian story is an old fairy-tale which they have put behind them. It is not even worth listening to. One shuts the door and turns back to the television screen where endless images of the 'good life' are on tap at all hours.

How can this strange story of God made flesh, of a crucified Savior, of resurrection and new creation become credible for those whose entire mental training has conditioned them to believe that the real world is the world which can be satisfactorily explained and managed without the hypothesis of God? I know of only one clue to the answering of that question, only one real hermeneutic of the gospel: a congregation which believes it.

Does that sound too simplistic? I don't believe it is. Evangelism is not some kind of technique by means of which people are persuaded to change their minds and think like us. Evangelism is the telling of good news, but what changes people's minds and converts their wills is always a mysterious work of the sovereign Holy Spirit, and we are not permitted to know more than a little of his secret working. But – and this is the point – the Holy Spirit is present in the believing congregation both gathered for praise and the offering up of spiritual sacrifice, and scattered throughout the community to bear the love of God into every secular happening and meeting. It is they who scatter the seeds of hope around, and even if the greater part falls on barren ground, there will be a few that begin to germinate, to create at least a questioning and a seeking, and perhaps to lead someone to inquire about the source from which these germs of hope came. Although it may seem simplistic, I most deeply believe that it is fundamental to recognize that what brings men and women and children to know Jesus as Lord and Savior is always the mysterious work of the Holy Spirit, always beyond our understanding or control, always the result of a presence, a reality which both draws and challenges – the reality who is in fact the living God himself. And God's presence is promised and granted in the midst of the believing, worshipping, celebrating, caring congregation. There is no other hermeneutic of the gospel.

The first priority, therefore, is the cherishing and nourishing of such a congregation in a life of worship, of teaching, and of mutual pastoral care so that the new life in Christ becomes more and more for them the great and controlling reality. That life will necessarily be different from the life of the neighborhood, but the important thing is that it be different in the right way and not in the wrong way. It is different in the wrong way if it reflects cultural norms and assumptions that belong to another time or place; its language and style must be that of the neighborhood. But yet if it is *not* different from the life around it, it is salt which has lost its saltiness. We ought to recognize, perhaps more sharply than we often do, that there *must* be a profound difference between a community which adores God as the great reality, and one where it is assumed that God can be ignored.

But here a problem arises which is perhaps specially pressing in deprived areas. It happens over and over again, and it has happened throughout history, that the effect of conversion and Christian nurture is that a man or woman acquires new energies, a new hope and a new sense of dignity. And it can follow that their next step is to leave the area where they see only depression and despair and seek a better place. They leave the inner city and move to the leafy suburb. The congregation which bears the good news is weakened by its very success.

This means, surely, that in all our preaching and teaching about the hope which the gospel makes possible, we have to keep steadily in view the fact that what the gospel offers is not just hope for the individual but hope for the world. Concretely I think this means that the congregation must be so deeply and intimately involved in the secular concerns of the neighborhood that it becomes clear to everyone that no one or nothing is outside the range of God's love in Jesus. Christ's message, the original gospel, was about the coming of the kingdom of God, that is to say God's kingly rule over the whole of creation and the whole of humankind. That is the only authentic gospel. And that means that every part of human life is within the range of the gospel message: in respect of everything, the gospel brings the necessity for choice between the rule of God and the negation of that rule. If the good news is to be authentically communicated, it must be clear that the church is concerned about the rule of God and not about itself. It must be clear, that is, that the local congregation cares for the well-being of the whole community and not just for itself. This will – in the contemporary situation of such areas as Winson Green – lead to much involvement in local issues of all kinds of which it is not necessary in an article of this kind to give examples.

But, and this reminder is very necessary, this involvement must not become something that muffles the distinctive note of the gospel. The church ought not to fit so comfortably into the situation that it is simply welcomed as one of the well-meaning agencies of philanthropy. I think this warning is necessary because of the frequency with which I hear 'kingdom' set against 'church' in discussions about our role in society. I have insisted that the church's message is about the kingdom. The church is called to be a sign, foretaste, and instrument of God's kingly rule. But it is the *church* to which this calling is given. We have too often heard 'kingdom issues' set against 'church issues' in a way which conceals the fact that 'kingdom issues' are being conceived not in terms of the crucified and risen Jesus, but in terms of some contemporary ideology. In the heyday of progressive liberal capitalism, 'advancing the kingdom' meant enabling more and more people to share in its blessings. Today the phrase is more generally colored by Marxist ideas about the oppressed as the bearers of liberation. One has much sympathy with this in view of the contemporary attempt to persuade us that the way to maximize public good is to give free rein to private greed. We live in a society which is being ideologically polarized by this attempt as never before. It is not easy to keep one's head. But it is essential to keep all our thinking centered in the fact that the kingdom of God is present in Jesus – incarnate, crucified, risen, and coming in judgment. The life of the church in the midst of the world is to be a sign and foretaste of the kingdom only in so far as its whole life is centered in that reality. Every other concept of the kingdom belongs to the category of false messiahs about which the Gospels have much to say.

To put it even more sharply: the hope, of which the church is called to be the bearer in the midst of a famine of hope, is a radically other-worldly hope. Knowing that Jesus *is* king and that he *will* come to reign, it fashions its life and invites the whole community to fashion its life in the light of this reality, because every other way of living is based on illusion. It thus creates signs, parables, foretastes, appetizers of the kingdom in the midst of the hopelessness of the world. It makes it possible to act both hopefully and realistically in a world without hope, a world which trades in illusions. If this radically otherworldly dimension of the church's witness is missing, then all its efforts in the life of the community are merely a series of minor eddies in a current which sweeps relentlessly in the opposite direction.

But if one insists as I am doing upon the radically other-worldly nature of the Christian hope, it is necessary at once to protect this against a misunderstanding which has brought this aspect of the Christian message into disrepute. A recognition of this other-worldly element has often been linked with a privatization of religion characteristic of our post-Enlightenment culture. When this happens, the church is seen not as a bearer of hope for the whole community, but as a group of people concerned about their own ultimate safety. It is thus seen as something essentially antisocial. And, especially in a religiously plural society, this attracts justifiable censure. 'Evangelism' is then easily identified as 'proselytism' – the natural attempt of every human community to add to its own strength at the expense of others. From the point of view of people concerned with the total welfare of a human community, 'evangelism' is seen as something at best irrelevant and at worst destructive of human unity.

Is there a valid distinction between 'evangelism' and 'proselytism'? It must be admitted that in many discussions of this subject I have sensed that the distinction was very simple: evangelism is what we do and proselytism is what the others do. But I think it is possible to get beyond this obvious illusion. Everything depends upon the point which I made at the beginning, namely that the conversion of a human mind and will to acknowledge Jesus as Lord and Savior is strictly a work of the sovereign Holy Spirit of God, a mystery always beyond our full comprehension, for which our words and deeds may be – by the grace of God – the occasions but never the sufficient causes. Anything in the nature of manipulation, any exploiting of weakness, any use of coercion, anything other than the 'manifestation of the truth . . . in the sight of God' (2 Cor. 4.2) has no place in true evangelism. Of course all who know Jesus as Lord and Savior will rejoice when the company of those who love him grows. But they will also know that Jesus is much greater than any single understanding of him and that it therefore behoves us to make no final judgments until the Judge himself comes. It is Jesus alone who decides who will be summoned to be with us in the company of his witnesses.

If we are clear about the distinction between evangelism and proselytism, we shall be in a position to say something constructive about the matter of evangelism among people of other faiths. I have mentioned the fact that in the area of my present pastoral charge there is a large proportion of families of Muslim, Hindu, or Sikh faith. I have said that I find it much easier to talk with them on matters of religious faith than with most of the natives. But I am also frequently told, sometimes by Christian clergymen, that evangelism among my neighbors of other faiths is an improper activity and that I ought to confine myself to 'dialogue'. I find this exceedingly odd. We live in one neighborhood. For weal or woe we share the same life. We wrestle with the same problems. It is, surely, a very peculiar form of racism which would affirm that the good news entrusted to us is strictly for white Anglo-Saxons! After the last annual assembly of the United Reformed Church which had given much attention to evangelism, one of the participants wrote to the church's monthly paper to ask why it was that this word was reserved for our relations with unchurched Anglo-Saxons while in respect of our relations with people of other faiths we spoke only of 'dialogue.' The question was not answered.

How has it come that 'evangelism' and 'dialogue' are presented as opposed alternatives? Surely because both have been misunderstood. Evangelism has been misunderstood as proselytism. There is reason for this and all of us who seek to be true bearers of the gospel need to take note. If evangelism is the attempt of a religious group to enlarge itself by cajoling or manipulating those unable to resist, then it is rightly suspect. But a believing, celebrating, loving Christian fellowship, fully involved in the life of the wider community and sharing its burdens and sorrows, cannot withhold from others the secret of its hope and certainly cannot commit the monstrous absurdity of supposing that the hope by which it lives applies only to those of a particular ethnic origin.

And the word 'dialogue' too needs to be examined. No sharing of the good news takes place except in the context of a shared human life, and that means in part, the context of shared conversation. In such conversation we talk about real things and we try both to communicate what we know and to learn what we do not know. The sharing of the good news about the kingdom is part of that conversation and cannot happen without it. But why do we have to substitute the high-sounding word 'dialogue' at this point? Is it because we fail in the simple business of ordinary human conversation? I confess that in the Winson Green neighborhood we have not established any 'dialogue' between representatives of the different faiths, but we do have quite a lot of conversation. It is a kind of conversation which is not an alternative to but the occasion for sharing our hope, and it leads some people to ask the sort of questions that lead further.

Some, but not many. I certainly cannot tell any story of 'success' in terms of numbers. I guess that this is the experience of many working in such areas. The church remains small and vulnerable. I do not find in this ground for discouragement. The kingdom is not ours. The times and seasons are not in our management. It is enough to know that Jesus reigns and shall reign, and to be privileged to share this assurance with our neighbors and to be able to do and say the small deeds and words that make it possible for others to believe.

Extract 2
The Gospel in a Pluralist Society *(1989)*[8]

[. . . .] The Church cannot accept as its role simply the winning of individuals to a kind of Christian discipleship which concerns only the private and domestic aspects of life. To be faithful to a message which concerns the kingdom of God, his rule over all things and all peoples, the Church has to claim the high ground of public truth. Every human society is governed by assumptions, normally taken for granted without question, about what is real, what is important, what is worth aiming for. There is no such thing as an ideological vacuum. Public truth, as it is taught in schools and universities, as it is assumed in the public debate about political and economic goals, is either in conformity with the truth as it is given in Jesus Christ, or it is not. Where it is not, the Church is bound to challenge it. When we speak of a time when public truth as it was understood and accepted in Europe was shaped by Christianity, we do not – of course – mean that every person's behavior was in accordance with Christ's teaching. In that sense there has never been and there can never be a Christian society. But Europe was a Christian society in the sense that its public truth was shaped by the biblical story with its center in the incarnation of the Word in Jesus.

What can it mean in practice to 'claim the high ground' for Christianity? Certainly it cannot mean going back to the past. The claim that I am making has often been and is now confused and corrupted by being represented as a conservative move, a move to restore the past. That is impossible and undesirable. We are – as always – in a new situation. The Church of the first three

[8] Newbigin 1989b: 222–33.

centuries was essentially a martyr Church, bearing witness against the public doctrine of the time. It could have accepted, but did not accept, the protection offered by Roman law to the private exercise of religion as a way of personal salvation. Though a small minority, it challenged the public doctrine of the time as false – and paid the price. When the old classical world view lost its confidence and disintegrated, it was perhaps inevitable that the ruling power should turn to the Church as the integrating power for a new social order. That had enormous consequences for good over the succeeding millennium. It created the Christian civilization of Europe. But it also led the Church into the fatal temptation to use the secular power to enforce conformity to Christian teaching. It is easy to condemn this with hindsight, but one has to ask: 'How can any society hold together against the forces of disruption without some commonly accepted beliefs about the truth, and – therefore – without some sanctions against deviations which threaten to destroy society?' These are agonizingly difficult questions and there are no simple answers valid for all circumstances. What is clear, however, is that the cohesion of European Christendom was shattered by internal dispute erupting into bloody warfare, and that in the seventeenth and eighteenth centuries Europe turned to another vision of public truth, a vision inspired by the achievements of the new science and eventually embodied in the idea of a secular state. No one, surely, can fail to acknowledge with gratitude the achievements of this period of human history. But no one can be blind to the evidence that the liberal, secular democratic state is in grave trouble. The attacks on it from powerful new religious fanaticisms are possible only because its own internal weaknesses have become so clear: the disintegration of family life, the growth of mindless violence, the vandalism which finds satisfaction in destroying whatever is comely and useful, the growing destruction of the environment by limitless consumption fueled by ceaseless propaganda, the threat of nuclear war, and – as the deepest root of it all – the loss of any sense of a meaningful future. Weakened from within, secular democratic societies are at a loss to respond to religious fanaticism without denying their own principles. What could it mean for the Church to make once again the claim which it made in its earliest centuries, the claim to provide the public truth by which society can be given coherence and direction?

Certainly it cannot mean a return to the use of coercion to impose belief. That is, in any case, impossible. Assent to the claim of Christ has to be given in freedom. But it is never given in a vacuum. The one to whom the call of Jesus comes already lives in a world full of assumptions about what is true. How is this world of assumptions formed? Obviously through all the means of education and communication existing in society. Who controls these means? The question of power is inescapable. Whatever their pretensions, schools teach children to believe something and not something else. There is no 'secular' neutrality. Christians cannot evade the responsibility which a democratic society gives to every citizen to seek access to the levers of power. But the issue has never confronted the Church in this way before; we are in a radically new situation and cannot dream either of a Constantinian authority or of a pre-Constantinian innocence.

What is to be done? How is it possible that the one who was nailed help-less to a cross should be seen by society as the ultimate source of power? Here is the piercing paradox at the heart of any attempt to talk about 'claiming the high ground.' No text of the Old Testament is more frequently quoted in the New than the terrible words of Yahweh to Isaiah: 'Go and say to this people: "Hear and hear but do not understand; see and see but do not perceive." Make the heart of this people fat and their ears heavy and shut their eyes, lest they see with their eyes and hear with their ears and understand with their hearts, and turn and be healed' (Isa. 6.9–10). It is quoted in all the Gospels, in Acts, by St Paul. Yet Paul is tireless in his effort to bring the gospel to the Gentiles, and is confident that God's purpose cannot fail. He is sure that in the end the fullness of the Gentiles will come in and all Israel will be saved (Rom. 11.25–26). How do we reconcile these elements in the New Testament teaching? It is only when we hold them both together that we begin to grasp the 'impossible possibility' of salvation. This ought to deliver us from being impressed by the various proposals which are frequently made to the effect that if we will adopt the proper techniques for evangelism, we can be assured of success. It ought to inoculate us against the Pelagianism which tends to infect missionary thinking, the Pelagianism which supposes that the conversion of the world will be our achievement. It ought to direct our minds away from our programs to the awesome reality of God whose sovereignty is manifest in what the world calls failure, and whose 'folly' is wiser than the wisdom of the world (1 Cor. 1.25). It ought to help us to understand why, at the end of his long discussion of these matters, St Paul can only exclaim: 'O the depth of the riches and wisdom and knowledge of God. How unsearchable are his judgments and how inscrutable his ways!' (Rom. 11.33). The conversion of the nations is, and can only be, the supernatural work of God. What, then, is our role?

In a necessary reaction against the idea of a Church which acts as God's viceroy on earth, a triumphalist Church, we have in recent years emphasized the servant role of the Church. We are here rightly seeking to follow the example of Jesus, who defined his role as that of servant (for example, Mark 10.45). But this servant role can be misunderstood. Jesus did not allow him-self to be simply at the disposal of others. The temptations at the outset of his ministry were temptations to do what people wanted the Messiah to do. While he responded instantly to the touch of human need, he yet retained the sovereignty in his own hands. He chose the times, place, and manner of his acts. Even at the end he was in control. 'No one,' he said, 'takes my life from me; I lay it down of my own accord' (John 10.18). The most sustained discussion of this issue is given in the Johannine account of the feeding of the multitude and its sequel (John 6).

The story begins with an act of pure compassion. A great crowd has gathered around Jesus, not because they believe his teaching but because they have seen his healing (vv. 1–2). They are hungry. Jesus sees that they are hungry and – without any request from the crowd – he provides enough and more than enough to satisfy them (vv. 3–13). The result is a surge of popular enthusiasm to make Jesus their leader. A real 'people's movement' is about to be born (v. 14)! The response of Jesus is to distance himself completely from this movement. He will have nothing to do with it (v. 15). The disciples, perplexed, set off for home. The crowds are determined to find him, and eventually succeed (vv. 16–25). Jesus tells them the real reason for their pursuit. They have been fed, but now they are hungry again. They should seek the food that gives not temporary but enduring life. When they (naturally) ask what work they must do to get this eminently desirable food, they are told that what is required is not a work, but faith. They are to believe the one whom God has sent (vv. 26–29). After further perplexed questioning the crowd is finally told that the food in question is Jesus himself (vv. 30–40). In response to the 'murmuring' (which forms the background to the story of the giving of manna in the desert) Jesus quietly replies that no one can come to him unless the Father draws him (vv. 41–44). In the ensuing debate the lines harden and the hearers refuse to hear more. Even many of Jesus' disciples leave him. Jesus is left with 'the twelve' and warns them that even in this group of his closest friends there is treachery (vv. 45–71).

If we take this as a picture of what is involved in the offering of the gospel to the world, we have something very different from the picture of a successful exercise in public relations. Jesus is both totally compassionate and yet totally uncompromising about what is involved in coming to the fullness of life. There can be no compromise with false ideas about what it is that makes for fullness of life. To give bread to the hungry is an action of divine compassion and as such a sign of that which alone can satisfy the infinite desires and needs of the human spirit. If the sign is confused with that which it signifies, the gift of life is forfeited. In serving human need, Jesus remains master. The servant who washes the feet of his disciples is their master and lord, and it is in serving that he exercises his lordship (John 13.13–14).

What does this say about the way in which the Church is authorized to represent the kingdom of God in the life of society? It excludes, certainly, the idea that it will be by exercising the kind of power which 'the rulers of the Gentiles' exercise (Luke 22.25–26). But it excludes also the idea that the Church simply 'responds to the aspirations of the people.' And it excludes ideas which have been too prevalent in 'evangelical' circles, ideas which portray the Church in the style of a commercial firm using modern techniques of promotion to attract members. How is it possible for the Church truly to represent the reign of God in the world in the way Jesus did? How can there be this combination of tender compassion and awesome sovereignty? How can any human society be both the servant of all people in all their needs, and yet at the same time responsible only to God in his awesome and holy sovereignty? How can the Church be fully open to the needs of the world and yet have its eyes fixed always on God? I think there is only one way.

One of the very few missionary leaders of this century who recognized at an early date that the greatest contemporary challenge to the missionary movement is presented by 'modern' Western society was J. H. Oldham. No one did more to shape the ecumenical movement in its early days and to direct the attention of the Churches to the need to challenge the assumptions of contemporary society. It was said of him by close colleagues that, when he spoke of 'the Church,' 'it was never quite clear whether he was talking about the ordinary, parson-led congregation, or about something more exciting but less visible'.[9] Oldham did not expect very much from the 'ordinary, parson-led congregation,' and one can scarcely blame him. Much of the vitality which was imparted to the early organs of ecumenical action was due to the fact that professional ecclesiastics were balanced by a goodly sprinkling of highly competent lay-persons from business, government, and the professions. And yet I confess that I have come to feel that the primary reality of which we have to take account in seeking for a Christian impact on public life is the Christian congregation. How is it possible that the gospel should be credible, that people should come to believe that the power which has the last word in human affairs is represented by a man hanging on a cross? I am suggesting that the only answer, the only hermeneutic of the gospel, is a congregation of men and women who believe it and live by it. I am, of course, not denying the importance of the many activities by which we seek to challenge public life with the gospel – evangelistic campaigns, distribution of Bibles and Christian literature, conferences, and even books such as this one. But I am saying that these are all secondary, and that they have power to accomplish their purpose only as they are rooted in and lead back to a believing community.

Jesus, as I said earlier, did not write a book but formed a community. This community has at its heart the remembering and rehearsing of his words and deeds, and the sacraments given by him through which it is enabled both to engraft new members into its life and to renew this life again and again through sharing in his risen life through the body broken and the lifeblood poured out. It exists in him and for him. He is the center of its life. Its character is given to it, when it is true to its nature, not by the characters of its members but by his character. In so far as it is true to its calling, it becomes the place where men and women and children find that the gospel gives them the framework of understanding, the 'lenses' through which they are able to understand and cope with the world. In so far as it is true to its calling, this community will have, I think, the following six characteristics:

1   It will be a community of praise. That is, perhaps, its most distinctive character. Praise is an activity which is almost totally absent from 'modern' society. Here two distinct points can be made.

---

[9] Letter from J. Eric Fenn to Newbigin (January, 1937).

(a)   The dominant notes in the development of the specifically 'modern' view of things has been [. . .] the note of scepticism, of doubt. The 'hermeneutic of suspicion' is only the most recent manifestation of the belief that one could be saved from error by the systematic exercise of doubt. It has followed that when any person, institution, or tradition has been held up as an object worthy of reverence, it has immediately attracted the attention of those who undertook to demonstrate that there was another side to the picture, that the golden image has feet of clay. I suppose that this is one manifestation of that 'disenchantment' which Weber regarded as a key element in the development of 'modern' society.[10] Reverence, the attitude which looks up in admiration and love to one who is greater and better than oneself, is generally regarded as something unworthy of those who have 'come of age' and who claim that equality is essential to human dignity. With such presuppositions, of course, the very idea of God is ruled out. The Christian congregation, by contrast, is a place where people find their true freedom, their true dignity, and their true equality in reverence to One who is worthy of all the praise that we can offer.

(b)   Then, too, the Church's praise includes thanksgiving. The Christian congregation meets as a community that acknowledges that it lives by the amazing grace of a boundless kindness. Contemporary society speaks much about 'human rights.' It is uncomfortable with 'charity' as something which falls short of 'justice,' and connects the giving of thanks with an unacceptable subservience. In Christian worship the language of rights is out of place except when it serves to remind us of the rights of others. For ourselves we confess that we cannot speak of rights, for we have been given everything and forgiven everything and promised everything, so that (as Luther said) we lack nothing except faith to believe it. In Christian worship we acknowledge that if we had received justice instead of charity we would be on our way to perdition. A Christian congregation is thus a body of people with gratitude to spare, a gratitude that can spill over into care for the neighbor. And it is of the essence of the matter that this concern for the neighbor is the overflow of a great gift of grace and not, primarily, the expression of commitment to a moral crusade. There is a big difference between these two.

2   Second, it will be a community of truth. This may seem an obvious point, but it needs to be stressed. As I have tried to show in these chapters, it is essential to recognize that all human thinking takes place within a 'plausibility structure' which determines what beliefs are reasonable and what are not. The reigning plausibility structure can only be effectively challenged by people who are fully integrated inhabitants of another. Every person living in a 'modern' society is subject to an almost continuous bombardment of ideas, images, slogans, and stories which presuppose a plausibility structure radically different from that which is controlled by the Christian understanding of human nature and destiny. The power of contemporary media to shape

---

[10]   (See e.g. Weber 1998: 155.)

thought and imagination is very great. Even the most alert critical powers are easily overwhelmed. A Christian congregation is a community in which, through the constant remembering and rehearsing of the true story of human nature and destiny, an attitude of healthy scepticism can be sustained, a scepticism which enables one to take part in the life of society without being bemused and deluded by its own beliefs about itself. And, if the congregation is to function effectively as a community of truth, its manner of speaking the truth must not be aligned to the techniques of modern propaganda, but must have the modesty, the sobriety, and the realism which are proper to a disciple of Jesus.

3   Third, it will be a community that does not live for itself but is deeply involved in the concerns of its neighborhood. It will be the church for the specific place where it lives, not the church for those who wish to be members of it – or, rather, it will be for them in so far as they are willing to be *for* the wider community. It is, I think, very significant that in the consistent usage of the New Testament, the word *ekklesia* is qualified in only two ways; it is 'the Church of God,' or 'of Christ,' and it is the church of a place. A Christian congregation is defined by this twofold relation: it is God's embassy in a specific place. Either of these vital relationships may be neglected. The congregation may be so identified with the place that it ceases to be the vehicle of God's judgment and mercy for that place and becomes simply the focus of the self-image of the people of that place. Or it may be so concerned about the relation of its members to God that it turns its back on the neighborhood and is perceived as irrelevant to its concerns. With the development of powerful denominational structures, nationwide agencies for evangelism or social action, it can happen that these things are no longer seen as the direct responsibility of the local congregation except in so far as they are called upon to support them financially. But if the local congregation is not perceived in its own neighborhood as the place from which good news overflows in good action, the programs for social and political action launched by the national agencies are apt to lose their integral relation to the good news and come to be seen as part of a moral crusade rather than part of the gospel. The local congregation is the place where the proper relation is most easily and naturally kept.

4   Fourth, it will be a community where men and women are prepared for and sustained in the exercise of the priesthood in the world. The Church is described in the New Testament as a royal priesthood, called to 'offer spiritual sacrifices acceptable to God' and to 'declare the wonderful deeds of him who called you out of darkness into his marvellous light' (1 Pet. 2.5, 9). The office of a priest is to stand before God on behalf of people and to stand before people on behalf of God. Jesus is himself the one High Priest who alone can fulfill and has fulfilled this office. The Church is sent into the world to continue that which he came to do, in the power of the same Spirit, reconciling people to God (John 20.19–23). This priesthood has to be exercised in the life of the world. It is in the ordinary secular business of the world that the sacrifices of love and obedience are to be offered to God. It is in the context of secular affairs that the mighty power released into the world through the

work of Christ is to be manifested. The Church gathers every Sunday, the day of resurrection and of Pentecost, to renew its participation in Christ's priesthood. But the exercise of this priesthood is not within the walls of the Church but in the daily business of the world. It is only in this way that the public life of the world, its accepted habits and assumptions, can be challenged by the gospel and brought under the searching light of the truth as it has been revealed in Jesus. It may indeed be the duty of the Church through its appointed representatives – bishops and synods and assemblies – to speak a word from time to time to the nation and the world. But such pronouncements carry weight only when they are validated by the way in which Christians are actually behaving and using their influence in public life. It is, of course, also true that individual Christians will be weakened in their efforts to live out the gospel in secular engagements if what they are doing does not have the support of the Church as a whole. There is a reciprocal relationship between official pronouncements and individual commitment. It has to be said, I think, that in recent years there has been a widely perceived disjunction between official pronouncements and individual commitment, and it is important to stress the fact that the former without the latter are ineffective.

Two implications of this need to be stated:

(a) The congregation has to be a place where its members are trained, supported, and nourished in the exercise of their parts of the priestly ministry in the world. The preaching and teaching of the local church has to be such that it enables members to think out the problems that face them in their secular work in the light of their Christian faith. This is very difficult. It is divisive. One pastor, trained in the kind of theology which is traditional, is not equipped to fulfill this function. There is need for 'frontier-groups,' groups of Christians working in the same sectors of public life, meeting to thrash out the controversial issues of their business or profession in the light of their faith. But there is also need to consider how far the present traditions of ministerial training really prepare ministers for this task. The report of the Archbishop's Committee on Urban Priority Areas contained devastating comments on the inappropriateness of current ministerial training as perceived by those working in these areas.[11] I realize how extremely difficult it is to find the way forward in this matter, but it seems clear that ministerial training as currently conceived is still far too much training for the pastoral care of the existing congregation, and far too little oriented towards the missionary calling to claim the whole of public life for Christ and his kingdom.

(b) A second implication is this: a Christian congregation must recognize that God gives different gifts to different members of the body, and calls them to different kinds of service. St Paul's letters contain many eloquent expositions of this fact. Yet there is a persistent tendency to deny this and to look for a

---

[11] Report 1985: 119 (para. 6:56).

uniform style of Christian discipleship. People look for a church which is all geared to explicit evangelism, or to radical social action; a church where all speak in tongues and dance in the aisles, or a church where all is decorous and staid. This is, of course, exactly the danger against which Paul warns in the long description of the body in 1 Corinthians 12. The ear should not demand that the whole body be ears, nor the eye that all should be eyes. A bagful of eyes is not a body. Only when a congregation can accept and rejoice in the diversity of gifts, and when members can rejoice in gifts which others have been given, can the whole body function as Christ's royal priesthood in the world.

5   Fifth, it will be a community of mutual responsibility. If the Church is to be effective in advocating and achieving a new social order in the nation, it must itself be a new social order. The deepest root of the contemporary malaise of Western culture is an individualism which denies the fundamental reality of our human nature as given by God – namely that we grow into true humanity only in relationships of faithfulness and responsibility towards one another. The local congregation is called to be, and by the grace of God often is, such a community of mutual responsibility. When it is such, it stands in the wider community of the neighborhood and the nation not primarily as the promoter of programs for social change (although it will be that) but primarily as itself the foretaste of a different social order. Its members will be advocates for human liberation by being themselves liberated. Its actions for justice and peace will be, and will be seen to be, the overflow of a life in Christ, where God's justice and God's peace are already an experienced treasure.

6   And finally it will be a community of hope. As I have already said, I think that one of the most striking features of contemporary Western culture is the virtual disappearance of hope. The nineteenth-century belief in progress no longer sustains us. There is widespread pessimism about the future of 'Western' civilization. Many Christian writers speak of our culture in accents of embarrassment, guilt, and shame. In his study of contemporary Western society, the Chinese Christian writer Carver T. Yu finds as its two key elements 'technological optimism and literary pessimism'.[12] Technology continues to forge ahead with more and more brilliant achievements; but the novels, the drama, and the general literature of the West are full of nihilism and despair. It is not surprising that many Western people are drawn towards Eastern types of spirituality in which the struggle to achieve the purpose of a personal creator is replaced by the timeless peace of pantheistic mysticism. As I have tried to suggest in an earlier chapter, the gospel offers an understanding of the human situation which makes it possible to be filled with a hope which is both eager and patient even in the most hopeless situations. I must repeat again that it is only as we are truly 'indwelling' the gospel story, only as we are so deeply involved in the life of the community which is shaped by this story that it becomes our real 'plausibility structure,' that we are able steadily and

---

[12] Yu 1987: 1.

confidently to live in this attitude of eager hope. Almost everything in the 'plausibility structure' which is the habitation of our society seems to contradict this Christian hope. Everything suggests that it is absurd to believe that the true authority over all things is represented in a crucified man. No amount of brilliant argument can make it sound reasonable to the inhabitants of the reigning plausibility structure. That is why I am suggesting that the only possible hermeneutic of the gospel is a congregation which believes it.

If the gospel is to challenge the public life of our society, if Christians are to occupy the 'high ground' which they vacated in the noontime of 'modernity,' it will not be by forming a Christian political party, or by aggressive propaganda campaigns. Once again it has to be said that there can be no going back to the 'Constantinian' era. It will only be by movements that begin with the local congregation in which the reality of the new creation is present, known, and experienced, and from which men and women will go into every sector of public life to claim it for Christ, to unmask the illusions which have remained hidden and to expose all areas of public life to the illumination of the gospel. But that will only happen as and when local congregations renounce an introverted concern for their own life, and recognize that they exist for the sake of those who are not members, as sign, instrument, and foretaste of God's redeeming grace for the whole life of society.

Further reading

Newbigin 1984: 1–14.
Newbigin 1990a: 148–57. (Reproduced on pp. 229–36 of this volume.)

9

The gospel and world religions

———◆◆◆———

From early on in his time at Kanchipuram in the 1930s, Newbigin's weekly readings and dialogue at the monastery of the Ramakrishna Mission brought him face-to-face with committed adherents of a living faith other than Christianity. This, alongside his wider experiences in India and beyond, bring a wealth of experience to his discussions of inter-faith dialogue. These are well illustrated by his 1977 article, 'The Basis, Purpose and Manner of Inter-Faith Dialogue', which is the first extract reproduced below. It was originally prepared in November 1975 for the Division for World Mission and Ecumenism of the Lutheran Church of America. In it, Newbigin holds together the firm belief that the grace of God is at work among the different world faiths with the fact that the only appropriate starting point for Christians in dialogue with others is the fact that they have been 'laid hold of by Jesus Christ' to be his witnesses. This is an act of pure grace that precedes even our knowledge of it, and becomes the deepest commitment, which transcends all others. The second part of the article outlines his approach to the practice of inter-faith dialogue in the light of this calling, and is developed in characteristically trinitarian terms.

   The second extract is a more recent piece, 'Religious Pluralism: A Missiological Approach', published in 1993. It originated as a contribution Newbigin gave to a symposium at the Pontifical Gregorian University in Rome in February 1993 on the theme of the 'Theology of Religions: Christianity and Other Religions'. Here Newbigin's approach to the question of other faiths is set in the broader context of the cultural transition from 'modernity' to 'postmodernity'. In this setting, the challenge of a world with many 'stories' to tell is further sharpened by the postmodern assumption that we have no ultimate criteria by which to judge between them. Newbigin develops his conviction that it is only from within the Christian framework of faith and conviction that Christianity can be defended. He then goes on to develop an appropriate understanding of inter-religious dialogue by distinguishing between an overbearing form of proselytism on the one hand, and an empty and uncommitted use of words on the other.

* * *

Extract 1
'The Basis, Purpose and Manner of Inter-Faith Dialogue'
(1977)[1]

I

All intellectual activity implies some presuppositions. Thoughts can only be formulated in words and these words have been formed by the previous thought of the community whose language they are. Even the most radical scepticism can only be formulated in terms of presuppositions which are – for the moment – unquestioned.[2]

In dialogue between representatives of different faiths the participants are called upon to submit their most fundamental presuppositions, the very grammar and syntax of their thought, to critical questioning. It is therefore essential at the outset to lay bare the presuppositions of the undertaking. No one enters into a conversation without presuppositions, and it is essential that these should be brought into the open. No one can bring a totally open mind to a dialogue except an imbecile who has not yet learned to use human language.

1   Modern interest among Western Christians in the comparative study of religion is a product of the eighteenth-century Enlightenment. Looking back upon this period it is easy to identify the presuppositions which lay behind the study. All religions, including Christianity, were required to make good their claims at the bar of reason, and reason was understood in terms of the tradition of thought which stemmed from Descartes. Lineal descendants of this type of thinking are the various theories of religion as illusion-theories which John Oman has classified under a threefold scheme: theories of a Hegelian type which see religion as a primitive, anthropomorphic science; theories of the Schleiermacher type which see religion as a product of human psychology; and theories of a Kantian type which see religion as the result of the moral pressure of the community upon the individual.[3] Theories of this kind are the logical development of the presupposition – implicit in many studies in comparative religion – that there are criteria drawn from outside of the religious experience itself by which the religious experience can be evaluated.

2   A much more ancient model of inter-religious dialogue takes as its basic presupposition that there is a common core of reality within all the varieties of religious experience. The classic statement of this position is the famous voice from the Rig Veda, 'The real is one, though sages name it variously.' In the long history of Indian religion this faith has been pressed to its farthest limit. Its most eloquent modern exponent has been Dr S. Radhakrishnan.[4]

---

[1]   Newbigin 1977a: 253–70.
[2]   Polanyi 1958: 269–98 (ch. 9, 'The Critique of Doubt').
[3]   Oman 1931: 29–46.
[4]   E.g. Radhakrishnan 1939.

More often it is present as an unexpressed and unexamined axiom. When W. Cantwell Smith[5] recommends that we should cease talking about different 'religions' and speak rather of the religiousness which is the human response to the one transcendent reality, and when John Hick[6] calls for a 'Copernican revolution' in our thought about religions so that we can see God as the one centre around which all the religions revolve, it is accepted as axiomatic that there is one reality behind or within all the forms of religion. Most frequently this has been identified with the mystical experience.

3   A third model for inter-religious dialogue is based on the practical need for political and social unity. One might find the classic example of this in the work of the Emperor Akbar (1556–1605), who encouraged representatives of different faiths to engage in dialogue and experimented with a universal religion designed to knit into one all the people of his empire. India since 1947 has again witnessed the strong pressure of the need for national unity upon the thinking of responsible people in the various religious communities. This pressure can be understood in a superficial way which simply subordinates a concern for truth in religion to a concern for political unity. But it can also be understood in a more fundamental way. Outstanding Indian Christian thinkers such as Paul Devanandan and M. M. Thomas saw that both the renaissance of Hinduism and the growth of a concern for nation-building were part of the consequences of the impact of Christ upon Indian society.[7] They therefore called their fellow Christians to the work of inter-faith dialogue in the context of the quest for national unity with the conviction that this was part of the continuing work of Christ in Indian society. The basis of their call to dialogue was in their Christian faith. It is a different matter when the basis of dialogue is simply the demand for national (or global) unity, without any deeper understanding of the reality on which the unity can be grounded. When dialogue is conducted in this way, religious truth is being subordinated to something else.

4   A Christian who participates in dialogue with people of other faiths will do so on the basis of his faith. The presuppositions which shape his thinking will be those which he draws from the Gospel. This must be quite explicit. He cannot agree that the position of final authority can be taken by anything other than the Gospel – either by a philosophical system, or by mystical experience, or by the requirements of national and global unity. Confessing Christ – incarnate, crucified and risen – as the true light and the true life, he cannot accept any other alleged authority as having right of way over this. He cannot regard the revelation given in Jesus as one of a type, or as requiring to be interpreted by means of categories based on other ways of understanding the totality of experience. Jesus is – for the believer – the source from whom

---

[5] Smith 1978.
[6] Hick 1993.
[7] Devanandan and Thomas 1960; Thomas 1969.

his understanding of the totality of experience is drawn and therefore the criterion by which other ways of understanding are judged.

In this respect the Christian will be in the same position as his partners in dialogue. The Hindu, the Muslim, the Buddhist and the Marxist each has his distinctive interpretation of other religions, including Christianity; and for each of them his own faith provides the basis of his understanding of the totality of experience, and therefore the criterion by which other ways of understanding – including that of the Christian – are judged.

The integrity and fruitfulness of the inter-faith dialogue depends in the first place upon the extent to which the different participants take seriously the full reality of their own faiths as sources for the understanding of the totality of experience.

II

If this is the basis upon which the Christian participates in the dialogue, what understanding of other faiths does this imply? Many different answers have been given and are given to this question. Many volumes would be needed to state and examine them. The following is only a series of headings for the purpose of orientation.

1   Other religions and ideologies are wholly false and the Christian has nothing to learn from them. On this three things may be said:

(a)   The sensitive Christian mind, enlightened by Christ, cannot fail to recognise and to rejoice in the abundant spiritual fruits to be seen in the lives of men and women of other faiths. Here we must simply appeal to the witness of Christians in all ages who have lived in friendship with those of other faiths.

(b)   In almost all cases where the Bible has been translated into the languages of the non-Christian peoples of the world, the New Testament word *Theos* has been rendered by the name given by the non-Christian peoples to the one whom they worshipped as the supreme being. It is under this name, therefore, that the Christians who now use these languages worship the God and Father of Jesus Christ. The very few exceptions, where translators have sought to evade the issue by simply transliterating the Greek or Hebrew word, only serve to prove the point; for the converts have simply explained the foreign word in the text of their bibles by using the indigenous name for God.[8] The name of the God revealed in Jesus Christ can only be known by using those names for God which have been developed within the non-Christian systems of belief and worship. It is therefore impossible to claim that there is a total discontinuity between the two.

---

[8] I owe this piece of information to a conversation with Dr Eugene Nida.

(c)   St John tells us that Jesus is the light that lightens every man. This text does not say anything about other *religions*, but it makes it impossible for the Christian to say that those outside the Church are totally devoid of the truth.

2   The non-Christian religions are the work of devils and their similarities to Christianity are the results of demonic cunning. This view is stated by Justin in his *Apology*, and is linked by him with the assertion that the Logos speaking through Socrates and others sought to lead men to the light and away from the work of demons – the Logos who was made man in Jesus Christ. A sharp distinction is here drawn between pagan religion (the work of demons) and pagan philosophy (in which the Logos was shedding his light). There are two points which should be made regarding this view.

(a)   It would be wise to recognise an element of truth here: the sphere of religion is the battlefield par excellence of the demonic. New converts often surprise missionaries by the horror and fear with which they reject the forms of their old religion – forms which to the secularised Westerner are interesting pieces of folklore and to the third-generation successors of the first converts may come to be prized as part of national culture. Religion – including the Christian religion – can be the sphere in which evil exhibits a power against which human reason and conscience are powerless. For religion is the sphere in which a man surrenders himself to something greater than himself.

(b)   Even the strange idea that the similarities to Christianity in the non-Christian religions are evidences of demonic cunning points to an important truth. It is precisely at points of highest ethical and spiritual achievement that the religious find themselves threatened by, and therefore ranged against, the Gospel. It was the guardians of God's revelation who crucified the Son of God. It is the noblest among the Hindus who most emphatically reject the Gospel. It is those who say, 'We see', who seek to blot out the light (John 9.41).

3   Other religions are a preparation for Christ: the Gospel fulfils them.[9] This way of understanding the matter was strong in Protestant missionary circles in the early years of this century and is fully expressed in the volume of the Edinburgh Conference of 1910 on 'The Missionary Message'. The non-Christian religions can be seen as preparation for the Gospel either as the 'revelation of deep wants in the human spirit',[10] which the Gospel satisfies, or as partial insights which are corrected and completed by the Gospel. Obviously such a view can be discussed only on the basis of an intimate and detailed knowledge of mankind's religions. There is, indeed, a vast missionary literature, mainly written in the first half of this century, which studies the religions from this point of view. (One could wish that modern Roman Catholic writers

---

[9] Perhaps the best-known example is Farquhar 1913.
[10] Farquhar 1913: 246.

who are now advocating something like the Preparation-Fulfilment view would study the earlier arguments.) Briefly one has to say that this view had to be abandoned because – in R. Otto's phrase – the different religions turn on different axes. The questions that Hinduism asks and answers are not the questions with which the Gospel is primarily concerned. One does not truly understand any of the religions by seeing it as a preparation for Christianity. Rather, each religion must be understood on its own terms and along the line of its own central axis.

4   A distinct but related view of the matter – the one dominant at the Jerusalem Conference of 1928 – seeks for 'values' in the religions and claims that while many values are indeed to be found in them, it is only in Christianity that all values are found in their proper balance and relationship. The final Statement of the Council lists such spiritual values as 'the sense of the Majesty of God' in Islam, 'the deep sympathy for the world's sorrow' in Buddhism, the 'desire for contact with ultimate reality' in Hinduism, 'the belief in a moral order of the universe' in Confucianism, and 'disinterested pursuit of truth and of human welfare' in secular civilisations as 'part of the one Truth'.[11] And yet, as the same statement goes on to say, Christ is not merely the continuation of human traditions: coming to him involves the surrender of the most precious traditions. The 'values' of the religions do not together add up to him who alone is the Truth.

5   A different picture of the relation between Christianity and the other religions is given in the Papal Encyclical *Ecclesiam Suam* (1964).[12] Here the world religions are seen as concentric circles having the Roman Catholic Church at the centre, and other Christians, Jews, Muslims, other theists, other religionists and atheists at progressively greater distances. In respect of this proposal one must repeat that the religions cannot be rightly understood by looking at them in terms of their distance from Christianity. They must be understood – so to speak – from within, on their own terms. And one must add that this model particularly fails to do justice to the paradoxical fact – central to the whole issue – that it is precisely those who are (in one sense) closest to the truth who are (in another sense) the bitterest opponents of the Gospel. Shall we say, that the Priest and the Levite – guardians of God's true revelation – are nearer to the centre than the semi-pagan Samaritan?

6   Recent Roman Catholic writing affirms that the non-Christian religions are the means through which God's saving will reaches those who have not yet been reached by the Gospel. Karl Rahner argues as follows.[13] God purposes the salvation of all men. Therefore he communicates himself by grace to all men, 'and these influences can be presumed to be accepted in spite

---

[11]   Report 1928: 1:491.
[12]   Chapter 3, 'The Dialogue'.
[13]   Rahner 1966: 115–34.

of the sinful state of men'. Since a saving religion must necessarily be social, it follows that the non-Christian religions have a positive salvific significance. In this respect they are parallel to the Judaism of the Old Testament, which – though it was a mixture of truth and error – was, until the coming of Christ, 'the lawful religion willed by God for them'. The adherent of a non-Christian religion is thus to be regarded as an anonymous Christian. But a Christian who is explicitly so, 'has a much greater chance of salvation than someone who is merely an anonymous Christian'.

This scheme is vulnerable at many points. The devout adherent of another religion will rightly say that to call him an anonymous Christian is to fail to take his faith seriously. The argument from the universal saving purpose of God to the salvific efficiency of non-Christian religions, assumes, without proving, that it is religion among all the activities of the human spirit which is the sphere of God's saving action. The unique relation of the Old Testament to Jesus Christ is not adequately recognised.

Its most serious weakness, however, is one which is shared in some degree by the other views we have examined: it assumes that our position as Christians entitles us to know and declare what is God's final judgment upon other people. On the question of the ultimate salvation of those who have never heard the Gospel, most contemporary Protestant writers are content to say that it is a matter to be left to the wise mercy of God. Some contemporary Roman Catholics (Hans Küng, for example) rebuke the attitude as a failure to do one's theological duty. On the basis of Luke 13.23f. one might reply that those who claim to know in advance the limits of God's saving action are going beyond their authority. The basis of our meeting with people of other faiths cannot be in this kind of claim to know their ultimate standing before God. All such claims go beyond what is authorised. The basis of our meeting can only be the much more humble acknowledgement that we have been chosen by one greater than ourselves to be witnesses to him. It is in this direction that we have to look for the basis of dialogue.

III

1   The starting point for my meeting with those of other faiths is that I have been laid hold of by Jesus Christ to be his witness. This is an act of his pure grace, prior to my knowledge of it, which I can only confess and acknowledge in thankfulness and praise to him.

2   This acknowledgment and confession means that I acknowledge and confess in Jesus Christ, in his life and teaching, his death and passion, his resurrection and exaltation, the decisive turning point of human history, the centre from which alone the meaning of my own personal life, and the meaning of the public life of mankind, is disclosed. It means that I acknowledge and confess Jesus as the Saviour of the world; the meaning and effect of what he

is and has done cannot apply to anything less than the totality of all that is. It is from this centre that I try to understand and participate in the common human history of which I am a part.

3   With this as my clue I expect to find and do find everywhere in the life of mankind signs of the kindness and justice of God which are manifested in Jesus. These signs are to be found throughout the life of mankind, not only – not even primarily – in his religion. The same clue enables me to recognise the fact that precisely these signs of God's goodness can be and are used as means by which men think to establish their own standing before God. Patterns of piety, of belief and of conduct drawn from the experience of God's grace then become the basis for a claim against God. The classic model of this is the role of the religious leaders of Judaism in the passion and death of Jesus. The same thing is repeated again and again both in the history of religions and in the history of the Christian Church. Thus the Cross of the risen Jesus, which is the centre of the Christian Gospel, stands throughout history over against all the claims of religion – including the claims of the Christian religion – to be the means of salvation. To put the matter in another way: the revelation of God's saving love and power in Jesus entitles and requires me to believe that God purposes the salvation of all men, but it does not entitle me to believe that this purpose is to be accomplished in any way which ignores or bypasses the historic event by which it was in fact revealed and effected.

4   The accomplishment of this saving purpose is to be by way of and through a real history – a history whose centre is defined by the events which took place 'under Pontius Pilate'. The end envisaged is the reconciliation of all things in heaven and earth in Christ (Col. 1.20), the 'summing up of all things in Christ' (Eph. 1.10), the liberation of the entire creation from its bondage (Rom. 8.19–21). The salvation which is promised in Christ, and of which his bodily resurrection is the first-fruit, is not to be conceived simply as the fulfilment of the personal spiritual history of each individual human being. To speak in this way is to depart both from Scripture and from a true understanding of what it is to be a person. We are fully persons only with and through others, and in Christ we know that our personal history is so rooted in Christ that there can be no final salvation for each of us until he has 'seen of the travail of his soul' and is satisfied (Isa. 53.11). The New Testament itself suggests at many points the need for the patience which this requires (e.g. Heb. 11.39–40; Rev. 6.9–11).

5   Because this salvation is a real consummation of universal history, and not simply the separate consummations of individual personal lives conceived as abstracted from the public life of which they are a part, it follows that an essential part of the history of salvation is the history of the bringing into obedience to Christ of the rich multiplicity of ethical, cultural spiritual treasures which God has lavished upon mankind. The way in which this is to be understood is shown in the well-known verses from the Fourth Gospel.

I have yet many things to say to you, but you cannot bear them now. When the Spirit of truth comes, he will guide you into all the truth; for he will not speak on his own authority, but whatever he hears he will speak, and he will declare to you the things that are to come. He will glorify me for he will take what is mine and declare it to you. All that the Father has is mine; therefore I said that he will take what is mine and declare it to you. (John 16.12–15)

We can spell out what is said here in a threefold form.

(a)   What can be given to and grasped by this group of first-century Jews is limited by the time and place and circumstances of their lives. It is true knowledge of the only true God and in that sense it is the full revelation of God (John 17.3, 6). But it is not yet the fulness of all that is to be manifested.

(b)   It will be the work of the Holy Spirit to lead this little community, limited as it now is within the narrow confines of a single time and place and culture, into 'the truth as a whole' and specifically into an understanding of 'the things that are to come' – the world history that is still to be enacted.

(c)   This does not mean, however, that they will be led beyond or away from Jesus. Jesus is the Word made flesh, the Word by which all that is came to be and is sustained in being. Consequently all the gifts which the Father has lavished on mankind belong in fact to Jesus, and it will be the work of the Spirit to restore them to their true owner. All these gifts will be truly received and understood when the Holy Spirit takes them and declares their true meaning and use to the Church.

We have here the outline of the way in which we are to understand the witness of the Church in relation to all the gifts which God has bestowed upon mankind. It does not suggest that the Church goes into the world as the body with nothing to receive and everything to give, quite the contrary. The Church has yet much to learn. This passage suggests a trinitarian model which will guide our thinking as we proceed. The Father is the giver of all things. They all belong rightly to the Son. It will be the work of the Spirit to guide the Church through the course of history into the truth as a whole by taking all God's manifold gifts given to all mankind and declaring their true meaning to the Church as that which belongs to the Son.

As we look back upon the story of the Church and trace its encounter first with the rich culture of the Hellenic world and then with one after another of the cultures of mankind, we can see, with many distractions and perversions and misunderstandings, the beginnings of the fulfilment of this promise.

6   The Church, therefore, as it is *in via*, faces the world not as the exclusive possessor of salvation, not as the fulness of what others have in part, not as the answer to the questions they ask, and not as the open revelation of what they are anonymously. The Church faces the world rather as *arrabon* of that salvation, as sign, first-fruit, token, witness of that salvation which God purposes for the whole. It can do so only because it lives by the Word and Sacraments of the Gospel by which it is again and again brought to judgment at the foot of the Cross. And the bearer of that judgment may well be, often is, a man or woman of another faith (cf. Luke 11.31f.). The Church is in the world as the

place where Jesus – in whom all the fulness of the godhead dwells – is present, but it is not itself that fulness. It is the place where the filling is taking place (Eph. 1.23). It must therefore live always in dialogue with the world – bearing its witness to Christ but always in such a way that it is open to receive the riches of God which belong properly to Christ but have to be brought to him. This dialogue, this life of continuous exchange with the world, means that the Church itself is changing. It must change if 'all that the Father has' is to be given to it as Christ's own possession (John 16.14f.). It does change. Very obviously the Church of the Hellenic world in the fourth century was different from the Church which met in the upper room in Jerusalem. It will continue to change as it meets ever new cultures and lives in faithful dialogue with them.

7   One may sum up – or at least indicate the direction of – this part of the paper by means of a picture. We have looked at and rejected a series of models which could be expressed in pictures. We will suggest (following Walter Freytag) a simple sketch which may serve to indicate the true basis for dialogue between Christians and those of other faiths.[14]

It will be something like this:

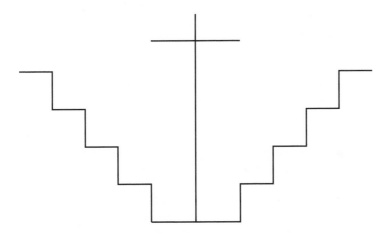

The staircases represent the many ways by which man learns to rise up towards the fulfilment of God's purpose. They include all the ethical and religious achievements which so richly adorn the cultures of mankind. But in the middle of them is placed a symbol which represents something of a different kind: a historic deed, in which God exposed himself in a total vulnerability to all man's purposes, and in that meeting exposed mankind as the beloved of God who is – even in his highest religion – the enemy of God. The picture expresses the central paradox of the human situation, that God comes to meet us at the bottom of our stairways, not at the top; that our (real and genuine) ascent

---

[14] Freytag 1957: 21.

towards God's will for us takes us farther away from the place where he actually meets us. 'I came to call not the righteous, but sinners.' Our meeting, therefore, with those of other faiths, takes place at the bottom of the stairway, not at the top. For 'Christianity' as it develops in history, takes on the form of one of these stairways. The Christian also has to come down to the bottom of his stairway to meet the man of another faith. There has to be a *kenosis*, a self-emptying. The Christian does not meet his partner in dialogue as one who possesses the truth and the holiness of God, but as one who bears witness to a truth and holiness which are God's judgment on him, and who is ready to hear that judgment spoken through the lips and life of his partner of another faith.

IV

On the basis which has been laid down one can speak briefly of the purpose with which the Christian enters into dialogue with people of other faiths. This purpose can only be obedient witness to Jesus Christ. Any other purpose, any goal which subordinates the honour of Jesus Christ to some purpose derived from another source, is impossible for the Christian. To accept such another purpose would involve a denial of the total lordship of Jesus Christ. A Christian cannot try to evade the accusation that, for him, dialogue is part of his obedient witness to Jesus Christ.

But this does not mean that the purpose of dialogue is to persuade the non-Christian partner to accept the Christianity of the Christian partner. Its purpose is not that Christianity should acquire one more recruit. On the contrary: *obedient* witness to Christ means that whenever we come with another person (Christian or not) into the presence of the Cross, we are prepared to receive judgment and correction, to find that our Christianity hides within its appearance of obedience the reality of disobedience. Each meeting with a non-Christian partner in dialogue therefore puts my own Christianity at risk.

The classic biblical example of this is the meeting of Peter with the Gentile Cornelius at Caesarea. We often speak of this as the conversion of Cornelius, but it was equally the conversion of Peter. In that encounter the Holy Spirit shattered Peter's own deeply cherished image of himself as an obedient member of the household of God. ('No, Lord; for I have never eaten anything that is common or unclean.') It is true that Cornelius was converted, but it is also true that 'Christianity' was changed. One decisive step was taken on the long road from the incarnation of the Word of God as a Jew of the first-century Palestine to the summing up of *all things* in him.

The purpose of dialogue for the Christian is obedient witness to Jesus Christ who is not the property of the Church but the Lord of the Church and of all men, and who is glorified as the living Holy Spirit takes all that the Father has given to man – all men of every creed and culture – and declares it to the Church as that which belongs to Christ as Lord. In this encounter the Church is changed and the world is changed and Christ is glorified.

V

What is to be said, on the basis of the preceding discussion, of the *manner* of inter-faith dialogue? We have already suggested that it is the doctrine of the Trinity which provides us with the true grammar of dialogue and we shall proceed accordingly.

1   We participate in dialogue with men of other faiths believing that we and they share a common nature as those who have been created by the one God who is the Father of all, that we live by his kindness, that we are both responsible to him and that he purposes the same blessing for us all. We meet as children of one Father, whether or not our partners have accepted their sonship.

This has at least three implications.

(a)   We are eager to receive from our partners what God has given them, to hear what God has shown them. In Karl Barth's words, we must have ears to hear the voice of the Good Shepherd in the world at large.

Eagerness to listen, to learn, to receive even what is new and strange will be the mark of one who knows the word of Jesus: 'All that the Father has is mine.' In our meeting with men of other faiths we are learning to share in our common patrimony as human beings made by the one God in his own image.

(b)   We meet in a shared context of things, of non-personal entities. The importance of this becomes clear if one recalls the distortion which arises when dialogue is conceived as the encounter of pure naked spirits. For those who regard the mystical experience of undifferentiated unity with pure Being as the core of religion, it will be natural to conceive dialogue as being directed towards a meeting of persons at a level 'deeper' than that which can be conceptualised. But, while fully acknowledging that there may be in such a personal meeting more than either of the partners can put into words, it must be insisted that truly personal relationships develop in the context of impersonal realities. We do not become more fully persons by trying to abstract ourselves from the world of things. The Christian in dialogue with men of other faiths rejoices to share with his partners the one common world which is the gift to both of the one God.

(c)   Moreover, in the dialogue we meet at a particular place in time in the ongoing history of the world, a history which we believe to be under the providence and rule of God. We do not meet as academics studying dead traditions from the past, but as men and women of faith struggling to meet the demands and opportunities of *this* moment in the life of our city, our nation, our world. To recognise this will prevent us from simply shooting at each other from old fortresses. We shall meet in the open country where all of us, of whatever faith, are being called upon to bring our faith to the test of decision and action in new and often unprecedented situations. It is in this open encounter in the field of contemporary decision that true dialogue takes place. This dialogue may, and often should, lead into common action on many matters of public life.

2   We participate in the dialogue as members in the body of Christ – that body which is sent into the world by the Father to continue the mission of Jesus. This has three consequences for the manner of the dialogue.

(a)   It means that we are vulnerable. We are exposed to temptation. We have no defences of our own. We do not possess the truth in an unassailable form. A real meeting with a partner of another faith must mean being so open to him that his way of looking at the world becomes a real possibility for me. One has not really heard the message of one of the great religions that have moved millions of people for centuries if one has not been really moved by it, if one has not felt in one's soul the power of it. Jesus was exposed to all the power of men's religious and ideological passion, to the point where he could cry, 'My God, my God, why did you forsake me?' and yet remain wholly bound to his Father and commit his spirit into his Father's hands. The true disciple will be exposed without defence in his dialogue with men of other faiths and yet will remain bound to Jesus.

(b)   One may put this point in the form of the model sketched on page 167. The Christian has to come down to the bottom of his stairway to meet his partner. Much of his 'Christianity' may have to be left behind in this meeting. Much of the intellectual construction, the piety, the practice in which his discipleship of Christ has been expressed may have to be called in question. The meeting place is at the Cross, at the place where he bears witness to Jesus as the Judge and Saviour both of the Christian and of his partner.

(c)   The implication of this is that the Christian who engages in dialogue must be firmly rooted in the life of the Church – its liturgy, teachings, sacraments and fellowship. The world of the religions is the world of the demonic. It is only by being deeply rooted in Christ that one can enter in complete self-emptying and with complete exposure into this world in order to bear faithful witness to Christ.

3   We participate in the dialogue believing and expecting that the Holy Spirit can and will use this dialogue to do his own sovereign work, to glorify Jesus by converting to him both the partners in the dialogue.

(a)   The Christian partner must recognise that the result of the dialogue may be a profound change in himself. We have referred to the story of the meeting of Peter and Cornelius, which is the story of radical conversion both for the apostle and for the pagan Roman soldier. Klaus Klostermeier writes as follows of his experience of dialogue with Hindus: 'Never did I feel more inadequate, shattered and helpless before God . . . all of a sudden the need for a *metanoia* in depth became irrepressibly urgent.'[15]

The Holy Spirit who convicts the world of sin, of righteousness and of judgment, may use the non-Christian partner in dialogue to convict the Church. Dialogue means exposure to the shattering and upbuilding power of God the Spirit.

---

[15] In Singh 1967.

(b)   The Christian will also believe and expect that the Holy Spirit can use the dialogue as the occasion for the conversion of his partner, to faith in Jesus. To exclude this belief and expectation is to reduce dialogue to something much less than its proper importance. What we have said about the 'conversion of Peter' in the encounter at Caesarea must not be used to overshadow the conversion of Cornelius, without which there would have been no conversion of Peter. A distinguished Hindu writer on religious and philosophical questions, Dr R. Sundarara Rajan of Madras, has recently commented on the current developments in the field of Hindu-Christian dialogue. He points out that the emphasis upon a self-critical attitude, the demand that each party should try to see things from within the mind of the other, and the disavowal of any attempt by either side to question the faith of the others, can easily mean that dialogue is simply an exercise in the mutual confirmation of different beliefs with all the really critical questions excluded. 'If it is impossible to lose one's faith as a result of an encounter with another faith, then I feel that the dialogue has been made safe from all possible risks.'[16] A dialogue which is safe from all possible risks is no true dialogue. The Christian will go into dialogue believing that the sovereign power of the Spirit can use the occasion for the radical conversion of his partner as well as of himself.

(c)   When we speak of the Holy Spirit we are speaking of the one who glorifies Christ by taking all the gifts of God and showing them to the Church as the treasury of Christ (John 16.14f.). The work of the Spirit is the confession of Christ (1 John 4.2f.; 1 Cor. 12.3). The Spirit is not in the possession of the Church but is Lord over the Church, guiding the Church from its limited, partial and distorted understanding of and embodiment of the truth into the fulness of the truth in Jesus who is the one in whom all things consist (Col. 1.17). Not every spirit is the Holy Spirit. Not every form of vitality is his work. There is need for the gift of discernment. Peter at Caesarea, and later the congregation in Jerusalem, had need of this discernment to recognise that this strange and (at first) shocking reversal of deeply held religious beliefs was the work of the Holy Spirit and not of the antichrist (Acts 11.1–18).

There is no substitute for the gift of discernment, no set of rules or institutional provisions by which we can be relieved of the responsibility for discernment. Dialogue cannot be 'made safe from all possible risks'. The Christian who enters into dialogue with people of other faiths and ideologies is accepting the risk. But to put *my* Christianity at risk is precisely the way by which I can confess Jesus Christ as Lord – Lord over all worlds and Lord over my faith. It is only as the Church accepts the risk that the promise is fulfilled that the Holy Spirit will take all the treasures of Christ, scattered by the Father's bounty over all the peoples and cultures of mankind, and declare them as the possession of Jesus to the Church.

---

[16] Rajan 1974: 74.

The mystery of God's reign can only be made safe against all risk by being buried in the ground. It can only earn its proper profits if those to whom it is entrusted are willing to risk it in the commerce of mankind.

Extract 2
'Religious Pluralism: a Missiological Approach' (1993)[17]

Religious pluralism is not a new experience for the Christian Church. Christianity was born in a religiously plural society and, if one takes a global viewpoint, it has never existed except in a religiously plural world. What is new, at least for Christians in the old Western Christendom, is the discovery that this is so. Western Christendom took its distinctive form during the long period in which it was the religion of a small region isolated from the religious worlds of Asia and sub-Saharan Africa by the massive power of Islam and from the religious world of the American peoples by the ocean. For these formative centuries Western Christendom was (except for the unsolved enigma of the Jewish people) a religiously monochrome society. It hardly needs to be said, of course, that Christianity in India has always been part of a religiously plural society. For Indian Christians, pluralism is nothing new. But, such is the dominance of Western thought in the modern world, the idea that religious pluralism is something new is accepted as though it were true.

However, and this is also part of the dominance of Western European thought in the modern world, the religious pluralism with which we are now familiar is new in the sense that it is part of a more fundamental pluralism. As I shall argue later in this paper, the kind of Western thought which has described itself as 'modern' is rapidly sinking into a kind of pluralism which is indistinguishable from nihilism – a pluralism which denies the possibility of making any universally justifiable truth-claims on any matter, whether religious or otherwise. It is this development which gives a distinctively new character to the contemporary debate about religious pluralism.

The apostolic Church was launched into a religiously plural world, a world where, as St Paul puts it, there were many gods and many lords (1 Cor. 8.5). This pluralism was tolerated, but only on one condition – namely that supreme lordship was ascribed to the emperor. Roman law distinguished between the exercise of private religious cults, ways of worship and practice claiming to offer personal salvation to the individual soul, and the public cult of the emperor, to which all were required to conform. It would have been possible for the early Church to accept the position of one of these religions of personal salvation, and thus escape any collision with the empire. It was the refusal of this option, the stubborn insistence that Jesus alone is the one to

---

[17] Newbigin 1993b: 227–44. (= Newbigin 1993c.)

whom the title of 'Lord' may be properly given, which put the Church on a collision course with the imperial power. The apostolic message confronted men and women with a choice about which there could be no compromise. For everyone to whom their message came there was posed a question to which an answer had to be given: 'Who, in fact, is Lord of all?' The answering of that question was, literally, a matter of life and death.

When the emperor finally bowed to the one who is truly Lord, and Constantine was baptized, the struggle did not end. It continued in the arena of theology and philosophy. The long and often arcane theological battles of the patristic period were, at heart, battles about the question whether Jesus is Lord in this absolute sense. For Greek philosophy to accept the full meaning of the apostolic message that the *logos* was identical with the man Jesus of Nazareth required nothing less than a complete abandonment of fundamental dualisms of matter and spirit, of time and eternity, of visible and invisible. One could, without a total break with traditional philosophy, accept the idea that Jesus was *like* God (*homoiousios*) but not that he was one in being with God (*homoousios*). The historian Gibbon mocked at the spectacle of Christians fighting over a diphthong, but that apparently minute difference concealed the whole difference between surrender to an ultimate pluralism and acknowledgement that God has actually made himself known by presence in the stuff of human history. It if is true that God has done this, then this has to be the starting point of all fundamental thinking and the criterion by which all ultimate truth-claims are judged. The whole existence of the Christian faith hung on that diphthong.

Christians in the modern world are not required to offer incense before a statue of the emperor on pain of death. They are, however, in typically 'modern' or 'modernizing' societies, expected to accept a lower place for the name of Jesus than that of supreme Lord of all things, *pantocrator*. They are normally expected to acknowledge, for practical purposes, that Jesus is the name of one among the symbols of religious affiliation in a society where religion itself is regarded as only one among the many optional activities in which people are free to engage or from which they are free to dissent. At this point it is difficult to speak in general terms because situations are different in different parts of the world. Until recently, in societies under the dominance of Marxist ideology, the affirmation of the absolute lordship of Jesus could indeed be a matter of life and death. The same is true in some Islamic states today. In societies where the religions of Indian origin prevail, it is taken for granted that God is ultimately unknowable and the Christian claim seems to pose no immediate threat. But in so far as the process of what is called 'modernization' continues in all parts of the world, the distinctive attitudes to religion which have prevailed in Western Europe since the eighteenth century are increasingly dominant.

For a thousand years Western Europe had been schooled in the Christian faith and had seen in the Bible, as mediated through the teaching and worship of the Church, the source of reliable truth. But another strand in European thought, deriving from the classical world of Greece and Rome, had also been present to question this biblical tradition. The seminal work of Thomas Aquinas had provided a synthesis of these two strands which shaped European thought during the high middle ages. But the breakdown of the unity of Christendom in the religious wars of the seventeenth century, and the emergence of the new scientific method exemplified in Galileo, Copernicus, Kepler and – above all – Isaac Newton, offered another paradigm of reliable knowledge to which Europe increasingly turned. The period of the mid-eighteenth century, which those who lived through it called the Enlightenment, was a time of profound conversion. It seemed to the thinkers of this 'Age of Reason' that the real light had come, that it was now possible to see things as they really are, and that the 'superstitions' of the past – above all those of religion – could be put aside. Reliable knowledge was now to be obtained with the tools of modern science. Claims to truth by religious traditions were to be accepted only in so far as they could be justified at the bar of reason as the new age understood it. Religion must abandon its claim to rule public life. It can only be a matter for the personal life of the individual. Provided it keeps within these limits it is to be tolerated. It cannot make claims to ultimate truth.

The immense confidence of the 'Age of Reason' was what fuelled the dramatic expansion of European power into the rest of the world. All the world was to be given the blessing of 'civilization' as understood by the thinkers of Europe. European science, technology, political institutions and commerce were to be taken to every part of the globe, and the new science gave Europe the military power necessary to achieve this benevolent mission. Christian missions also, not without critical reservations, shared in this global expansion. They were among the major carriers of Western education and medicine to the rest of the world, and they are still involved in this activity. It is inevitable that, as this process of 'modernization' goes on all over the world, the 'enlightened' view of religion tends to prevail. The various kinds of religious belief and practice, Christian or other, are to be tolerated as permitted activities for the benefit of the individual soul, but are not to claim a role in public affairs. Religious pluralism is, quite naturally, an integral part of this picture. If the religions are not making ultimate truth-claims which would challenge the assumptions of 'modernity', then there is no obstacle to peaceful co-existence.

This picture of the spread of 'modernity' describes with reasonable accuracy the period from the mid-eighteenth to the mid-twentieth centuries. In the later decades of this century, two important changes have been taking place to modify this picture. One is the rise of religious fundamentalism. This affects all the religions, including Christianity. The accepted wisdom of 'modernity' was that religion must gradually die out. Modern science, modern rational organization of industry and management – including the management of national governments by the techniques of modern bureaucracy – must necessarily push religion more and more to the margin of public life. 'Secularization' was a process which must inevitably continue and gather strength. What is happening, however, is that a strong counter-movement is taking place. Peoples everywhere are finding that 'modernity' does not provide a world in which the human person can flourish. There is a passionate return to traditional religious certainties, and there is every sign that this movement will continue, and that 'modernity' does not have the spiritual resources to contain it.

The second development is the rise of what is often called 'postmodernism'. This is a somewhat slippery word, but it is easy to identify the movement of thought which it denotes. Its main feature is the abandonment of any claim to know the truth in an absolute sense. Ultimate reality is not single but diverse and chaotic. Truth-claims are really concealed claims to power, and this applies as much to the claims of science as to those of religion. The father of this whole movement is the German philosopher F. W. Nietzsche. Nietzsche was the one who foresaw, in the closing years of the nineteenth century, that the methods of the Enlightenment must in the end lead to total scepticism and nihilism. Enlightenment thought had broadly accepted the lead of Descartes, who had exalted the 'critical principle' to a position of priority in the search for reliable knowledge. Reliable knowledge is that which starts from indubitable statements (such as 'I think, therefore I am') and develops from them propositions which can be demonstrated with the precision, clarity and certainty of mathematics. Everything which cannot be so demonstrated is to be doubted. Reliable knowledge will be obtained by distinguishing that which can be certainly known by a kind of reasoning of which mathematics is the model, from that which cannot be so demonstrated and which is therefore a matter of faith. Descartes claimed, of course, like Aquinas before him, to demonstrate the existence of God so that belief in God is not merely a matter of faith but knowledge. But it is clear that the position achieved in this way is unstable. Doubt is not an autonomous activity; one can only rationally doubt a statement on the basis of something else which one believes to be true. That belief can, of course, also be doubted, but only on the basis of something else which is believed to be true. The critical principle destroys itself. If it is given primacy in the search for reliable knowledge, the end can only be total scepticism and nihilism. Truth-claims lose their justification; they can only be regarded as exercises of the will, the will to power.

This critique applies to the claims of the Enlightenment as much as to the claims of religion. One of the most famous statements of the Enlightenment was the dictum of Lessing that accidental happenings of history cannot prove eternal truths of reason. This, of course, removed the Bible and the Christian tradition from the place of eternal truth. What Nietzsche and his modern disciples have done is to demonstrate that the so called 'eternal truths of reason' are in fact products of particular histories. There is no such thing as a suprahistorical 'reason' standing above all actual human reasoning, which is always the reasoning of human beings in a particular cultural and historical situation. So we do not have any 'eternal truths'; we have only narratives of how beliefs and ideas have been born and developed. There is no overarching 'reason' by which all particular claims to truth might be tested; there is only a vast variety of stories. No story can claim 'truth' in an exclusive sense. Ultimate reality (if such a phrase means anything) is incoherent. This is the radical pluralism with which we now have to deal.

The response of many Christians at this point is to speak about dialogue. I shall discuss this again later, but here two points may be made. The first is that we must recognize the situation in which the dialogue takes place. If it is in a 'modernist' (as distinct from a postmodernist) context, then perhaps the Socratic idea of dialogue might be appropriate. The central idea of dialogue is that one is brought nearer to truth by allowing truth-claims to be questioned by other truth-claims, leading to modifications which, at each step, bring the participants nearer to the truth. If the 'truth' which one is seeking is understood to be timeless, eternal truth of the kind of which Lessing spoke, then this method can be valid. The problem here is that the message of Christianity is essentially a story, a report of things which have happened. At its heart is the statement that 'the word was made flesh.' This is a statement of a fact of history which the original evangelists are careful to locate exactly within the continuum of recorded human history. A fact of history does not arise out of a dialogue; it has to be unilaterally reported by those who, as witnesses, can truly report what happened. Of course there will then be dialogue about the way in which what has happened is to be understood, how it is to be related to other things which we know, or think that we know. But the story itself does not arise out of dialogue; it simply has to be told.

If, secondly, our dialogue is in the context of a postmodernist culture, the situation is different. We tell our story, but it is only one among the many stories. We accept the postmodernist position that all human reasoning is socially, culturally, historically embodied. We have left behind the illusion that there is available some kind of neutral standpoint from which one could judge the different stories and decide which is true. The 'Age of Reason' supposed that there was available to human beings a kind of indubitable knowledge, capable of being grasped by all human beings which was more reliable than any alleged revelation, and which could therefore provide the criteria by which any alleged divine revelation could be assessed. This immensely powerful hangover from the 'modernist' position still haunts many discussions of religious pluralism. Much so-called 'natural theology' is devoted to the enterprise of finding grounds which are variously described as 'rational', 'neutral' and 'secular' on which the Christian story could be shown to be more acceptable than others. The assumption is, apparently, that these grounds are more reliable as sources of knowledge than God's revelation of himself in Jesus Christ. But in a postmodernist context all this is swept away. There are only stories, and the Christian story is one among them.

These stories are, as the postmodernists correctly perceive, also claims to power. If, for example, one accepts the story which is told in the normal European school or university, where world history is taught as the history of the development of 'civilization', then one is committed to shaping one's life in accordance with this story. In that case, the stories told by the different religions will be seen as disrupting. One will wish to see them subordinate their stories to the main story. Rival religious claims will be judged in accordance with their positive or negative contributions to the progress of human 'development' understood in terms of this story.

Among the stories which the religions tell, the one which Nietzsche singled out for the most violent attack was the Christian story, which he saw as undermining human power. Christianity, with the story of the crucifixion at its centre, would create a world of slaves rather than of masters. In that also, Nietzsche's perception was acute. What is unique in the Christian story is that the cross and resurrection of Jesus are at its heart. Taken together (as they must always be) they are the public affirmation of the fact that God rules, but that his rule is (in this age) hidden; that the ultimate union of truth with power lies beyond history, but can yet be declared and portrayed within history. The fact that the crucifixion of the incarnate Lord stands at the centre of the Christian story ought to have made it forever impossible that the Christian story should have been made into a validation of imperial power. Any exposition of a missionary approach to religious pluralism must include the penitent acknowledgement that the Church has been guilty of contradicting its own gospel by using it as an instrument of imperial power.

Why does religious pluralism pose a problem to us? I suppose that it is because deep in the heart of every human being there is a desire for harmony, for coherence, for the mental security which comes from knowing that there is no threat from what is radically alien. We all want unity because of the security which it brings. The problem is that we seek unity on our own terms. As André Dumas has said, every proposal for the unity of humankind, unless it explicitly specifies the centre of that unity, has the self of the proposer as its implicit centre. One could tell the story of the human race as the story of successive attempts to impose unity on larger and larger areas of human life. When we are the authors of these efforts they appear in a benevolent light; when they are the projects of others, we label them 'imperialism'. It is very hard to recognize the imperialist element in our own projects for human unity.

Why is it that our projects for human unity become rival imperialisms? It is because of that deep corruption in human nature which leads me to see myself as the centre of the world and to judge everything from this centre. That corruption has been met, exposed and dealt with in the atoning work of Jesus Christ. It is the dying of Jesus for the sin of the world which brings me to the point where I can say with St Paul: 'I have been crucified with Christ and I no longer live but Christ lives in me. The life I live in the body, I live by faith in the Son of God who loved me and gave himself up for me' (Gal. 2.20). The self is displaced by a new centre, and that can only be so because the One who so displaced my self is the one through whom and for whom all things exist and in whom they hold together. That is why Jesus can say, as he looks towards Calvary, 'I when I am lifted up from the earth will draw all to me' (John 12.32). The one place where our self-centred human wills can be drawn

177

together is the place where this radical corruption has been met and dealt with, where sin has been forgiven and atonement made, the mercy-seat where we can meet together as common debtors to the immeasurable grace of God.

I am, of course, using confessional language, the language of one among the contending confessions which make up the multiple conversations of our pluralist society. I know that this will be objected to as improper for a discussion of pluralism. But if I am asked to use another and more 'objective' kind of language I shall have to decline the invitation. For, as I have been saying already, there is no language which is 'neutral', no language which does *not* arise out of a particular tradition of reasoning. I could, of course, use the language which I was trained to use in my school and university education. I could use the kind of language used in the comparative study of world religions. But this language is, of course, the language which belongs to another story, another way of understanding the human situation, another belief about what is ultimately reliable knowledge. I can, of course, use this language, for it is the language I learned at school. But its use necessarily implies that Jesus is *not* the one of whom the Scriptures and the Christian tradition speak – the one who is the Word made flesh, the one who is the source and goal of all that is.

And, of course, this other 'non-confessional' language embodies imperial claims which those who use it do not notice but which are obvious to others. During 1992 there was considerable excitement in the English-speaking world over the writings of a US civil servant named Francis Fukuyama, who claimed that with the collapse of Marxist socialism as a world power, we had reached the end of history.[18] There were no more great battles to be fought. The future belonged to the victorious liberal free market economies of the west. All the world would come to recognize that this is the only future for humanity. He did make passing reference to Islam as a possible contender for world dominance, but no reference – as far as I know – to Christianity as a possible player in the game. This is the language of 'enlightened' Europe, and if this is our story, then dialogue among the world religions will naturally be conducted in the languages of Europe (mainly English, Spanish and German) and within the conceptual framework which these languages embody. The imperialist claims of this particular project for human unity are, as usual, concealed from those who share this story but obvious to those who do not. Once again I am making the obvious, but often unrecognized point that there is no 'neutral' or 'objective' approach to religious pluralism. Any claim to such neutrality conceals an imperialism which is more dangerous for being unacknowledged.

I am, of course, aware that this position will be challenged. It will be seen as arbitrary and irrational. It may be dismissed as 'fideism', or as a blind 'leap of faith'. But these charges have to be thrown back at those who make them.

---

[18] (Fukuyama 1992.)

Every claim to show grounds for believing the gospel which lie outside the gospel itself can be shown to rest ultimately on faith-commitments which can be questioned. There is, indeed, a very proper exercise of reason in showing the coherence which is found in the whole of human experience when it is illuminated by the gospel, but this is to be distinguished from the supposition that there are grounds for ultimate confidence more reliable than those furnished in God's revelation of himself in Jesus Christ, grounds on which, therefore, one may affirm the reliability of Christian belief. The final authority for the Christian faith is the self-revelation of God in Jesus Christ. If I am pressed to give reasons for being a Christian, I can only reply by speaking of the calling of Jesus Christ which has come to me through his Church and is authenticated by the working of the Holy Spirit as mediated to me through the word and sacraments of the gospel and the life of the believing community. If I have accepted that calling, I cannot agree to place the name of Jesus as one among a class of names to be subsumed under some more inclusive category. If Jesus is the Word made flesh, then there is no more inclusive category. In particular, I cannot accept the widely prevalent custom of putting the cross in a whole list of symbols of the world's religions. The cross is not a mere symbol like the OM often used to denote Hinduism, or the crescent denoting Islam. The crucifixion of Jesus was an event in history, the mighty act of God by which at infinite cost he reconciled the fallen world to himself and rescued it from perdition. To suggest that there is a reality more inclusive than this is to deny it.

How, then, from this standpoint, does one approach the devout adherents of the world's religions? I suggest the following as guiding principles.

1   The first is that one approaches the adherents of another faith (whether 'religious' or not) with an eagerness to discover and welcome all the evidence of the work of God's grace in the life of that person. If our starting point is God's revealing and atoning work in Jesus Christ, we know that Jesus is the eternal word of God active in all creation and in all human life. We know that as the ascended Lord, at the right hand of the Father he reigns over all and there is no limit to the reach of his gracious work. We know that he is the light that illuminates all being. We will rejoice in every reflection of that light wherever it is found. To put it in the negative form, it will *not* be our endeavour to probe the soul of the other person in order to discover the sins, the weaknesses, the anxieties which might provide the 'point of contact' for the gospel. Human beings have a natural desire to protect themselves against this kind of probing. The recognition of need, of weakness, of sin will indeed come, but it will be the work of the Holy Spirit mediated through the telling of the gospel story which brings this about. As St Paul argues in the letter to the Galatians, the promise of God comes before the law. It is in the light of God's immeasurable mercy in Christ that we learn how deep is our need and how dark our sin. The Church must acknowledge with thankfulness and without reservation all that is of God in the world outside the walls of the Church and beyond the sound of the gospel.

2   But the Church must also tell the story which has been entrusted to her. There is no substitute for this story. There are several places in Scripture where we see both the apostolic recognition of the work of God outside the Church, and the necessity to tell the story. To the pagan crowd at Lystra St Paul speaks of the blessings they have received from God, but immediately insists that he is bringing them good news of something new. To the citizens in Athens he affirms their great religious devotion and quotes with approval from one of their poets, but immediately goes on to tell them that he has news; God has done a new thing which confronts them with a radically new situation (Acts 14.8–18 and 17.22–31). Perhaps the most striking illustration of this point is provided by the encounter of St Peter and his colleagues with the household of Cornelius (Acts 10). Here it is explicitly stated that God hears the prayers and accepts the gifts of a pagan Roman soldier (vv. 4, 31, 34f.). Nevertheless Peter is commanded to go to him and to give him the news of what God has done in Jesus Christ, and as the story is told, the Holy Spirit is given to Cornelius and his household. The matter is expressed in precise terms in the opening verse of St John's Gospel where we read both that the Word who was made flesh in Jesus was already in the world, because all things were made through him and he is the light that gives light to everyone, and also that he came into the world and the world did not know him. Both sides of this paradox must be affirmed. It is the paradox of our fallen nature, both made in the image of God and also alienated from God. It is vital that we do not use either side of the paradox to deny the other; neither use the reality of God's universal grace to deny the necessity and the uniqueness of his action in Jesus Christ, nor use the uniqueness of his action in Jesus Christ to deny the reality of his universal presence and action. Much of the debate about religious pluralism arises from falling into this trap.

3   There is no substitute for telling the story. It is necessary to say this because it is sometimes said that 'Christian presence' rather than 'evangelization' is the proper form of Christian response to religious pluralism. This is a confusing half-truth. It is indeed true that the message with which the Church is entrusted cannot be faithfully delivered by a company of people who do not follow the incarnate Lord in his total commitment to our human condition. The Church has both to embody and to proclaim the gospel. When Jesus commissioned his apostles he said to them 'As the Father sent me, so I send you', and he showed them his hands and his side (John 20.19–23). It was surely an unforgettable reminder to them that they would be recognizable as truly his representatives if their corporate life bore the scars of his encounter with the ruler of this world. The gospel as Jesus proclaimed it was that the kingdom, the active reign of God, is at hand, present in his life of healing and teaching, and present supremely in his final conflict with and victory over the powers of sin and death. The commission to the Church is to be his body, the place where the reign of God is present and therefore where the battle with the powers of darkness is joined. Mere words, proceeding from a company which is in peaceful co-existence with the world will not truly represent

the Saviour. But words are not dispensable. Jesus himself preached and commanded his apostles to preach. We deceive ourselves (but nobody else) if we imagine that our mere presence is sufficient to do the whole work of Jesus. Certainly there are times when words are not appropriate, yet – even in these circumstances – our presence will be a witness to Christ only because we are known to represent a Church which does preach the gospel. And there are also times when silence is betrayal.

4   It is important to distinguish between pluralism as an ideology and plurality as a fact. Plurality of religious communities is a present fact, and I do not find in Scripture grounds for believing that, within this age, all human beings will be Christians. Rather the New Testament clearly suggests that the normal attitude of the world towards the Christian Church will be one of hostility. The fulfilment of Jesus' promise to draw all people to himself belongs to the consummation and not – surely – to terrestrial history. And given the fact of religious plurality, it is important that Christians should do everything possible to create and maintain good relationships between the religious communities. There are very many social and ethical issues on which there can be cordial co-operation, based on mutual respect. This will be furthered if Christians are eager, as they should be, to recognize and give thanks for the work of God's grace in the lives of those outside the Church. It is also very desirable that members of the different religious communities should understand as fully as possible the beliefs and practice of their neighbours of other faiths. Christians who engage in this kind of sharing find their own understanding of the Christian faith deepened and enlarged, and this experience is of course not confined to Christians.

The acceptance of this fact of plurality must not be confused with acceptance of the ideology of pluralism if that means the abandonment of the human responsibility to seek and know the truth. There is a proper kind of pluralism which affirms the freedom of people to seek for truth without being coerced, although this freedom is empty unless it is combined with a sense of responsibility to a cultural tradition. But a pluralism which simply abandons the struggle to distinguish truth from falsehood can only lead to the kind of society to which we are sadly becoming accustomed in the 'developed' world – a society which loses any sense of meaning and therefore can find no higher goal than the multiplication of amusements.

It is characteristic of the 'postmodern' situation that claims to truth are regarded as concealed assertions of power. In this perspective, evangelism is seen as an expression of the will to dominate, and dialogue is seen as the renunciation of this desire. Dialogue is seen not as a means of coming nearer to the truth but as a way of life in which different truth-claims no longer conflict with one another but seek friendly co-existence. An 'instrumental' view of dialogue is rejected. One speaks rather of the dialogue of cultures and of dialogue as a celebration of the rich variety of human life. Religious communities are regarded as varieties of human culture rather than as bearers of truth-claims. In this perspective, of course, dialogue is seen as the preferred alternative to evangelization. But we have to ask whether we are not dealing here with another example of the failure of nerve of Christians who are too much controlled by the collapse of Western European culture into scepticism and nihilism.

5　In a religiously plural world it is sometimes regarded as arrogant for the adherents of one religion to claim a unique relation to the truth and therefore to seek to make disciples of the faithful adherents of others. 'Proselytism' is, for most people, a word of condemnation. And there have been enough examples of a kind of arrogance which might justify this condemnation. But a few elementary observations are enough to show that this cannot be the last word, however annoyed we may sometimes be by a certain kind of religious proselytising. No religious community would exist unless at some time there were men and women who went out and made disciples. Moreover the arrogance is not all on one side. To assert that there are no such discrepancies between the truth-claims of different religions as to justify the attempt to persuade people of the truth of one's own is – in fact – to claim a knowledge superior to that of the adherents of these religions. It is to relativize all their truth-claims on the authority of a supposedly superior truth. In many other areas of human discourse we are continually engaged in seeking to persuade others in the truth of what we believe: it would be odd if, in this area alone, such persuasion were ruled out of order. And, finally, it is plain that Jesus commissioned his apostles to go and make disciples, and that the Christian Church would not exist if they had not obeyed this command. To deplore the effort to bring others to faith in Christ is to desire the extinction of Christianity.

But, when all this has been said, there are understandable reasons for the condemnation of proselytism. We are commissioned to bring good news, to tell the story of God's marvellous and mighty acts for the salvation of the world. We must not withhold this story from anyone. To keep it to ourselves, as though it were a private 'in-house' story of the Church, as though Jesus were the lord of Christians but not the lord of all, would be intolerable sectarianism. We have no right to keep silent about it, and if we try to do so we deny its truth. But it is not our work to convert any human soul to Christ. That is the work of the Holy Spirit. It is impossible to overstate the importance of this. The New Testament repeatedly affirms that it is the Holy Spirit who is the primary witness to Christ. It is he only who can 'convict the world in respect of sin, of righteousness and of judgment' (John 16.8). The faithful witness of the Church gives the occasion for the witness of the Holy Spirit, but it is that witness which alone can truly convert the heart. When the Christian thinks that he or she can convert another to Christ, there is something badly wrong. The ways in which men and women (and children too) are brought to faith in Christ are mysterious and almost infinitely various. It is perhaps enough to refer to the great number of people in all times and cultures who have come to faith through a vision or a dream, to remind us that the business is not in our hands. The life of the Church, its words, its deeds, its corporate life and – above all – its worship may in the providence of God provide the occasions for the inner witness of the Holy Spirit in the heart of an unbeliever. Christians must pray and hope for that. But the answering of the prayer is in the hands of God alone.

6   This is the context in which we should speak about inter-religious dialogue. If dialogue is understood in its broadest sense as referring to any kind of conversation between human beings, then it is hardly necessary to say that we cannot live without dialogue. But in the context of a discussion of religious pluralism, the word dialogue is often introduced as though it were the preferred alternative to evangelism. I have already argued that dialogue in its classical Socratic sense cannot be a substitute for the telling of the story which is the gospel. It can lead up to the telling of the story – as in the conversation between Jesus and the woman at the well in Samaria. It can follow from it as we try to understand the meaning of the story – and much of the Pauline correspondence is one side of such a dialogue with the young churches which he had brought to birth. What is the place of inter-religious dialogue in a religiously plural society where Christianity is already well established? There is, I believe, an important place. It is a way of enabling the participants to learn about and to enter into the religious experience of others, of creating mutual understanding and so building friendship. It can also be a way of exploring the possibilities of common action on contemporary social and political issues – issues on which different faith-communities may have many shared objectives.

Such dialogue should not be seen as an occasion for evangelism, but rather as the proper precondition for it. But nor is it a substitute for evangelism. What is important is that the Christian participant in such conversations is, and is known to be fully committed to and loyal to the Church which is publicly preaching the gospel and calling people to conversion and faith. There are very many of our daily activities in which we are not (and should not be) engaged in direct evangelism, and inter-religious dialogue is one of these. But we engage in dialogue as members of a Church which is publicly confessing Jesus Christ as Lord of all and publicly calling men and women to give their allegiance to him.

To put the matter in another, if perhaps very obvious way, the participants in dialogue should be truly representative of the faiths for which they speak. To enter into dialogue without a proper understanding of one's own faith-tradition is to sell our partners short. And to enter into dialogue with one's own faith held – as it were – in suspension, as though for purposes of dialogue one could subordinate it to some higher more inclusive principle, is equally to make the dialogue sterile. A dialogue in which the participants are *not* truly representing the claims to truth which their traditions make cannot be truly fruitful, nor can it enhance real mutual respect.

7   In speaking about proselytism I touched on the matter which is most important of all. At the heart of the Christian faith is the affirmation that God so loved the world that he gave his beloved Son to be incarnate among us, to die for us and to rise victorious so that we might be delivered from the

bondage of sin and death. If these things are true, they cannot be subordinated to anything else. They cannot be bracketed within some more inclusive category. The response which they call for is primarily that of worship. The centre of Christian witness is worship. It is the presence of a truly worshipping community which draws people to Christ by the power of the Holy Spirit. The kind of proselytism which hardens the hearts of others against the gospel arises from the confusion into which Christians have often fallen by thinking too much of themselves as the agents of mission. We are indeed called to bear witness to what has been given to us. But our witness is subordinate to the witness of the Spirit. We are not in control. We are not the final judges. We await the final judgment and meanwhile point men and women to him who is both the Saviour and the Judge. We know from our Lord's teaching that there will be many surprises on that day. We know that some who have said 'Lord, Lord' will be left outside and that many who were far off will be in the Father's kingdom. We are only witnesses, not judges. But we who have been redeemed as the first-fruit of God's new creation must be above all concerned that his name is honoured. In a religiously plural world we cannot offer any other centre for human unity except the one which he has provided in the atoning work of Jesus. The life of a Church wholly devoted to honouring him in worship, loving obedience and faithful witness is the human means through which he will fulfil his promise to draw all peoples to himself. The heart of our praying is that he should see of the travail of his soul and be satisfied.

Further reading

Newbigin 1978b: 181–214. (Reprinted as Newbigin 1995b: 160–89.)
Newbigin 1989a: 310–40.
Newbigin 1994a: 125–36.

10

The missionary crisis in the West

10.1 Background to the crisis

Newbigin had been aware of the profound changes taking place within the culture of the West even before he set out for missionary service in India in 1936. In his autobiography, for example, he recalls the impact of an address given by the missionary statesman Joe Oldham at the 'Edinburgh Quadrennial' conference in 1933, in which he had referred to the radical departure of Europe from the Christian faith that had resulted from its succumbing to the thought of Descartes and other leading thinkers of the Enlightenment.[1]

But it was on Newbigin's return to the UK in 1974 – some forty years later – that the reality of these changes really hit home. By the time he came to write The Other Side of 1984 *in the early 1980s, he was referring to 'the dramatic suddenness with which, in the space of one lifetime, our civilization has so completely lost confidence in its own validity'.[2] During his travels around the UK during this period, he was frequently asked what was the greatest difficulty he faced in moving back from India. He always replied that it was 'The disappearance of hope'.[3] As a result of these experiences, Newbigin set out to try to understand how these cultural changes had come about, and to make his own contribution to what he called the 'development of a truly missionary encounter with this very tough form of paganism'. He came to regard this task – which was to occupy his considerable energies for the rest of his life – as 'the greatest intellectual and practical task facing the Church'.[4]*

The following extracts describe something of this journey. The first is taken from the revised edition of his autobiography and describes how the process of reflection and discovery came about. The second is from his 1983 book The Other Side of 1984. *This was his first book to deal with the challenge of Western culture to the Church, and it was seen by Newbigin as very much a 'draft' document, setting out the questions rather than offering any kind of solutions. He thought that it contained 'nothing new or revolutionary',[5] and resembled 'a small blast not of the trumpet but of the tin whistle'.[6] He was therefore rather 'puzzled about the fact that such a brief,*

---

[1] Newbigin 1993d: 26.
[2] Newbigin 1983: 3.
[3] Newbigin 1983: 1.
[4] Newbigin 1993d: 236.
[5] Newbigin 1993d: 256.
[6] Newbigin 1994b: 69.

hastily written paper could have such a reception'.[7] It quickly sold out of its original print-run of 500 copies, and when the World Council of Churches reprinted it, it soon sold over 20,000 copies. Newbigin later wrote in his autobiography: 'I was quite astonished at the volume and range of correspondence that descended on me. Clearly the questions had touched a nerve, even if answers were still to be found.'[8] He later acknowledged that it was the impetus of this reception that was instrumental in 'pitchforking' him into further reflection on the missionary challenges facing the Church in the West.[9]

* * *

Extract 1
Unfinished Agenda *(1993)*[10]

During the decade of the 1980s I continued to wrestle, very ineffectually, with the problem of relating the Christian faith to public issues. In 1984 I was invited to give the Gore Lecture in Westminster Abbey on 'The Welfare State: A Christian Perspective' and I spent many months on reading in preparation for this. I was only beginning to understand the dimensions of the changes that were being forced through under the leadership of Mrs Thatcher. [. . . .] Things which had been simply taken for granted in the years following the war were being swept aside. The idea that we have obligations to fellow citizens, that public service is a good way to spend one's life and that public consensus is something to be sought – all these were swept contemptuously aside in favour of commitment to private gain. Market forces were to have final sovereignty over our lives. People would only work effectively if they were subject to the pressures of a competitive market. Teachers, doctors, nurses, social workers and others in public service could not be trusted to acknowledge good professional standards; they had to be bribed or threatened. The BBC, previously respected (even if sometimes laughed at) as among our greatest institutions, was the target of constant attack. Long-term planning, such as only governments can afford, was to be replaced by the rush for short-term profit. We were out of the era of pragmatic politics and into an era of ideology. We were seeing (at a less violent level) a replay of what happened in the 1930s when British people, with their long liberal tradition, simply could not grasp the dimensions of what was happening in Italy and Germany. We had been thinking of Britain as a secular, liberal democracy. It was only slowly that one began to see that the terms of the Church's mission had to change. We

---

[7] Newbigin 1993d: 253.
[8] Newbigin 1993d: 252.
[9] Newbigin 1992d: 22.
[10] Newbigin 1993d: [. . . .] 250–2 [. . . .].

were dealing not with a political programme but with an idolatry. We were coming into a confessional situation.

During all this time I was still having in the back of my mind the challenge which I had been unable to meet from the committee on 'Mission and Other Faiths'. How can one find a perspective on one's own culture? I had asked for a Christian approach to contemporary Western liberal capitalism, in fact to the culture of which I was a part and by which I had been formed. Could there be an Archimedean point, so to speak, from which one could look critically at one's own intellectual and spiritual formation? It happened that I was invited to spend a few days leading bible studies at St Deiniol's library in Hawarden, North Wales. This is the magnificent library bequeathed by W. E. Gladstone, splendidly maintained under a series of wardens, one of whom had been Alec Vidler. I had been greatly impressed by Vidler's book *The Orb and the Cross*,[11] which was a study of a work written by Gladstone before he switched from his earlier high Tory views to the liberalism of his public career. It was entitled *The State in its relation to the Church*. I took the chance of being at St Deiniol's to read quickly through this work. What was striking was the perspective – so foreign to present ways of thinking – which saw the Church as the great, solid enduring reality in comparison with which the state is a fragile and ephemeral affair.

While at St Deiniol's I naturally spent time browsing among the books. The title of one caught my eye: *La Crise de la Conscience Européenne* by Paul Hazard. The title was striking. It was a study of the eighteenth century Enlightenment, a subject about which I had never thought. I found and read the English translation.[12] It seemed to provide the perspective I was looking for. Here was the critical moment in which one could say that, after a very long period of gestation, modern Europe came to birth and to consciousness of its own unique character. I bought and read other books on the period and began to see the outlines of what might be a Christian critique of things which I had taken for granted. The stimulus to think further along these lines came from an unexpected quarter.

The British Council of Churches had sponsored the formation of the Foundation for the Study of Christianity and Society. But its new general secretary, Philip Morgan, was becoming increasingly uneasy about what the Council was doing and failing to do. It was continually being asked to react to particular political and ethical issues, making quick responses to whatever was the issue dominating the headlines for the moment. It was not making time and space for more fundamental thinking. This concern was brought to a focus by a remark made by the Dean of Salisbury (Sydney Evans) in the course of a sermon preached before the General Synod of the Church of

---

[11] (Vidler 1945.)
[12] (Hazard 1973.)

England in 1982. He had spoken of 'the end of Renaissance man'. The phrase sharpened the conviction in Philip Morgan's mind that we were, perhaps, at a moment of profound change and that we needed to do some fundamental thinking about the direction in which we were going. He convened a gathering of distinguished Christians, lay and clerical, for a day's 'brainstorming'. Out of this came a decision to hold a conference of 1,000 people at Nottingham in 1984. The imminence of this date naturally evoked thoughts about the vision of a future society sketched by George Orwell in his famous book. A committee was appointed to prepare for the conference, and I was included in its membership.

I was not able to attend the first meeting of the committee. At the second meeting on 3 September 1982 I found that a programme for the conference had already been drafted. I was very unhappy about it, as I did not think it began to deal with the underlying issues. I did not have the courage at that moment to question it but when I went home I phoned another member of the committee, David Jenkins (Bishop of Durham), and told him of my feelings. He encouraged me to challenge the proposed programme and at the next meeting (8 October) I did so. I suggested that we should follow the example of J. H. Oldham when (in the 1930s) he was trying to rouse the Churches in Britain to a recognition of the significance of what was happening in Europe. In 1934 he published a small pamphlet entitled 'Church, Community and State', raising the fundamental issues.[13] He then initiated a three-year study programme which provided the substance on which the 1937 Oxford Conference was able to work – with far-reaching results. The committee was generous enough to accept my suggestion, agreed to postpone the conference and instructed me to write a pamphlet raising the questions which needed to be discussed. Three weeks later I sent the results of my scribbling to Philip Morgan suggesting that (if it was not destined for the waste-paper basket) it might be sent to 25 or 30 people for comment and necessary revision. In due course comments were received, some of them incorporated, and the pamphlet published under the title 'The Other Side of 1984: Questions to the Churches'. The BCC's publishing department thought that it would be risky to print more than 500 copies, but it was taken up by the World Council of Churches and quickly sold 20,000. I was quite astonished at the volume and range of correspondence that descended on me. Clearly the questions had touched a nerve, even if answers were still to be found. I was moved by letters from lay people who told me that it had illuminated their situation. A lawyer told me that he felt as if the sun had risen and he could see the landscape. But what gave me the deepest satisfaction was a brief note from Wim Visser't Hooft: 'You have written many good things, but *The Other Side*

---

[13] (Oldham 1935.)

of 1984 is the best'. Ever since then I have puzzled about the fact that such a brief, hastily written paper could have such a reception.

Extract 2
The Other Side of 1984 *(1983)*[14]

I have been speaking about 'our culture' and I must now try to say what I mean by this phrase. A convenient dictionary definition of the word is as follows: 'The sum total of ways of living built up by a human community and transmitted from one generation to another.' Culture thus includes the whole life of human beings in so far as it is a shared life. It includes the science, art, technology, politics, jurisprudence and religion of a group of people. Fundamental to any culture is language which embodies the way in which a people grasps and copes with experience, sharing it with one another within the group. So long as one lives one's life within one culture, one is hardly aware of the way in which language provides the framework in which experience is placed, the spectacles through which one 'sees'. It is when one lives in a completely different culture and learns a new language that one discovers that there are other ways of grasping experience and coping with it. One discovers that things are seen differently through different spectacles. When, as happened during the past two centuries, the culture of Western Europe in-vaded the cultures of what we now call the 'third world', an essential element in that invasion was the introduction of European languages as media of educa-tion. As a result, for example, whole generations in India have grown up with English as their language of public life, and have therefore become accustomed to grasping and coping with experience through the categories of European thought instead of those developed in the ancient cultural traditions of India.

But this European culture which has so forcibly inserted itself into almost every culture of the world is a relatively recent arrival on the stage of history. During most of the history of the world of which we have knowledge, the tribes inhabiting the western peninsulas of Asia have been surpassed in the arts of civilization by the peoples of India, China and the Arab world. Yet during the past three centuries the descendants of these same tribes have extended their culture into every part of the world, dominating and often destroying more ancient cultures, and creating for the first time a common civilization which embraces the whole earth – not in the sense that it includes everyone, but in the sense that it has a dominating role, at least in nearly all the great cities of the world. To most of the world's people it has appeared as the bearer of 'modernity' – with all its implications of technical mastery and unlimited powers of discovery, innovation and control.

---

[14] Newbigin 1983: 5–16.

W. E. Hocking, writing in 1956, could still speak with unshaken confidence of the almost timeless and universal validity of this culture:

> Today we seem to be standing on the threshold of a new thing, civilization in the singular . . . For the first time our entire world-space is permeated with ideas which, as Locke said about truth and the keeping of faith, 'belong to man as man and not as a member of a society'. Here and there in the Orient there is still revulsion from the clinging localisms of Western thought and practice, but none towards what we may call the Clean Universals, the sciences, the mathematics, the technics – these it claims not as borrowings from the west, but as its own. In giving birth to the universal, the west has begotten something which can never again be private property.[15]

Hocking's words express the assurance of a culture which was still confident of the universal validity of its way of seeing things. Today we are required to look afresh at this 'way of seeing things' which is in fact being questioned, and to enquire about its origins and credentials.

I have referred to the eighteenth-century 'Enlightenment' as the proximate source of our culture, but of course its roots lie much further back in history. All movements of thought are continuous because the thinkers live through the changes, even when the changes are as sharp as wars and revolutions. Any decision about where to mark the emergence of something new must be somewhat arbitrary. The movement of which we are speaking had its earlier beginnings in the ferment of thought introduced into Western Europe by the translation of Arabic writings into Latin, the impact of Aristotelian philosophy, the flood of classical ideas at the time of the Renaissance, the passionate debates of the Reformation, and the beginnings of modern science in the seventeenth century. But it is clear that by the middle of the eighteenth century there was a widespread feeling that Europe had reached a turning point. Developments which had been going on continuously for several centuries seemed to have reached a point of clarification such that people could only use the word 'enlightenment' to describe what had happened. Light had dawned. Darkness had passed away. What had been obscure was now clear. Things would henceforth be seen as they really are. 'Enlightenment' is a word with profound religious overtones. It is the word used to describe the decisive experience of the Buddha. It is the word used in the Johannine writings to describe the coming of Jesus: 'The light has come into the world' (John 3.19). The leading thinkers of the mid-eighteenth century felt themselves to be at such a moment of enlightenment, and this moment provides a proper point from which to begin an understanding of our culture.

The feeling of the time is well expressed in some words of D'Alembert, written in 1759:

---

[15] Hocking 1956: 51f.

If one examines carefully the mid-point of the century in which we live, the events which excite us or at any rate occupy our minds, our customs, our achievements, and even our diversions, it is difficult not to see that in some respects a very remarkable change in our ideas is taking place, a change whose rapidity seems to promise an even greater transformation to come. Natural science from day to day accumulates new riches. Geometry, by extending its limits, has borne its torch into the regions of physical science which lay nearest at hand. The true system of the world has been recognized, developed, and perfected . . . In short, from the earth to Saturn, from the history of the heavens to that of insects, natural philosophy has been revolutionized; and nearly all other fields of knowledge have assumed new forms . . . The discovery and application of a new method of philosophizing, the kind of enthusiasm which accompanies discoveries, a certain exaltation of ideas which the spectacle of the universe produces in us – all these causes have brought about a lively fermentation of minds. Spreading through nature in all directions like a river which has burst its dams, this fermentation has swept with a sort of violence everything along with it which stood in its way.[16]

By the end of the century the leading thinkers in Western Europe were convinced that a light had indeed dawned compared with which the preceding centuries of European history and the previous history of most of the human race were darkness. Whatever might have been the achievements of the Greeks and the Chinese, they had not progressed. Modern Europe had surpassed them all. The European peoples were now the vanguard of history. They had mastered the secret of a true scientific method which would banish old superstition and lay bare the real nature of things as in the light of day. They were the bearers of light in a world still largely dark. They had therefore both the duty and the capacity to carry their civilization into every corner of the world. And they proceeded to do so.

What, exactly, was it that happened at that momentous turning point? The French historian Paul Hazard[17] describes it as the replacement of a society based on duties by a society based on rights. That, as we shall note later, is part of the truth, but it is not the root of the matter. Basil Willey has, it seems to me, come much closer to the real answer when he says that the feeling of exhilaration which so manifestly marked the birth of modern European culture came from the conviction that things which had previously been obscure were now being 'explained'. In place of 'dogmatic' or 'unscientific' explanations which no longer satisfied the mind, the 'true explanation' of things was now coming to light. That was the heart of the matter, says Willey, and that was why 'enlightenment' was felt to be such an appropriate word at the point when this movement became fully conscious of itself.

---

[16] D'Alembert, *Eléments de philosophie* (1759), quoted in Cassirer 1951.
[17] Hazard 1973.

But we have to go on to ask: 'What do we mean by "explanation"?' Basil Willey tries to answer this question:

> The clarity of an explanation seems to depend upon the degree of satisfaction that it affords. An explanation 'explains' best when it meets some need of our nature, some deep-seated demand for assurance. 'Explanation' may perhaps be roughly defined as a restatement of something – event, theory, doctrine, etc. – in terms of the current interests and assumptions. It satisfies, as explanation, because it appeals to that particular set of assumptions, as superseding those of a past age or of a former state of mind. Thus it is necessary, if an explanation is to seem satisfactory, that its terms should seem ultimate, incapable of further analysis. Directly we allow ourselves to ask 'What, after all, does this explanation amount to?' we have really demanded an explanation of the explanation, that is to say, we have seen that the terms of the first explanation are not ultimate, but can be analyzed into other terms – which perhaps for the moment do seem to us to be ultimate. Thus, for example, we may choose to accept a psychological explanation of a metaphysical proposition, or we may prefer a metaphysical explanation of a psychological proposition. All depends upon our presuppositions, which in turn depend upon our training, whereby we have come to regard (or to feel) one set of terms as ultimate, the other not. An explanation commands our assent with immediate authority when it presupposes the 'reality', the 'truth', of what seems to us most real, most true. One cannot, therefore, define 'explanation' absolutely; one can only say that it is a statement which satisfies the demands of a particular time or place.[18]

If one has lived at different times in different places, one becomes aware of the relativity of all 'explanations'. One of the first things I did on arrival in India was to be involved in a bus accident which laid me off for two years. How to 'explain' it? The Indian pastor said: 'It is the will of God.' A Hindu would have said: 'The karma of your former lives has caught up with you.' In some cultures the explanation would be that an enemy had put a curse on me. If I, as an 'enlightened' European, had said that it was because the brakes were not working properly, that would have been – for the others – no explanation at all. It would have been simply a restatement of what had to be explained. To speak of an 'explanation' is to speak of the ultimate framework of axioms and assumptions by means of which one 'makes sense of things'. 'Explanations' only operate within an accepted framework which does not itself require explanation. What happened at the Enlightenment was that one framework was felt to be inadequate and another took its place.

It is because the 'Enlightenment' framework is now proving inadequate that we are enabled to look critically at it, and that we are obliged to do so.

What was the 'framework' which enabled the thinkers of the eighteenth century to feel satisfied with a new 'explanation' of experience? I realize that

---

[18] Willey 1979: 10f.

it is foolish to oversimplify profound and complex movements of thought, but surely it is safe to begin the answer by referring to the enormous impression created on the eighteenth-century mind by the work of scientists, and very specially by that of Isaac Newton. Alexander Pope's famous lines express what the eighteenth century felt:

> Nature and Nature's laws lay hid in night.
> God said: 'Let Newton be', and all was light.

Newton did not begin from alleged revelation or alleged 'innate ideas'. He began from observation of the phenomena, and sought thus to formulate general 'laws', subsuming the largest possible range of phenomena. The outcome of this method was a picture of the world which was to dominate European thinking for the next two hundred years. In this picture, the 'real' world is a world of moving bodies which have a totally 'objective' existence apart from any human observer. All reality is ultimately intelligible in these terms. The most fundamental of all 'laws' are those of mathematics which are applicable to all that really is. By analysing all the data of experience into the smallest possible components one can discover the laws which govern their movements and mutual relations. Analysis is the necessary instrument of all thinking and enables human thought to penetrate behind appearances and so discover how things really are. This enterprise is cumulative and infinite in its range. It leads on to a steadily growing capacity to exploit the processes of nature for human ends.

The totality of all observable phenomena is 'Nature'. 'Nature' in effect replaces the concept of God, which is no longer necessary. The characteristic position of the eighteenth century, known as 'Deism', did indeed retain the concept of God as a sort of Prime Mover standing behind the processes of nature. But even in that century there were plenty of critics who defined a deist as 'a person who is not weak enough to be a Christian and not strong enough to be an atheist'. The nineteenth century drew the obvious conclusion: there was no place for 'God'.

Since 'Nature' has replaced 'God', the scientist who is learned in the ways of nature becomes the priest who can mediate between the human person and this new god. It is science alone which can enable men and women to understand nature, and can unlock nature's bounty for the benefit of humanity. And science cannot accept any authority other than the authority of the observable facts. Therefore the different sciences, while sharing a common method, are all autonomous as regards their own subject matter. No alleged revelation can be allowed to interfere. The study of astronomy or of biology or of literature (including that segment of literature which has been canonized as 'The Word of God') is to be pursued according to the scientific principles of which Newton's physics provide the most brilliant example. Economics (and here the Enlightenment was to have perhaps its most far-reaching consequences) is no longer a part of ethics and therefore ultimately

dependent on theology; it is an autonomous science for which ethical principles derived from alleged divine revelation can have no authority.[19, 20]

The replacement of 'God' by 'Nature' involved a new understanding of
'Law'. There is no longer a divine lawgiver whose commands are to be obeyed
because they are God's. Laws are the necessary relationships which spring from
the nature of things (Montesquieu). As such they are available for discovery by
human reason. Reason is a faculty common to all human beings and is in
principle the same everywhere. Provided it is not perverted by the imposition
of dogmas from without, reason is capable of discovering what the nature of
things is and what therefore are 'Nature's laws'. The most dangerous and
destructive of all the dogmas which have perverted human reason is the
dogma of original sin. To destroy this wicked slander against humanity is the
first essential for the liberating of human reason and conscience to do their
proper work. But this dogma is only the centrepiece of a whole structure of
dogma which has to be destroyed. Any authority – of dogma, of scripture or
of 'God' – which purports to replace human reason is to be rejected as false
and as a treason against the dignity of the human being.

The word 'dignity' is used advisedly. The medieval world spoke of a person's 'honour', and this was related to his or her status in society.[21] After the
Enlightenment one spoke of human 'dignity' – something which belongs to
every human being simply from the person's birth and apart from any question of social status. Every human being is possessed of reason and conscience,
and is therefore capable of distinguishing truth from error, right from wrong.
In this sense, every human being is 'autonomous', not subject to an external
law-giver, ruling his or her own life in accordance with the real 'laws' – which

---

[19] The very important shift in this respect from the seventeenth to the eighteenth century is
described by Cassirer as follows: 'The systematic concepts developed by seventeenth-century
metaphysics are still firmly anchored in theological thinking with all their originality and independence. For Descartes and Malebranche and for Spinoza and Leibniz there is no solution of
the problem of truth independently of the problem of God because knowledge of the divine
being forms the highest principle of knowledge from which all other certainties are deduced.
But in eighteenth-century thought the intellectual centre of gravity changes its position. The
various fields of knowledge – natural science, history, law, politics, art – gradually withdraw
from the domination and tutelage of traditional metaphysics and theology. They no longer
look to the concept of God for their justification and legitimation; the various sciences themselves now determine that concept on the basis of their specific form. The relations between
the concept of God and the concepts of truth, morality, law are by no means abandoned, but
their direction changes. An exchange of index symbols takes place, as it were. That which formerly had established other concepts, now moves into the position of that which is to be established, and that which hitherto had justified other concepts, now finds itself in the position of
a concept which requires justification. Finally even the theology of the eighteenth century is
affected by this trend. It gives up the absolute primacy it had previously enjoyed; it no longer
sets the standard but submits to certain basic norms derived from another source which are furnished it by reason as the epitome of independent intellectual forces.' Cassirer 1951: 158f.
[20] Cassirer 1951: 163.
[21] Berger, Berger and Kellner 1973: ch. 3 – Excursus.

are the laws of nature discoverable by the exercise of reason and the moral law which is written in the conscience of every person. In the later developments which followed the Enlightenment (and reacted against some of its features) this vision of the autonomous human person became more and more important. The Romantic Movement developed the idea of the 'personality', and it became part of the unquestioned assumptions of a western European that every human person has the 'right' to develop his or her own potential to the greatest possible extent, limited only by the parallel rights of others. Medieval society had emphasized the idea of the duties involved for each person by his or her position in society. From the Enlightenment onwards, it was the 'rights of man' which seemed axiomatic. To the founding fathers of the new republic created in the New World to embody the principles of this new philosophy, it seemed necessary and natural to begin with the famous words: 'We hold these truths to be self-evident, that all men are created equal, that they are endowed by their Creator with certain inalienable rights; that among these are life, liberty and the pursuit of happiness; that to secure these rights governments are instituted among men, deriving their just powers from the consent of the governed.' The rights of the human person are the unquestioned starting point from which all else follows.

These rights include the right to the pursuit of 'happiness'. Happiness (*bonheur*) was hailed by the eighteenth-century philosophers as 'a new word in Europe'. In place of the joys of heaven to which the medieval person was encouraged to look forward, Enlightenment people looked forward to 'happiness' here on earth. This would come within the reach of all through the cumulative work of science, liberating societies from bondage to dogma and superstition, unlocking the secrets of nature and opening them for all. Once again Pope is the spokesman of his age:

> Oh happiness, Our Being's End and Aim.
> Good, Pleasure, Ease, Content, Whate'er thy Name.

Hannah Arendt[22] has pointed out that, for some at least of the American founding fathers, the happiness intended was the 'public happiness' of actively shared responsibility for public life. She also shows, however, that while any sort of private hedonism was very far from their purposes, the course of events led inexorably to an interpretation of their language as meaning the pursuit of private wellbeing. The result is that the world becomes (as in the contemporary Western world it has become) a place where each individual has the 'right' to pursue 'happiness' in the domestic and privatized sense, and it is the responsibility of the state to see that this right is honoured. It follows, of course, that any consideration of what lies beyond death is both unreliable and subversive. It is unreliable because the methods of science do not provide any reliable knowledge of what lies beyond death. It is subversive because it

---

[22] Arendt 1963: ch. 3.

deflects attention from the 'happiness' which is the right of every person in this life, to an alleged happiness in another life for which we have only the authority of the clergy who themselves live very comfortably in this life at the expense of the unenlightened poor.

Once the concept of 'human rights' has established itself as an axiom, the question inevitably arises: How and by whom are these rights to be secured? With growing emphasis, post-Enlightenment societies have answered: by the state. The nation state, replacing the old concepts of the Holy Church and the Holy Empire, is the centrepiece in the political scene in post-Enlightenment Europe. After the trauma of the religious wars of the seventeenth century, Europe settled down to the principle of religious coexistence, and the passions which had formerly been invested in rival interpretations of religion were more and more invested in the nation state. Nationalism became the effective ideology of the European peoples, always at times of crises proving stronger than any other ideological or religious force. If there is any entity to which ultimate loyalty is due, it is the nation state. In the twentieth century we have become accustomed to the fact that – in the name of the nation – Catholics will fight Catholics, Protestants will fight Protestants, and Marxists will fight Marxists. The charge of blasphemy, if it is ever made, is treated as a quaint anachronism; but the charge of treason, of placing another loyalty above that to the nation state, is treated as the unforgivable crime. The nation state has taken the place of God. Responsibilities for education, healing and public welfare which had formerly rested with the Church devolved more and more upon the nation state. In the present century this movement has been vastly accelerated by the advent of the 'welfare state'. National governments are widely assumed to be responsible for and capable of providing those things which former generations thought only God could provide: freedom from fear, hunger, disease and want. In a word: 'happiness'.

If it is true that we are now compelled to look critically at the 'conversion' which brought our modern world into existence, it would be perverse and misleading to do so without first acknowledging our enormous debt to the Enlightenment. One cannot fail, even now, to be moved by the words in which Immanuel Kant answered the question: 'What is Enlightenment?' 'Enlightenment is man's exodus from his self-incurred tutelage. Tutelage is the inability to use one's understanding without the guidance of another person . . . "Dare to know" (*sapere aude*)! Have the courage to use your own understanding; this is the motto of the Enlightenment.'[23] Who can deny the liberating consequences which flowed from this robust summons? For Christians it is particularly necessary to acknowledge that the Bible and the teaching office of the Church had become fetters upon the human spirit; that the removal of barriers to freedom of conscience and of intellectual enquiry

---

[23] Cassirer 1951: 163. (The quotation comes from Kant's 1784 essay 'An Answer to the Question: What is Enlightenment?', reprinted in Kant 1983: 41–8.)

was achieved by the leaders of the Enlightenment against the resistance of the churches; that this made possible the ending of much cruelty, oppression and ignorance; and that the developments in science and technology which this liberation has made possible have brought vast benefit to succeeding generations. It would be dishonest to fail to recognize our debt to the Enlightenment.

Moreover there is much to be said for the view that the unfinished work of the Enlightenment is still a large part of our contemporary agenda. The leaders of the Enlightenment by no means completed the tasks they set themselves. They were not exempt from the human sin which invokes eternal truths to justify selfish interests. The 'human rights' which the eighteenth-century philosophers espoused were mainly the rights of the rising bourgeoisie. Freedom meant primarily freedom to hold property, to trade and to travel. It was not freedom for workers to organize trade unions, for blacks to vote, for Aboriginal peoples to retain their lands, or for women to have equal rights with men. Late in the twentieth century we are still struggling with this unfinished agenda.

Yet epochs in history always overlap, and while we work to complete the unfinished business of the Enlightenment, we have also – I believe – to recognize that its way of understanding the world can no longer satisfy us. The 'explanations' of the eighteenth century no longer provide meaning for us. We have, beyond this unfinished agenda, the new task of seeking an understanding of 'how things are' which will meet our sense of being at a dead end and open new horizons of meaning.

Further reading

Newbigin 1985b: 6–8.
Newbigin 1988b: 30–41.
Newbigin 1994b: 66–79. (Reproduced on pp. 207–17 of this volume.)

10.2 *Profile of a culture*

Newbigin's analysis of Western culture was informed by his many years of cross-cultural experience in India as well as by his extensive knowledge of the wider world Church gained over decades of intercontinental travel. As a result of this, there is a deep awareness of the cross-cultural nature of missionary engagement at the heart of his writings, which enables him to bring unique insights to bear upon the missionary challenges facing the Church in the West. The following two extracts illustrate something of this experience. The first is taken from his 1986 book Foolishness to the Greeks, *which was the follow-up to* The Other Side *of 1984. The cross-cultural character of the book is immediately apparent. 'The angle from which I am approaching the study', he writes on page one, 'is that of a foreign missionary.'[24] Chapter 2 of the book is entitled 'Profile*

---

[24] Newbigin 1986b: 1.

of a Culture' and is Newbigin's descriptive analysis of the culture of the West as he saw it. The first extract is the introductory section of this chapter in which he traces the origins of the Enlightenment's elevation of 'Reason' at the expense of more traditional sources of authority. The second extract is taken from a collection of studies published in 1989 under the title Mission and the Crisis of Western Culture, *and is part of a lecture given to the annual conference of the German Home Missions 'umbrella' organization, the Arbeitsgemeinschaft Missionarische Dienste. Here Newbigin takes the analysis a stage further, uncovering the cultural distinction between 'facts' and 'values', and identifying a rejection of the idea of 'purpose' as the prime category by which to understand human life in favour of a more mechanistic approach that concentrates on* how *things* work. *In a way that is highly characteristic of his later writings, Newbigin traces the cultural malaise brought about by these developments to a crisis in our understanding of 'knowledge'. In the writings of Michael Polanyi he finds a helpful ally not only in the criticism of these developments, but also in pointing the way out of the impasse produced by them.*

* * *

Extract 1
Foolishness to the Greeks *(1986)*[25]

A missionary going to serve in another country is advised to make a thorough study of its culture. When I was preparing to go to India, and during my years there, I spent much time in trying to understand the whole complex of ideas and practices that make up what Western peoples during the past 150 years have called 'Hinduism.' (*Hinduism* is just as useless or useful a word as *Europeanism* might be in the mouth of a Japanese person summarizing everything thought and said in Europe from Pythagoras to Whitehead.) Obviously, I studied Indian religion and culture with the intellectual tools of a twentieth-century European. But with what tools could I study my own culture? There is a Chinese proverb that says, 'If you want a definition of water, don't ask a fish.' Indians had no word for 'Hinduism' until Europeans imposed it on them. They spoke of *dharma* – which is simply the ultimate principle of how things are and therefore the rule that should govern our lives. Until I had spent many years in India, I was an innocent specimen of modern European culture. I had learned from childhood through school and university how things really are, and it was on this basis that I could begin to understand and evaluate the world of *dharma* under the name of Hinduism. Where shall I find the stance from which I can study Europeanism? On the basis of what perceptions can I evaluate my own perceptions of 'how things really are' – perceptions that are part of my mental make-up from childhood?

---

[25] Newbigin 1986b: 21–5 [. . . .].

As a young missionary, I was confident that the critical evaluations I made about Hindu beliefs and practices were securely founded on God's revelation in Christ. As I grew older, I learned to see that they were shaped more than I had realized by my own culture. And I could not have come to this critical stance in relation to my own culture without the experience of living in another, an Indian culture. The assumption of these chapters is that the gospel provides the stance from which all culture is to be evaluated; but the gospel [. . .] is always embodied in some cultural form. The typical apologetic for Christianity in our Western culture has been one that attempts to 'explain' it in the terms of our culture, to show that it is 'reasonable' in terms of our ultimate beliefs about how things really are. But what is meant by the word *explain*? We accept something as an explanation when it shows how an un-explained fact fits into the world as we already understand it. Explanation is related to the framework of understanding we inhabit, the firm structure of beliefs we never question, our picture of how things really are. Explanation puts a strange thing into a place where it fits and is no longer strange. Thus it comes about that one person can give a psychological explanation for a polit-ical stance and another a political explanation for a theory in psychology. Whether you accept the explanation depends upon the way in which you understand how things really are. What may be an explanation for one is no explanation for another. The question with which I am wrestling [. . .] is this: As people who are part of modern Western culture, with its confidence in the validity of its scientific methods, how can we move from the place where we explain the gospel in terms of our modern scientific world view to the place where we explain our modern scientific world view from the point of view of the gospel?

Part of the answer will be to listen to the witness of Christians from other cultures. [. . .] The difficulty is that most of us are not able to listen to them until they can speak to us in our language. Only those who have been co-opted into our culture by receiving what we call a modern scientific educa-tion are able to join in dialogue with us. The others, however charming they may be, however profitable to the tourist industry, are not potential partners in dialogue. They are still candidates – often eager candidates – for what is called 'modernization.'

A more useful way of starting is to look at the genesis of our modern cul-ture and especially at the decisive point where it becomes fully conscious of itself, the point which those who experienced it called 'the Enlightenment.' That word is itself a very significant pointer to the nature of the experience that created modern Western culture. It expresses the joy and excitement of those who have seen the day dawn over a dark world, for whom what was obscure and confusing is now clearly seen as it is, for whom the unexplained has been explained – or at least made explicable. It is a conversion word; not, however, the experience of an individual – like the enlightenment of the Buddha – but one of whole peoples. Europe, or at least the community of its thinkers in those decisive years, went through a kind of collective conversion.

'We were blind, now we see. The iron grip of dogma has been loosened. The mists of superstition are dissolving in the warmth of the dawning day. Now we see landscape as it really is.' If we want to grasp the essential elements in what we call modern Western culture, the best place to begin is with that exhilarating feeling that light has come into the world and banished the darkness, the experience Paul Hazard has called 'the crisis of Europe's consciousness.'

Of course, like all conversion experiences, this one has a prehistory. It was prepared for by events and movements of thought many centuries before. One could mention especially the ferment introduced into the Western world by the translation of Arabic texts into Latin through which Greek science and metaphysics, and especially the thought of Aristotle, were brought into contact with the Western Christian world. Following this came the rise of the universities, the flood of classical ideas in the Renaissance, the fierce theological and political controversies of the Reformation, the wars of religion, and – above all – the new developments in science associated with the names of Bacon, Galileo, and Newton, and the new method in philosophy opened up by Descartes. However one assesses the role played by all these factors, it is clear that around the middle of the eighteenth century there was a profound and widely shared feeling among thinking people in Western Europe that a new age had come, and that its essential nature was 'Enlightenment.' It was, in fact, a conviction that Europeans now knew the secret of knowledge and therefore the secret of mastery over the world.

What were the elements in the new vision? Central and fundamental was the vision of the nature of reality opened up by science and above all by the work of Isaac Newton. Greek physics had worked with the idea that change and movement in the world of nature are to be explained in terms of purpose. Medieval thought saw divine purpose manifest everywhere in the world of nature. The revelation of that purpose had been given in those events confessed in the church's creed, and thus all study of nature had its place within the framework that the creed articulated. The condition for entry into the world of scholarship was the acceptance of that framework.

The effect of the work of the new scientists, and above all the brilliant vision of Newton, was to replace this explanatory framework with another. The real world disclosed by the work of science was one governed not by purpose but by natural laws of cause and effect. Teleology had no place in physics or astronomy. All the movements of tangible bodies and the changes in the visible world could be explained without reference to purpose and in terms of efficient cause. The rotation of the planets manifested not the perfection of the divine will but the uniform operation of the laws of inertia and gravitation. As the methods of science achieved greater and greater triumphs, both theoretical and practical, the old picture of how things are, the picture derived from the Bible and vividly sketched, for example, in the medieval mystery plays, was replaced by a quite different one. The real world, as distinct from the world of appearances, was a world of material bodies – as vast as the sun or as small as an atom – moving ceaselessly according to unchanging and mathematically stable laws in a fixed and infinite space through time, which moved with unvarying velocity from an infinite past to an infinite future. All causes, therefore, are adequate to the effects they produce, and all things can be in principle adequately explained by the causes that produce them. To have discovered the cause of something is to have explained it. There is no need to invoke purpose or design as an explanation. There is no place for miracles or divine intervention in providence as categories of explanation. God may be conceived, as in eighteenth-century Deism, as the ultimate author of it all, but one does not need to know the author personally in order to read the book. Nature – the sum total of what exists – is the really real. And the scientist is the priest who can unlock for us the secrets of nature and give us the practical mastery of its workings.

Science, so understood, does not work by deduction either from revelation or from first principles. It works by observation of the phenomena and induction from the results of observation. But it does not simply take the phenomena at their face value, so to speak. It uses the tools of analysis to dissect, separate, and observe each of the elements that constitute the phenomena. This process of analysis has no limit in principle, and any appearance of ultimate unity is a challenge to further analysis. Analysis is followed by reconstruction, and for this mathematics provides the tools. Mathematics enables all reality to be quantified and arranged in a relatively comprehensible structure. What the eighteenth century celebrated as 'the geometric spirit' is thus applied to all forms of human knowledge.

The thinkers of the Enlightenment spoke of their age as the age of reason, and by reason they meant essentially those analytical and mathematical powers by which human beings could attain (at least in principle) to a complete understanding of, and thus a full mastery of, nature – of reality in all its forms. Reason, so understood, is sovereign in this enterprise. It cannot bow before any authority other than what it calls the facts. No alleged divine revelation, no tradition however ancient, and no dogma however hallowed has the right to veto its exercise. Immanuel Kant, in answer to the question of what Enlightenment was, used the famous phrase 'dare to know.' The eighteenth century accepted the challenge, and from that day to the present, even though so much in the philosophy of science has changed, this phrase of Kant has defined the central thrust of our culture.

Extract 2
Mission and the Crisis of Western Culture *(1989)*[26]

Our culture, increasingly dominant throughout the world, is showing signs of disintegration at the point of its origin, Western Europe. The confident

[26] Newbigin 1989c: [. . . .] 1–7 [. . . .].

expectation of progress towards an ever better world no longer exists. The literature of our time is filled with a sense of pessimism; the Chinese theologian Carver Yu, looking at Europe from the East, sums up our contemporary cultural scene as 'technological optimism and literary despair'.[27]

A most sobering thought is that Christian missions have themselves been powerful bearers of the process of modernisation. During the past two centuries, missionaries have introduced Western education, science and technology wherever they have gone; indeed they are still doing so. There is a strange blindness here both to the inner relationship between Christianity and Western culture and also to the profound crisis of Western culture itself. Thus missionaries have unwittingly laid the foundations for an emphatic repudiation of the gospel!

Diagnosis

1   If we look at Western culture from the perspective of other, older cultures, its most obvious feature is that it is split into two parts: there is a public world of what are called 'facts', and a private world of what are called 'values'. 'Facts' are what everyone has to accept whether they like it or not, 'values' are a matter of personal choice. Facts are what every child in school must learn and accept, e.g. that the development of the human person depends on the programme encoded in the DNA molecule; values, whether expressed in religious terms or otherwise, are matters for the Church and the home. Indeed there is often a sexist overlay – facts are for the world of men, values are for the world of women.

Even as recently as 100 years ago, every child in school in Scotland learned as a fact that 'Man's chief end is to glorify God and enjoy him for ever'; this was as much a fact as anything in biology or physics. Today such teaching, if permitted, would be confined to a small part of R(eligious) E(ducation) under the heading of 'Christian beliefs and values'.

We do not teach as public truth any particular belief about the purpose of human life, we take pride in being a pluralist society where many different creeds can flourish. But this pluralism does not extend to the world of 'facts'. Where there is disagreement about what are called 'facts' we do not celebrate the glories of pluralism. No! We argue, we conduct experiments, we try to convince each other of error and we do not rest until we reach agreement about the 'facts'. In this public world of 'facts', pluralism does not reign!

2   The root of this dichotomy between a public world of facts and a private world of values is to be found at a crucial turning-point in European history. The scientific enterprise did not deny the existence of God, but viewed God as a clockmaker who had made the universe and left it to run according to its own 'laws of nature', which it was the task of scientists to explore. Lord Bacon advised his contemporaries to avoid speculation and collect facts; by

---

[27] (Yu 1987: 1. Yu's actual phrase is 'technological optimism and literary pessimism'.)

speculation he meant ideas about the purpose of human life – the stuff of theology and philosophy; facts, by contrast, could be known with certainty.

Purpose, of course, was not denied by the early scientists. Rather, they said, it lies in the sphere of revelation; only God can reveal the 'why' of things, and such revelation has to be accepted in faith. It is a matter of personal decision, not public truth. 'How' statements are different. So, it follows that statements about the DNA molecule, and how it governs human life, are facts, part of public truth. But statements about the purpose of human life being to glorify God are not facts; they are private opinion. Here is the fundamental split in our culture.

The older science had at least asked questions about purpose; the new science asked questions about cause. And this has opened up for us enormous vistas of knowledge and power. But there is a price to pay. If we eliminate questions about purpose, the 'why' questions, there is no way to find a factual basis for values; no way of moving from the statement, 'This is' to 'This is good'. If I say, 'My clock has not lost ten seconds in two years', most people would say 'That is a really good clock!', that is, they would move from a statement of fact to one of value without realising what they were doing. But of course, whether the clock is a good one in terms of values, depends entirely on its purpose – if it is for decorating the hall, or for throwing at a burglar, the conclusion does not follow. If we eliminate questions of purpose, then facts are value-free and we cannot call them good or bad; and such 'value-free facts' are the currency with which the public world does its business.

3   It follows from this that 'values' are relegated to a private world where one cannot speak of certain knowledge but only of personal belief. This was made explicit in the philosophy of John Locke which has had such a dominant role in all subsequent thinking in the English-speaking world. Locke defined belief as that which we fall back on when we do not have knowledge. Thus 'I believe' means 'I do not know'; statements about God and his purpose are prefaced by the words 'We believe' because we do not know; statements in a physics text-book require no such preface, as they are impersonal statements of fact!

The developments of modern physics have shown how misleading this is. All scientific knowledge rests upon faith commitments, upon beliefs (e.g. in the 'rationality of things') which cannot be demonstrated by science itself. Faith is not a substitute for knowledge, but its starting point; as Anselm used to say, 'I believe in order to understand'. In a classic sentence, Einstein said, 'In so far as the statements of mathematics are certain, they make no contact with reality; in so far as they make contact with reality, they are not certain.' The idea of a kind of knowledge which is totally impersonal, which involves no commitment on the part of the knower, is an illusion. But it dominates our culture.

4   There is illumination to be had by looking at the contribution to the discussion which is being made by the sociology of knowledge. The earlier sociologists were in general dismissive of religion, seeing it only as a reflection of psychological or social conditions. Recent writings by sociologists have been more positive. Peter Berger, for instance, uses the sociology of religion to

undergird rather than undermine the Christian claim. Berger identifies three strategies adopted by Christian thinkers: deductive (affirming Christian belief in a loud voice), reductive (dismissing Christian belief in the light of a 'modern world view'), and inductive (taking all religious experience seriously, and weighing it in 'the sober light of reason').[28] Barth, Bultmann and Schleiermacher would exemplify these three strategies. Berger himself opts for the third, taking religious experience seriously, but basing his approach on the thought of the Muslim theologian Al-Ghazali, who compared religious experience with a (happy!) state of inebriation. For Berger, religious certainty is located 'only within the enclave of religious experience itself', and cannot be had except 'precariously in recollection' in the ordinary life of the world.

While this is a much more positive affirmation of the value of religion, it still relegates it to the private sphere. In other words, Berger himself is working with the assumption of his culture that there is a public world to which religion relates only as a medicine and motivation for individuals; the question of its truth or falsity is confined to its own private world.

5   Clearly in this cultural split an early casualty would be biblical authority. How could the Bible survive in this world of 'value-free facts'? During the eighteenth century, at least in the English-speaking world, the defence of biblical authority took the form of demonstration that its teaching was in accord with 'reason', as the Enlightenment understood it. But this defence crumbled in the nineteenth century, as the encounter between Darwin's supporters and Bishop Wilberforce showed.

The result we inherit in the twentieth century is a split within the Christian community which corresponds precisely to the split down the middle of our culture. On both sides the dichotomy between 'facts' and 'values' is accepted. On the one side are fundamentalists who assert the factual inerrancy of Scripture and who regard statements of Christian doctrine as factually correct propositions of the same kind as the statements of physics or astronomy (see the 'Creation Science' advocated in the USA). On the other side are liberals who see theological statements as symbols of religious experience which is essentially inward and personal; for the latter, theology is not concerned with factual statements about the world and its history, and the Bible is simply a record of religious experience, a divine quarry of ideas. Both sides, fundamentalist and liberal, are operating within the assumptions of our culture. As C. S. Lewis used to say, when two equally sincere and intelligent people disagree, look for what they hold in common, and there you will find the fallacy.

What is reality?

How then can we know what is real, how do we come to know the truth? If 'truth' is not confined to the world of 'facts' alone, or of 'values' alone, how do

---

[28] (Berger 1980: 66–156.)

the two relate and how can we know anyway? How can we put both sides of the brain together? These are questions of epistemology.

In his bestseller entitled *The Closing of the American Mind*,[29] the Jewish philosopher Alan Bloom sees a total relativism dominating culture. Instead of speaking of 'right' and 'wrong', one speaks of 'values', 'life-styles', 'authentic persons'. We ask of a statement not 'Is it true?' but 'Are you sincere?' Bloom traces this back to Nietzsche, who saw with great clarity that the Enlightenment methods had made firm statements about absolute values impossible; the only thing left was the will, the will to power; and all this talk of values is simply Nietzsche wrapped up in cotton wool. Values, as distinct from facts, are what some people want; they are a matter of the will, not of truth; the only question is, whose will dominates?

The Hungarian physicist and philosopher Michael Polanyi expresses this in a vivid metaphor. The last 250 years of European culture, he says, have been the most brilliant in human history, but their brilliance was created by the combustion of the heritage of a thousand years of Christian civilisation in the oxygen of Greek rationalism; the fuel is now exhausted, and pumping in more oxygen cannot produce more light.

So is it possible to say with Paul, 'I know whom I have believed'? Is it possible to announce the gospel not just as an option for private choice, but as public truth for all?

Polanyi approaches our problem with a profound analysis of what is involved in the enterprise of knowing. Most discussion of epistemology in the past three centuries has approached the issue through the visual sense, the sense of sight – Polanyi approaches the matter through the sense of touch. Take the example of a surgeon who uses a probe to investigate a cavity into which he cannot look. A medical student using the probe for the first time will be conscious for a time of the pressure of the probe on the palm of his hand; as he grows in experience, he will forget this, and all his attention will be directed to what the tip of the probe is discovering in the invisible cavity; the probe becomes a kind of additional finger, an extension of his body. The surgeon feels what the tip of the probe is finding, he indwells the probe in the same kind of way that he indwells his finger.

Polanyi takes this as a way in to understanding how we know things. Like the surgeon using the probe, we explore reality by indwelling a whole range of instruments: words, concepts, images, ideas. We have to learn how to use these, and while we are learning how to use them we focus upon the new words, the new concepts; but once we have become familiar with their use we no longer focus upon them. We are tacitly aware of them, but focally aware of the reality they enable us to probe; we indwell the words, the concepts in order to focus on the reality we wish to explore. The same is true of learning

---

[29] (Bloom 1987.)

a language. For a while we have to focus on the words, the grammar, the pronunciation, but after a while we 'take off' and use the new language to talk about things without always having to pause and think, 'Am I saying it the right way?' Of course at times we find we are not communicating properly, then we have to pause and check the words and expressions we are using, looking critically at them and perhaps finding new words; but then we return to focus on the meaning. And the key point is this – we cannot at the same moment take a critical attitude to the words and use them to convey meaning.

This is true also of our culture. As we grow up we learn a whole set of tools with which we probe the world around us; these tools include books, maps, theories, dictionaries, computers and much more. When we first come across them we have to concentrate on the tools, then we learn to indwell them in order to focus on reality. And these tools are taken for granted. It usually takes a severe shock, personal or national, for us to question the assumptions of our culture. And if we do take a critical look at the assumptions of our own culture, we can only do so by relying (uncritically!) on some other way of grasping things. We cannot have a critical approach to everything at the same time! It is strictly impossible to doubt anything except on the basis of something we do not doubt, some set of beliefs we hold tacitly.

All knowing involves the uncritical acceptance of a language, of concepts, ideas and images, which we indwell and through which we seek to probe the world around us. This uncritical acceptance is at first not a matter of choice; it is in this sense that one is 'brought up a Christian' or 'brought up a Hindu'; to start with there is no other stance from which we might question our beliefs. In due course, as we meet other people, this framework of belief will be called in question by those who inhabit a different framework. From this point onwards, my personal choice is involved; I can step outside the framework and look at it critically from within another; and I can be so impressed by the clarity and coherence of the view I get that I am drawn into this other framework. Conversion is all about moving from one set of beliefs to another. Personal choice is involved – to step outside your whole framework of thought, and look at it critically from within another. This is a decision, and with it the possibility of being wrong. But it involves a commitment to reality, not just a personal preference.

[. . .] 'Can the West be converted?' That is the question underlying Christian mission today. Can the Church offer, in the context of our culture, a new 'framework of belief', a new way of grasping the totality of things? Such a framework has to challenge not only the private religious worlds of individuals, but the public world into which all of us educated in a European language have been inducted since childhood. For two and a half centuries theologians have laboured to understand the Bible from within the framework of belief of Western culture. Can we now undertake the operation in reverse, and critically examine our culture from within the framework of Scripture and the tradition of Christian thought?

Further reading

Newbigin 1986b: 25–41.
Newbigin 1988e: 98–112.
Newbigin 1989b: 1–38.

10.3 Responding to the challenge

Newbigin's response to the challenges facing the Church in the West were developed on two main levels. First, he sought to engage with the theoretical and intellectual challenges posed by the impact of the seventeenth- and eighteenth- century era of 'the Enlightenment' on the cultural consciousness of the West. Newbigin's response to the critical developments of this era is focused in his critique of the Enlightenment's overconfident search for certainty in the field of knowledge: a confidence that – owing to its shaky foundations – threatened to lead to nothing but an arid nihilism. Newbigin sought repeatedly to show that what was needed in an era in which the 'fuel' of Enlightenment thinking appeared to be running out was a proper recovery of the place of 'faith' as being essential to the quest for true knowledge – whether scientific or religious. In arguing this way, he sought to show on the one hand that 'scientific' knowledge is not as objective *as our culture assumes, and on the other that 'religious' knowledge is not as* subjective *as its Enlightenment opponents might wish to claim. The second level at which Newbigin responds to the missionary challenge is characterized by his exhortations to Christians to become truly countercultural. Only as Christians free themselves from the kind of assumptions that betray a domestication to the prevailing culture will an alternative vision be made available. This will involve a deep renewal of Christian thinking and practice in relation to faith, vocation and witness.*

The following extract brings some of these elements together. It was ori-ginally given as a lecture to members of the Evangelische Missionswerke organization in Stuttgart, Germany in October 1994, in connection with the issues arising from the publication of The Other Side of 1984 *ten years earlier.*

* * *

Extract
'The Cultural Captivity of Western Christianity as a Challenge to a Missionary Church' (1994)[30]

Twelve years ago, at the Bangkok Conference on 'Salvation Today,'[31] I was sitting in a plenary session next to General Simatoupong. Simatoupong was the

---

[30] Newbigin 1994b: 66–79.

[31] (Sponsored by the Commission on World Mission and Evangelism (CWME) of the World Council of Churches, and held in January 1973. Newbigin appears to have got his maths wrong – it would have been 21 years previously.)

general who commanded the Indonesian forces that threw the Dutch out of Indonesia, and when there was no more fighting to be done, he naturally took up theology. We were discussing the global missionary situation, and Simatoupong had just made an intervention in the debate. And as he returned to his seat beside me, I heard him say sotto voce, 'Of course the number one question is: Can the West be converted?' I have often thought of that since. I am sure he was right. What we call the modern Western scientific world view, the post-Enlightenment cultural world, is the most powerful and persuasive ideology in the world today. As we know, it operates in two forms, Eastern and Western, which are in many ways mirror images of each other. Everywhere in the world it penetrates and disrupts the ancient religious systems with 'the acids of modernity.' The Christian gospel continues to find new victories among the non-Western, premodern cultures of the world, but in the face of this modern Western culture the Church is everywhere in retreat. Can there be a more challenging frontier for the Church than this?

Simatoupong's question has reverberated in my mind ever since. Most of my life has been spent as a 'foreign missionary,' and my thinking has been shaped by this experience. Now I am a pastor, along with an Indian colleague, of an inner-city congregation in Birmingham, and I find myself, as my Indian colleague also finds himself, faced with a kind of paganism much more resistant to the gospel than anything that one can find in India. And so the question becomes a burning one: 'Can the West be converted?'

Everyone with experience of cross-cultural mission knows that there are always two opposite dangers, the Scylla and Charybdis, between which one must steer. On the one side there is the danger that one finds no point of contact for the message as the missionary preaches it, to the people of the local culture the message appears irrelevant and meaningless. On the other side is the danger that the point of contact determines entirely the way that the message is received, and the result is syncretism. Every missionary path has to find the way between these two dangers: irrelevance and syncretism. And if one is more afraid of one danger than the other, one will certainly fall into its opposite.

Since I came to live in England after a lifetime as a foreign missionary, I have had the unhappy feeling that most English theology is falling into the second danger – syncretism. Ours is an advanced case of syncretism. In other words, instead of confronting our culture with the gospel, we are perpetually trying to fit the gospel into our culture. In our effort to communicate, we interpret the gospel by the categories of our culture. But how can we avoid this? How can we, who are part of this culture, find a standpoint from which we can address a word, the word of the gospel, to our culture? Archimedes said: Give me a point outside of the earth and with a lever I will move the earth. Where is the Archimedean point from which we can challenge the culture of which we are ourselves a part? Can the experience of cross-cultural mission help us in this task?

When I went as a young missionary to India, I could find the elements of syncretism in Indian Christianity. I saw how, inevitably, the meaning of sentences spoken by my Christian friends was shaped by the Hindu background of the language. The words used, the only available words for God, sin, salvation, and so on, are words that have received their entire content from the Hindu religious tradition. I thought that I was in a position to correct this syncretism. Only slowly did I come to see that my own Christianity was also profoundly syncretistic. Many times I sat with groups of Indian pastors and evangelists to study together a passage of Scripture. Over and over again their interpretation of the text, as it spoke to them in their language, called my interpretation into question. And it was not always clear that my interpretation was in fact more faithful to the text. Many times I had to confess that my reading of the text, which I had hitherto taken for granted, was wholly shaped by my own intellectual formation in what we call the modern scientific world view. My Christianity was syncretistic, but so was theirs. Yet neither of us could discover that without the challenge of the other. Such is the situation in cross-cultural mission. The gospel comes to the Hindu embodied in the form given to it by the culture of the missionary. That form is both a way of thinking and a way of living. It challenges the traditional Hindu form. The first converts will naturally accept it in the form in which it came from the missionaries, and the form and content cannot be immediately distinguished. But as the second and third and later generations of Christians make their own explorations in Scripture, they will begin to test the Christianity of the missionaries in the light of their own reading of the Scripture. So the missionary, if he is at all awake, finds himself, as I did, in a new situation. He becomes, as a bearer of the gospel, a critic of his own culture. He finds there the Archimedean point. He sees his own culture with the Christian eyes of a foreigner, and the foreigner can see what the native cannot see. We do not see the lenses of our spectacles; we see through them, and it is another who has to say to us, 'Friend, you need a new pair of spectacles.' The question therefore is this: 'How can the European Churches, whose life and thought is shaped so completely by this post-Enlightenment culture, become bearers of a mission to that culture?'

I know that we are all very enthusiastic about dialogue with people of other faiths and cultures. It is interesting that we use this word *dialogue*. When I talk with my non-Christian neighbor across the garden fence, I just have a conversation, but when I am really serious, then of course it is a dialogue. And that is good, but the problem is that all this dialogue is conducted exclusively in the languages of Europe – German, English, Spanish. No one is qualified to take part in this kind of dialogue without having a full education in a European language and therefore being fully co-opted into the post-Enlightenment world view. That becomes very explicit in a little aside in Hans Küng's book *Christsein*, where he says that we cannot have real deep-going dialogue with the great world religions until they develop 'a scientific theology.'[32] In other words, the dialogue is only possible within the parameters of

---

[32] Küng 1976.

the post-Enlightenment world view. That view remains unchallenged. We do not see it as our ideology. It is just how things are when you are properly educated! The gospel, along with all other religions, is simply co-opted as one equal partner within that ideology.

And that brings me to the crux of the matter. In the little pamphlet – a small blast not of the trumpet but of the tin whistle – called *The Other Side of 1984*,[33] I said that it seemed to me that while the Roman Catholic Church had attempted to erect barriers against the Enlightenment, the Protestant Churches had, in effect, surrendered the public field – politics, education, industry, economics – to the ideology of the Enlightenment and sought refuge in the private world of the home and the soul. This sharp dichotomy between the public and the private world is one of the distinctive features of our culture. Such a dichotomy is not found in traditional premodern cultures. It corresponds to the distinction we draw between 'facts' and 'values.' The public world of our culture is the world of what we call 'facts,' which do not depend upon the beliefs of the individual; 'values' on the other hand are personal beliefs, and in the world of values pluralism reigns. Each one must be free to cherish the values that he or she chooses. No one, no state or Church or party, has the right to dictate common beliefs regarding values. Everyone has the right to the pursuit of happiness, and – what is more important – everyone has the right to define happiness as he will. It is to this world of personally chosen values that religion is thought to belong. And Christianity is one among the options offered for personal choice. It has freedom to compete with others, provided it makes no claim to absolute truth. In contrast to this is the public world of what we call facts. Here pluralism emphatically does not reign. Here all are expected to agree. Where there are apparent contradictions between statements of alleged facts, we do not celebrate this as a good example of pluralism. We argue and experiment and test until we arrive at a point where all agree; and for those who cannot agree we have, of course, our mental hospitals. In the school textbook these agreed-upon conclusions will be simply stated as facts without the use of the prefix 'I believe' or 'We believe.' Thus every student will be expected to know that the development of the human person is governed by the program encoded in the DNA molecules. This is a fact. But that every human person is made to glorify God and enjoy him forever is not a fact – it is a belief, one among many possible beliefs. It is not part of the school curricula. And yet, clearly the question of truth is at stake as much in the second matter as in the first. It either is or is not true that every human being must finally appear before the judgment seat of Christ. If it is true, it is universally true, just as the statement about the DNA molecule is true; if it is true at all, it is true for everyone. It belongs to the public sector as much as to the private.

---

[33] Newbigin 1983; Newbigin 1993d: 252f.

What is the source of this dichotomy between the public world of facts and the private world of beliefs? It is a complex story, and I am not an expert in the history of philosophy. Certain things can, I think, be said with confidence. Ever since Galileo turned his telescope on the heavens and showed that the universe is not what it seems to be, there has been a passionate search for a kind of certainty, a kind of knowledge that does not depend on fallible human beliefs. Descartes sought it in the certainty of his own thought; the new scientists sought it in the precise observation of the data of the senses without reliance on the traditional beliefs of religion and philosophy, and particularly without reliance on the traditional concept of purpose through which the Greeks and the medieval scholars had tried to interpret phenomena. This new observation of the phenomena was held to give knowledge of what Francis Bacon called the facts. And a fact in this sense has no value. A thing can only be called good or bad if it is or is not fitted for the purpose for which it was made. And this purpose is real in the mind of the one who purposes, but it is not yet fully realized in the world of objects. It can, in principle, only be grasped by an act of faith. That faith enables us to understand the world of objects, not as mere facts about which no value judgment can be made, but in relation to the purpose for which they exist. And that gives a different kind of certainty from the certainty our culture seeks. It is not a certainty that relieves me of personal responsibility for my beliefs. It is a personal trust. It relies on grace. It does not claim – in contrast to the search of our culture – the kind of knowledge only God can have. It is the certainty of faith, not of omniscience. John Locke – whose thinking, I suppose, has shaped the Anglo-Saxon world almost more than any other since the Enlightenment – John Locke defined belief as something we fall back on when certain knowledge is unattainable.[34] I say 'I believe' only when I am not in a position to say 'I know.' As I heard a philosopher put it wittily the other day, 'If I believe, then I don't know.' So I *know* the facts in the physics textbook, but I only *believe* what the gospel promises. The public world is the world of what we know, and here pluralism is excluded. The private world is the world of what we believe, and here pluralism rules.

But of course, this is profoundly false. Scientists themselves know that science rests on a faith-commitment that cannot be demonstrated, on the faith that the universe is both rational and contingent. If the universe were not rational, science would be impossible. If the universe were not contingent, science would be unnecessary. Faith therefore is not a substitute for knowledge. It is the precondition of knowledge. And the kind of certainty that our post-Enlightenment culture has aspired to is an illusion. The idea that brute facts simply imprint themselves on our minds apart from our deliberate and fallible efforts to grasp them is an illusion. And so also the idea that there is a body of objective value-free facts against which the Christian claims and the

---

[34] Locke 1975. Originally written in 1690.

claims of all other religions have to be tested is nonsense. The Christian faith in God as creator and sustainer of a world that is both rational and contingent made possible the rise of modern science. Today, if I am not mistaken, our great danger is a total skepticism about any possibility of knowing the truth. I find among young people, and I think I understand and sympathize with them, a profound skepticism about any claim to the truth. Our danger is of a new irrationalism and nihilism. It is the despair that doubts there is anything worth believing and preserving. And even Christians are encouraged to think of their faith as only one among a number of options available for personal choice. We may be convinced that it is a source of comfort, of hope, of inner peace. And when we try to commend it to others, we try to show that it is not incompatible with the modern scientific world view that controls public life; but we commend it as a responsible and respectable option for the private sector. Am I wrong? Is this a caricature?

If I think of the English Church scene, I do not think so. Like others who have returned to the West after a lifetime as a foreign missionary, I am moved to ask, Who will be the missionaries to this culture? Who will confront this culture of ours with the claim of absolute truth, the claim that Jesus Christ is the truth? Who will be bold enough to say, not that the Christian message can be explained in terms of the facts as we know them, but rather that *all* so-called knowledge must be tested against the supreme reality: God incarnate in Jesus Christ, present yesterday, today, until the end, in the power of the Spirit? What will it mean to call for a missionary confrontation with this culture?

I confess that as I ask these questions I am alarmed. I do not know where they will lead us. I say that in all honesty: I do not know where they will lead us. And yet I am bound to ask these questions. Certainly we cannot expect or desire to return to the *Corpus Christianum*. We cannot reconstruct the total synthesis of Christian belief and public order that finally broke down in the religious wars of the seventeenth century. But equally, I think, and this may be more unpopular, we cannot simply go back to the New Testament and the primitive Church. We cannot aspire now, after these nineteen centuries, to a kind of pre-Constantinian innocence. That kind of nostalgia is dangerous. I hear too many Christians saying, in effect, that the Church can have nothing to do with power, that its only function is to protest and demonstrate against all the powers. We cannot do without a theologically grounded Christian doctrine of the state. We must not fall into the error of dividing physical force as bad from soul force (*satyagraha*) as good. That is the old Manichean heresy. There is no going back. We are in a new and unprecedented situation, a new missionary frontier. How do we approach this task? As I said, I am puzzled and even frightened. I do not know what this will involve. I see dangers on all sides. But so that I may not end with a set of unanswered questions, let me try to make five constructive points:

1   If what I have been saying is true, there is need for what I would call a declericalizing of theology. Theology has been largely the preserve of clergy

and academics. What is needed is the co-operative work of Christian laymen and women in specific sectors of public life: industry, politics, medicine, education, local government, welfare, administration, the media, literature, drama, and the arts. In each of these and other sectors of public life there is a need to examine the accepted axioms and assumptions that underlie the contemporary practice, to examine them in the light of the gospel. That will not happen as long as theology is the preserve of the clergy or, what is equally dangerous, simply an enclave within a secular academic community. There is an immense intellectual and pastoral task in which the experience of the foreign missionary movement could, I believe, be of great help to the Churches in making this move towards a more truly missionary relationship with our culture.

2   It is obvious that this can only be done by the Churches acting together. It can only be done as the Church *in* each place becomes recognizable as the Church *for* that place. But what is a denomination? Perhaps I could refer to the somewhat uncomfortable question raised by Ulrich Duchrow in his book *Conflict in the Ecumenical Movement*.[35] This is a question that will not go away. A denomination is not a Church, it is not a sect, it does not make the claim to the allegiance of society as a whole. It has been defined by one of its apologists, the American sociologist Sidney Mead, in the following terms: 'It is a voluntary association of like-minded and like-hearted individuals who are united on the basis of common beliefs for the purpose of accomplishing tangible and defined objectives. One of the primary objectives is the propagation of its point of view.' In that description we recognize the American denominational model, but it is clearly a model that is tending to reproduce itself everywhere, especially through the increasingly powerful operation of the world confessional bodies. And, as the sociologists have pointed out, the denomination is simply the institutional form of privatized religion. It is a voluntary association of individuals. It is to put it simply – the outward and visible form of an inward and spiritual surrender to the ideology of our culture. It follows that, in strict logic, neither the denomination alone nor denominations federated in what is now, I believe, called 'reconciled diversity' can become the instrument of a missionary challenge to our culture, because they are themselves the institutional form of a surrender to our culture. They cannot confront our culture as Jesus confronted Pontius Pilate with the witness to the truth, since they do not claim to be more than associations of individuals who hold the same opinion. We do not see clearly what the form of a restored and reunited catholic Church would be. That is our great task in the ecumenical movement. But I believe that it is possible to act effectively in each local situation in such a way that the Christians together in each place begin even now to be recognizable as the Church for that place.

3   If we are to escape from the ideology of the Enlightenment without falling into the errors of the *Corpus Christianum*, we must recover a doctrine

---

[35] Duchrow 1981.

of freedom of thought and conscience that is founded not on the ideology of the Enlightenment but on the gospel. At this point I think I must admit that my use of the word *dogma* in my little book was perhaps a tactical mistake. It was intended to shock people into recognizing the fact that we all operate with dogmas. The difference is whether we recognize that we do. The freedom of conscience, the freedom of thought that was won for us by the men and women of the Enlightenment against the resistance of the Church, is a gift we cannot surrender. We must remember penitently our past in that respect. But if we now ask that the Christian faith claim the whole public life of the nation, of society in the name of truth, how can we safeguard that freedom?

What we must seek for is a doctrine of freedom based on the gospel and not on the ideology of the Enlightenment. And we must begin by distinguishing tolerance from neutrality or indifference. There is a beautiful description of Roman society in Gibbon's *Decline and Fall of the Roman Empire* that I think exactly describes ours. He said that in Roman society all religions were to the people equally true, to the philosophers equally false, and to the government equally useful. It would be difficult to deny that that is a true account of some modern developed societies. But that kind of neutrality is evidence either of impending collapse or else of the fact that some other ideology has taken the place usually occupied by religion as the overarching 'plausibility structure' within which public life is conducted. Since total skepticism about ultimate beliefs is impossible, in that no belief can be doubted except on the basis of some other belief, indifference is always in danger of collapsing into skepticism or fanaticism. Tolerance in respect of what is not important is easy. How is it possible to combine real commitment to the truth in matters of supreme importance with tolerance of falsehood?

Clearly, if we are to be consistent, the answer has to be given from within our commitment to the truth as it is in Jesus, not sought from outside of that truth. It can be given in the form of three statements.

First, let us recall the fact that the risen Jesus, whose kingship was defined as bearing witness to the truth, also warned his Church against the temptation to expect immediately the manifestation of the truth in coercive power. 'Lord, will you at this time restore the kingdom of Israel?' The answer is: It is not for you to know the times and seasons that the Father has set in his own authority, but you will receive the Spirit, the foretaste, the *arrabon* of the kingdom and you will be my witnesses (Acts 1.6–7). In other words, it is the will of the Father to provide a space and a time wherein men and women can give their allegiance to the kingship of God in the only way that it can be given, that is, in freedom. To use the God-given authority of the state to deny this freedom is therefore to violate the space that God himself has provided and that he has put into the care – if I understand the New Testament rightly – of earthly governors, of the powers that be.

Second, the Church, which is entrusted with the truth, is also a body of sinful men and women who falsely identify their grasp of truth with the truth

itself. Here we have that paradox of grace that the Church is a body of forgiven sinners, which applies equally to the Church's understanding of the
truth. That is brought out with brilliant clarity in that incident in the Gospel
where Jesus has to say to Peter, 'You are the rock and on this rock I will build
my church,' and in the next breath, 'Get behind me, Satan' (Matt. 16.18, 23).
This deep fundamental paradox of the Church is real because sin remains a
reality in the life of the forgiven community. The Church can and does allow
the truth that is entrusted to her to become an ideological justification of her
own human interest. And God consequently has to use his other servants, and
especially the state, to bring the Church to repentance and renewal.

Third, I return to the Johannine discourses in which our Lord tells his disciples that they have yet much to learn of the truth that cannot be told them
immediately, and that it is the Spirit who will be given to them who will lead
them into the truth. The context of that saying is of course the long account
of the missionary experience that lies ahead of the Church, its rejection by the
world, and the witness that the Spirit will give in speaking for the Church, in
confusing the wisdom of the world, and in glorifying Jesus by taking what
belongs to the Father and showing it to the Church (John 15.18—16.15).
This promise is being fulfilled as the Church goes on its missionary journey
to the ends of the earth and to the end of time, entering into dialogue with
new cultures and being itself changed, as parts of the Father's world are
brought through the Spirit into the Church's treasury of truth. In this missionary dialogue the Church both learns new things and provides the place
where witness is borne to Christ as head of the human race – Christ, who is
so much more than any of us can yet grasp or state, who is seen more and
more through the missionary experience of the Church as he truly is, but who
will only be seen in his fullness when every tongue confesses that he is Lord.

Thus, if I am right, a true understanding of the gospel itself ought to enable
Christians both to be firm in their allegiance to Christ as the way, the truth,
and the life, and also to be ready to hear and enter into dialogue with those
who do not give that allegiance but from whom the Church has still to learn
of all that belongs to the Father. The mind that is firmly anchored in Christ,
knowing that Christ is much greater than the limited understanding that each
of us has of him, is at the same time able to enter freely into the kind of missionary dialogue I have described. This is the foundation for a true tolerance,
not indifference to the truth. True dialogue is as far as possible from neutrality or indifference. Its basis is the shared conviction that there is truth to be
known and that we must both bear witness to the truth given to us and also
listen to the witness of others.

4   I want to make a strictly theological point. There can be no missionary
encounter with our culture without a biblically grounded eschatology, without a recovering of a true apocalyptic. The dichotomy that runs through our
culture between the private and the public worlds is reflected in the dissolution of the biblical vision of the last things into two separate and unrelated
forms of hope. One is the public hope for a better world in the future, the

heavenly city of the eighteenth-century French philosophers, the utopia of the evolutionary social planners, or the classless society of the revolutionary sociologists. The other is the private hope for personal immortality in a blessed world beyond this one. This dissolution is tragic. It destroys the integrity of the human person. If I pin my hope to a perfect world that is to be prepared for some future generations, I know that I and my contemporaries will never live to see it, and therefore that those now living can be – and if necessary must be – sacrificed in the interests of those as yet unborn; and so the way is open for the ruthless logic of totalitarian planners and social engineers. If on the other hand I place all my hope in a personal future, I am tempted to wash my hands of responsibility for the public life of the world and to turn inwards towards a purely private spirituality.

That tragic split runs right through our lives and our society, and only the biblical understanding of the last things can heal that dichotomy. The apocalyptic teaching that forms such an important part of the New Testament has generally in our culture been pushed to the margins of Christian thought. It has been treasured, of course, by small oppressed groups on the margins of our society, but it has been generally silenced in the mainstream of our established Christianity. Essentially this says to us: If I ask what in all my active life is the horizon of my expectations, the thing to which I look forward, the answer, it seems to me, cannot be some social utopia in the future and cannot be some personal bliss for myself, it can only be, quite simply, the coming of Jesus to complete his Father's will. He shall come again. He is the horizon of my expectations. Everything from my side, whether prayer or action, private or public, is done to him and for him. It is simply offered for his use. In the words of Schweitzer, it is an 'acted prayer for His coming.' He will make of it what he will. My most vigorous and righteous actions do not build the holy city. They are too shot through with sin for that. But they are acted prayers that he will give the holy city. And that embraces both the public and the private world. The holy city, as its name indicates, is on the one hand the crown and perfection of all that we call civilization. Into it the kings of the nations bring their cultural treasures. But it is also the place where every tear is wiped from our eyes and we are the beloved children of God who see him face to face. Only in that vision and hope is the tragic dichotomy of our culture healed.

5   Finally, I want to argue the need for a certain boldness that was evidently a characteristic mark of the first apostles. Some time ago I happened to have the privilege of sitting next to Cardinal Suenens at a conference, and he asked me what I thought of contemporary English theology. I replied 'timid syncretism.' Perhaps that was unfair. I am sure it cannot be true of German theology. What I am pleading for is the courage to hold and proclaim a belief that cannot be proved to be true in terms of the accepted axioms of our society, that can be doubted by rational minds, but that we nevertheless hold as the truth. It may sound simplistic to say that. Our modern scientific culture has pursued the ideal of a completely impersonal knowledge of a world of so-called facts that are simply there and cannot be doubted by rational minds,

facts that constitute the real world as distinct from the opinions, desires, hopes, and beliefs of human beings. Now, this whole way of trying to understand the world rests upon beliefs that are simply not questioned. Every attempt to understand and cope with experience has to begin with some act of faith. Every such belief is of course open to critical question, but no criticism is possible except by relying on beliefs that in the act of criticism are not criticized. All understanding of reality involves a venture of faith. No belief system can be faulted by the fact that it rests upon unproved assumptions. What can and must be faulted is a blindness to the assumptions one is relying upon. The gospel is not a set of beliefs that arise or could arise from empirical observation of the whole human experience. It cannot be based upon inductive reasoning. It is the announcement of a name and a fact that offer the starting point for the whole lifelong enterprise of understanding and coping with experience. It is a new starting point. To accept it means a new beginning, a radical conversion. We cannot side-step that necessity. It has always been the case that to believe means to turn around and face in a different direction, to be a dissident, to swim against the stream. The Church, it seems to me, needs to be very humble in acknowledging that it is itself only a learner, needing to pay heed to all the variety of human experience in order to learn in practice what it means that Jesus is King and Head of the human race. But the Church also needs to be very bold, bold in bearing witness to him as the one who alone is that King and Head. For the demonstration of the truth we have to wait for the end. Till then we have to be bold and steadfast in our witness and patient in our hope, for, to quote the letter to the Hebrews, we are partakers of Christ if we hold our first confidence firm to the end (Heb. 3.14).

Further reading

Newbigin 1986a: 57–68.
Newbigin 1985a: 25–37. (Reprinted as Newbigin 1987a: 355–68.)
Newbigin 1990b: 162–6.

11

The gospel and public life

11.1 Proclamation and persuasion

The conviction that lies at the heart of Newbigin's writings – and is especially prominent in the pieces he wrote towards the end of his life – is that the gospel of Jesus Christ is 'public' news. It is not merely a private 'opinion' held by those who happen to be religiously inclined, but rests upon certain facts which surround God's self-disclosure in history in the person of his Son Jesus Christ. But upon what authority do these facts rest? And on what grounds are Christians able to declare this good news to others? The following extracts illustrate Newbigin's answers to these questions. They show a combination of his skills in addressing the prevailing intellectual climate, as well as offering more practical guidance for Christians in their work and witness.

The first extract is from The Gospel in a Pluralist Society *(1989), and addresses the question of how Christians are justified in their beliefs. In a culture that has largely dismissed Christian faith from the public realm, is it now the case that belief must simply be regarded as a private option? Newbigin's response to this question is to look deeply at the issue of 'truth' – not just in religious matters, but also in the realm of science. In this lengthy but important argument he draws once more on the work of Michael Polanyi, who argued that at the heart of all kinds of knowing lies the indispensable exercise of faith. Newbigin draws parallels between scientific and religious 'knowing', and argues that both are held – in Polanyi's words – 'with universal intent'. By this, he means that they make contact with a reality exterior to the knower, and therefore touch upon matters of universal truth and significance that are necessarily 'public'. It is because of this that truth-discoverers are impelled to make known (or to 'publish') what they have discovered, in the confidence not only that such insights are important in themselves, but that they will in turn lead to further truth.*

The second extract was originally published in the Dutch journal Kerk en Theologie *in 1990. Beginning with an attack on the modern myth that a 'secular' society is one in which 'facts' are 'value-free', Newbigin explores the question of what the practice of 'evangelism' means in this kind of society. The final extract is taken from Newbigin's later book,* Proper Confidence, *published in 1995. Here, he specifically addresses the subject of apologetics, arguing that for too long our approach to the defence of Christian faith has rested on the attempt to make it sound rationally 'plausible' to the ears of our contemporaries. In contrast to this Newbigin develops the argument that* true apologetics must start not from some supposedly 'neutral' foundation but from the revelation of the gospel itself.

***

Extract 1
The Gospel in a Pluralist Society *(1989)*[1]

The movement of the Enlightenment in the eighteenth century, the movement which brought our contemporary Western culture to its distinctive self-consciousness, was in an important respect a movement of rejection of tradition and its authority. Immanuel Kant summed up the central theme of the Enlightenment in the famous phrase 'Dare to Know.' It was a summons to have the courage to think for oneself, to test everything in the light of reason and conscience, to dare to question even the most hallowed traditions. That robust determination remains operative as perhaps the central thrust of our culture, of what is happening now in every part of the world under the name of 'modernization.' Any attempt to affirm and defend the Christian faith within our modern scientific world view has necessarily to answer the questions the Enlightenment put to tradition and the authority of tradition.

The first thing to be said is that a movement of this kind is irreversible. One cannot go back. It is one thing to say 'The Church has always taught' or 'The Bible teaches,' if one is part of a culture which accepts these as authoritative. But it is quite a different thing to say these things in a culture which does not. If, in a modern society today, I say 'The Bible teaches,' I will at once have to answer the question: 'But why should I believe the Bible?' In this culture an appeal to the Bible is simply an expression of my personal choice of this particular authority among the many which I might choose from. This is the point Peter Berger makes in the title of his book *The Heretical Imperative.*[2] In a pre-Enlightenment society there are only a few heretics in the original sense of the word, that is to say, only a few people who make their own decisions about what to believe. For the vast majority faith is not a matter of personal decision: it is simply the acceptance of what everybody accepts because it is obviously the case. There is no alternative and no personal choice. By contrast, Berger rightly says, in a post-Enlightenment society we are all required to be heretics, we are all required to make a personal choice. Everyone, as the saying goes, has to have a faith of his or her own. If, then, I appeal to the authority of the Bible or the Church, that is simply my personal choice. It does not settle any argument.

---

[1] Newbigin 1989b: 39–51.
[2] (Berger 1980.)

Of course one could point out, in response to Peter Berger, that his heretical imperative is not universal. There are elements in our culture where tradition is operative. No one, in our culture, suggests that each of us should have a physics of his own or a biology of her own. We know, of course, that there are arguments among physicists and biologists, just as there have always been arguments among biblical scholars and Church theologians. But where there is a consensus among physicists, as there is across the vast range of matter which is included, for example, in a school textbook of physics, we accept that as authoritative. In this field, the statement 'All physicists are agreed that . . .' is normally enough to settle an argument. There is no significant proportion of our society which simply dismisses the findings of the physicists as merely private, subjective preferences. In the case of statements about Christian belief, however, the situation is obviously different. A very large section of society simply dismisses the statements of theologians as expressions of personal opinion – opinion which they are entitled to hold but which does not rank as public truth, as factual knowledge in the sense that the statements of physicists do. If Christians then appeal to the authority of Scripture or of the Church, they know that others will regard this appeal as simply the expression of a personal choice. How, in this situation, can Christians affirm their statements as public, factual, objective truth?

My own first teacher in theology was John Oman, and there was no issue about which Oman felt so passionately as the issue of individual freedom and responsibility in pursuing and grasping the truth. His book *Vision and Authority*,[3] with its subtitle 'The Throne of St Peter,' was a passionate assertion of the right and duty of individual search for truth over against the claims of ecclesiastical authority. He takes Jesus' command that we are to become as little children to be his authorization of a spirit of endless and relentless curiosity which refuses to be fobbed off with authoritarian answers. And in an unforgettable chapter entitled 'The Authority of the Optic Nerve' he contemplates the fragility of the instrument through which we perceive the world, so small and so liable to failure, and asks the question: 'Why is the channel of sight a nerve and not a sinew, a thread and not a cable? Why, if the Creator would grant a vehicle of knowledge of the outer world, is it so weak and delicate?'[4] It would seem, in other words, that the Creator had intended fallibility to be part of our human nature, and that the appeal to an authority beyond our own fallible vision is an offense against our Creator. And so, in a chapter entitled 'The Essential Attitude,' Oman writes: 'All man's faculties afford their own demonstration and require no external guidance, nay, err if they are subjected to any such interference.'[5]

There is surely a vital element of truth in this, and there are situations in which it is this element which needs to be emphasized. But it is a one-sided

---

[3] (Oman 1902.)
[4] Oman 1902: 44.
[5] Oman 1902: 40.

emphasis. A teacher of mathematics who has tried to teach her pupils the elements of geometry will not be content until the pupil can see for himself or herself that it is true that the three angles of every triangle add up to 180 degrees. The teacher will not be content if the child simply accepts it on her authority and – when questioned by someone who does not understand – can only say, 'My teacher says so.' And yet the child will certainly not reach the point of understanding without first accepting the authority of the teacher. We do not expect each fresh generation of schoolchildren to discover the whole of Euclid by the unaided exercise of native curiosity.

It is instructive to compare at this point the differing approaches to learning which are currently used in science and in religion. There is a great deal of contemporary literature about the teaching of religion which emphasizes almost exclusively the freedom and autonomy of the child, and which strongly condemns any attempt to impose on the mind of the child any particular view of religious truth. One may take as an authoritative example the report entitled 'Understanding Christian Nurture,' produced by the British Council of Churches in 1981 under the chairmanship of Bishop John Gibb.[6] The report affirms as the purpose of Christian nurture the development in children of 'critical openness' or 'autonomy.' Tillich's concept of theonomy as something distinct both from heteronomy and from autonomy is rejected, since either God must give me reasons for submitting to him or else theonomy is simply heteronomy. In the words of the report: 'Either divine authority is presented to us with reasons, in which case we must discern them in critical openness in order to obey God, or, on the other hand, God is a dictator'.[7] Children are to be taught to use their critical faculties in respect of any claim to truth, and to be open to new truths which might call in question their previous ideas of truth. The Christian must learn to 'act as if it were possibly the case that his beliefs were false'.[8] The problem, of course, is that one can only entertain rational doubt about a proposition on the basis of some belief which, at that moment, one does not doubt. To doubt all one's beliefs at the same time is impossible. The report recognizes this in a later section where it is said that 'a certain element of dogmatism is necessary to balance the critical principle since without this the criticism itself would seldom be sufficiently sustained and penetrating'.[9] The problem here is that it is not possible to be both dogmatic and doubtful about the same beliefs at the same time. One can only be doubtful about some beliefs if one is at the same time firm in holding others. In spite of this concession to dogma, the report overwhelmingly emphasizes the critical principle as the one which is to be fostered in the nurture of children. The approach corresponds to the succinct statement made by the legal representative of the school board in a recent case in the US courts, a

---

[6] (Report 1981.)
[7] Report 1981: 19.
[8] Report 1981: 26.
[9] Report 1981: 26.

case in which Christian parents were objecting to the things their children were learning in the state schools. 'The schools seek to teach students to be autonomous individuals who can make their own judgments about moral questions. The schools believe that students should be able to evaluate and make judgments on their own, based on their experience and beliefs, not on those of their teachers.'

The contrast between this approach and the approach to the teaching of science in schools is obvious. The science teacher has a clear and firm view of what is the case about – for example – the laws governing the expansion of gases, and he expects that as a result of the teaching the pupils will also believe the same thing. This 'believing' must mean, of course, that the pupil has really understood it, believes it to be true because he or she sees that it is true; it will not be enough that the pupil learns to repeat what the teacher says; the pupil must also understand it as true. And that means that the pupil will have to be encouraged to ask critical questions. There is no other way by which the new truth can really be grasped. But the teacher will certainly not be satisfied if, at the end, the pupil has an open mind on the truth or otherwise of what is taught, nor will the teacher at any stage give the pupils the impression that the truth or otherwise of Boyle's Law is a matter of private opinion.

This 'understanding' is more than a matter of logical argument. It is much more a kind of intuition. Most of us can, perhaps, remember early struggles with school mathematics. There is a time, sometimes a long time, when one simply cannot see what the point of it is. The teacher's words are clear and simple, but one cannot see the point. And then, suddenly, the penny drops. One sees that there is something true and beautiful and satisfying. Afterward it is impossible to see how we could not see it before. The logical steps the teacher took in explaining it are now quite clear, and we wonder why they were not clear before. It is a little like trying to learn how to ride a bicycle. You can be told all about the way balance is kept by turning the front wheel this way or that, but you still fall off. But then, suddenly, you know how to do it, and after that you soon reach the point where the actions needed to keep your balance are no longer a matter of deliberate decision. You have so internalized them that you no longer attend to them but think only about where you are going. While you are still learning and falling off, you have to accept in faith the belief that people *can* ride a two-wheeled machine without falling off. You have to submit yourself to the tradition of bicycle-riding until the point comes when you have internalized the tradition and it has become part of your own self. The same is true in respect of our learning in mathematics and science. As Michael Polanyi has said, 'The authority of science is essentially traditional'.[10]

The statement of Polanyi stands in sharp contrast to the way science is popularly understood. One could quote as typical of the popular understanding

---

[10] Polanyi 1969: 66.

of science some words of Bertrand Russell: 'The triumphs of science are due to the substitution of observation and inference for authority. Every attempt to revive authority in intellectual matters is a retrograde step . . . One of the great benefits that science confers upon those who understand its spirit is that it enables them to live without the delusive support of subjective authority'.[11] How is one to explain these contradictory views of the place of authority in science? The answer is partly by reference to history. At the critical time when the new science was developing it was necessary to reject elements in the traditional teaching of the Church. It was necessary to set the actual visibility of the moons of Jupiter through the telescope against the traditional teaching that there could not be such moons. In this sense observable facts had to be set against the authority of a tradition. And such oppositions are obviously necessary at many points in the development of human thought. But it is an elementary mistake to assume, therefore, that the authority of tradition has no necessary part to play in the quest for truth. The actual practice of science shows that Polanyi is right. Polanyi has followed the advice of Einstein, who said that if you want to understand science you should not listen to what scientists say but watch what they do. In other words, we will get a better understanding of science if we look behind the finished product to the workshop, the laboratory where the creative work on the frontiers of science is done.

I began by looking at the experience we have all had in our first attempts to learn mathematics or physics. We have to rely on the authority of the teachers, but the purpose for which this authority is exercised is that we should come to see for ourselves that what is being taught is true. Clearly also the teacher herself has had to rely and continues to rely on the authority of the scientific tradition as embodied in the standard textbooks. But behind these textbooks lies a whole range of material – articles in learned journals, lectures and seminars in which the frontiers are being pushed back and new ideas are being explored. It is through this work that the tradition is being continually developed and reshaped – sometimes by gradual adjustments, sometimes by dramatic changes which Thomas Kuhn calls 'paradigm shifts.' But how do these changes, these new discoveries, take place? [. . .] There are no logical rules by which one can learn how to make new discoveries. There are certainly no logical steps by which one could argue from the premises of Newton's physics to the formulations of the special and general theories of relativity. It has much more to do with intuition and imagination – the intuition that there is a problem waiting to be tackled, a configuration of things waiting to be discerned, an orderliness not yet manifest but hidden and waiting to be discovered. And it is a matter of personal judgment between alternative possibilities for experiment and research, personal judgment also in distinguishing between a meaningful pattern and a set of random events.

---

[11] Bertrand Russell, *The Impact of Science on Society*, 1952; quoted in Polanyi 1969: 94.

None of this can be embodied in formal rules which could be applied without taking the risks involved in personal judgment. That is why the scientific tradition can only be passed on through personal contact between teachers and learners. This is true even at elementary levels. A child cannot grasp even elementary mathematics simply by reading a textbook; the help of a teacher is essential. A medical student is not qualified to become a doctor simply by reading all the textbooks on physiology, anatomy and the like. When she has completed this she has to go through a long period of clinical training in which she learns through hour-by-hour contact with an expert as he does his work. She may have learned all she can from a textbook on diseases of the lungs, but she will still need this clinical practice with an experienced doctor before she can learn to interpret the lights and shades of an X-ray picture. She has to acquire this skill through a long period of practice, and there is no way of acquiring it except by submitting herself to the authority of a practitioner who is already acknowledged as possessing this skill, and certified by the scientific community as a competent teacher.

The same holds true from this elementary level right through to the highest levels of original research. Only after a long period in which the student has submitted herself to the authority of the tradition is she qualified to work alongside a scientist who is doing original research on problems which are not only unsolved, but perhaps not even recognized except by this scientist. It will only be by watching this scientist at work, seeing how he tackles difficulties, chooses lines of inquiry, evaluates ambiguous evidence, and projects fresh and original ideas that the student will learn the skill of research. There are no impersonal and mechanically applicable rules by which such original research can be guided. There are no objective criteria by which the work of the scientist can be judged: he, along with his peers, is the one who sets the standards and determines the criteria, and – in doing so – accepts the risks of failure as well as the possibility of success. The question of success or failure may not be settled for a long time. Einstein's theories were, after much debate, accepted on the basis of their intrinsic beauty and completeness, but it was only long afterward that there was any experimental verification of their truth. In fact, a great many attempts were made to test their truth by repetitions of the Morley Michelson tests, and they did not give the results required by Einstein's theory. Polanyi records that in a broadcast discussion with Bertrand Russell they both agreed that Einstein's theory was never likely to have any practical consequences. Only a few days later the first atomic bomb was exploded, and since that fateful date we have learned of many more practical consequences that have flowed from his theory. Yet the theory was held as true by scientists even in the absence of proof or of practical utility. This is an example of an important feature of scientific discovery. The theory was held to be true because of its intrinsic beauty, rationality, and comprehensiveness. These qualities were taken to indicate that it corresponded with reality, and that therefore it would open the way for new discoveries. The holding of the theory for truth is an act of faith in the rationality of the cosmos. The justification – if one may put it so – is by faith; only afterward, as a spin-off, does one find that it is also justified because it works. The analogy with Christian faith hardly needs to be pointed out.

A major paradigm shift, such as that from the Newtonian physics to that of Einstein, does not take place easily. Perhaps it will come mainly through the conversion of younger scientists to the new view. A similar long debate took place before the Copernican paradigm replaced the Ptolemaic. For such paradigms form the world within which scientists work for generations. They form the lenses through which things are perceived. They are not easily or lightly abandoned. I spoke [. . .] about Polanyi's use of the example of a probe. In the act of using the probe we do not attend to the probe but to the lumps and cavities which are being explored by the tip of the probe. The probe becomes an extension of my hand. I indwell it, just as I indwell all the bodily functions – eyes, ears, fingers, and so on – through which I explore the world. I do not attend to them, but through them I attend to the world I am seeking to understand. My relation to them is a-critical. I may have to be told by a doctor that my eyes need attending to, and in that sense I have to take a critical attitude to them. But while I am using them to examine things – for example, to read a book – I do not and cannot take a critical attitude. I indwell them a-critically. Clearly the scientific tradition as a whole, and the many concepts, classifications of data, and theoretical models which are the working tools of science, form as a whole a tradition *within* which scientists have to *dwell* in order to do their work. Without such an enduring tradition, science would collapse. At any moment in history several parts of the tradition may be under critical review and alternatives may be proposed; but this critical review would be impossible without the a-critical acceptance of the tradition as a whole. The progress of science depends, therefore, on the authority of this tradition.

The authority of this tradition is maintained by the community of scientists as a whole. This community is held together by the free acceptance by its members of the authority of the tradition. Attempts to organize science from a single center, such as those made at certain times in Russia, have failed and are bound to fail. The authority of the tradition is maintained by the free assent of its members. But it is, nonetheless, a powerful authority. It is exercised in practice by those who determine which articles will be accepted for publication in scientific journals and which rejected, and by those who determine appointments to teaching and research posts in universities and other institutions. There is no appeal within the scientific community against this authority, and any appeal outside falls on deaf ears. Polanyi in various writings has given a number of examples of theories put forward with a considerable body of evidence to support them but which have been rejected without examination or discussion by the scientific community. Among the many examples given I quote just one. In 1947 Lord Rayleigh, a distinguished member of the Royal Society, published an account of an experiment which demonstrated that a hydrogen atom impinging on a metal wire releases energies ranging up to a hundred electron volts. If this were true, it would have enormous implications for physics. But the article was ignored. No one attempted to repeat the experiment or to discuss it. It was simply implausible within the existing frame of understanding. And, says Polanyi, scientists were right to ignore it. If every experiment which purported to show novel results was followed up by detailed examination and debate, science would evaporate into futility. Great numbers of articles offered to scientific journals are rejected without discussion simply because they fall outside the accepted tradition. Without this careful protection of the tradition, science could not develop. Yet if the tradition did not make room for radical innovation, science would stagnate. The point to be made seems to be twofold: first, innovation can only be responsibly accepted from those who are already masters of the tradition, skilled practitioners of whom it could be said both that the tradition dwells fully in them and that they dwell fully in the tradition; and second, that one alleged new fact, or even a number of new facts, does not suffice to discredit an established paradigm. That can only happen when a new and more compelling paradigm is offered, a vision of reality which commends itself by its beauty, rationality, and comprehensiveness.

The acceptance of such a vision is a personal act, an act of personal judgment to which one commits oneself in the knowledge that others may disagree and that one may be proved wrong. It involves personal commitment. But it is not therefore merely subjective. The scientist who commits himself to the new vision does so – as Polanyi puts it – with universal intent. He believes it to be objectively true, and he therefore causes it to be widely published, invites discussion, and seeks to persuade his fellow scientists that it is a true account of reality. As I have already said, he may have to wait many years before there is convincing experimental verification of his vision. It is his personal belief to which he commits himself and on which he risks his scientific reputation. But at no stage is it merely a subjective opinion. It is held 'with universal intent' as being a true account of reality which all people ought to accept and which will prove itself true both by experimental verification and also by opening the way to fresh discovery. It is offered not as private opinion but as public truth.

On what does the authority of this tradition rest? Obviously on nothing outside itself. Like all visions of ultimate truth, science is necessarily involved in a circular argument. It has to assume from the beginning the truth of that which it seeks to prove. It begins from the conviction that the universe is accessible to rational understanding, it refuses to accept as final evidence that which seems to contradict this faith, and it seeks with a passion which is one of the glories of human history to prove that the faith is true. It can only pursue this task within a tradition which is authoritative. The maintenance of the tradition depends on the mutual trust which scientists have in one another, in the integrity with which each does her work, for no one scientist can have direct knowledge of more than a tiny fraction of the whole. But the authority of the tradition is not something apart from the vision of truth which the tradition embodies. It would be a violation of the tradition if authority were to be substituted for the personal grasping of the truth. The scientist, from the pupil just beginning to study physics, to the pioneer on the frontiers of research, accepts the authority of the tradition not to replace personal grasp of the truth but as the necessary precondition for gaining this grasp. He accepts the authority of the tradition in order to reach the point where he can say, 'I see for myself'. In Augustine's phrase, his program is *Credo ut intelligam* – 'I believe in order to understand.' And if the scientist is a pioneer who has reached the point where he has to challenge the tradition and to propose a drastic innovation, it is not in order to undermine the authority of the tradition, but to strengthen it by making it more truly congruent with the truth. In so far as his innovation proves acceptable to the scientific community, it will itself become part of the authoritative tradition.

Before I move on to consider the bearing of this discussion on the question of the authority of the Christian tradition, one further remark may be in order. I have emphasized the character of scientific knowledge as – in Polanyi's phrase – 'personal knowledge.' It is knowledge to which the scientist commits herself personally and on which she stakes her professional reputation. She accepts the risk that she might be wrong. If this is so, must we not say that it is part of the deep sickness of our culture that, ever since Descartes, we have been seduced by the idea of a kind of knowledge which could not be doubted, in which we would be absolutely secure from personal risk? And has not this seduction taken two forms which, even if they disclaim all relationship with each other, are really twin brothers? One is a biblical fundamentalism which supposes that adherence to the text of the Bible frees me from the risk of error and therefore gives me a security which does not depend on my own discernment of the truth. The other is a kind of scientism which supposes that science is simply a transcript of reality, of the 'facts' which simply have to be accepted and call for no personal decision on my part, a kind of knowledge which is 'objective' and free from all the bias of subjectivity. With that question I move to look briefly at the role of an authoritative tradition in Christian believing. Here I suggest only a few broad generalizations which will have to be developed in the later chapters.

When we are received into the Christian community, whether by baptism as infants or by conversion as adults, we enter into a tradition which claims authority. It is embodied in the Holy Scriptures and in the continuous history of the interpretation of these Scriptures as they have been translated into 1,500 languages and lived out under myriad different circumstances in different ages and places. This tradition, like the scientific tradition, embodies and carries forward certain ways of looking at things, certain models for interpreting experience. Unlike the scientific tradition, at least in its present form, this tradition is not confined to a limited set of questions about the rational structure of the cosmos. Specifically, unlike science, it concerns questions about the ultimate meaning and purpose of things and of human life – questions which modern science eliminates as a matter of methodology. The models, concepts, and paradigms through which the Christian tradition seeks to understand the world embrace these larger questions. They have the same presupposition about the rationality of the cosmos as the natural sciences do, but it is a more comprehensive rationality based on the faith that the author and sustainer of the cosmos has personally revealed his purpose.

Like the scientist, the Christian believer has to learn to indwell the tradition. Its models and concepts are things which he does not simply examine from the perspective of another set of models, but have to become the models through which he understands the world. He has to internalize them and to dwell in them. And, as in the case of the pupil learning physics or mathematics, this has to be in the beginning an exercise of faith. He has to trust the tradition and trust the teacher as an authorized interpreter of it. In an established Christian community the first teachers will be parents, followed perhaps by teachers in school and church. In the beginning the child has simply to accept what is told on the authority of parent or teacher. There is no alternative to this. But if the parents and teachers are wise, they know that their work is not truly done until the child has reached the point where he or she can say, 'Now I see for myself. Now I know the Lord Jesus Christ as my personal Lord and Savior.' And this 'knowing' is of course not a matter only of the mind, but also of the heart and will. It is a personal and practical discipleship within the tradition.

But being personal does not mean that it is subjective. The faith is held with universal intent. It is held not as 'my personal opinion,' but as the truth which is true for all. It must therefore be publicly affirmed, and opened to public interrogation and debate. Specifically, as the command of Jesus tells us, it is to be made known to all the nations, to all human communities of whatever race or creed or culture. It is public truth. We commend it to all people in the hope that, by the witness of the Holy Spirit in the hearts of others, it will come to be seen by them for themselves as the truth.

The integrity and fruitfulness of this continuing learning and communicating will require (as in the case of science) the recognition and honoring of the authority of a tradition. There will be proposals which are simply so implausible within the tradition that they do not deserve serious attention. But, on the other hand, those who have learned to indwell the tradition and to become skilled interpreters of it will also be called from time to time to propose modifications in the tradition, modifications which must be submitted to the judgment of the Christian community as a whole, and which may be the subject of debate and dispute for many years. The purpose, however, should always be that the community as a whole should advance towards a more complete understanding of and living by the truth.

Thus far, I have suggested, there is a close parallel between the ways in which the authority of tradition works within the scientific community and within the Christian community. The parallel, however, is by no means complete. In the case of the scientific community, the tradition is one of human learning, writing, and speaking. In the case of the Christian community the tradition is that of witness to the action of God in history, action which reveals and effects the purpose of the Creator. These actions are themselves the reality which faith seeks to understand. Thus the Christian understanding of the world is not only a matter of 'dwelling in' a tradition of understanding; it is a matter of dwelling in a story of God's activity, activity which is still continuing. The knowledge which Christian faith seeks is knowledge of God who has acted and is acting. [. . . .]

Extract 2
'Evangelism in the Context of Secularization' (1990)[12]

One must begin with some examination of the concept of secularization. Many sociologists now agree that the idea that has been dominant during the past half-century, namely that the progress of modern science and technology must increasingly eliminate religious belief, has proved to be false. The present century has in fact witnessed a marked growth in religiosity in Europe. It is true that this has not been expressed in Christian terms. But in the forms of many new religious movements, in the enthusiasm for Eastern types of religious belief and practice, in the revival of various ancient forms of pagan religion, and in the enormous popularity of astrology among European peoples, there is a luxuriant growth of religion in what is called the secular society. Moreover, in those parts of Europe where people have lived for forty years or more under the control of the Marxist ideology with its claim to replace religion completely by a 'scientific' doctrine of human nature and history, the Christian churches have shown a power of survival and renewal much more impressive than what has been seen in the areas that called themselves the 'free world.'

And there is a farther point to be made. Leaving aside movements that are recognizably religious in the sense that they affirm realities not available for investigation by the methods of empirical science, it is clear that there are, even in the most secularized societies, forces that have a religious character in the sense that they have the status of dogma and command total trust. In the great debates about secularization in the decade of the 1960s, when many Christians (such as Arend van Leeuwen) welcomed the process of secularization as a form of liberation made possible by the Christian gospel, it seemed to be taken for granted that secularization created a space free of all ideological or religious control. In this space, human beings (and Christians among them) would find the freedom to exercise their own rational and moral powers without coercion from any dominant belief system. The secular society was hailed as the free society. Writers such as Harvey Cox in the United States and Denis Munby in England encouraged the Christians of their day to welcome

---

[12] Newbigin 1990a: 148–57.

the process of secularization as a proper fruit of the Christian message and a farther stage in human emancipation.

But a candid look at the societies that call themselves 'secular' must surely dispel such illusions. Dogma does not vanish when the name is dropped. It is impossible to pretend that children in the state schools of Europe are not being taught to accept certain beliefs about human origins, human history, all shaped by certain assumptions. The loud complaints of Muslim parents that I hear in England are directed against precisely the claim that what their children are being taught to believe are simply 'the facts,' while everyone must know that they are in reality beliefs that a Muslim must reject. They quite rightly see that their children are being taught (not in the classes on 'religious education' but in the classes on science, history, literature, and sociology) to believe that human life can be satisfactorily understood and managed without any reference to God. They protest against the arrogance that assumes that things taught in school are simply 'the facts,' while religious beliefs are merely private opinion.

The apostles of secularization in the 1960s seemed to believe that human societies can flourish without any shared beliefs. But this is obviously not so. The societies we know in Europe share the belief that what human beings need to know in order to manage their lives is the body of assured knowledge that is available through the methods of science. Perhaps those critics are right to see Descartes as the key figure. The attempt to find a kind of certitude that left no room for doubt, and the discovery of that certitude in the existence of the thinking self (*cogito ergo sum*),[13] constitute the deliberate choice of a position that is open to doubt. Why should we imagine that human beings should have available to them a basis for certitude other than the one provided by a trustful dependence on the Author of our being? Descartes' starting point already begs that question. But the secular societies that have developed in Europe since the seventeenth century share the common belief that reliable knowledge about human nature, and therefore about how human life is to be managed, is to be found not by reliance upon divine revelation and grace but by reliance upon the methods of empirical science. This, broadly speaking, is the dogma that controls public life, as distinct from the private opinions that individuals are free to hold.

But the dogma does not measure up to the realities of human nature. If there is no answer to the question 'But why did this happen to me?' people will turn to astrology. If there is no answer to the question 'What is human life really for? What is the purpose of human life and of the whole creation?' people will seek to fill the void with the search for instant pleasure in drugs, in sex, in mindless violence through which one can express the sense of meaninglessness. We have to be endlessly entertained and we have to have idols to fill the

---

[13] ('I think therefore I am'.)

empty space from which the living God has been removed. In the end, the society we have is not a secular society but a pagan society, a society in which men and women are giving their allegiance to no-gods. The rational part of us puts its trust in the findings of science but is left with no answer to the question of ultimate meaning. The way is open for the irrational part of us to develop a pantheon of idols.

The 'secular' society is not a neutral area into which we can project the Christian message. It is an area already occupied by other gods. We have a battle on our hands. We are dealing with principalities and powers. What, then, is evangelism in this context?

To our 'secular' contemporaries the answer to this question is quite simple. The Christian Church is a voluntary association of people who wish to promote certain 'values' for themselves and for society. These 'values,' like all others, are matters of personal choice. They are not matters of 'fact' that everyone has to accept. It follows that the success of these 'values' depends on the number of people who support them. There is a diminishing number of people who identify themselves with the Christian churches. The churches are therefore in danger of collapsing. Evangelism is an effort by the churches to avert this collapse and to recruit more adherents to their cause. It is even possible that this way of understanding evangelism may be in the minds of some church members. It then becomes impossible to conceal the element of anxiety that infects the enterprise. It becomes very important that *we* should succeed. The shadow of Pelagius hangs over the enterprise. In contrast to this way of seeing things, it is a striking fact that nowhere in the letters of St Paul does the apostle lay upon the Church the duty of evangelism. The gospel is such a tremendous reality that he cannot possibly keep silent about it. 'Woe is me if I do not preach the gospel' (1 Cor. 9.16). He seems to take it for granted that the same will be true for his readers. He is not slow to warn, persuade, rebuke his friends; it is a matter of life or death for him that they should be utterly faithful to Christ. But he never lays upon them the duty to go out and evangelize. Why should this be so?

The first evangelism in the New Testament is the announcement by Jesus that the Kingdom of God is at hand. This, if one may put it so, is not ecclesiastical news but world news. It is not about 'values' but about 'facts.' It is, strictly speaking, news, and it requires an immediate response in action. There is immediate excitement. People flock to hear. But it seems as if God's reign was not what we expected. There is both enthusiasm and rejection. In the end there is betrayal, condemnation, and death. God's reign has not appeared after all. There is despair and suicide. But what seemed to be the end is the new beginning. The tomb is empty, Jesus is risen, death is conquered, God does reign after all. There is an explosion of joy, news that cannot be kept secret. Everyone must hear it. A new creation has begun. One does not have to be summoned to the 'task' of evangelism. If these things are really true, they have to be told. That, I suppose, is why St Paul did not have to remind his readers about the duty of evangelism.

But can this have any relevance to the ordinary comfortable, respectable Christian congregation in the suburbs of a contemporary European city? There is, let us admit, a big gulf between them. We have largely domesticated the gospel within our culture. We have quietly accepted, for practical purposes, the dogma that controls public life. We have accepted as the 'real' history the story that is told in the school classrooms about the history of 'civilization', which means the interpretation of the human story from the point of view of *this* moment and *this* place in the whole story. We have allowed the Bible to be inserted into this history as a very minor strand in the whole human story, one element in the history of religions, which is itself only one element in the whole fabric of human history. We have not had the boldness that, for example, our black-led churches in Birmingham show, to recognize the story that the Bible tells as the real story, the true story, the story that explains who we really are, where we come from and where we are going. If we were faithful to our best traditions, if we took the Bible seriously over the years by the constant reading of it, expounding it, meditating on it, then we would see the story that is told in the schools as a story that misses the real point. What is the real point of the human story, in which my life is only a small part? It is not in the achievement, somewhere in the distant future, of a perfect human civilization. It is not in the achievement of my personal ambition, after which I decline into senility. The point of the whole story has been made once and for all in the events that the New Testament tells. If we believe that, then we live by a different story from the one that is told in our society. And the difference will become clear and will provoke questions. I have taken the example of St Paul to suggest that we may be missing an essential point if we speak about evangelism as a duty. One could also point to the striking fact that almost all of the evangelistic sermons that are recorded in the Acts of the Apostles are responses to questions asked, rather than discourses given on the initiative of the speaker. It would seem that if the Church is faithfully living the true story, the evangelistic dialogue will be initiated not by the Church but by the one who senses the presence of a new reality and wants to inquire about its secret.

How will the presence of the new reality become known? I suggest by three things: by a certain kind of shared life, by actions, and by words that interpret the actions. The first and fundamental one is a certain kind of shared life. At the heart of that life will be praise. St Luke tells us that the first response of the first disciples to the resurrection of Jesus was that 'they returned to Jerusalem with great joy and were continually in the Temple, praising God' (Luke 24.51). A community of people that, in the midst of all the pain and sorrow and wickedness of the world, is continually praising God is the first obvious result of living by another story than the one the world lives by. In our own century we have the witness of the churches in the USSR, who for three generations were denied the opportunity of any kind of outward witness by word or action, but who sustained through those years a life of praise, reflecting in their worship the glory of the triune God. It was that reality, the presence of something that by its very existence called into question the official story by which the nation was required to live, that drew men and women to faith in Christ through the darkest years of tyranny.

We know that the worship of a Christian congregation can become a dead and formal thing, having the outward form but lacking the inward joy of adoration. When that has happened, our duty is to pray for the reviving work of the Holy Spirit to kindle into flame the embers that are always there. We know that this prayer has been answered many times in ways beyond expectation. And where there is a praising community, there also will be a caring community with love to spare for others. Such a community is the primary hermeneutic of the gospel. All the statistical evidence goes to show that those within our secularized societies who are being drawn out of unbelief to faith in Christ say that they were drawn through the friendship of a local congregation. There is, of course, a kind of 'loving' that is selfish – merely the desire to have more members for the congregation. This kind of 'love' is quickly recognized. But a congregation that has at its heart a joyful worship of the living God and a constantly renewed sense of the sheer grace and kindness of God will be a congregation from which true love flows out to the neighbors, a love that seeks their good whether or not they come to church.

Second, the presence of a new reality will be made known by the acts that originate from it. Jesus' announcement of the gospel, that the Kingdom of God is at hand, was immediately implemented by actions of healing and deliverance. These actions are portrayed as simple evidence that the power of God, his kindly rule over all powers, is present. They are acts of sheer compassion. A victim of leprosy, sensing the presence of this reality, says, 'If you will you can make me clean.' Jesus replies: 'I will; be clean,' touches him and heals him (Mark 1.40–41). There are no conditions attached. Nothing is said about faith and repentance. It is the love of God in action. The reign of God has come near.

When the Christian congregation is filled with the Spirit and lives the true story, such actions will flow from it. Primarily they will be the actions of the members in their several vocations every day. While there are also actions that a congregation or a wider church body may undertake, these are secondary. The primary action of the Church in the world is the action of its members in their daily work. A congregation may have no social action program and may yet be acting more effectively in secular society than a congregation with a big program of social action.

What is important in these actions – whether the personal actions of individual members or the corporate programs of a congregation – is that they spring out of the new life in Christ. It can be otherwise. They can be designed to attract new members, or to justify the congregation in the eyes of society by its good works. The Gospels make it clear that Jesus resolutely refused to make for himself a public reputation as a healer and a worker of miracles. His mighty works were indeed signs of the presence of the Kingdom, but when he was asked for a sign, he refused. When a multitude of people who had gathered around him were hungry, he fed them. But when they pursued him, he sternly told them that they must seek for the bread that does not perish with the eating (John 6.25). A program of church action may arise not from sheer compassion but from an ideological commitment to some vision of society shaped by the story that the world tells and not by the story that the Bible tells. The Church then becomes one among a number of agencies for promoting justice and peace, rather than the sign and foretaste of the new reality where alone justice and peace embrace, the sign pointing to the crucified and risen Jesus in whom alone we can receive both God's justice and God's peace.

Third, then, the presence of the new reality will be attested to by words. The Church has to speak, to announce the new reality, to preach. Here we have to reject two false positions. On the one hand there is the view that 'actions speak louder than words,' the view that the Church will win people's allegiance to the gospel by good lives and good works and that preaching is unacceptable and unnecessary. The word *mission* is used to describe a range of activities in which explicit naming of the name of Jesus has no place. On this two things may be said. The first is that Jesus himself preached and instructed his disciples to preach. Not, as we have seen, that each act of healing or deliverance was accompanied by a sermon. Not at all. But the acts of healing and deliverance were not self-explanatory. They might even be the work of the devil (Mark 3.21ff.). And when Jesus sent out the 12 with the authority to heal and deliver, he also told them to preach. It is clear that the preaching is an explanation of the mighty works, and that the mighty works are evidence that the preaching is true. They are not separable (Mark 6.7). Second, therefore, we have to say that the preaching of the Church carries no weight if it does not come from a community in which the truth of what is preached is being validated (even though always imperfectly) in the life of the community. But the life of even the most saintly community does not by itself tell the story, the story in which the name of Jesus has the central place.

If these general affirmations are true, I would suggest that in thinking of evangelism in a secular society and – in particular – in thinking of the re-evangelization of Europe, the following five points may be helpful.

1   Evangelism is not the effort of Christians to increase the size and importance of the Church. It is sharing the good news that God reigns – good news for those who believe, bad news for those who reject. Evangelism must be rescued from a Pelagian anxiety, as though we were responsible for converting the world. God reigns and his reign is revealed and effective in the incarnation, ministry, death, and resurrection of Jesus. As we grow into a deeper understanding of this fact, as we learn more and more to live by the other story, we become more confident in sharing this reality with those who have not yet seen it.

2   The clue to evangelism in a secular society must be the local congregation. There are many other things of which one could speak – mass evangelism of the Billy Graham type, Christian literature, radio and television, study and training courses, and so on. These are auxiliary. Many of them can be very valuable. But they are auxiliary to the primary center of evangelism, which is

the local congregation. The congregation should live by the true story and center their life in the continual remembering and relating of the true story, in meditating on it and expounding it in its relation to contemporary events so that contemporary events are truly understood, and in sharing in the sacrament by which we are incorporated into the dying and rising of Jesus so that we are at the very heart of the true story. The congregation that does this becomes the place where the new reality is present with its heart in the praise and adoration of God and in the sharing of the love of God among the members and in the wider society. And here, of course, an immense amount depends upon the leadership given through preaching, pastoral encouragement, and public action by those called to ministry in the congregations.

3   It will be a major part of the work of such congregations to train and enable members to act as agents of the Kingdom in the various sectors of public life where they work. This kind of 'frontier' work is very difficult, and although many promising starts have been made during the years since the last war, there is still much to do. It must become a part of ordinary congregational life that members are enabled to think through and discuss the ways in which their Christian faith impinges on their daily life in their secular work. Here is the place where the real interface between the Church and the world, between the new creation and the old, takes place. Here is where there ought to be a discernible difference in behavior between those who live by the old story and those who live by the story the Bible tells. It ought at many points to lead to differences in behavior, to dissent from current practice, to questioning. And this, of course, will be the place where the counter questions arise. The Christian will be asked, 'Why do you do this? Why do you behave like this?' Here is where the true evangelistic dialogue begins. At present it is very rare to find this kind of situation because the churches have so largely accepted relegation to the private sector, leaving the public sector to be controlled by the other story.

4   From this it follows that it will also be the task of the local congregation to equip members to enter into this dialogue, to explain the Christian story and its bearing on daily life. And of course the explanation will be not be complete without the invitation to become part of the community that lives by the other story and to learn there what it means to do so. Here is where the call to conversion comes, but it is not only a call addressed to the heart and the will, and not only concerned with personal and domestic life; it is also a call addressed to the mind, a call to a radically different way of seeing things, including all the things that make up daily life in the secular world.

5   If this approach is right, evangelism is not just the call to personal conversion, although it is that. It is not just a program for church growth, although it is that also. It is not just preaching, although it is that, and it is not just action for changing society, although it is that too. It is not a program for the re-establishment of the *Corpus Christianum* in Europe with the Church in the supreme position. Most certainly it is not that. But I believe it is possible to hope for and to work for something different – a Europe (a 'common

European home') that is a Christian society, not in the sense that it is ruled by the Church, and not in the sense that everyone is a Christian, but in another sense, which I would indicate as follows. It is possible to envision a society in which Christians have engaged so seriously over several decades with the consequences of the Enlightenment (good and bad) and with the kind of society that has developed at the end of the twentieth century that those who achieve the highest standards of excellence in all the sectors of public life – politics, industry, learning, and the arts – may be shaped in their public work by the Christian story. Then the worship of the triune God as he is made known to us in Jesus may again be the focus of ordinary life in our towns and villages.

Whether or not that is in the purpose of God for our continent, the main point is quite simple. We are entrusted with good news, the news that God reigns. That must be the starting point of all our thinking, and our evangelism will be an overflow of that joyful faith. Who knows, perhaps God has in store for our poor old secularized Europe a new birth of faith in the twenty-first century.

Extract 3
Proper Confidence (1995)[14]

I am writing this [. . .] as a missionary who is concerned to commend the truth of the gospel in a culture that has sought for absolute certainty as the ideal of true knowledge but now despairs of the possibility of knowing truth at all, a culture that therefore responds to the Christian story by asking, 'But how can we know that it is true?' There is a long tradition of Christian theology that goes under the name 'apologetics' and that seeks to respond to this question and to demonstrate the reasonableness of Christianity. The assumption often underlying titles of this kind is that the gospel can be made acceptable by showing that it does not contravene the requirements of reason as we understand them within the contemporary plausibility structure. The heart of my argument is that this is a mistaken policy. The story the church is commissioned to tell, if it is true, is bound to call into question any plausibility structure which is founded on other assumptions. The affirmation that the One by whom and through whom and for whom all creation exists is to be identified with a man who was crucified and rose bodily from the dead cannot possibly be accommodated within any plausibility structure except one of which it is the cornerstone. In any other place in the structure it can only be a stone of stumbling. The reasonableness of Christianity will be demonstrated (in so far as it can be) not by adjusting its claims to the requirements of a preexisting structure of thought but by showing how it can provide an alternative foundation for a different structure. The title of one of the most famous writings of the Enlightenment was *Religion within the Limits of Reason*.[15] The

---

[14] Newbigin 1995c: 93–105.
[15] (Written by Immanuel Kant and published in 1793.)

American philosopher Wolterstorff has reversed the title with his book *Reason within the Limits of Religion*.[16] The reversal of words is justified if one remembers that all human reasoning is embodied in a specific culture and that, through most of human history, religion has been the most powerful factor in the shaping of culture. To look outside of the gospel for a starting point for the demonstration of the reasonableness of the gospel is itself a contradiction of the gospel, for it implies that we look for the *logos* elsewhere than in Jesus.

The obvious implication of this argument, therefore, is that the proper form of apologetics is the preaching of the gospel itself and the demonstration – which is not merely or primarily a matter of words – that it does provide the best foundation for a way of grasping and dealing with the mystery of our existence in this universe. Needless to say, this demonstration can never be more than partial and tentative. It is, according to the gospel, only on the day of judgment that the demonstration will be complete and decisive. Until then, my commitment to the truth of the gospel is a commitment of faith. If I am further pressed to justify this commitment (as I have often been), my only response has to be a personal confession. The story is not my construction. In ways that I cannot fully understand but always through the witness of those who went before me in the company of those called to be witnesses, I have been laid hold of and charged with the responsibility of telling this story. I am only a witness, not the Judge who alone can give the final verdict. But as a witness I am under obligation – the obligation of a debtor to the grace of God in Jesus Christ – to give my witness. I cannot pretend to anticipate the final judgment by offering any proof other than the fact that my life is committed to the truth of this witness.

In my own experience, I find that this position is questioned from three sides: from the Catholic tradition of natural theology, from Protestant fundamentalism, and from liberal theology of all kinds. At the risk of going over ground already partially covered, it may be helpful to look at these three criticisms in order:

The first critical standpoint comes from the long tradition of natural theology. From this standpoint, the stance I have suggested is attacked as being an abandonment of the responsible use of reason. It is a blind leap in the dark. It requires more rational justification. How, it is asked, am I to believe that Jesus is the Word of God if I do not have rational grounds for believing that the word 'God' stands for any actual reality?

In reply to this, four points are in order:

1   We are not speaking of a blind leap into darkness but of a personal response to a personal calling. When Jesus called the first disciples with the words: 'Follow me,' he was certainly calling for an act of faith. He did not offer any demonstrable certainties. And so it is with everyone who has been so

---

[16]   (Wolterstorff 1984.)

called through the faithfulness of the first apostles and their successors. To regard this as cognitively inferior to the rational demonstration of supposedly certain truths is to assume that the ultimate reality with which we have to deal is not personal but impersonal. In the investigation of impersonal realities we may ask for the kind of indubitable certainties that the Age of Reason demanded, even though subsequent history has shown that they are not attainable. But if the ultimate reality with which, or rather with whom, we have to deal is the being of the triune God, then the response of personal faith to a personal calling is the only way of knowing that reality. To rule this out as unreasonable is to make an a priori decision against the possibility that ultimate reality is personal.

2   The objection from natural theology also seems to rest on the assumption that there is available a kind of knowledge which does not rest on any faith commitment. It denies the truth of Augustine's slogan, 'I believe in order to know.' I have already argued that this setting of reason against faith is absurd. Reason is not an independent means for finding out what is the case. It is not a substitute for information. In order to be informed, we have to make acts of trust in the traditions we have inherited and in the evidence of our senses. Moreover, as has already been said, all systematic reasoning has to begin by taking for granted certain things that are accepted without argument. There must be data without argument or, at least, without prior demonstration. I have already referred to the argument of Roy Clouser in his book *The Myth of Religious Neutrality*.[17] There exists no neutral reason that can decide impartially on the truth or falsehood of the Christian gospel. On the contrary, if it is true that Jesus *is* the Word made flesh, then to know Jesus must be the basis for all true knowledge. We therefore have to recognize that the ancient words 'The fear of the Lord is the beginning of wisdom' have a wider range of reference than is often supposed.

3   Having said this, it is now important to add that it follows from the above argument that there is a proper kind of theology that deals with the area natural theology addresses. If one may put it so, it covers the same field but starts from the other end. It does not start from somewhere outside the gospel in order to demonstrate the truth of the gospel but starts from the gospel itself, seeking to show how this starting point illuminates all our other experience. This is a true and necessary form of apologetics. In preaching the gospel, it is our business to show, in so far as our knowledge and experience equip us to do so, how the Christian story enables us to understand and deal with the whole range of human experience in both public and private life. Once again we follow the path suggested in Augustine's slogan: we believe in order to understand. We do not argue from experience to the gospel. On the contrary, it is the gospel accepted in faith which enables us to experience all reality in a new way and to find that all reality does indeed reflect the glory of God.

---

[17] (Clouser 1991.)

4   The points made in the three preceding paragraphs refer to the role of natural theology in Christian apologetics. There is, of course, a long pre-Christian tradition of natural theology. If, as for most of the great thinkers of classical antiquity alleged divine revelation is not a reliable source of certain truth or if we disallow the Christian claims regarding God's revelation of himself in Jesus Christ, then natural theology is surely a perfectly legitimate enterprise. But for those who have become believers in the gospel of the Word made flesh, there is something improper, as I have argued, in supposing that this faith can be validated by the arguments of natural theology. This has special poignancy if we remember, as we must always remember, that when we speak of God's self-revelation in Christ, we are speaking of an immeasurably costly act of self-giving for our redemption and reconciliation. When we know that God has done this infinitely gracious thing, is it not inappropriate for us to respond, to put it crudely, 'Thank you, but I have other collateral sources of information'? The truth surely is not that we come to know God by reasoning from our unredeemed experience but that what God has done for us in Christ gives us the eyes through which we can begin to truly understand our experience in the world.

In addition to the attack from natural theology there is a second attack. It comes from what I have called Protestant fundamentalism. I hesitate to use the word 'fundamentalism,' since it has become common to label anyone who firmly believes in the truth of his or her religion a fundamentalist. In this sense, I am myself happy to be called a fundamentalist. But I am referring to something more specific. I have argued (in agreement with the post-modernists) that all truth claims are culturally and historically embodied. The Christian gospel arises out of the culture of one people among all the peoples of the world, the people of Israel. The claim, of course, is that within this particular culture there was present, in the man Jesus, the eternal Word through whom and for whom all things exist. But those who make this claim do not occupy a position above other particular cultures or histories. I have found myself attacked at this point on the ground that this is a surrender to subjectivity. The safety of the church and of the Christian confession requires, it is said, that we affirm the 'objective' truth of what the gospel affirms. If the word 'objective' here means 'really true,' then I am happy. But the claim is made that we must affirm the factual truth of every statement in the Bible as a matter of indubitable certainty and that, if this position is surrendered, we are in a world of subjectivity and relativism along with the rest of contemporary society. I have been told that there are context-independent criteria of truth on the basis of which one can undertake to demonstrate the truth of the gospel.

One can understand this anxiety that the gospel should not be allowed to sink into the swamp of relativism where there are no firm footholds, and what is true for you may not be true for me. But this way of defending the truth of the gospel will not work. Two things can be said in reply to the fundamentalist stance:

1   In seeking a kind of supracultural and indubitable certainty these Christians have fallen into the trap set by Descartes. They are seeking a kind of certainty that does not acknowledge the certainty of faith as the only kind of certainty available. The only one who has a context-independent standpoint is God. The fundamental error of Descartes, surely, was the supposition that we ourselves can have such a standpoint. Christian faith is not a matter of logically demonstrable certainties but of the total commitment of fallible human beings putting their trust in the faithful God who has called them. I believe and trust that the Bible is the true rendering of the story of God's acts in creation and redemption and therefore the true rendering of the character of God. At the core of the biblical story there is a record of events in history. The biblical accounts of the beginning and the end of the world are, however, obviously not of the kind of accounts which rest upon indubitable Cartesian certainty since no human evidence is available. The stories of the beginning are reshapings of the contemporary, available cosmologies to reflect that knowledge of God's ways and purposes that had been given to the prophets of Israel by God. Likewise, the vision of the end of the world in the last book of the Bible uses the images that Israel and the church had learned to use through their experience of God's dealing with them, his people. It is a confusion of categories to use the constantly changing modern views of cosmology to call into question the unchanging truth about God and his relation to the world and human life, a truth embodied in the protology and eschatology of the Bible.

The heart of the Christian faith from the first apostles onward has been that the story told in the Bible is the true story of God's dealings with the people he had chosen to be the bearers of his purpose for the world, and that those through whom the story has come down to us were enabled by his Holy Spirit – the same Spirit by whom Jesus was anointed and empowered – to interpret truly his dealings with his people. But the Bible is also the work of sinful and fallible human beings whose sins had to be constantly rebuked and whose misunderstandings had to be corrected. The very heart of the Bible is in this long, patient wrestling of God with a sinful and fallible people. The writer of the letter to the Hebrews summarizes the whole story as the story of a faith that grasps what cannot yet be seen, and he calls upon his readers to exercise the same faith. To convert the Bible into a compendium of indubitably certain facts is to impose upon it a character alien to itself, a character that is the typical product of minds shaped by the Enlightenment.

2   This way of understanding the Bible can and does often lead to a kind of hard rationalism that is remote from grace. Christian discipleship is a kind of life lived by faith in the grace of God. The arrogance of supposedly indubitable certainties is uncongenial to it. Indubitable certainties call for the submission of the intellect even if the heart is unpersuaded. (And indubitable certainties, as we have been reminded, make no contact with reality.) But the gospel is not a matter of indubitable certainties; it is the offer of a grace that can only be accepted in faith, a faith in which both heart and intellect join.

In addition to being criticized by natural theology and Protestant fundamentalism, the position I am seeking to establish comes under attack from a third tradition: theological liberalism. The assertion that the biblical story with its crucial turning point being the events concerning Jesus, must be accepted in faith as the starting point for all our thinking – such an assertion is unacceptable dogmatism in the eyes of many in the liberal tradition. And it is fundamental to the liberal tradition that all such dogma must be open to critical evaluation. Clearly anyone who claims the name 'Christian' has to take the Bible, or at least the New Testament, very seriously. But in the liberal tradition, the Bible cannot have the kind of ultimate authority I have suggested. It is, after all, the product of human experience; and, like all records of human experience, it must be tested in the light of the wider experience of the human race. It must take its place along with other records of human religious experience and be subject to the same kind of critical questioning as are the others. Liberals will, therefore, gladly acknowledge that God may speak to the human mind and conscience through the Bible, but they are uncomfortable with any identification of the Bible as the word of God.

The great value of the liberal tradition is its readiness to listen to new truth and to be open to questioning. There are many times when one has to be thankful for this, in contrast to the kind of dogmatism incapable of hearing anything that calls present beliefs into question. Precisely because it concerns our whole being and destiny religious belief can be so tightly held that the mind is closed to anything new. Against this, the liberal tradition is a refreshing protest. But theological liberalism can itself become a dogmatic position that is closed to the witness of the gospel. The principle that every dogma must be open to question is itself a dogma open to question. I suggest four lines along which questions should be raised against the central dogma of theological liberalism:

1   Liberalism has accepted the critical principle of Descartes and his successors as an integral part of its method. In the preceding pages, I have tried to show how this inevitably leads to nihilism. All grasping of the truth concerning the world beyond our consciousness is the work of minds shaped by a tradition that uses a language and a set of concepts and models developed over many generations. The historical-critical method upon which liberal theologians rely in their use of Scripture is one part of such a tradition. Those who are shaped by this tradition work with certain, quite specific presuppositions, which I have discussed in a previous chapter. These presuppositions are so much a part of the reigning plausibility structure of contemporary modern society that it is hard for those who accept them to recognize that these presuppositions are only a few among a whole possible set of presuppositions, and that there are no rational grounds on which it could be shown that they have a superior epistemological status to the presuppositions that a Christian (or Jewish) reader brings to the Scriptures. They form part of a particular cultural tradition that has had a relatively short life, showing many signs of disintegration.

In contrast to the liberal reader of the Bible, who stands within the tradition of the historical-critical principle, the confessional reader stands within the tradition of the Christian church. The presuppositions here are those of the gospel itself, namely that in Jesus the Word of God was made flesh, lived a human life, died for the sin of the world, and rose again. These presuppositions govern Christians' reading. They read as members of that same community whose story is told in the Bible. It is that community that has put the Bible into their hands and has taught them how to understand it. They read as believers. The difference between this way of reading the Bible and the historical-critical way is not that the latter is neutral or scientific whereas the former is confessional or sectarian; rather, it is the difference between two confessions, two traditions of interpretation developed in two different human communities. From the perspective of the much longer and wider experience of the Christian church, the historical-critical approach to the Bible is part of a cultural movement that has been fruitful in many respects but that is now in the process of disintegration. From a Christian point of view, there is something naive about the confidence of liberal theologians who suppose that the critical method provides a standpoint more secure than that offered by the historical faith of the universal church.

2   The principle that every dogma must be open to question runs into the difficulty that, in human affairs, action is required before all questions can be asked and answered. In his famous essay *The Will to Believe*,[18] William James gives us a parable that illustrates the point I am making: A man climbing a cliff finds his hold slipping. Close by there is a tree growing out of a cleft in the rock. If he transfers himself to the tree, will it hold his weight? There is no way of deciding the matter in advance of action. There is no possibility of keeping an open mind. The climber has to make a decision on the evidence available, and that will be the final decision. The proposition that every dogma must be open to question is a typical product of that separation of thought from action, which we have traced to Descartes. We are continually required to act on beliefs that are not demonstrably certain and to commit our lives to propositions that can be doubted. The liberal who discounts the Christian interpretation of the biblical narrative on the ground that its truth cannot be demonstrated continues nevertheless to act on other beliefs whose truth cannot be demonstrated but are accepted anyway because they are part of the plausibility structure. Since the birth of the church, it has never been a secret that the acceptance of the full truth of the gospel announcement – that in the events concerning Jesus, God was himself performing those acts that are determinative for the history of the world – meant a radical questioning of the presuppositions of the majority of mankind. To decline the evangelical invitation to do exactly that is not to have the security of objective truth as opposed to confessional prejudice. It is to have chosen another confession.

---

[18] (Reprinted in James 1979. The essay was first published in 1896.)

3   Liberal theologians speak much of experience and frequently describe the Bible as a particular record of human religious experience. But experience can be of many kinds, and we have to make distinctions. The experience of having a stomach-ache does not provide us with any information about a world of realities beyond the sufferer – only perhaps something about the eating habits of the person concerned. But the experience of seeing a great work of art does tell us something about a world beyond ourselves. Of course the Bible describes human experiences, but it does not speak of them in those terms; it speaks of the mighty acts of God. Of course these acts are understood and made part of the reader's awareness through the experience of human beings who were witnesses of them. But their witness concerns what God has done and not just what they have felt. And if God did indeed do the things of which the gospel speaks, then these accounts of them cannot be filed away in a catalogue of the varieties of religious experience. The story must either be disbelieved or it must become the fundamental presupposition of all our thought and action.

4   But perhaps the fundamental flaw in the tradition of theological liberalism lies at the point of its most attractive feature. The liberal mind is at its best in challenging us to be open to new truth, to be fearless in exploring all reality, and to be humble in recognizing the vastness and mystery that we try to comprehend with our finite minds. But even the language about the greatness and the unfathomable depths of the mystery of God can be the cloak for a calamitous error. The error is the supposition that it is we who are the explorers, that the real questions are the ones we formulate and put to the universe, and that our minds have a sovereign freedom to explore a reality waiting to be discovered. Our peril is that, out of the vastness of the unplumbed mystery, we summon up images that are the creations of our own minds. The human heart, as Calvin said, is a factory of idols.

The gospel challenges liberals' thinking in the sharpest possible way and perhaps this is the hardest thing for them to accept. It exposes as illusion the liberal picture – the picture of ourselves as sovereign explorers who formulate the real questions in a search for a yet-to-be-discovered reality. The gospel undermines our questions with a question that comes to us from the mystery we thought to explore. It is a question as piercing and shattering as the voice that spoke to Job out of the whirlwind. It exposes our false pretensions. We are *not* honest and open-minded explorers of reality; we are alienated from reality because we have made ourselves the center of the universe. Before we continue with our questions, we have to answer a question put to us from the heart of the mystery. We have to answer that anguished question, 'Adam, where are you?' We have to learn that we are lost and that we have to be rescued. We have to answer the call of the one who has come to rescue us and learn that it is only in him and through him that we shall be led into the truth in its fullness. There is still mystery, but it is not the mystery of an empty infinity of space and time. It is the mystery of the incarnation and the cross, of the holiness that can embrace the sinner, of a Lord who is servant, and of the deathless one who can die. There is still the vast ocean of what we do not know and do not understand. But we know the way and the way is Jesus. In the words of Dietrich Bonhoeffer that stand at the head of this essay 'Jesus Christ alone is the certainty of faith.' To look for certainty elsewhere is to head for the wasteland.

Both faith and doubt have their proper roles in the whole enterprise of knowing, but faith is primary and doubt is secondary because rational doubt depends upon beliefs that sustain our doubt. The ideal that modernity following Descartes, has set before itself, namely the ideal of a kind of certainty that admits no possibility of doubt, is leading us into skepticism and nihilism. The universe is not provided with a spectator's gallery in which we can survey the total scene without being personally involved. True knowledge of reality is available only to the one who is personally committed to the truth already grasped. Knowing cannot be severed from living and acting, for we cannot know the truth unless we seek it with love and unless our love commits us to action. Faith is the only certainty because faith involves personal commitment. The point has often been made that there is a distinction between the cognitive and the affective elements in belief, between 'I believe that . . .' and 'I believe in. . . .' But faith holds both together; to separate them is to deny oneself access to truth.

The confidence proper to a Christian is not the confidence of one who claims possession of demonstrable and indubitable knowledge. It is the confidence of one who had heard and answered the call that comes from the God through whom and for whom all things were made: 'Follow me.'

Further reading
Newbigin 1989b: 128–40.
Newbigin 1988c: 158–76.

11.2 The gospel as public truth

Newbigin's description of the Christian gospel as 'public truth' is highly characteristic of his later writings, and came to represent something of a catchphrase for his programme of missionary engagement with Western culture during the 1980s and 1990s. The phrase occurs frequently in his published writings during this period, often serving as the title given to lectures and articles.[19] *The title 'The Gospel as Public Truth' became the theme for the conference at Swanwick in Derbyshire in July 1992 that was the culmination of a process of reflection and discussion aimed at addressing the challenges facing the Church in the West. The conference was international in flavour and drew 400 delegates, whose task was to develop 'realistic strategies for Christian action to penetrate areas of public life with the gospel'. The first extract reproduced below is the Conference Call issued to delegates prior to the Consultation itself, in which Newbigin lays out*

---

[19] For example: Newbigin 1991b; 1991a; 1992b; and 1997.

what is meant by the phrase, drawing attention to the gospel as the 'announcement' of things that have happened – a starting point for the kind of dialogue out of which the implications of the happenings may be discerned.

The second and third extracts explore the implications of this gospel for public life. The first of these is part of a lecture given at King's College, London in 1995, entitled 'Can a Modern Society be Christian?' Here Newbigin traces the origins of Christendom and sees its roots in a fusion of classical and biblical elements within European culture. He argues that the era of modernity effectively removed the theological underpinning for public life that had characterized the earlier period, leaving religious faith relegated to the private realm. The lecture sets out the unique challenges that face the Church in the light of past experience. 'If we are to get our bearings for the future', he argues, 'we need to pay attention to the past, not to return to it but to learn from it.'

The final extract is one of the last pieces Newbigin wrote before his death. It is part of his contribution to a book outlining a Christian vision for Britain at the end of the millennium. Along with fellow contributors Lamin Sanneh and Jenny Taylor, he discusses the public role of Christian faith in an increasingly multi-cultural society – particularly in relation to the challenge to the Church's retreat from the public sphere raised by Islam. In this extract, Newbigin outlines in practical terms what would be involved in the 'activation' of a Christian vision for society. Though he is writing with the British scene particularly in mind, his words have a much wider relevance.

* * *

Extract 1
'Conference Call: The Gospel as Public Truth' (1992)[20]

The Consultation called to meet under this title at Swanwick in July 1992 is invited to consider a thesis. It is not a meeting for the pooling of ideas from whatever quarter, but for the testing of a thesis proposed by those who have convened the meeting. The thesis is that the Gospel is public truth. Critics have (very reasonably) asked for clarification at several points. What is meant by 'the Gospel'? What is meant by speaking of it as 'public truth'? And what kind of authority can 'the Gospel' have in a secular pluralist society? This paper is an attempt to offer clarification with the hope that it will facilitate the work of the Sections during the Consultation.

The Gospel is an account of things which have happened. It is not a proposition in metaphysics or a programme for ethics and politics, though it has implications in both these spheres. It is narrated history, and (like all narrated history) it is told with a belief about its meaning. This belief is that the story

---

[20] Newbigin 1992a.

tells what God has done for the redemption of all creation and its reconciliation to the source of all being.

The story is made available to us through the living memory of the Church, the community which from its beginning has been enabled by the work of the Holy Spirit to recognize in Jesus the one sent by the Father for the salvation of the world. This community has kept the memory alive by preserving, cherishing and handing on from generation to generation the earliest records of Jesus, the words and acts of the earliest witnesses, and that body of writing which was sacred scripture for the Jewish people and therefore for Jesus and his disciples and which tells the story for which the ministry of Jesus is the hermeneutic key. This whole corpus of writings has been recognized and accepted by the Church as providing the norm by which subsequent developments in the interpretation of the Gospel and of its implications are to be tested.

The first communicators of the Gospel were the eye-witnesses who could say: 'That which we have seen and heard . . . we declare to you'. They were well aware that their story could be and would be rejected, and that only the word of the Holy Spirit could convince people of its truth. But they did not draw the conclusion that its truth was a private matter for the individual. They did not avail themselves of the protection which Roman law provided for the exercise of religions of personal salvation. They affirmed that the message which had been entrusted to them was one which concerned the destiny of the whole human race. The one who had died and risen again was the saviour and judge of the world. The news was of vital concern to every human being. It was public truth. Fidelity to it required the momentous decision to withhold acknowledgement of the emperor as supreme power. They accepted the price which had to be paid for this fidelity.

To affirm the Gospel as public truth does not mean, therefore, that belief in the truth of the Gospel is to be ensured by the use of political power. It has been made clear from the beginning, though often forgotten in subsequent centuries, that the form of the affirmation is given once and for all in the witness which Jesus bore in his dying. The fact that the cross is at the heart of the Gospel, and that it was the powers of state, Church and popular opinion which sought to silence the divine word, must forever forbid the Church to seek an identification of the Gospel with political power. But the Gospel, the good news with which the Church is entrusted, is that God raised the rejected Jesus from the dead and that he is now alive and at work in the community which he sent forth to tell the story. This means that he is the rightful bearer of God's rule even though that rule is now veiled in weakness. With all its weakness, sinfulness and compromise, the Church is the body entrusted with the responsibility of bearing witness to the fact that the one whom Jesus called Father is the Lord and will be the judge of all without exception. This is public truth.

In contemporary 'modern' culture, the model of public truth is to be found in timeless law-like statements, ideally capable of being stated in mathematical form. From its early roots in Greek thought this model has been powerful in European culture. Perhaps the most important example is to be found in the enormous influence of the work of Isaac Newton on the thinkers of the 'Age of Reason' in which modern Western culture was shaped. Since that time it has been common to identify 'public truth' with matters which can be stated in this form. The word 'scientific' is used to distinguish knowledge of this kind from claims to know which rest on faith. What is forgotten is that the entire 'scientific world view' rests on assumptions which are accepted in faith but cannot be proved true otherwise than in the actual practice of science. To affirm the Gospel as public truth is to invite acceptance of a new starting point for thought, the truth of which will be proved only in the course of a life of reflection and action which proves itself more adequate to the totality of human experience than its rivals. To claim that the Gospel is public truth is, therefore, certainly not to seek some kind of dominance for the Church. It is to embark on a journey of faith which looks for final justification only at the end. It is not to seek for the Gospel any coercive power in the arena of public debate but it is to insist that the Gospel must be heard as an affirmation of the truth which must finally govern every facet of human life. It is not to ask that the Gospel should exclude all other voices, only that it should be heard. The universal recognition that Jesus is Lord is something promised for the end, not for the present age.

To affirm the Gospel as public truth is not to assert dominance but to invite dialogue. The announcement of things which have happened is not the fruit of dialogue but its starting point, for the meaning and implications of what is announced have to be learned in dialogue. For news of things that have happened we depend upon competent witness. Dialogue is not a substitute for reliable information. The first responsibility of the Church is to give faithful witness to the things that have happened. But this must lead on to dialogue, for the witnessing community does not know in advance what the message will entail, what will be the consequences of its acceptance in the several areas of human life. The New Testament itself shows that the Church, as it moved out from its roots in Israel to all the nations, had to learn (and be surprised by) what its implications would be (e.g. Acts 10 and 11). In the same way the Church has to learn what the implications of the Gospel might be for the worlds of (for example) economics, education and healing. This can only come about through dialogue in which, as Jesus promised, the Church must learn new things (John 16.12–15). And it is important to remember that, in this same context, Jesus told his disciples that they must expect hostility and rejection. The Church must not aspire to any other kind of authority than that of the crucified and risen Jesus. The final 'proof' of the thesis can only be at the end of history, at the final consummation of which the resurrection of Jesus is pledge and first-fruit.

The Swanwick Consultation is an opportunity for dialogue in which we seek to discover the implications of the Gospel for the various sectors of public life. The starting point is the Gospel itself, the narrative of those events in which the Author of all being has acted to redeem and reconcile an alienated creation and to direct it towards its true end. And since the super-abundant grace and glory of God surpasses all our powers of thought and imagination, we may confidently expect and pray for new understandings of the scope of God's purpose for our society and new energy for the doing of our part in it.

Extract 2
'Can a Modern Society be Christian?' (1995)[21]

Modernity is a product of Western Christendom. Many historians of thought have traced its roots in the ongoing history of the interaction between the classical and the biblical elements in European culture, and it is a fascinating story. It is clear that the particular form of human culture which calls itself modernity could not have arisen from within the cultures of Asia or Africa. And it seems clear that modern science, that form of human knowledge which we have learned to distinguish from the rest of our knowledge by giving it a special name, would not have developed without the fresh input of biblical thinking at the Reformation which challenged the dominance of Aristotelian rationalism in the later Middle Ages.

Many of the earliest apostles of modernity – from Voltaire onwards – were clear that Christianity was part of the old baggage which would have to be thrown away. Scepticism about the possibility of combining the 'modern' world view with Christianity grew through the nineteenth century and became clamorous in the twentieth. Yet churchmen and theologians continued to explore ways of adjusting the conflicting claims of modernity and the Gospel in such a way that Christianity would survive.

Its survival depended upon its being confined to an inner world of religious experience, making no claim to control, or even address the public realm of political, scientific and cultural discourse. The public realm was to be the realm of the secular. Any talk of a Christian society was taken to be the nostalgic dreaming of disoriented Christians seeking a return to the Middle Ages, to those happy days when witches were burned and inquisitors turned their thumb-screws. At the strange climax of this wave of thought, in the decade of the 60s, we heard the secular celebrated as a great achievement of Christianity in such books as Harvey Cox's *The Secular City*,[22] and van Buren's *The Secular Meaning of the Gospel*.[23] It is rare, but not unique, to witness a defeat being so splendidly celebrated as a victory.

Both Christianity and modernity make global claims. Both are necessarily missionary faiths, because they claim to give the true understanding of the human situation, valid for all peoples at all times. During the past two centuries these two faiths have expanded from their place of origin to penetrate

---

[21] Newbigin 1995a: 1–10 [. . . .].
[22] (Cox 1965.)
[23] (van Buren 1968.)

all the cultures of the world. But, of course, to speak in that way is an anachronism. Until well into this century we did not speak of 'cultures' in the plural. We spoke of societies which were more, or less, civilised. Europe was the home-base of civilisation. Europe's mission was to extend the blessings of civilisation to the world. Most Christians went along with this and saw Christian missions as part of this grand design. Looked at from the point of view of the non-European societies, this meant that they received from the missionaries a package in which Christianity and modernity were parcelled up together in a way which it was as difficult for them as it was for Christians in Europe to unpack.

Another way of describing what was happening is to speak, as the early pioneers of the ecumenical movement such as Joe Oldham and Visser't Hooft did, of the domestication of Christianity within European culture. The cuckoo's egg was, as happens in nature, mistakenly supposed by the original owner of the nest, to be one of her own young with whom there could be a happy family life. She had yet to learn that the cuckoo would claim the whole nest. To use a different sort of language, there was the illusion that the meta-narrative of the Gospel and the meta-narrative of the Enlightenment could be fused into a single story of the march of Christian civilisation.

It seems often to be forgotten now that it was the recognition of this illusion and this danger which was at the heart of the passion with which these men and others with them threw themselves into the ecumenical movement. The slogan of the 1937 Oxford Conference on Church, Community and State – 'Let the Church be the Church' – was a call to recognise the unique, distinct and God-ordained reality of the Church as standing over against the state and call it to account in the name of God. In the background, but not far in the background, was the German Church's struggle, and the English title of the conference was a translation of the key German words of that struggle – *Volk, Stadt, Kirche*.

The slogan of 1937 hardly rings bells for us today, but it is impossible to understand the passion that drove the early ecumenical leaders, including very specially our own Bishop George Bell, without realising that the background of their thought was always the terrible struggle going on in the heart of Europe. It was a passion to rescue the Church from its Babylonish captivity to European culture.

Perhaps it was an inevitable reaction to this that, when the terrible struggle was over the new slogan should be 'Let the Secular be the Secular'. If the Church asserts its freedom over against the State, let the State and all the organs of public life affirm their independence over against the Church. Under the shadow of the coming conflict, T. S. Eliot had ventured to write of 'The Idea of a Christian Society'. Twenty years later the Christian economist Dennis Munby wrote *The Idea of a Secular Society*[24] – a book which laid the

---

[24] (Munby 1963.)

line that was to be followed in ecumenical thinking for several decades. It is extraordinary that this idea has had such a long run among Christians. A much more recent work of Michael Novak, *The Spirit of Democratic Capitalism*,[25] celebrates as the glory of our secular society that, in his words, 'the central shrine is empty'. There is no icon to tell us what is most to be desired. There is no table of the law preserved in the sanctuary. The secular society creates its own norms.

Even if we are blind and deaf to the multiplying signs of a descent into moral anarchy, we might at least be awakened by the angry voices of our young Muslim neighbours who attack with increasing fury what they rightly see as a pagan society which openly defies the laws of God.

To speak in most gatherings of liberally minded Christians about the idea of a Christian society is, in my experience, to invite the immediate question: 'Do you want to go back to the Middle Ages?' But this knee-jerk reaction is absurd. Of course we cannot go back, nor should we wish to. But also, we cannot remain as we are. We are carried along by a tide that sweeps us towards increasing moral anarchy and social disintegration.

Certainly we cannot go back; but we can and we should look back on the way we have come. A society which has lost its memory is like a ship which has lost its rudder. It can only drift with the tides. I find it very alarming that history seems to have such a diminishing place in our public education. We know, and we do not like, the symptoms of Alzheimer's disease when we meet it among our friends. It sometimes looks as if the dissemination of a sort of national Alzheimer's disease is part of the present agenda. If we are to get our bearings for the future, we need to pay attention to the past, not to return to it but to learn from it.

Let us begin by posing a question which is central to any fundamental debate about Christianity in the public realm. It is the question: 'How is power legitimated?' By what right do some people, calling themselves 'the State', exercise coercive power over others? It has been alleged of Los Angeles that it is a city governed by four gangs, one of which is called 'Police'. What entitles this one to claim authority over the others? In all ancient societies, as far as we know, the legitimation is held to come from powers higher than human. The ruler in some way represents a more-than-human reality, whether conceived in terms of a personal divine being or otherwise. There is therefore an indissoluble link between acknowledgment of this power and acknowledgement of the authority of the ruler. What Professor Lamin Sanneh calls the 'territorial principle' in religion[26] is in operation. Being a subject of the earthly ruler involves acknowledgment of the power which lies behind the legitimacy of his rule.

Obviously the Roman Empire, within which Christianity came to birth, was an order of this kind. Political and religious obligations were fused. There

---

[25] (Novak 1982.)
[26] (E.g. Sanneh 1993: 185ff.)

could be private religious cults offering personal salvation through various rites, teachings and practice, but these could not replace, or be allowed to threaten, the public cult by which the empire was held together.

When the point came at which the Roman world was collapsing from its own inner weakness and was being threatened with destruction from the barbarian enemies from without, and when the Emperor Constantine took the step of baptism, it was necessarily both a political and religious act. It opened the way for the Church, evidently the only body capable of giving some renewal of order to a disintegrating society, to take increasing responsibility for public life. But this assumption of responsibility did not alter the fundamental character of that society. It was still, to use van Leeuwen's term, an 'ontocratic' society,[27] a society based on the acknowledgment of a more-than-human power. Certainly that power was now invoked under another name and had a different character. But it is easy, with hindsight, to see that the figure of Christ as the Byzantine Pantocrator has been more shaped by the image of imperial power than by the image of the crucified Jesus. The important point is that the 'territorial principle' still operates. How could it be otherwise? Society is still held together by acknowledgment of a more-than-human power, represented in the human figure of the earthly ruler. It would surely be hopelessly anachronistic to imagine a modern 'free Church in a free State' emerging full-grown from that critical change in the fourth century.

The territorial principle in religion operated through Europe for the next 13 centuries. In much of the old eastern Christendom the Arab armies ensured that a new territorial regime, at once political and religious, would be established so securely that it is still in place.

The division of Western Christendom at the Reformation did not end the territorial principle, in spite of the Anabaptist protest against it. Lutherans, Calvinists, Anglicans and Roman Catholics each made territorial claims on the principle of *Cuius regio, eius religio*. But the terrible religious wars of seventeenth-century Europe opened the way for the conversion of Western Europe to the new faith of the Enlightenment, and so for the ending of territorial religion. The decisive event, marking a radically new departure within the story of Christianity, was that experiment in an altogether new kind of political and religious order which was, and is, the United States of America. Here both the new ideas of the Enlightenment and also the enduring power were both at work to create a new kind of society based on a new principle of legitimation.

Not that the ontocratic note was entirely silenced. According to the foundation documents of the new republic it is the Creator who has endowed all persons with equal rights to life, liberty and the pursuit of happiness. The political order thus still rests upon a more-than-human authority. But in the ensuing development of this new kind of society, the face and the voice of

---

[27] (van Leeuwen 1964: 158ff.)

the Creator do not remain centre-stage. The equal rights of every individual human being, understood as something belonging to human beings as such apart from any divine ordering, move to the centre. It is the duty of the State to safeguard these rights. In doing so it necessarily exercises power. But whence comes its authority to do so? Evidently from the will of the people.

Here we come, I think, to the central problem which now faces the liberal democratic state. In so far as the older biblical meta-narrative still pervades society, the concept of human rights still has some anchorage in the will of the Creator who is their author and upon whose character as a holy and loving God they rest. But in so far as the biblical story fades from public memory, the intrinsic self-contradiction of the liberal vision shows itself. This self-contradiction has been set out with admirable clarity by Ian Markham in his recent book *Plurality and Christian Ethics*.[28] If there is no more-than-human source for the rights of the individual person; if, in other words, nothing exists except the sum total of human persons and all things visible, there are no grounds for affirming that one individual human person has rights which can limit the rights of all human beings considered collectively. There is no ground for affirming the rights of an individual as limiting the rights of the collective. The liberal democracies of Western Europe are still haunted by memories, even if fading memories, of that formidable being whom Moses encountered on Mount Sinai, and by the figure of Jesus, even if only in a mist of childhood memories. So long as this is so, the logic of the liberal state is checked from exercising its full rigour. But when this fades still further into the background of memory, or when – as in Central Europe during the inter-war years – it is swept away by the re-emergence of pre-Christian pagan myths, there is no check against anarchy except tyranny.

Before we turn to look at the alternatives before us, we should pause to reflect on the ending of the territorial principle. It would be ungrateful and unrealistic to move on without recognising what has been achieved in this ending. The separation of political power from religious belief has made possible the freedom of thought and speech which we rightly prize as something we are ready to defend at all costs. Whatever our present problems and perplexities, we must affirm and defend this freedom. And the ending of the territorial principle has also brought a positive gain for religion. We now recognise that being a Christian is much more than being a citizen of a 'Christian' country, or subjects of a Christian ruler. This is not universally recognised even now. You can still find people in parts of the Third World who assume that a visitor from Europe or North America is a Christian until the contrary is proved. It is one of the positive fruits of the Enlightenment that we recognise that to be a Christian is to be personally committed to Jesus Christ as a matter of deliberate and sustained willing and doing. In that sense,

---

[28] (Markham 1994.)

the ending of the territorial principle has been a cleansing experience for Christendom, and we should be thankful for it. But this proper gratitude cannot absolve us of the responsibility of asking about the adequacy of that which has replaced the old territorial principle. We still have to ask about the legitimation of political power.

I have referred to the internal contradiction which besets the liberal answer to this question. If political power is legitimated by 'the will of the people', and if at the same time one holds that every individual among those who make up 'the people' has inalienable human rights, how can these rights be secured against the will of a majority? As we have noted, in the classic political statement about human rights, these are said to have been given by the Creator. But, as we well know, the Creator has long been retired from the public square. These rights are held to be part of the substance of human nature, even though it is obvious that the definition of these rights (as in the documents of the United Nations and the European Union) are matters of ad hoc political negotiation. The problem with human rights cut off from their source in the will of the Creator, is that they are things to be desired rather than secure possessions. The concept of rights belongs to the language of law. It is a juridical term. Rights exist only if there is an agreed framework in which there are parties who acknowledge the corresponding responsibility to honour the claim for a right. Since these claims are – in the modern world – usually made against the nation state, it is natural that the definition of these rights becomes a matter of political negotiation. Individuals have rights only to the extent to which governments are prepared to acknowledge them. Anyone who regularly writes 'Urgent Action' letters for Amnesty International knows about this.

But if human rights are a gift from the Creator, then they cannot be severed from their context in what we may know of the Creator's purpose for human life. One cannot take the gift on an 'à la carte' basis, ignoring the purpose for which these rights were bestowed. In the biblical tradition which has shaped Western Christendom into a coherent and distinct culture, this context is the covenant relation established by God, first with the people of Israel, and then extended to all nations through the new covenant in the blood of Jesus. And here we come to what seems to me to be an extraordinary feature of the whole debate about the relation between political power and Christian belief. At the heart of the political debate is always the question: 'How shall justice be effective; how shall power be just?' One might almost say that this agonised question is the pervasive theme of the Old Testament, above all of the Psalms. How, when, where shall God's holy and just rule take effect in the life of this world of violent wrong-doing? When, where and how, in other words, shall we see the kingdom of God, his kingly rule manifest in the life of the world?

The answer which the Gospel gives to this is an astonishing one. God's kingly rule *has* been decisively manifest: it is there in the dying of Jesus, and we know it is there because the crucified and humiliated Jesus has been raised from the dead. We know, in other words, that God's kingly rule *is* the final reality with which we have to deal, and which must therefore shape all our thinking and acting, but that the full manifestation of this rule is an event beyond history, an event by which all human living – personal or political – is to be guided and judged.

The political implications of this must be that, when Christians are in a position to exercise political authority, they must do so on the basis of that which has been revealed in Jesus Christ as God's purpose for human life, but in doing so they are required to give to all under their political authority the same freedom to dissent as God gives to us in the incarnation of his word in Jesus. This freedom to dissent is required not in spite of, but because of, what God has revealed to us as the truth. I have said that the freedom of dissent which the Enlightenment brought is something that we can never surrender. But we have now to recognise that it was based upon an insecure foundation. The liberal doctrine of the free society has no adequate safeguard against the twin dangers of moral anarchy and political tyranny.

We must surely now recognise that it is an illusion to suppose that the State can be totally neutral in respect of fundamental beliefs. All deliberate action presupposes some belief about what is the case, about the meaning and direction of human life. The ideologically neutral state is a myth, and a very dangerous one. In so far as Christians are in positions of political responsibility, they are bound to use the power entrusted to them in accordance with the Christian understanding of God's purpose for human life. This means that there will be resistance from those who take other views. For the reason just stated, namely for the reason that in Christ God has given us a space of freedom for dissent and disobedience, but also for witness to the kingly rule of God, a government shaped by Christian belief will ensure the preservation of this space. It will recognise that there is unending need for the spiritual warfare which is required if the truth of the Gospel is to prevail in the public realm. But it will not pretend to neutrality. It will use the power entrusted to it in accordance with its understanding of God's will as revealed in the Gospel.

I have in mind here, of course, the alternative vision for modern society which is being vigorously offered today by Islam, the only contemporary ideology which seriously challenged the reigning idea of the liberal secular state. Islam seeks legitimation for political power in the will of Allah as understood to be embodied in the Qur'an and the Sharia law. Here there is no question of freedom to dissent. Political and religious authority are fused. Growing numbers of our Muslim contemporaries in Western Europe correctly perceive the slide towards moral anarchy in our society and claim that only Islam can save us. On university campuses, and in those areas of our cities where Muslims are strongly represented in the population, this claim is proving increasingly credible. To suppose that we can meet it by repeating the slogans of secularity and neutrality would be blind and foolish. If there were no contemporary challenge from Islam, Christians would still have to face up to the manifest failures of the liberal secular state. We should be grateful that the powerful challenge of Islam makes it impossible for us to evade the issue.

I referred earlier to the early slogan of the ecumenical movement, 'Let the Church be the Church'. In the context of that time – the 1930s – this was a summons to the European churches to extricate themselves from the position of domestic chaplains to Western society. That was a necessary summons. But we need to add a corollary: 'Let the Church be the Church and therefore let it take proper responsibility for the civic community'. This means addressing the question of power.

The main Christian tradition, following the teaching of the New Testament, has acknowledged the use of power by the civic authorities as something ordained by God for the preservation of justice. But this tradition is explicitly or implicitly questioned in much contemporary Christian discourse. The words 'dominance' and 'violence' are routinely used to denote what has traditionally been regarded as the normal use of power by governing authorities. Those who resist governments are routinely regarded as occupying higher moral ground than those who govern.

Certainly the Church, according to the main tradition, has the duty to admonish the civic authority when it abandons justice and serves injustice. But it is foolish to suppose that anything can be accomplished in the political order without power. Those who exercise power need constantly to be reminded that power tends to corrupt, but it would be an evasion of their calling if Christians refused to take the responsibility of power when its use is needed for the maintenance of justice. Christians will not fulfil their respons-ibilities to the civic community merely by protesting. They have to take the responsibility of government, knowing well the dangers which this involves. And, if my argument is right, when they have this responsibility, they will have to use the powers entrusted to them in accordance with the understanding of the purpose of human life which we have in Christ.

They will therefore seek a kind of government which is not neutral but Christian, knowing that those who hold other beliefs will protest, and ensuring that they have the freedom to protest, to dissent, and to engage in public argument. Their vision would be not that of a neutral, secular society, nor that of a theocratic society of the type sought by Islam, but of a Christian society, a society whose public life is shaped by the Christian beliefs about the human person and human society. And because at the heart of these Christian beliefs is the knowledge that in Christ God has given us the freedom to dissent, and has entrusted to his Church the responsibility of bearing witness to the truth in face of dissent, it would be a society in which there is provided the maximum of opportunity at all levels of society for open discussion of the matters which have to be decided in the public arena.

Extract 3
'Activating the Christian Vision' (1998)[29]

What is offered in the following paragraphs is addressed to the Church. It is not a political programme. Long before we can think of formulating political changes which might be recommended to governments and political parties, there is a need to address Christians about their understanding of the relation of the gospel to the public square. There are, in the first place, some false assumptions to be identified and rejected.

1   The first concerns the idea of religious neutrality. A state can be religiously neutral in the sense that it does not have to support or to suppress any particular religious belief or practice. This concept of religious neutrality has, as we all know, been classically embodied in the Constitution of the United States of America, which has been the great pioneer and paradigm of the attack on the territorial principle and the development of religious pluralism. But, as has been impressively shown by the writing of Stephen Carter, the effect of this has been to favour non-religious beliefs and practice against religion.[30] Here the problem is with the very term 'religion'. How is this to be defined? In a famous definition, Paul Tillich defined religion as 'ultimate concern'. Whatever is the cause or belief for which you would put everything else aside, that (in this definition) is your religion. In a bizarre case which went to the US Supreme Court, a group of citizens of the State of Arkansas successfully sued a local school board on a charge of violating the Constitution by teaching religion in schools – the religion in question being 'secular humanism'. The case was decided by the Supreme Court in favour of the school board. Everything turns on the definition of religion. In another case, the court overruled a decision by another state to permit the teaching of 'creation science' along with Darwinism as alternatives. The court decided that the former was 'religion' while the latter was 'science', and this settled the matter.

This judgement highlights the problem in a very clear way. 'Science' is another word for 'knowing' and we have come to use it exclusively for one way of knowing. What is embodied in this and other judgements of the Supreme Court is that one way of knowing is operative in public life and children are required to be trained in it in the state schools, while another way of knowing is a matter for personal and parental choice. Thus the state may be 'religiously neutral' provided we accept a definition of religion (determined by the courts) which separates it from the ways of knowing embodied in 'science'. But the state is not neutral in respect of worldviews, meta-narratives or whatever term one may use for the framework which gives overall coherence to our understanding of what it is to be human.

These legal rulings bring to clear sight the fact that the secular liberal society rests in part on the assumption that there is available a body of 'objective' truth

---

[29] Newbigin 1998: [. . . .] 150–61, 162, 164–5.
[30] Carter 1993.

which is not a matter of personal or sectarian opinion but is true for all, and has to be understood and accepted by all.

There is today an understanding of the limitations of the scientific method much more widespread than a few decades ago. The nineteenth-century attempt to portray science as the modern replacement for religion as the key to human happiness has faded into the past. There is wider recognition that the methods of science, while brilliantly successful in enabling us to understand how things are produced and function, excludes from its reach the questions of ultimate meaning and purpose. The rise of post-modernism with its scepticism towards all 'meta-narratives' and comprehensive explanations has led also to scepticism regarding the claims of science. But, in spite of these developments, there remains widespread in the popular mind the idea that there is some standpoint from which the claims of religions could be adjudicated and they could be proved to be either true or false. Science is still widely seen as being part of this body of public truth to be acknowledged by all. The effect of this absolutizing of the distinction between two ways of knowing, between science and religion, is (as Stephen Carter shows) to create a bias against religion and to suppress its role in the life of society.

One by-product of this dichotomy between two ways of knowing is the radical difference between the rules which govern inter-religious discussion and those which govern discussion on other matters. In most areas of culture there is vigorous discussion in which the proponents of different views challenge one another and seek to persuade one another. This kind of active debate is the very oxygen which keeps culture alive and fruitful. But different rules are generally applied in the world of interfaith relations. Here 'dialogue' is the order of the day, and the agenda is not a matter of mutual challenge but of sharing and comparing 'experience'. I am not denying all value to this, far from it. Nor am I blind to the dangers of vigorous debate between believers of different faith communities, debates which can easily degenerate into polemics which obscure the truth rather than advance it. But the point is worth making as an illustration of the effect of the removal of religion from the arena of debate about truth.

The first step, therefore, in approaching the idea of a Christian society is a negative one. We have to question the assumption that a secular state is neutral. It does not establish any of the world's religions, but it does establish a world-view which embodies truth-claims which Christians cannot accept and which must be brought into the open and challenged.

This way of understanding the world is very seldom brought out into the open. It is simply assumed because it is the way we are taught to think from our earliest schooldays, and by the unstated assumptions which underlie what we read, watch and hear through the mass media. It is only when we take the difficult step back and reflect from a Christian point of view on what is being said that we recognize what is happening. Our public world is being continually shaped by a certain set of beliefs about what is the case, and these beliefs certainly do not include the belief that the reality with which we finally have to do and to which we shall all finally give an account of our lives, is God as he is made known to us in Jesus Christ. Society is being continually shaped by a set of beliefs which have a privileged position as against other beliefs. We must assume that a Christian society, if such were possible, would be one in which the Christian faith has this privileged position.

2 The obvious implication of this is that a Christian society would be one in which Christians formed a sufficiently large proportion of the total population to exert a preponderant influence on public life. But this statement needs to be filled out in several respects.

(a) 'Believing the Christian faith' means believing that it is true and is therefore public truth, truth for all, truth which all people ought to accept because it is true. It does not mean taking the Christian faith as a personally preferred option for oneself which, like other personal preferences, we refrain from pressing upon our friends. Once again we must make clear exactly what is being said. We do not seek to impose our Christian beliefs upon others, but this is not because (as in the liberal view) we recognize that they may be right and we may be wrong. It is because the Christian faith itself centred in the message of the incarnation, cross and resurrection, forbids the use of any kind of coercive pressure upon others to conform. Of course we know, or ought to know, that there are many matters, including matters of religious belief in respect of which we must recognize that our unbelieving friends may be right and we may be wrong. But our personal commitment to Jesus as Lord and Saviour is not a matter for negotiation or compromise. And it carries with it the obligation to affirm Him as Lord and Saviour of the world, even though we know that we are still faltering and fumbling in our struggle to carry that belief into our daily conduct in the public realm.

(b) This belief carries with it the implication that part of our Christian obedience is the acceptance of our share of responsibility for the life of our city, our nation, the world. This is not an option which one may choose or reject. To ignore it is a dereliction of duty. Here it is necessary to talk about eschatology. During the period when Christianity in both catholic and evangelical forms was flourishing in England (I am thinking especially of the latter half of the nineteenth century), the taunt was often flung at Christians that they offered the victims of the industrial revolution only an other-worldly recompense for their present sufferings, that they offered 'pie in the sky when you die' rather than justice now. This is a gross distortion of the real facts, but it does point to the danger of a privatized eschatology which thinks only of the destiny of the individual soul and not (as the Bible does) of the consummation of God's universal purpose for his whole creation. In the years since the 1914–1918 war many Christians have sought to redress the balance by active involvement in issues of social justice and world peace, to the point at which it sometimes becomes difficult to distinguish the Church from a political pressure group. At the present time there is again some reaction.

More and more Christians are tempted to give up hope in the political process, to recognize that the rival promises of political parties are simply empty charades, that there are really no political solutions to our major social ills. There is a danger of retreat into a politically irresponsible concentration on 'religious experience'. The recovery of an authentic and holistic biblical eschatology is essential if we are to speak realistically of a Christian vision for society.

The focus of the biblical vision is on the final vindication of God in the gift of his perfect reign, symbolized in a city of perfect beauty and glory into which all the nations are to bring their honour and glory. This gift of God's blessed reign is both imminent, in the sense that it is the proper horizon of all our actions here and now, whether in the public or the private realms, and at the same time a secret whose timing is wholly in the keeping of God who alone can know what possibilities there remain for repentance, faith and obedience. Our actions do not create this new order, nor do they bring it about. They are, in Albert Schweitzer's fine words, acted prayers to God that he may give us the Kingdom. We act now (in the public realm as in our personal and domestic life) in ways which correspond to the reality which is to be the final reality, the judgement which will be the final judgement. These actions do not directly solve the world's problems. They may fail. They will probably be forgotten after a few years or generations. They are simply committed to God, entrusted to his wise hands, in the faith that nothing entrusted to him is lost. There is an analogy, indeed a continuity here with our most intimate personal acts of discipleship. We know that our mortal bodies will, before many years, be nothing but dust and ashes. Yet we cherish them and care for them, so that they may be instruments useful for God's service for such years as may be given to us. We do not neglect or despise them because they are so transient. So also with the social, political and cultural products of our thought and labour. We are right to recognize that politics will not solve the world's problems. But we would be wrong if we concluded that politics are not part of the substance of Christian discipleship.

(c)   The third condition for a Christian contribution to the shaping of society will be that Christians understand the nature of the political order in the way in which the Christian tradition affirms, in spite of the apparent absurdity of talking about 'the Christian tradition' in view of the long history of disagreement among Christians on this matter. Some of our contemporary debates are too much shaped by the fact that Western peoples have been accustomed for so long to living in relatively stable societies where law is administered and enforced in a way which, though open to criticism, is generally accepted. This we have taken for granted. It is when we see such developments as those in Lebanon in the 1980s and in Yugoslavia and Central Africa in the 1990s that we are compelled to see the fact that even a tyrannous and despotic regime can be preferred to chaos and anarchy. In the former situation there are ways by which most individuals can live relatively peaceful lives free from sudden eruptions of violence. When the political order breaks down, peace and security vanish. One can therefore understand, from a purely natural point of view, why St Paul can see even the despotic government of the Roman Empire as a ministry appointed by God.

[In spite] of the ambivalence of the picture of kingship as it is portrayed in the Old Testament [. . . .] the kingship is ordained by God and the king is anointed by God's servant. However many debates may circle around the enigmatic saying of Jesus on the subject of taxes paid to the Emperor Caesar, it is clear, both from this saying and from the words spoken to Pontius Pilate in the story as told by St John (John 19.11) that Jesus acknowledges the authority of the Roman rule as coming from God. Political power is not simply the exercise of brute force by those who have succeeded in crushing their rivals. However political power may have been obtained, those who wield it are responsible to God, and it is the responsibility of the Church to remind them of this fact. When the state fails to use the necessary power to suppress and punish forces of evil and to encourage and sustain movements of good, it fails in its responsibility to God from whom its authority comes.

If we affirm, as I have done, that the function of the state is to punish bad conduct and to reward good conduct, assuming that there are accepted criteria of good and bad, this in turn implies some set of beliefs by reference to which these judgements of good and bad may be made. A state controlled, for example, by Benthamite beliefs will make these judgements in a manner different from a state controlled by Christian beliefs. The idea of neutrality at this point is sheer illusion. All the actions of the state are obviously shaped by the beliefs of those who are, for the time being, in the seats of power, and these in turn reflect, in greater or lesser degree, the beliefs of those who put them in power. In a society where Christians, committed to the truth of their faith and to its expression in the public square, are sufficiently numerous to shape the policy, the state will tend to act upon principles congruent with the Christian faith.

(d)   I am assuming that the society of which I speak will be a democratic society. But it will be a democracy shaped more by Christian beliefs than by those of the Enlightenment. It will not see the individual with his or her inalienable rights as the vis-à-vis of the state. When there is nothing between the individual and the state, the inevitable result is the coercion of minorities. A society shaped by Christian beliefs would recognize that, since human being and flourishing is to be understood not in terms of the self-fulfilment of the individual but in terms of the development of interpersonal relationships of trust and responsibility, there will be a multitude of societies intermediate between the individual and the state; places where people meet one another on a face-to-face level and, by argument and persuasion, seek to convince one another about the good and the right. As A. D. Lindsay and others have shown, the deep roots of democracy in England lay in the experience of those Puritan Christians who, in their rejection of the divine right of an autocratic kingship, believed that the will of God could be found in serious engagement with one another under the authority of Scripture.[31] The result hoped for was not

---

[31]   Lindsay 1935.

simply the rule of the majority over the minority, but the rule of God over all. This is of course a hope which can never be fully realized in a fallen world, but it points to the essential character of a democratic state as Christians would wish to envisage it: a state in which governance is dispersed as widely as possible so that the maximum participation of all in matters of the common good is enlisted.

3   A third element in the Christian vision for society concerns the role of lay men and women in the life of society and of the Church. From what has been said already, I hope it is clear that Christians ought not to hope for a society controlled by bishops or church synods. The Church can only fulfil its God-given responsibilities by being clearly distinct from the state. The state is required to use coercive power: the Church is forbidden to do so. It is through the presence and activity of committed and competent Christian men and women in the various areas of the common life of society that the Christian vision for society could become effective in practice. The twentieth century has seen a strong anti-clerical movement in most of the churches. The Second Vatican Council has been widely held to mark a watershed in Catholic think-ing about the Church as the people of God rather than as a hierarchy of clergy to whom the laity have the duty of humble and unquestioning obedience. In the Anglican and Protestant churches there has been a strong assertion of lay responsibility for the life of the Church and a rejection of clerical dom-inance. But unfortunately this tends to miss the point. Bishops, priests, and other ordained ministers are set apart for particular functions in enabling the whole Church to fulfil its priestly role as the body of Christ in the world. But the priesthood of the whole membership is not primarily exercised by sitting on church committees or in church assemblies. It is exercised in the life of the world, as the first letter of Peter says, by showing forth the mighty acts of God and by offering up sacrifices worthy of God (1 Pet. 2.5, 9). This is to be done in the midst of the life of the world. The reality of the reign of God, hidden from the eyes of unbelievers, is to be made visible to the world through the obedience of believers in the midst of their daily work. The sacrifices accept-able to God are to be made in all the acts of loving obedience, small or great, which a believer is called upon to make in the course of daily work in the world. The priesthood of the people of God is to be exercised in the midst of the secular world of business, labour, politics and culture. And for this, as the Apostle reminds us, we need to be equipped (Eph. 4.11–12).

It is here that we must recognize our greatest deficit. In spite of many courageous attempts by groups of Christians, it must be said that in general the Church has not given the necessary attention to equipping all its mem-bers for these tasks. To do so is very difficult because we quickly run into sharp differences of judgement. However difficult it may be, the churches must give a very high priority to the development of strategies to help its members in various sectors of public life to form some judgements about their course of action. The long tradition of Catholic social work developed in the past hundred years is one great resource. There are groups of Christians engaged in the worlds of economics, philosophy, literature, medicine and the natural sciences who have worked hard to develop Christian insights into the ways in which these disciplines should develop. But these are only the beginnings, and the Church as a whole has not given to these matters anything like the attention that they need.

In any discussion on the nature of society and of our vision for it, education must have a central place. Societies exist, cohere and flourish in so far as they embody a reasonably coherent understanding of existence within which they can make sense of their personal lives. Education, in its broadest sense, is the initiation of new members of society into this tradition. In contemporary British society the tradition into which young people are initiated in school and college is the set of assumptions which have controlled Western society since the Enlightenment. In a minority of homes – Christian, Islamic, Jewish and others – children are initiated into other traditions. In so far as these are at odds with the tradition into which children are initiated in school and college, they obviously fight a losing battle. Even in homes where the parents are committed Christians, it is hard, to the point of impossibility, for children to sustain belief in the meta-narrative of the Bible over against that understanding of the meta-narrative – the picture of the origins and development of nature, of human society as a whole – which is being offered to them at school. It is possible to maintain the telling of the biblical story in the privacy of home and church, but in so far as this story contradicts the meta-narrative of the schools, young people are placed in an impossible situation. The question 'which is the true story?' must ultimately be faced.

To illustrate the point, one may ask what would be the position of a young scientist who insisted that, whatever the findings of contemporary biologists (always changing) the existence of human life on this earth cannot ultimately be explained without belief in some pre-existing intelligence, and that therefore the neo-Darwinian explanation of the evolution of living organisms and of human beings cannot be the last word on the subject. Such a person would have almost no possibility of appointment and promotion in the academic world. He would be told that such beliefs are permissible as private opinions but that they cannot form part of public opinion. But this *modus vivendi* is ultimately untenable. One has to ask which is true. A belief which is permitted only to exist in a bunker may survive for a time, but it must finally be obliterated. For the sake of the well-being of civil society as a whole, I believe that Christians have a duty to share with those who hold other beliefs, whether religious or secular, to create a public educational system which will train future citizens to live in mutual respect and mutual responsibility while acknowledging their differences in fundamental belief. In this sense I accept what I understand to be the intention of the American writer Os Guinness when he speaks of a 'chartered pluralism'. But this pluralism cannot be sustained if one of these belief systems, namely 'secular humanism', uses its present hegemony to exclude from the curriculum of public education the belief system which is embodied in the Bible. It is only the gospel which enables us to affirm both that the Sovereign Lord of all has made his will and purpose known in Jesus Christ for the whole of our life, private and public, and yet at the same time, not in spite of this but because of this, to affirm that God has ordained a space in which disbelief can have the freedom to flourish. Thus chartered pluralism can only exist where there is a sufficiently large, vigorous and articulate Christian community to sustain the basis on which it rests. To put the same point negatively, if the present erosion of Christian belief continues beyond a certain point, it will become impossible to offer any alternative to the present dominant secularist ideology, since [. . . .] this ideology is ultimately self-destructive, and the way would be open for other powerful or seductive alternatives.

Perhaps the point can be made clearer by putting it in another way. [. . . .] [The] phrase 'a secular society' can be understood in two radically different ways. It may on the one hand refer to a society or an educational system in which different religious beliefs are given equal opportunity to flourish, but may on the other hand refer to a society or an educational system which is dominated by the ideology of secularism, by the belief that all things can be satisfactorily explained without any reference to divine revelation or to any supra-natural realities. I am affirming that in the last analysis it is only the Christian gospel which can sustain a secular society or a secular educational system in the former and proper sense.

[. . . .]

Is it proper to speak of 'a Christian society'? If by that phrase we mean a society in which the Christian belief so controls all public life as to suppress and exclude alternative beliefs, we must answer that we ought not to have any such goal in mind. The age-long domination of the territorial principle was decisively ended at the Enlightenment, and there can be no going back on that crucial event in the history of the world. Two centuries of religious freedom have taught us so to value it that we can never surrender it. But now, two centuries after the Enlightenment, we are discovering that the principles developed at the Enlightenment cannot in the long run sustain religious freedom. This freedom is increasingly threatened by religious movements which claim absolute control over all life. The only ultimate secure ground for religious freedom is in the fact that Almighty God, in the act of revealing his sovereign power and wisdom in the cross and resurrection of Jesus Christ, has at the same time established for his world a space and a time during which faith is possible because unbelief is also possible. And if we are tempted to cry out to God in impatience because he allows so much wickedness still to flourish in his world, we know that the answer to our cry is in his long, long patience which, as the Apostle tells us, is to lead us to repentance. I am sure that this is the critical point for all debate about the gospel as public truth.

[. . . .]

To the end of history we are called upon to be witnesses to the truth in a world where it is contradicted, to engage in the kind of discourse in which through our struggle we learn more of the truth, and always to remain thankful to the God whose providence creates a world in which falsehood can still exist without destroying us. [. . . .] We are in that period between Christ's coming and his coming again when we are called upon to put upon us the whole armour of God, and to fight not against human beings ('flesh and blood') but against those spiritual powers which so subtly, and yet often so blatantly, take over the great institutions and movements of public life.

[. . . .]

We do indeed look forward with eager longing to that Christian society which is the final goal of all God's creative and redemptive love, but until that day we are called upon to seek on earth a society which, as far as may be granted to us, reflects the glory of the city to which we look forward.

Further reading

Newbigin 1985d: 173–82.
Newbigin 1991b: 1–13.
Newbigin 1997: 1–8.

Bibliography

❖◆❖

Referenced works by Lesslie Newbigin

Newbigin, J. E. Lesslie. (1936) 'Revelation'. Unpublished Essay. (*Lesslie Newbigin Papers*, Library Special Collections, The University of Birmingham, UK.)

—— (1937) *Christian Freedom in the Modern World*. London: SCM Press.

—— (1941) 'The Kingdom of God and the Idea of Progress.' In G. Wainwright (ed.), *Signs amid the Rubble: The Purposes of God in Human History*. Grand Rapids, MI/Cambridge, UK: William B. Eerdmans Publishing Company, 2003, 1–55. (Originally given as lectures in 1941.)

—— (1948) 'The Duty and Authority of the Church to Preach the Gospel.' In *The Church's Witness to God's Design: An Ecumenical Study Prepared under the Auspices of the World Council of Churches*. London: SCM Press, 19–35.

—— (1951) *A South India Diary*. London: SCM Press.

—— (1953) *The Household of God: Lectures on the Nature of the Church*. London: SCM Press.

—— (1955) 'The Quest for Unity through Religion.' *Journal of Religion* 35: 17–33.

—— (1956) *Sin and Salvation*. London: SCM Press.

—— (1958) *One Body, One Gospel, One World: The Christian Mission Today*. London: International Missionary Council.

—— (1960a) 'The Pattern of the Christian World Mission.' In E. Jackson (ed.), *A Word in Season: Perspectives on Christian World Missions*. Grand Rapids, MI/Edinburgh: William B. Eerdmans Publishing Company/Saint Andrew Press, 1994, 7–20.

—— (1960b) *The Reunion of the Church: A Defence of the South India Scheme*. 2nd edn. London: SCM Press. Original publication 1948.

—— (1961) *A Faith for this One World?* London: SCM Press.

—— (1962a) 'The Missionary Dimension of the Ecumenical Movement.' *Ecumenical Review* 14: 207–15.

—— (1962b) 'Missions in an Ecumenical Perspective.' Unpublished Manuscript. (World Council of Churches, Ecumenical Centre Library, Geneva, Switzerland.)

—— (1962c) 'Unfaith and Other Faiths.' Unpublished Address. (World Council of Churches, Ecumenical Centre Library, Geneva, Switzerland.)

—— (1963) *The Relevance of Trinitarian Doctrine for Today's Mission*. CWME Study Pamphlets, No. 2. London: Edinburgh House Press.

—— (1966) *Honest Religion for Secular Man*. London: SCM Press.

—— (1968) *Christ Our Eternal Contemporary*. Madras: Christian Literature Society of India.

—— (1969) *The Finality of Christ*. London: SCM Press.

—— (1976) 'All in One Place or All of One Sort? On Unity and Diversity in the Church.' In R. W. A. McKinney (ed.), *Creation, Christ and Culture: Studies in Honour of T. F. Torrance*. Edinburgh: T & T Clark, 288–306.

—— (1977a) 'The Basis, Purpose and Manner of Inter-Faith Dialogue.' *Scottish Journal of Theology* 30: 253–70.

—— (1977b) 'The Future of Missions and Missionaries.' *Review and Expositor* 74: 209–18.

—— (1977c) 'What is "a local church truly united"?' *Ecumenical Review* 29: 115–28.

—— (1978a) 'Christ and the Cultures.' *Scottish Journal of Theology* 31: 1–22.

—— (1978b) *The Open Secret: Sketches for a Missionary Theology.* Grand Rapids, MI: William B. Eerdmans Publishing Company.

—— (1981a) 'Integration – Some Personal Reflections 1981.' *International Review of Mission* 70: 247–55.

—— (1981b) 'The Missionary Dimension of the Ecumenical Movement.' *International Review of Mission* 70: 240–6. (Originally published in *The Ecumenical Review* 14 (1962): 207–15.)

—— (1982) *The Light has Come: An Exposition of the Fourth Gospel.* Grand Rapids, MI: William B. Eerdmans Publishing Company.

—— (1983) *The Other Side of 1984: Questions for the Churches.* Geneva: World Council of Churches.

—— (1984) 'The Sending of the Church – Three Bible Studies.' In *New Perspectives on World Mission and Unity.* Vol. 1. Edinburgh: Church of Scotland Board of Mission and Unity, 1–14.

—— (1985a) 'Can the West be Converted?' *Princeton Seminary Bulletin* 6/1: 25–37.

—— (1985b) 'How I Arrived at the Other Side of 1984.' *Selly Oak Journal* 2: 6–8.

—— (1985c) *Unfinished Agenda: An Autobiography.* London: SPCK.

—— (1985d) 'The Welfare State: A Christian Perspective.' *Theology* 88: 173–82.

—— (1986a) 'A British and European Perspective.' In M. Hill (ed.), *Entering the Kingdom: A Fresh Look at Conversion.* Bromley: MARC Europe/British Church Growth Association, 57–68.

—— (1986b) *Foolishness to the Greeks: The Gospel and Western Culture.* London: SPCK.

—— (1987a) 'Can the West be Converted?' *Evangelical Review of Theology* 11: 355–68.

—— (1987b) 'Evangelism in the City.' *Reformed Review* 41: 3–8.

—— (1988a) 'The Enduring Validity of Cross-Cultural Mission.' *International Bulletin of Missionary Research* 12: 50–3.

—— (1988b) 'Interview with Bishop Lesslie Newbigin.' In A. Walker (ed.), *Different Gospels.* London: Hodder & Stoughton, 30–41.

—— (1988c) 'Mission in a Pluralist Society.' In E. Jackson (ed.), *A Word in Season: Perspectives on Christian World Missions.* Grand Rapids, MI/Edinburgh: William B. Eerdmans Publishing Company/Saint Andrew Press, 1994, 158–76.

—— (1988d) 'On Being the Church for the World.' In G. Ecclestone (ed.), *The Parish Church? Explorations in the Relationship of the Church and the World.* Oxford: Mowbray, 25–42.

—— (1988e) 'Our Missionary Responsibility in the Crisis of Western Culture.' In E. Jackson (ed.), *A Word in Season: Perspectives on Christian World Missions.* Grand Rapids, MI/Edinburgh: William B. Eerdmans Publishing Company/Saint Andrew Press, 1994, 98–112.

—— (1989a) 'The Christian Faith and the World Religions.' In G. Wainwright (ed.), *Keeping the Faith: Essays to mark the Centenary of Lux Mundi.* London: SPCK, 310–40.

—— (1989b) *The Gospel in a Pluralist Society.* London: SPCK.

—— (1989c) *Mission and the Crisis of Western Culture.* Edinburgh: The Handsel Press.

—— (1990a) 'Evangelism in the Context of Secularization.' In E. Jackson (ed.), *A Word in Season: Perspectives on Christian World Missions.* Grand Rapids, MI/Edinburgh: William B. Eerdmans Publishing Company/Saint Andrew Press, 1994, 148–57.

—— (1990b) 'A Mission to Modern Western Culture.' In F. R. Wilson (ed.), *The San Antonio Report: Your Will be Done – Mission in Christ's Way*. Geneva: WCC, 162–6.

—— (1991a) 'The Gospel as Public Truth.' *The Gospel and Our Culture Newsletter* 9 (Spring): 1–2.

—— (1991b) *Truth to Tell: The Gospel as Public Truth*. London: SPCK.

—— (1992a) 'Conference Call: The Gospel as Public Truth.' *The Gospel and Our Culture Newsletter* 12 (Spring): Insert.

—— (1992b) 'The Gospel as Public Truth.' *Touchstone* 5/3: 1–2.

—— (1992c) 'A Riverside Sermon.' In E. Jackson (ed.), *A Word in Season: Perspectives on Christian World Missions*. Grand Rapids, MI/Edinburgh: William B. Eerdmans Publishing Company/Saint Andrew Press, 1994, 1–6. (Approximate original date.)

—— (1992d) 'Way Out West: The Gospel in a Post-Enlightenment World.' *Touchstone* 5/3: 22–4.

—— (1993a) 'Culture and Theology.' In A. E. McGrath (ed.), *The Blackwell Encyclopedia of Modern Christian Thought*. Oxford: Blackwell Publishers, 98–100.

—— (1993b) 'Religious Pluralism: a Missiological Approach.' *Studia Missionalia* 42: 227–44.

—— (1993c) 'Religious Pluralism: A Missiological Approach.' In *Theology of Religions: Christianity and Other Religions*. Roma: Pontifical Gregorian University, 227–44.

—— (1993d) *Unfinished Agenda: An Updated Autobiography*. 2nd edn. Edinburgh: Saint Andrew Press.

—— (1994a) 'Confessing Christ in a Multi-Religion Society.' *Scottish Bulletin of Evangelical Theology* 12: 125–36.

—— (1994b) 'The Cultural Captivity of Western Christianity as a Challenge to a Missionary Church.' In E. Jackson (ed.), *A Word in Season: Perspectives on Christian World Missions*. Grand Rapids, MI/Edinburgh: William B. Eerdmans Publishing Company/Saint Andrew Press, 1994, 66–79.

—— (1994c) 'Ecumenical Amnesia.' *International Bulletin of Missionary Research* 18: 2–5.

—— (1995a) 'Can a Modern Society be Christian?' Given as 1995 Gospel and Culture Lecture, King's College London. 1–12. (Lecture transcript.)

—— (1995b) *The Open Secret: An Introduction to the Theology of Mission*. 2nd edn. London: SPCK.

—— (1995c) *Proper Confidence: Faith, Doubt and Certainty in Christian Discipleship*. London: SPCK.

—— (1996) *Truth and Authority in Modernity*. Valley Forge, PA: Gracewing/Trinity Press International.

—— (1997) 'The Trinity as Public Truth.' In K. J. Vanhoozer (ed.), *The Trinity in a Pluralistic Age: Theological Essays on Culture and Religion*. Grand Rapids, MI: William B. Eerdmans Publishing Company, 1–8.

—— (1998) 'A Light to the Nations: Theology in Politics.' In Newbigin et al. (eds.), *Faith and Power: Christianity and Islam in 'Secular' Britain*. London: SPCK, 133–65.

Other referenced publications

Arendt, Hannah. (1963) *On Revolution*. London: Faber & Faber.

Barrett, David B. (1968) *Schism and Renewal in Africa: An Analysis of Six Thousand Contemporary Religious Movements*. Nairobi: Oxford University Press.

Berger, Peter L. (1980) *The Heretical Imperative: Contemporary Possibilities of Religious Affirmation.* London: Collins. Original publication 1979.

Berger, Peter L., Berger, Brigitte and Kellner, Hansfried. (1973) *The Homeless Mind: Modernization and Consciousness.* New York: Random House.

Bloom, Allan. (1987) *The Closing of the American Mind: How Higher Education has Failed Democracy and Impoverished the Souls of Today's Students.* Harmondsworth: Penguin.

Buber, Martin. (1958) *I and Thou.* 2nd edn. Trans. R. G. Smith. New York: Charles Scribner's Sons.

Carter, Stephen L. (1993) *The Culture of Disbelief: How American Law and Politics Trivialize Religious Devotion.* New York: Basic Books.

Cassirer, Ernst. (1951) *The Philosophy of the Enlightenment.* Trans. F. Koelln and J. Pettegrove. Princeton: Princeton University Press.

Clouser, Roy A. (1991) *The Myth of Religious Neutrality: An Essay on the Hidden Role of Religious Belief in Theories.* Notre Dame, IN: Notre Dame University Press.

Cochrane, Charles N. (1940) *Christianity and Classical Culture: A Study of Thought and Action from Augustus to Augustine.* Oxford: The Clarendon Press.

Cox, Harvey. (1965) *The Secular City: Secularization and Urbanization in Theological Perspective.* London: SCM Press.

Denney, James. (1904) 'St Paul's Epistle to the Romans.' In W. R. Nicoll (ed.), *The Expositor's Greek New Testament.* London: Hodder & Stoughton, 555–725.

Devanandan, David Paul and Thomas, Madathilparampil M. (eds.). (1960) *Christian Participation in Nation-building: The Summing up of a Corporate Study on Rapid Social Change.* Social Concerns Series, no. 9. Bangalore: National Christian Council of India and the Christian Institute for the Study of Religion and Society.

Duchrow, Ulrich. (1981) *Conflict over the Ecumenical Movement: Confessing Christ Today in the Universal Church.* Trans. D. Lewis. Geneva: World Council of Churches.

Farquhar, John Nicol. (1913) *The Crown of Hinduism.* London: Oxford University Press.

Freytag, Walter. (1957) *The Gospel and the Religions: A Biblical Enquiry.* IMC Research Pamphlets. Vol. 5. London: International Missionary Council.

Fukuyama, Francis. (1992) *The End of History and the Last Man.* New York: Free Press.

Hazard, Paul. (1973) *The European Mind, 1680–1715.* Trans. J. L. May. Harmondsworth: Penguin University Books. Original publication in French 1935.

Hick, John. (1993) *God and the Universe of Faiths: Essays in the Philosophy of Religion.* Reissued edn. Oxford: Oneworld Publications. Original publication 1973.

Hocking, William Ernest. (1956) *The Coming World Civilization.* New York: Harper.

Hoerschelmann, Werner. (1977) *Christliche Gurus: Darst. von Selbstverstäendnis u. Funktion indigenen Christseins durch unabhäengige, charismat. geführte Gruppen in Südindien.* Frankfurt: Lang.

Hunsberger, George R. (1998) *Bearing the Witness of the Spirit: Lesslie Newbigin's Theology of Cultural Plurality.* Grand Rapids, MI/Cambridge: William B. Eerdmans Publishing Company.

James, William. (1979) *The Will to Believe: and Other Essays in Popular Philosophy.* Cambridge, MA: Harvard University Press.

Kant, Immanuel. (1983) 'An Answer to the Question: What is Enlightenment?' In T. Humphrey (ed.), *Perpetual Peace and Other Essays.* Trans. T. Humphrey. Indianapolis, IN: Hackett Publishing, 41–8. Original publication 1784.

Kraemer, Hendrik. (1938) *The Christian Message in a Non-Christian World.* London: Edinburgh House Press. 2nd edn 1947.

Küng, Hans. (1976) *On Being a Christian.* Trans. E. Quinn. Garden City, NY: Doubleday. Original publication in German (*Christ sein*), 1974.

Lindsay, Alexander D. (1935) *Essentials of Democracy.* 2nd edn. London: Oxford University Press.

Locke, John. (1975) *An Essay on Human Understanding.* Edited by P. Nidditch. Oxford: The Clarendon Press. Original publication 1690.

Markham, Ian S. (1994) *Plurality and Christian Ethics.* Cambridge: Cambridge University Press.

Munby, D. L. (1963) *The Idea of a Secular Society: and its Significance for Christians.* Oxford: Oxford University Press.

Niebuhr, H. Richard. (1952) *Christ and Culture.* London: Faber & Faber.

Novak, Michael. (1982) *The Spirit of Democratic Capitalism.* New York: Simon & Schuster.

Oldham, Joseph H. (1935) *Church, Community and State: A World Issue.* London: SCM Press.

Oman, John. (1902) *Vision and Authority: or The Throne of St Peter.* London: Hodder & Stoughton.

—— (1931) *The Natural and the Supernatural.* Cambridge: Cambridge University Press.

Polanyi, Michael. (1958) *Personal Knowledge: Towards a Post-Critical Philosophy.* Chicago: University of Chicago Press.

—— (1969) *Knowing and Being: Essays by Michael Polanyi.* Edited by M. Grene. Chicago: University of Chicago Press.

Radhakrishnan, Sarvepalli. (1939) *Eastern Religions and Western Thought.* Oxford: The Clarendon Press.

Rahner, Karl. (1966) *Theological Investigations: Volume 5 – Later Writings.* Trans. K.-H. Kruger. Baltimore/London: Helicon Press/Darton, Longman & Todd.

Rajan, R. Sundarara. (1974) 'Negations: an article on dialogue among religions.' *Religion and Society* 21/4. (Published in Bangalore.)

Report. (1928) *Report of the Jerusalem meeting of the International Missionary Council, March 24th–April 8th, 1928.* 8 vols. London: Oxford University Press.

—— (1981) *Understanding Christian Nurture.* London: British Council of Churches.

—— (1985) *Faith in the City: A Call for Action by Church and Nation.* The Report of the Archbishop of Canterbury's Commission on Urban Priority Areas. London: Church House Publishing.

Richardson, Alan. (1947) *Christian Apologetics.* London: SCM Press.

Sanneh, Lamin. (1993) *Encountering the West – Christianity and the Global Cultural Process: The African Dimension.* London: Marshall Pickering/Harper Collins.

Schmidt, Karl Ludwig. (1965) 'Ekklesia.' In G. Kittel (ed.), *Theological Dictionary of the New Testament.* Vol. III. Trans. G. W. Bromiley. Grand Rapids, MI: William B. Eerdmans Publishing Company, 501–36.

Singh, Herbert Jai (ed.) (1967) *Inter-Religious Dialogue.* Bangalore: The Christian Institute for the Study of Religion and Society.

Smith, Wilfred Cantwell. (1978) *The Meaning and End of Religion.* London: SPCK. Original publication 1963.

Thomas, Madathilparampil Mammen. (1969) *The Acknowledged Christ of the Indian Renaissance.* London: SCM Press.

Tillich, Paul. (1959) *A Theology of Culture.* Edited by R. C. Kimball. New York: Oxford University Press.

—— (1963) *Christianity and the Encounter of the World Religions.* New York: Columbia University Press.

van Buren, Paul. (1968) *The Secular Meaning of the Gospel.* Harmondsworth: Pelican Books. Original publication SCM Press, 1963.

van Leeuwen, Arend Theodoor. (1964) *Christianity in World History: The Meeting of the Faiths of East and West.* Trans. H. Hoskyns. London: Edinburgh House Press.

Vidler, Alec Roper. (1945) *The Orb and the Cross: A normative study in the relations of church and state with reference to Gladstone's early writings.* London: SPCK.

Wainwright, Geoffrey. (2000) *Lesslie Newbigin: A Theological Life.* Oxford: Oxford University Press.

Weber, Max. (1998) *From Max Weber: Essays in Sociology,* trans. and ed. H. H. Gerth and C. Wright Mills. London: Routledge. Original publication 1948.

Willey, Basil. (1979) *The Seventeenth-Century Background: Studies in the Thought of the Age in Relation to Poetry and Religion.* London: Routledge & Kegan Paul. Original publication 1934.

Wink, Walter. (1984) *Naming the Powers: The Language of Power in the New Testament.* Philadelphia, PA: Fortress Press.

—— (1986) *Unmasking the Powers: Invisible Forces that Determine Human Existence.* Philadelphia, PA: Fortress Press.

Wolterstorff, Nicholas P. (1984) *Reason within the Bounds of Religion.* 2nd edn. Grand Rapids, MI: William B. Eerdmans Publishing Company. Original publication 1976.

Yu, Carver T. (1987) *Being and Relation: A Theological Critique of Western Dualism and Individualism.* Edinburgh: Scottish Academic Press.

For further study of Newbigin's work, see the website <www.newbigin.net> – a searchable database concerned with the writings and life of Bishop J. E. Lesslie Newbigin. It includes both a comprehensive bibliography of his writings and a wide-ranging collection of texts written by him.

Biblical index

271

General index

Akbar, Emperor 160
Al-Ghazali, A. H. 204
Amsterdam (WCC, 1948) 8, 48, 70, 121–2
Anselm 24, 203
apartheid 44
apologetics 199, 218–19, 236–9
Aquinas, T. 174, 175
Archimedes 208
Arendt, H. 195
Aristotelian philosophy 190, 248, 260
Aristotle 200, 259–60
Athanasius 84, 90
atonement *see* cross of Christ: as atonement
Augustine 90–2, 227, 238, 259–6
authority 39–43, 193–4, 250–5; in the church 78–9; for mission 84–92, 102–6, 148–57, 178–82; political 250–5; of revelation 160–1, 179, 204, 245–8; of science 193–4, 201, 222–3; of traditions of knowledge 219–29
axioms, fundamental 75–6, 90–1, 103, 106, 160, 192, 195–6, 213, 216; myth of neutral starting-points 176, 178, 219, 238, 240, 254, 256–7

Bacon, F. 200, 202, 211
Bangalore 54
Bangkok (CWME, 1973) 11, 207
baptism 28, 35, 116, 119; of Jesus, 86–8
Barmen Declaration 64
Barrett, D. 97
Barth, K. 5, 12, 20, 169, 204
Berger, P. L. 45n, 194, 203–4, 219–20
Bible: authority of 71, 204–6, 241; and hermeneutics 99–106, 227–8, 241–4; and historical–critical method 105; as 'story' 28, 49, 62, 232, 240–2, 245–6; *see also* revelation

Bloom, A. 205
Bonhoeffer, D. 244
British Council of Churches (BCC) 13, 187–8, 221
Buber, M. 25–6
Buddhism 56, 68, 163
Bultmann, R. 204

Calvin, J. 243
Calvinism 251
capitalism 146, 187
Carr, E. H. 60
Carter, S. L. 256–7
Cassirer, E. 194n
Celsus 132
chance 43–4
Christendom 56, 75–6, 83, 90–1, 112, 117–20, 172, 148–51; breakdown of 115–17, 149, 174; and 'corpus Christianum' 115–16, 212–14, 235–6
Christianity: as 'anonymously' Christian 163–4; as 'demonic' 162; as false 161–2; and other faiths 158–84; as 'preparation' for Christ 162–3
Church 114–57; Anglican 76–8, 251; and culture 96–100, 117–20, 146 *see also* gospel and culture; doctrine of 115–25; fellowship of 76–7, 99–100, 106, 124; as 'hermeneutic' of the gospel 142, 144, 148–57; missionary character of 59, 117–20, 207–17 *see also* election; Orthodox 70–1, 76–7, 139; Presbyterian 5, 7, 70; Roman Catholic 76, 141, 163–4, 210; as sign, foretaste and instrument of the Kingdom of God 138–40, 146, 166; United Reformed 12, 130, 147; unity of 8, 51–2, 66–80, 82, 120–5 *see also* ecumenical movement; as visible community 72, 74–7, 126–7

272